Nepal and the Geo-Strategic Rivalry between China and India

T0418160

The importance of the Himalayan state of Nepal has been obscured by the international campaign to free Tibet and the vicissitudes of the Sino-Indian rivalry. This book presents the history of Nepal's domestic politics and foreign relations from ancient to modern times.

Analyzing newly declassified reports from the United States and Britain, published memoirs, oral recollections and interviews, the book presents the historical interactions between Nepal, China, Tibet and India. It discusses how the aging and inevitable death of the Fourteenth Dalai Lama, the radicalization of Tibetan diaspora, and the ascendancy of the international campaign to free Tibet are of increasing importance to Nepal. With its position between China and India, the book notes how the focus could shift to Nepal, with it being home to some 20,000 Tibetan refugees and its chronic political turmoil, deepened by the Asian giants' rivalry.

Using a chronological approach, the past and present of the rivalry between China and India are studied, and attempts to chart the future are made. The book contributes to a new understanding of the intricate relationship of Nepal with these neighboring countries, and is of interest to students and scholars of south Asian studies, politics and international relations.

Sanjay Upadhya is a Nepalese journalist specializing in his country's politics and foreign relations. He has contributed to BBC Radio, *The Times* of London, *World Politics Review*, Inter Press Service and *Khaleej Times*.

Routledge Studies in South Asian Politics

Nepal and the Geo-Strategic Rivalry between China and India
Sanjay Upadhya

Nepal and the Geo-Strategic Rivalry between China and India

Sanjay Upadhya

Routledge
Taylor & Francis Group

LONDON AND NEW YORK

First published 2012
by Routledge
2 Park Square, Milton Park, Abingdon, Oxfordshire OX14 4RN

Simultaneously published in the USA and Canada
by Routledge
711 Third Avenue, New York, NY 10017

First issued in paperback 2015

Routledge is an imprint of the Taylor & Francis Group, an informa business

British Library Cataloguing in Publication Data
A catalogue record for this book is available from the British Library

Library of Congress Cataloging in Publication Data
Upadhya, Sanjay.
  Nepal and the Geo-Strategic Rivalry between China and India/Sanjay
  Upadhya.
    p. cm. – (Routledge studies in South Asian politics; 1) Includes
  bibliographical references and index.
    1. Nepal–Politics and government. 2. Nepal–Foreign relations–China. 3.
  China–Foreign relations–Nepal. 4. Nepal–Foreign relations–India. 5.
  India–Foreign relations–Nepal. 6. Geopolitics–South Asia. I. Title.
  DS494.7.U63 2012
  327.5496051–dc23

                                                            2011040911

ISBN13: 978-1-138-11934-5 (pbk)
ISBN13: 978-0-415-69572-5 (hbk)

Typeset in Times
by Wearset Ltd, Boldon, Tyne and Wear

To my mother, Sarala Upadhya, for ceaselessly inspiring me to tell this story of a nation's quest to live

Contents

Preface

This book draws heavily from the abundant literature available on the subject it addresses. Older, more familiar, events and episodes reflect the chroniclers' views colored by the geo-strategic and commercial imperatives of their times. Vital elements of narratives of subsequent phases are scattered across diverse publications, while newer accounts tend to be more speculative and less amenable to thorough analysis. A retelling of the story becomes important in light of newer complexities that are either already evident or are on the horizon.

Newly declassified files from U.S. and British archives shed new light on Nepal's place in Cold War international politics. Reminiscences by key players in India and the United States, in particular, offer deeper external insights to specific events. Published memoirs by Nepalese protagonists, thriving in the intellectual and academic openness of the past two decades, have enriched the discourse. An abundance of academic, journalistic and personal writings on China exists where Nepal tends to appear in passing. In proper context, they provide revealing insights. Technology has made these easier to access across the language barrier. I have attempted to weave these diverse materials to widen the perspective of the Nepal–China–India relationship, buttressed by my own discussions with some key personalities in Nepal's royalist, democratic and communist camps over the past three decades.

At the conclusion of each chapter, I have endeavored to highlight Tibet's role and influence in the Sino-Indian-Nepalese relationship for that particular period in keeping with the general theme of the volume. While no attempt is made here to address the international legal status of Tibet, the reality that the region has been under Chinese political influence or outright control for much of the period discussed remains central to the inquiry. Conversely, the periods when Tibet has been able to act more independently of China have been treated for their impact on the regional relationships. Thus, at times, Nepal's relationship with Tibet and that with China seem to run parallel, while at others they converge. As far as possible, I have attempted to present the Nepalese, Tibetan, Chinese and (British) Indian versions of principal events.

If this volume appears to treat the China side of the rivalry more exhaustively, it is out of recognition that scholarship seems to be lacking there. India's attitude towards, and perceptions of, Nepal are more widely known because of the deep social, cultural, religious and political ties the two countries share. The factors driving China's challenge to India's "special relations" in Nepal are relatively obscure and likely to become more prominent. For someone who has not set foot on Chinese soil, this is surely an enormous – and perhaps even audacious – undertaking. This shortcoming becomes even more telling in view of the paucity of Chinese perspectives on Nepal in the English language. My bypassing of China was not for want of effort, which began in an abortive attempt to travel to that country as a student more than two decades ago. I have tried to compensate by bringing in perspectives garnered through interactions with Chinese diplomats, academics and journalists over the course of my quarter-century career as a journalist.

I have drawn heavily from the works of people around the world who are too numerous to name. Some have been kind enough with their time to clarify their points and respond to specific questions. I hope I have conveyed all academic, specialist and general views correctly. I owe much to my late father, Devendra Raj Upadhya, who spent months in China during three visits in the 1980s and early 1990s researching the dynamics of the Nepal–China–India relationship. Before that, his participation in the crafting and conduct of Nepal's foreign policy as a diplomat and administrator yielded a treasure trove of personal papers. Transcribing his notes and typing the preliminary drafts of his own contributions on the subject provided a monumental education enriched by the countless hours of discussion on historical and contemporary aspects of the regional relationships.

As a practitioner of a skill described as the first draft of history, I must acknowledge that the chapters of more recent events may tend to lack a sense of detachment. As for the earlier chapters, my views may have been colored by the re-evaluation time affords and the perspective of a Nepalese on a subject hitherto treated largely by foreign academics and experts. At other places, they may appear to be either a regurgitation of accepted wisdom or a challenge mounted from the vantage point of those living the consequences of decisions, events, or ideas. Finally, the author's biases are bound to become apparent in their manifold forms. All errors of fact are certainly my own.

I would like to express my gratitude to editors Dorothea Schaefter and Leanne Hinves, and senior editorial assistant Jillian Morrison of Routledge Asian Studies for their tireless assistance in all phases of this book's production. This volume benefited immensely from the thorough scrutiny and incisive suggestions of two anonymous reviewers. I would like to thank my wife, Ranu, and children, Jay and Nilu, for yielding the time that was surely theirs. Without their patience, understanding and encouragement, this book would have been impossible.

Sanjay Upadhya
Plymouth, Michigan
United States
August 2011

SOUTH ASIA

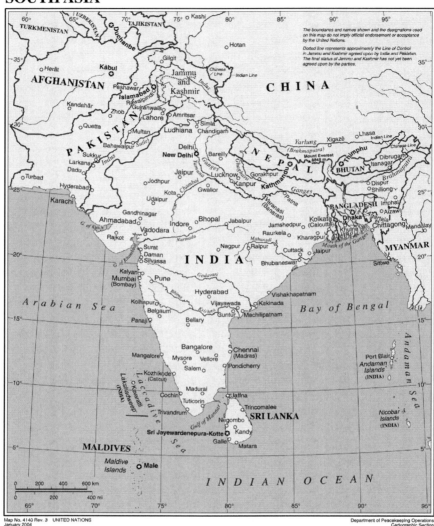

Map 1 Nepal in South Asia (source: United Nations Cartographic Section. Reprinted by permission).

Map 2 Nepal between China and India (source: Perry-Castañeda Library Map Collection/ The University of Texas at Austin. Reprinted by permission).

Introduction

Despite its centrality to the Tibet saga and the geo-strategic rivalry between China and India, Nepal remains a relatively obscure part of recent studies in either field. This book is a modest attempt not only to fill the gaps but also to bridge these two critical areas of modern Asian studies. The aging and inevitable death of the Fourteenth Dalai Lama, the radicalization of Tibetan diaspora and the fervor of the international campaign to free Tibet are bound to keep the Himalayan dispute on the world's front pages as the Tibetans and Chinese each seek to determine a successor they consider legitimate. India, which has offered refuge to the Dalai Lama and tens of thousands of his followers for more than half a century, today increasingly sees Tibet as a bargaining chip with China in its overall bilateral relationship. Nepal, which shares a 1,415 km border with China and one of 1,751 km with India, is home to some 20,000 Tibetan refugees. Wedged between the rising and assertive Asian giants, Nepal is likely to become an even more important news peg also because of its chronic political turmoil deepened by elements of the Sino-Indian rivalry.

An issue going beyond Tibet

The issue of Tibet goes beyond the freedom of a land, the liberation of a culture, and a celebration of a way of life. From the Nepalese perspective, at least, Tibet has been and continues to be an instrument through which major external protagonists have sought to pursue wider objectives. The British Empire, which first saw Tibet as a commercial prize and, later, a back door to more lucrative opportunities in the western Chinese market, went on to consider the region a critical part of the imperial chessboard. That legacy lives on in today's geo-strategic milieu where Tibet has become a vital front in what China sees an effort to contain its rise. Nepal, which has had its own designs on Tibetan territory and treasure, has become a willing tool of external powers. At other times, Nepal has been drawn against its will into the regional vortex at great cost to its internal stability and cohesion. In either case, it has sought to make the best of the situation, sometimes with greater success than at other times.

While the Nepalese and Tibetan experiences have long been intertwined, today's storyline has an atypical psychological subtext in Nepal. Some of the same people who profess the greatest admiration for the Dalai Lama and his cause also hope that Tibet remains under Chinese control. Beneath this glaring paradox lies a gripping parochialism: an independent Tibet would leave Nepal without a border with China. That, in the view of many Nepalese, would allow India to tighten its already asphyxiating grip on the landlocked nation.

Nepal's Tibet challenge

This peculiar feature of Nepal's Tibet challenge emerged in full public display in Kathmandu in the spring of 2008, as Beijing prepared to host the Olympic Games. The Nepalese government, led by parties that only two springs earlier had vanquished the royal army to re-establish democracy, cracked down hard on Tibetan exiles as Tibet itself saw some of its worst unrest in decades. As western governments and human rights organizations condemned what they considered Kathmandu's eagerness to appease Beijing, China accused Nepal of not doing enough.

The Tibetan protesters suspended their protests, allowing Nepalese to vote in crucial elections. Defying pundits and pollsters, the Maoists emerged as the largest political party in an exercise most international observers certified as free and fair. Once the results came in the Tibetan protests resumed, Chinese anger surged, western condemnation soared, and Nepal's geo-strategic precariousness resurfaced. The Chinese took a new look at the Nepalese Maoists, whom they had long shunned for having tarnished the image of the Great Helmsman. The former rebels, who had consistently denigrated Mao's successors as revisionists, reciprocated by warning Tibetan exiles not to violate Nepal's long-standing 'one China' policy.

The Qing's last tributary

Nepalese legend has it that a sage from China, Manjusri, created today's Kathmandu Valley by draining a giant lake and establishing the first settlements. While there is geological evidence that Kathmandu indeed was once a lake, experts believe the valley may have been drained in phases over tens of thousands of years. The historicity of Manjusri and his purported feat would be subordinated to the symbolism attached to him on both sides of the Himalayas. Although Tibet has been central to the Sino-Nepalese relationship, Nepal's formal contacts with China did not originate through the region. It began with China's thirst for Buddhist texts, artifacts and codes from the wider Gangetic heartland.

In the mid-seventh century, a powerful Tibetan king extracted consorts from Chinese and Nepalese royal households on the principle of peace through kinship. The two wives helped bring Buddhism to Tibet and opened a direct Himalayan route between Nepal and China, bypassing the more arduous one across Central Asia. As religion and trade began traversing the same Himalayan passes, peace and goodwill began losing ground. As the British sun rose higher over India, Nepal fought two wars with Tibet, precipitating a Chinese invasion. The Nepalese gained peace by entering into a tributary relationship with the Middle Kingdom, a duty they would discharge with utmost diligence. The Nepalese became the last foreigners to pay tribute to the Qing, as the arrangement helped maintain their independence as most of modern south Asia fell under the sway of the British Empire.

Nepal, which fought a third war with Tibet in 1855–1856, refused to aid the Tibetans against a British invasion in 1904, but helped secure the withdrawal of the invaders. The diplomatic triumph was short-lived as the tottering Qing formally claimed suzerainty over Nepal. Seeking to preserve its interests in Tibet – and demonstrate its independence – Nepal mediated between Beijing and Lhasa in 1912, after which Tibet enjoyed a period of de facto independence. For all their antipathy for the Qing – and for each other – Chinese nationalists and communists pressed their country's claims on Nepal: Sun Yat-sen and Mao Zedong both included Nepal among territories China had lost to imperialism.

Tibet and Nepalese democracy

The Chinese invasion of Tibet in 1950 impelled the leaders of independent India, successors to more than 500 princely states they considered an anachronism, to restore the monarchy at the top of a multiparty democracy in Nepal to forestall a communist advance southward. On the eve of Nepal's first democratic elections in 1959, Tibetans rose up in a failed revolt against Beijing, prompting the Dalai Lama's flight into exile in India. Nepal's first elected prime minister sought to consolidate democracy by asserting Nepalese independence from India and China, but the country had become a key – but largely unseen – front of the Cold War. The king dissolved parliament, jailed the prime minister and most of the elected leaders, and abolished multiparty democracy claiming it was incompatible with Nepalese traditions and needs. Recently declassified documents in the United States suggest that much more than royal ambition and assertiveness was at play. Nepal had become a center of Cold War intrigue where the United States and India – two democracies – were working to undermine each other as were the communist giants China and the Soviet Union. By the end of the 1960s, Sino-American rapprochement put the two nations on the same side in Nepal for the duration of the Cold War.

A new round of unrest in Tibet merged with student unrest in Beijing, culminating in the bloody crackdown in Tiananmen Square. The fall of the Berlin Wall inspired the Nepalese to bring down the palace-led partyless Panchayat system in 1990, with Beijing a bystander. As Nepalese democracy turned rancorous, parties – like the courtiers of yore – saw China as a political expedient. The annual March 10 anniversary of the Lhasa uprising became an occasion for the opposition to embarrass the government.

China's Nepal policy transcends Tibet

The cause of Tibetan independence has proved resilient, picking up momentum among international celebrities and the public at large, as governments have withdrawn backing in deference to China's growing power. Yet the fact that the Dalai Lama has reconciled for autonomy within China perhaps underscores his own doubts over whether Tibet can ever be a viable independent nation. That is a question few Nepalese want to consider. The 'nationalist' strand in both the royalist right and the radical left continues to view China as a guarantor of independence and sovereignty.

Chinese policy toward Nepal has been marked by much ambiguity, which both Beijing and Kathmandu have benefited from. One school of thought – which has resonated throughout history – sees limited Chinese interest in Nepal, where phases of Beijing's assertiveness are the exception. Beijing could thus easily concede Nepal as part of New Delhi's sphere of influence. I contend otherwise. Chinese assertiveness is bound to grow as its interests in Nepal go beyond the issue of Tibet to encompass its wider south Asian strategy. Nepal is the only country that maintains diplomatic representation in Lhasa, and Beijing reminds Kathmandu with ever-greater regularity the responsibility that flows with that privilege. Enticing Nepal with promises of greater commercial benefits as part of its massive investments in Tibet, Beijing is intent on committing Nepal to political, security, economic and cultural agreements governments of every ideological orientation would honor. Should tradition become a more dominant part of Chinese regional diplomacy – as seems likely – Nepal's status as a former tributary to the Middle Kingdom is likely to drive Beijing's policy. It may be impossible to see precisely what the future holds for Nepal, but studying the past and present – through the chronological case study approach I have adopted – can provide important pointers.

1   Trails of truth and trade

Meditating in his abode in northern China's Wutai Mountains, Nepalese legend has it, the sage Manjusri was seized by the extraordinary vision of the primordial Buddha in the form of a flame rising from a lotus on a lake in some distant land. Intent on finding the miraculous flare, Manjusri led a group of followers thousands of miles southwest on a grueling journey. He finally stopped in front of a lotus flower studded with precious stones – just as it had appeared in his vision – at the center of a lake swirling with serpents. After circumambulating the area and paying his obeisance, Manjusri decided he would settle his followers there.

The sage swung his scimitar to slice a deep gorge on a southern ridge, draining the water and creating what is today, Kathmandu Valley. The flower turned into Swayambhu Hill, which stands today as a sacred site for Nepalese Buddhists and Hindus alike. Through that cavernous cleft, the Bagmati River continues to flow southward into India before emptying itself into the Bay of Bengal. Manjusri stayed on in the valley until farmers from surrounding areas established the first settlement. Before returning home, the sage named an escort the first king of the valley.

The nebulous narrative of the early links between China and Nepal is then picked up by Chinese annals. By this time, the Kiratas, a people of Mongoloid origin who also appear in the Hindu epic *Mahabharata*, were ruling Kathmandu. However, it was a kingdom further southwest that would draw the attention of the Chinese. In the year 6 BC, during Han Aidi's reign, an envoy from the country of the Great Yuezhi, adjacent to modern day Afghanistan, traveled to China and narrated to his court counterpart some comforting *sutras* attributed to a wise man. The visitor spoke of a kingdom called Lumni Guo, the birthplace of the master they called Gautam Buddha. The enthusiastic Han official spread the news among his superiors, associates and friends, triggering a wave of curiosity. While Buddhism is believed to have entered China two centuries earlier, this exchange is said to have been the first reference of Lumbini there.[1]

Monks and manuscripts

Buddhism would receive its next major boost in China under Ming Ti, the second emperor of the Eastern Han dynasty, who sent a delegation to the land of the Great Teacher in AD 54. The team returned eleven years later with texts, figures and shamans who would formally introduce Buddhism to the Chinese. Although the collapse of the Han dynasty in AD 220 plunged China into disunion, Buddhism continued to grow. As emperors built monasteries and propagated texts, Chinese monks began translating *sutras* from the great canon called the *tripitaka*, often with great difficulty. Sanskrit was polysyllabic, highly inflected, and alphabetic like English and other Indo-European languages, while the script of China was monosyllabic, uninflected and ideographic. If conveying the highly imaginative and metaphysical abstractions of Indian mysticism into a terse and concrete medium proved its own challenge, Chinese Buddhists also lacked disciplinary codes for monastic life.[2] Monk and scholars began hazardous journeys to the land of the Buddha to seek complete authentic sources.

By the fourth century, a new state had emerged in Kathmandu valley under the Licchavis, whose patronage of religion, the arts and culture would attract more truth-seekers from China. Around AD 350, Sheng-tsai arrived in Nepal as part of an extended tour of the subcontinent. The Chinese monk, who did not travel to Kathmandu valley, visited Lumbini and wrote about the precise location of Siddhartha Gautam's birth and the topography of the adjacent regions.[3]

Half a century later, another Chinese monk, Fa Xian, set out for India to obtain a complete copy of the *vinaya*, or book of monastic rules. Like his predecessor, Fa Xian traveled across the oasis kingdoms of Central Asia, spent years studying languages, collecting texts, and visiting famous sites in India, before arriving in Lumbini in AD 406. Fa Xian found abandoned monasteries and shrines there, and the city of Kapilvastu lying in ruins. His work, *The Record of Buddhist Lands*, provides insightful accounts of early Buddhism and the countries along the Silk Roads. Sheng-tsai's and Fa Xian's descriptions would go on to enrich the great Chinese tome, *Commentary to the River Classic*.

As Fa Xian toured south Asia, a Nepalese monk set out in the opposite direction. Invited by the Chinese clergy, Buddhabhadra, a descendant of Gautam Buddha, arrived in the capital city of Changan in AD 408, where he started preaching a new blend of meditation and mysticism, gaining popularity among monks, scholars and laymen.[4] Although Buddhabhadra clashed with followers of the renowned foreign translator, Kumarajiva, over matters of style and substance, he would go on to translate chief Buddhist manuscripts into Chinese, 15 of which are still preserved.[5]

Buddhism inspired Chinese architects, painters and sculptors, attracting patrons from all backgrounds. Then came the first of the backlashes recorded as "The Three Disasters of Wu," named for the common posthumous or temple name of the three emperors who carried them out. After re-uniting China in AD 589, the Sui dynasty reversed the proscription on Buddhism, but almost another century elapsed before China and Nepal recorded their first official relations.

Tang–Licchavi relations

After rising to power in AD 618, the Tang dynasty inaugurated a period of progress and stability in China. In Kathmandu the Licchavis had laid the groundwork of what would become the golden age of the valley's art and culture. In AD 628 Xuanzang, a monk in Changan who had heard of Fa Xian's travels, decided to set out on a journey to south Asia. An itinerant student, Xuanzang shared Fa Xian's concern about the incomplete and misinterpreted nature of the Buddhist scriptures that had reached China. Unable to secure official backing for his mission because of an imperial edict banning non-essential foreign travel, Xuanzang furtively took the perilous Central Asian route through what is modern-day Kyrgyzstan, Uzbekistan, Tajikistan, Afghanistan and Pakistan to India and Nepal. Among his key destinations were Nalanda, the great north Indian center of Buddhist learning that Emperor Ashoka and his Gupta successors had built, as well as Lumbini. Xuanzang located the ruins of the palace of the Buddha's father, King Suddhodana, and saw a broken pillar with an inscription stating that King Asoka had worshipped on the spot where the Buddha was born.[6]

Although he did not visit Kathmandu, Xuanzang wrote about the valley based on accounts of informants, suggesting the pervasiveness of Buddhism there. Amsuvarma, an influential officer of the court, had risen to become a co-ruler with Siva Dev. In Xuanzang's words, Amsuvarma had established himself as a man of bravery, learning and piety.[7] While he spent much of his 17-year journey on the road, Xuanzang lived among the greatest teachers and thinkers of his time.[8] After returning to Changan in AD 645, Xuanzang wrote to the Taizong emperor about the results of his 16,000 km journey on the northern and southern Silk roads. Impressed, the emperor named him an advisor on Asian affairs, but Xuanzang refused all high civil appointments. The emperor then suggested that he write about his journey, which he did in the form of *Record of the Western Regions*. Xuanzang would become a main character in the great Chinese epic *Journey to the West*.

Nepal and Tibet open political ties

In AD 639, while Xuanzang was still touring the region, the Nepalese ruler gave his daughter, Bhrikuti, in marriage to Srong-tsen Gampo, the powerful ruler of Tibet.[9] Srong-tsen Gampo had unified the many feuding Tibetan fiefdoms into a single expanding empire that eventually reached the frontiers of Nepal and China. Threatened by invasion, the Nepalese concluded a peace-through-kinship marriage alliance with Tibet, a union that also created a direct land route across the Himalayas through the Kerong pass, west of Kathmandu. Two years later, after a succession of vicious battles, the Tang emperor, too, gave a daughter, Wencheng, in marriage to Srong-tsen Gampo. The Tibetan minister who had escorted Bhrikuti to Lhasa was sent to the Chinese court to receive Princess Wencheng.[10] The Nepalese and Chinese princesses, who carried a treasure trove of Buddhist idols and artifacts as part of their dowries, helped to expand Buddhism in Tibet. Together, they inspired the construction of Lhasa's Jokhang Temple, Tibet's most sacred shrine, and converted Srong-tsen Gampo to Buddhism.

Amsuvarma was believed to have adopted Siva Dev's son, Udaya Dev, as his heir. Shortly after ascending the throne, Udaya Dev was overthrown by a brother and led his family into exile in Tibet, where he died.[11] In AD 643, Srong-tsen Gampo helped Crown Prince Narendra Dev ascend to the throne in exchange for which, Chinese and Tibetan sources state, Tibet exercised some form of authority over Kathmandu valley until the late ninth century,[12] a claim Nepalese historians deny.[13]

While Xuanzang was returning to China by way of the Pamirs, a 22-member Chinese mission, led by Li Yibiao and Wang Xuance, headed to India on a complimentary mission through the new Himalayan route. Crossing the Kerong pass, the team arrived in Kathmandu in AD 644 to an enthusiastic reception. Three years later, Narendra Dev sent an envoy to the Tang court to establish friendly relations. This envoy also met representatives from Rome and Persia in Changan.[14]

In AD 648, the Taizong emperor sent Wang Xuance on a complimentary mission to visit devout Buddhist, King Harsha Vardhan of the northern Indian empire of Magadha. But before the mission reached its destination, Harsha died and a courtier seized the throne. After the new ruler ordered an attack on the approaching 30-strong Chinese convoy, Wang and his deputy fled to Nepal where they recruited a 7,000-strong army complemented by 1,000 men from Tibet.[15] Returning to Magadha, the Nepalese–Tibetan army killed thousands of Indians, deposed the usurper, and took him prisoner to China. Nepal won China's gratitude for having protected its honor, prestige and power.[16]

After Srong-tsen Gampo's death in AD 650, Tibet and China descended into renewed hostilities. The following year, Narendra Dev sent a political mission to the new emperor, Gaozong, in a move possibly aimed at checking Tibet's growing influence in Nepal. The Chinese reciprocated in AD 657 by sending another delegation under Wang Xuance. Tang dynasty annals mentioned the great wealth of the cities of Kathmandu valley and the important role of the local mercantile community. Wary of the growing Chinese–Nepalese contacts, Tibet, by AD 665, had imposed a total restriction on movements of monks and officials between China and Nepal.[17] When Tibet blocked the Kashmir and Kabul routes as well, contacts between Nepal and China ceased. The rupture would last several centuries, and during this time references to Nepal virtually disappeared from the history of Chinese dynasties.

After almost 300 years in power the Tang dynasty collapsed in AD 907, giving way to the Five Dynasties and Ten Kingdoms Period. Buddhism was to suffer another blow in AD 955, when the Shizong emperor of the Later Zhou Dynasty, desperate for copper to mint coins, ordered the destruction of Buddha statues. Almost coinciding with the Tang decline, Kathmandu valley saw a gradual weakening of central authority, resulting in the Licchavis' collapse around

AD 880. While the state's territory and power declined, Buddhism's role and influence continued to grow and Nepal served as a conduit between Tibet and centers of Buddhist learning in northern India. Nepalese Buddhists played an important role in the rebuilding of Tibetan Buddhism in the tenth century after the collapse of the Tibetan empire.[19]

China's contacts with Nepal resumed through Tibet during the Song dynasty (960–1279). The Taizu emperor sent 300 monks to India in AD 964 to seek Buddhist relics and scriptures, and the monks visited Lumbini and Swayambhu in Kathmandu on their way back home.[20] In an effort to revive the faith the Tibetans invited Atisha, an elder at Vikramasila monastery in Magadha (the chief seat of Buddhist learning), to accompany them. He duly set out for Tibet in 1041 with 24 disciples.

The early Mallas and the Mongols

As three main centers, Kathmandu, Patan and Bhadgaon, emerged in the valley, Ari Malla took power in 1200 ushering in a near six-century long period known by his surname. Around this time, Genghis Khan united the Mongol tribes and his hordes spread out in all directions. Having vanquished the Jin empire in northern China in 1234, the Mongols conquered the Southern Song 45 years later. Genghis' ablest grandson, Khubilai, became emperor of China in 1271, calling his dynasty Yuan. He built his capital at Dadu, near modern-day Beijing. Since the Mongols were too few and too ill equipped to govern a state of such size and complexity, Khubilai Khan allowed the Chinese to rule themselves under Mongol supervision. In order to avoid ensnarement by the Chinese bureaucracy, Khubilai recruited foreign advisers and experts who would be entirely dependent on his favor.[21]

Despite having subordinated the Tibetans, Khubilai chose not to rule them directly and sought a special relationship. The *cho-yon*, or patron-priest, relationship was strengthened when Khubilai was initiated into the rites of Buddhism by the state tutor, Phagspa, a member of Tibet's most powerful family. Phagspa acknowledged Khubilai as a universal Buddhist ruler as well as the reincarnation of Manjusri, while Khubilai put Phagspa in charge of Tibet. This arrangement would enable Khubilai to dominate Tibet politically without having to use force, while assuring Tibetan religious leaders local autonomy.[22]

Realizing the need for visual representations of gods and ideas in his role as the patron of Buddhism, Khubilai asked Phagspa to send him artists to make images for the temples. Nepal sent 80 Newar craftsmen under the leadership of Arniko, a native of Patan. Personally interviewing Arniko, Khubilai gave him complete authority over all artists working in metal.[23] Arniko had expected to return to his family after two years, but during the consecration of a stupa he had just built, he took the robes of a monk.[24] Ordering Arniko to revert to lay status, Khubilai made him controller of the court of imperial manufacturers. The Nepalese artisan's most renowned work lives on in the form of the White Stupa of Miaoying Temple in Beijing.[25]

Arniko drew heavily from the Buddhist heritage that had enriched Kathmandu valley by then. During the Muslim invasions of India, almost the entire body of Buddhist Sanskrit texts there were lost. Eminent Indian monks from such great universities as Nalanda fled northward, bringing along the texts they could gather. Nepalese Buddhists began copying them as an act of merit. As ordinary Buddhists purchased them for religious purposes, the texts found reflection in Nepalese artistic styles.

The Ming reach out

After Khubilai Khan's death, Mongol control of China weakened amid succession struggles, court rivalries and natural calamities. The Yuan were finally driven out by an uprising led by Zhu Yuanzhang, who founded the Ming dynasty in 1368. While Chinese rule was now established throughout the empire after four centuries of foreign rule in the north, the new emperor, who took the name of Hongwu, still confronted the Mongols. Anxious to avoid a threat from Tibet, which still had special ties with the Mongols, the Ming evolved a complex and multi-dimensional policy that contained elements of politics, commerce and war. They also re-established diplomatic relations with Nepal, ostensibly hoping to outflank and pacify Tibet.[26]

The Ming engaged not with the Mallas but with the Rama family, a powerful section of the nobility that the Malla palace was unable to subdue militarily so garnered its support by entrusting them with handling relations with China. The Ramas were Buddhists with whom Chinese monks and scholars were more comfortable, and it was they who controlled the region between the Tibet border and Kathmandu.[27] Chinese annals of the time describe the country of "Ni-ba-la being situated west of Tibet, quite far from China [and ruled by] Buddhist monks."[28] In 1384 Hongwu dispatched a monk to Nepal with an imperial edict professing friendship, and presents. The Nepalese king reciprocated three years later by sending a delegation carrying gifts of a golden statue of the Buddha, and five horses, for the emperor. In 1390 another mission from Nepal arrived in China.[29]

These contacts would be part of a general Ming trend of outreach. Between 1405 and 1433, the Chinese government sponsored a series of seven naval expeditions under the legendary eunuch-admiral Zheng He. The Yongle emperor designed these voyages to establish a Chinese presence, impose imperial control over trade, and impress foreign peoples in the Indian Ocean basin. He also might have wanted to extend the tributary system, which, at its height under the Ming, had some 38 states regularly sending missions to China.[30] In the spring of 1413, Hou Xian, a eunuch of outstanding ability who had accompanied Admiral Zheng on two voyages, traveled to Nepal to make gifts of brocade and silk to its ruler. The Nepalese ruler, whom the emperor appointed as king and to whom he awarded a seal of gilded silver and a patent, delegated a high official to accompany Hou back to China.[31] In 1418, Yongle, who claimed to be a living incarnation of Manjusri, the legendary creator of Kathmandu Valley, dispatched another eunuch, Deng Cheng, with a load of brightly hued brocade and satin to the king of Nepal.[32] Hou Xian's last mission was to Tibet and Nepal in 1427.[33]

Once they unified Kathmandu valley and consolidated their power by way of subduing the Rama nobility, the Malla family ceased diplomatic contacts with the Ming.[34] Yet China itself was withdrawing from the world, as the rise of Confucian-trained scholar-officials, who opposed trade and foreign contact on principle, brought the sea voyages to a halt. The revival of Mongol power and border raids would eventually turn the Ming inward.[35] By 1482, unified Malla rule in Kathmandu valley had broken down and Kathmandu, Patan and Bhadgaon emerged as independent city-states.

Fateful confluence of events

The sixteenth century brought a confluence of events from the north and south that would have a lasting impact on Nepal. Babur, a descendent of Genghis Khan in Central Asia, invaded India in 1526 and founded the Mughal dynasty. A little over three decades later, Drabya Shah, a descendant of Rajput rulers who had fled Muslim conquests of northern India, established the kingdom of Gorkha. The Mongols, driven northeastwards after the Ming conquest, and fragmented into rival groups, produced a prince who would redefine Tibet's identity and regional influence.

Altan Khan was converted to Buddhism by two lamas he had won as war booty. Having heard of an eminent sage in Tibet, Altan sent a mission to the region in 1576 to invite him to a meeting. Sonam Gyatso was legitimized from childhood as the third re-incarnation of a line of masters belonging to the Gelugpa (Yellow Hat) sect of Tibetan Buddhism. The two men met in 1578 in the Yanghua temple in Qinghai and sealed a pact that was to bring important benefits to each. Altan Khan bestowed on Sonam Gyatso the title of "Ocean of Wisdom," or Dalai Lama, and the Tibetan applied the appellation retrospectively to his two previous incarnations. Sonam Gyatso announced that he and Altan were reincarnations of Phagspa and Khubilai respectively, who had come together again to propagate Buddhism.[36] In 1588, while returning to Tibet from a visit to the Ming emperor, Sonam Gyatso died, and the following year the Dalai Lama reincarnated as a Mongol boy named Yonten Gyatso. He was the great-grandson of Altan Khan, the first time the Dalai Lama manifested in a non-Tibetan body. Amid growing regional and sectarian conflicts, the Fourth Dalai Lama died in 1616.

The Fifth Dalai Lama, Ngawang Lozsang Gyatso, was born the following year in what is now Lhokha in the province of U in central Tibet. He was identified at the age of six by Lobsang Choekyi, a leading cleric, who brought him to Drepung monastery and served as the child's religious tutor. In gratitude, the Dalai Lama bestowed on Lobsang Choekyi the title of Panchen Lama, or "Wise Teacher." After initiating the Fifth Dalai Lama into full monkhood in 1637, the Panchen Lama was to guide his young pupil through the critical next steps in the consolidation of Gelugpa power. Rivalries among the key Buddhist sects meshed into power struggles between the rising Manchu and various Mongol and Oirat factions. Gushri Khan of the Khoshud Mongols, having ousted Altan Khan's descendants, overthrew the prince of Tsang in 1642, displacing the rival dominant school of the Karmapas, and seated the Fifth Dalai Lama on the throne. Ngawang Lozsang Gyatso, who gave Gushri Khan the title of king of Tibet, became the first Dalai Lama to enjoy supreme political authority. General administration was handled by the desi, the equivalent of prime minister, who referred matters of special significance to the Dalai Lama.[37]

At this time, the kings of Gorkha and Kathmandu were competing for control of the lucrative trans-Himalayan trading passes. Gorkhali King Ram Shah led soldiers into Tibet, probably between 1625 and 1630 after conquering the territories between Gorkha and Kerong, but was repulsed. He led another army into Kerong, defeating the Tibetans this time, and imperiling Kathmandu's traders who relied on the route. Instead of confronting the Gorkhalis, King Pratap Malla of Kathmandu sent his soldiers to Kuti in the northeast to gain control of the second major trade route to Tibet.

The early Gorkhalis and the Qing

The Ming enjoyed comparative peace for three centuries, largely by restoring ancient Chinese customs and traditions. Confronted by the revived Mongol and growing Manchu empires, and crippled by a series of ineffectual rulers, the Ming were eventually swept away. The non-Han Qing dynasty completed its conquest of China in 1644, applying a method of military organization that grouped fighting men and their families in divisions identified by different colored banners. Seeking acceptance as legitimate heirs to the "mandate of heaven" and not foreign usurpers, (the Qing were Manchus and hence considered as foreigners by the Chinese) they adopted Chinese ways. Since the new emperor, Shunzhi, was a minor, his uncle, Dorghon, ran the state. In 1646, the eastern provinces of Fujian and Zhejiang were brought under Qing control and Sichuan fell in the southwest, while Canton was taken the following year.

The Fifth Dalai Lama decided to build a palace in his newly designated capital city, Lhasa. On a hill stood the ruins of the palace Srong-tsen Gampo had built for his Nepalese wife, Bhrikuti, a millennium earlier. There the foundations were laid in 1645 for what stands today as the Potala.[38] In 1648, Dorghon invited the Fifth Dalai Lama to Beijing forge an alliance. Although the Tibetan leader promptly accepted, the meeting did not occur until 1653, by which time Shunzhi had assumed power. The two leaders met and established a modified *cho-yon* relationship. The Manchu sought such a relationship in view of the lamas' strong influence among the Mongols, whose submission Beijing sought.[39]

The Dalai Lama recognized the emperor as patron, which allowed the Qing to claim they had displaced the Mongols as Tibet's most important ally. The emperors also began to identify themselves with Manjusri.[40] Still controlling most of the country, the Dalai Lama was no longer in authority of all of Tibet. The Great Fifth had made the Panchen Lama the official ruler of the Tashilhunpo region in a division of power that would lead to the disintegration of the *cho-yon* relationship. The emergence of rival power centers would work to the advantage of a succession of foreign powers.

Coins and conspiracies

Foreign travelers now began speaking not only of a flourishing trade between Bengal, Nepal, Bhutan and Tibet but also of the caravans of merchants coming from China, Tatary and Persia. After the king of Ladakh prohibited foreign caravans through his territory, the bulk of the India–Tibet trade shifted to the Patna–Kathmandu–Lhasa route.[41] Kashmiri merchants carried their goods to the Kuti pass and procured wool. From here their manufactured goods were sent to Tibet, to China via Sining and to Patna through Nepal. The Tibetan merchants brought woolen cloths, ponies, shawl goats, yaks, sheep, musk, salt, borax, gold, silver and paper to Kathmandu. The lamas of Tibet also sent large quantities of bullion to the Nepal mints. The Indian merchants carried cotton cloth, cutlery, glassware, coral, pearls, spices, camphor, betel and hardware.[42] On each of the trade routes a toll station collected duty on exports and imports based on their character, value, weight, load, or number.[43]

Pratap Malla, hoping to increase Kathmandu's share of that prosperity, ordered troops into Tibet a second time, between 1645 and 1650. Overrunning the border districts, the Malla army advanced toward Shigatse before the Dalai Lama's representatives proposed peace. Kathmandu gained joint authority over Kuti and Kerong and its Newar merchants were permitted to establish 32 trading houses in the Tibetan capital. Pratap Malla won the right to post a representative in Lhasa, while the Tibetans agreed to direct all trade with India through Kathmandu valley. Nepal would mint coins for the Tibetans, who would either provide the silver or pay for them in gold.[44] Of the 34 mountain passes available for the trans-Himalayan trade, only 24 were in use. Kuti and Kerong were located at the lowest altitude, and could remain open all year long.[45] However, Kathmandu's joint authority over Kuti and Kerong ended 25 years later when the Dalai Lama regained them.

When the Fifth Dalai Lama died in 1682 the desi concealed it from the general population. Claiming the leader had entered an extended period of meditation, he skilfully manipulated events. The Qing were preoccupied in other directions, having recently occupied the island of Taiwan and begun concentrating on defining border and trading rights with Russia. The desi, now ruling as regent, was able to carry on his deception for 14 years. Encouraging the powerful Dzungars to work toward unifying all the Mongol tribes, he hoped to increase the power and prestige of Lhasa. However, collaboration with the last remaining challengers to Qing authority put him on a collision course with Beijing.

When a Chinese delegation arrived in Lhasa, the desi was no longer able to maintain the charade, and produced a new Dalai Lama. But the Sixth Dalai Lama, Tsangyang Gyatso, rejected his monastic vows and refused to play the role of celibate religious leader. Using the Dalai Lama's behavior as an excuse,

Lhazang Khan, the king of the Khoshud Mongols and an ally of the Qing emperor of China, killed the regent and kidnapped the Sixth Dalai Lama, who died soon afterwards whilst on the way to China. Lhazang Khan installed Ngawang Yeshey Gyatso as the Sixth Dalai Lama in 1707, claiming that he was the true rebirth of Lozang Gyatso, a choice that Gelukpa dignitaries and the Tibetan people rejected. The Tibetans appealed to the Dzungar Mongols, who invaded Tibet and killed Lhazang Khan in late 1717. However, the Dzungars themselves soon began to loot, rape and kill throughout Lhasa, destroying Tibetan goodwill toward them. An expedition sent by Emperor Kangxi, together with Tibetan forces, expelled the Dzungars from Tibet in 1720. They brought Kelzang Gyatso with them from Kumbum to Lhasa, and he was enthroned as the Seventh Dalai Lama.

Emperor Kangxi, the fourth emperor of the Qing dynasty, was anxious to prevent Tibet's fractious leaders from using their influence with the Mongols to harm Qing interests, and moved to reassert China's role in Tibet. Mounting a purge against a Tibetan elite that had dominated power during the preceding decades, the Qing built a military garrison in Lhasa and introduced collective rule by four ministers, or *kalon*. The emperor withdrew the garrison in 1722 after Tibetan ministers complained that the region's subsistence economy was incapable of feeding several thousand troops.[46] Meanwhile, the rulers of the three Kathmandu valley principalities sent missions to congratulate the new Dalai Lama,[47] demonstrating that Nepal continued throughout this period to have nominal political relations with Tibet and an awareness of Chinese involvement there.

By the time the Yongzheng emperor assumed power in 1723, China had become the largest and one of the most prosperous unified empires on earth, and Tibet its virtual protectorate. However, Beijing's decision to replace a single all-powerful regent with a council of ministers created dissensions in Lhasa. When civil war broke out in 1727, the Qing emperor had to dispatch the imperial army to Lhasa for the third time in a decade. Sending the Seventh Dalai Lama into exile in Kham, the Chinese installed the Panchen Lama as a political figurehead and re-established the military garrison in Lhasa with two thousand troops. The emperor also stationed in Lhasa two Manchu imperial residents, known as ambans, to keep a careful eye on Tibetan leaders and supervise the garrison. Over time, the ambans' duties would include overseeing Tibet's relations with Nepal.

The Tibetans brought the Seventh Dalai Lama back from exile in 1735, but he would serve as little more than a spiritual figurehead. Lhasa officials lodged a complaint with the new emperor, Qianlong, against the ambans' growing interference. Since Tibet had remained largely peaceful during the previous decades, the emperor reduced the Lhasa garrison to a token one hundred troops and instructed the ambans to cease their interference. Qianlong also sanctioned additional funds to cover the expense of the ambans and the troops, thereby easing the forced acquisition of goods and services. When the ambans resisted and violence broke out again, Qianlong sent troops back in. By the time they reached Lhasa, the Dalai Lama had restored order. The Qing commander now drew up a formal reorganization plan to stabilize Tibetan politics. Acknowledging its failure to control Tibet through lay aristocratic leaders, Beijing restored the Dalai Lama as ruler,[48] but under the closer supervision of the ambans. The powers of the ambans were gradually increased while the authority of the *kalon* was curtailed.[49]

Across the Himalayas an ambitious young king in Gorkha had advanced on a campaign of territorial conquest that had eluded his forefathers. After Prithvi Narayan Shah overran the principality of Nuwakot in 1744, cutting off access to the Kerong pass, Kathmandu's trade with Tibet was interrupted once again. Increased military spending had created financial problems for the Gorkhali king, and few of his new territories brought significant additional revenue. Prithvi Narayan hoped to raise money by sending his own silver coins to Tibet in exchange for pure bullion which he expected to sell to Indian merchants at a profit.[50] Ultimately, though, the king signed a treaty with Kathmandu that promised both states equal benefit from the trans-Himalayan trade, an arrangement Tibet refused to recognize.

A crisis was already developing over the quality of the coins the Mallas had been minting for Tibet. The bullion from Lhasa was turned in at the mints in Kathmandu, Patan or Bhadgaon in exchange for coins of a corresponding weight. The profit for Nepal lay in the difference between the weight of the pure bullion turned in and the weight of silver in the alloy of the coin, which varied according to the government's financial needs or the ruler's avarice. The disparity was a perennial source of friction not only between Tibet and Nepal and but also among the Malla kings.[51] The shortage of silver resulting from the Gorkhali blockade of the valley only served to exacerbate the practice and resulting tensions.

Shadow looms large from the south

The shadow on Nepal was looming larger from the south after the British conquest of Bengal in 1757. In the same year Prithvi Narayan mounted his first assault on Kirtipur, the first major front in his long and bloody campaign to conquer the valley. Barring a brief period of unified resistance, the Malla kings had been reaching separate deals with the Gorkhalis. When Ranjit Malla, the king of Bhadgaon, sought Gorkha's help against Kathmandu, Prithvi Narayan saw a major opening and swept on Kirtipur. Kathmandu's Jaya Prakash Malla sent a strong force that crushed the Gorkhalis.

The valley kingdoms were each wealthier and bigger than Gorkha and stood protected by their mountain perimeter. Unable to face Jaya Prakash on the battlefield, Prithvi Narayan moved to cut off supplies into the valley from the vital passes. Encouraged by the internecine quarrels among the Malla kings, Prithvi Narayan bought new weapons, including some European-made muskets, and assiduously wooed Jaya Prakash Malla's opponents, but another Gorkhali offensive on Kirtipur failed in 1764.

The Tibetans and the Mallas had been able to contain their political and commercial tensions. Alarmed by the belligerent Gorkhalis' territorial ambitions, the

Tibetans now feared for their own land, while the Mallas began cultivating the British. When Prithvi Narayan finally captured Kirtipur in 1766, the Mallas pleaded for military assistance from the British East India Company. The British sent a small expeditionary force under Captain Kinloch, but the men were forced to retreat following an assault by the Gorkhalis and an outbreak of malaria. On September 29, 1768, as Kathmandu residents were celebrating the traditional *Indra Jatra* festival in honor of the rain god, Gorkhali soldiers entered the city almost without opposition, and Prithvi Narayan Shah took the throne.

Conclusion

The religious and cultural influences invigorating Nepal's early relationships with China and Tibet had, by the time of the Gorkhali conquest of Kathmandu valley in the mid-eighteenth century, given way to a bitter trade and territorial contest with the Tibetans. Although Qing emperors had tightened control over Tibet, they were largely detached from events beyond the Himalayas. To Nepal's south the British East India Company, officially a private trading corporation with its own army, had obtained from a decaying Mughal Empire the right to govern all of Bengal. In search of additional sources of revenue, the Company saw Kathmandu's traditional entrepot trade as a possible source.

Those atop the disparate regimes across Nepal's northern and southern frontiers were united in their distrust of the belligerent and militaristic Gorkhalis. Cherishing the importance of isolationism to the survival of his regime, Prithvi Narayan Shah also recognized the work in progress his nation-building enterprise represented. Thus the nascent state required a coherent foreign policy in place of the contrasting and often conflicting pronouncements and practices of the principalities it had begun to replace.

2   Bubbling between boulders

As Prithvi Narayan Shah's armies pushed into Kathmandu valley's other two cities, Patan and Bhadgaon, during 1768–1769, the East India Company struggled to respond. The failure of the Kinloch expedition had not diminished British eagerness for reopening the trade routes to Tibet through Nepal, and the Company sent an envoy to Kathmandu in the winter of 1769. But Prithvi Narayan's sentiments had now hardened against all foreigners. Suspecting foreign traders, ascetic Hindu travelers and Christian missionaries of complicity with the Mallas in soliciting British military assistance, Prithvi Narayan expelled them from the valley. Shutting his passes to all European merchandise, the king proposed to the Tibetans that, in return for free access to Indian goods, they join with him in a ban against everything associated with the Company.[1]

Although Kathmandu valley had had no formal ties with China since the mid-Malla period, the Gorkhali ruler recognized the implications of the Qing's growing power in Tibet. Prithvi Narayan would go on to describe his new country as a "yam between two boulders," a phrase that continues to epitomize its geo-political precariousness. "Maintain friendly relations with the emperor of China," the king would counsel his people, adding:

> Great friendship should also be maintained with the emperor beyond the Southern Seas (i.e., the British), but he is very clever. He has kept India suppressed and is entrenching himself on the plains. One day that army will come.[2]

Prithvi Narayan would codify such thinking later in life, but a key tenet of his foreign policy had emerged with clarity: he considered the threat from the south more serious, another perception that would endure. Acknowledging the fragility of his triumph, however, he sought Company acquiescence to his rule at the very least. Prithvi Narayan began corresponding with Governor Warren Hastings, who now saw co-operation with the Gorkhalis, rather than with their displaced foes, as potentially more beneficial to the Company.

As he set out to conquer the principalities to the west, Prithvi Narayan intended to shut off the active trade routes there. But an active army drained the treasury. Seeking to reconcile his political and economic imperatives, the king hoped to establish trade marts on the main route from India to Kathmandu and along several points on the Tibetan border, where Nepalese merchants would purchase goods and ship them on. Rejecting the policy, Tibet closed the trade routes to Nepal in 1770 and suspended all commercial transactions.[3]

The Tibetans had grown increasingly distrustful of Prithvi Narayan's motives, especially after he adopted Hinduism as a central element of state policy. When Prithvi Narayan sent emissaries to Tibet with new and purer coins, Lhasa insisted the Gorkhalis first buy back at face value the debased coins in circulation. The Gorkhalis, insisting they bore no responsibility for the actions of their vanquished predecessors, argued that the coins should be exchanged on the basis of their relative value. As Lhasa prepared to wield its most effective weapon, in the form of a salt embargo, the Gorkhalis perceived an organized Tibetan resistance to their wider campaign of military expansion.[4]

Britain sees back door to China

Nepalese obstructionism had forced the British to contemplate trade with Tibet through alternative routes, an imperative that grew with the Company's acknowledgment of the access the region provided to the vast and lucrative markets of western China. But the window of opportunity was narrowing, as Bhutan grew more assertive in the region. Shortly after the Gorkhali conquest of Kathmandu valley, Bhutan seized the Chumbi valley from Sikkim, taking control of the routes into Tibet through that area. By 1772 Prithvi Narayan's armies, repulsed by the western principalities, had turned eastward.

That year Bhutan attacked the principality of Cooch Bihar, north of Bengal, then mired in a succession dispute. Asserting their traditional right to appoint the rulers, the Bhutanese seized control of the state and installed their own candidate on the throne. This brought part of the access area between Sikkim and the plains under Bhutanese control. Receiving pleas of help from the ousted ruler, Governor Warren Hastings responded, in his words, "from a love of justice and desire of assisting the distressed."[5] Company forces drove out the Bhutanese from Cooch Bihar in 1773, while internal rivals deposed Bhutan's Desi Shidariva. The prospect of growing British influence in the eastern hills goaded Prithvi Narayan to seek the Panchen Lama's mediation between the Bhutanese and the Company.[6] The new Bhutanese ruler, anxious to forestall a fully fledged British invasion, also appealed to the lama who, in a formal letter, urged Hastings to show leniency.

In 1774 Bhutan signed a treaty with the head of the British mission, George Bogle (a close aide to Hastings) and in so doing it became the first hill state to enter into a formal agreement with the East India Company. Hastings, who had just been promoted from Governor of Bengal to Governor-General of all Company possessions in India, was quick to detect the commercial and political opening the Panchen Lama's intercession offered. The gifts the lama had sent with his letter offered Hastings evidence of Tibet's wealth and artisanship, and suggested that the region was at the heart of the central Asian trading networks.[7]

Seeing the possibility of sending a mission to Tibet, a country no Briton had ever visited, Hastings chose Bogle for the job.

There was one big problem. The Qianlong emperor had decreed that no "Moghul, Indian, Pathan or Englishman should be admitted to Tibet without royal authority."[8] Here, too, help came from the Panchen Lama, who seemed prepared to exercise some independence from Beijing. While the Bogle mission was delayed in Bhutan, as the Panchen Lama sought Lhasa's official approval for the visit, Nepalese forces crossed into the Morang region in the Terai, cutting off the route to Tibet through the vital Walung Chung pass. The number of trans-Himalayan routes the British could hope to use without Kathmandu's acquiescence was dwindling.

Tibetan–British contacts

The Panchen Lama received Bogle in Shigatse in October 1774 and the two men struck a close companionship. Yet the Qing grip on Tibet proved too powerful and Bogle was unable to obtain the Panchen Lama's approval for either a commercial treaty or a visit to Lhasa. The lama used the visit to discuss developments in the wider region, including the policies of Prithvi Narayan, who had sent another envoy to inform Lhasa and Shigatse that he had subjugated the eastern territories. The king, according to Bogle, insisted that he did not wish to quarrel with the Tibetans, "but if they had a mind for war, he let them know he was well prepared."[9] The Panchen Lama complained that the Gorkhalis' oppressive tolls and levies had virtually snuffed out the flourishing trade between Tibet and India through the Nepalese mountain passes.[10]

While negotiating with the Panchen Lama, the Gorkhalis were embroiled in hostilities with Sikkim. The soldiers Nepal had sent in aid of the Bhutanese the previous year had massed on the frontier with Sikkim after being denied passage eastward. Now they crossed the border to occupy large parts of Sikkim, breaking a promise the Panchen Lama insisted Prithvi Narayan had made to Lhasa that he would not threaten Tibet or its tributary states. Bogle told the lama that he saw nothing "more likely to make the Gorkha Rajah ... confine himself to his own country than the knowledge of a connection between the government of Tibet and that of Bengal."[11]

On his return from Tibet, Bogle reported to Hastings:

> The opening of the road through Nepal and obtaining the abolition of the duties and exactions which have lately been imposed on trade in that country appears an object of great importance towards establishing a free communication between Bengal and Tibet.[12]

Despite his failure to grant Britain's commercial wishes, the Panchen Lama sought to keep open channels of communication with Calcutta. It was an endeavor fraught with peril. Opposition from both the Qing court and Lhasa could be expected not only to grow, but also to provide the two common cause to rally against Tashilhunpo, the seat of the Panchen Lama and the spiritual and political center of western Tibet. Settling the trade and coinage questions with Kathmandu thus became a growing priority for the Panchen Lama. The death of Prithvi Narayan Shah in January 1775 presented him with a new opportunity.

After hearing of the enthronement of Pratap Singh Shah – who he considered less belligerent than his father – the Panchen Lama wrote to Kathmandu offering to maintain their ancient ties. Pratap Singh dispatched a delegation to Lhasa, which signed a treaty in August 1775 stipulating that the rate of exchange between gold and silver would be either fixed jointly between the two governments or determined by the merchants. Nepal would send coins of the proper alloy to Tibet, while the privileged position of the Newar merchants and shopkeepers in Lhasa would be maintained. Tibet pledged to guarantee Kuti and Kerong as the only points for trade with Bengal and closed the eastern and western plains-mountain routes to Hindu ascetic traders as well as regular Indian merchants. Both, however, would be allowed free movement in Kathmandu valley as part of their transactions. Any party violating the treaty would have to pay the other side a fine of 120 kg in gold.[13]

The treaty did not settle the original dispute over the debased Malla currency or provide the precise trading arrangements the signatories had sought. Instead, new discord set in. A representative of the Sikkimese ruler was also present at the treaty deliberations, during which Nepal and Sikkim also fixed their boundary. Tibet consented to pay 4,000 rupees in compensation to Nepal for the death of four emissaries it had sent to the Sikkim court, while Kathmandu agreed to refrain from further aggression against Sikkim and to sever all connections with the Bhutanese. Privately, Kathmandu chafed at what it considered unwarranted intervention by the Tibetans on behalf of Sikkim. The Nepalese court was infuriated by the Panchen Lama's effort to pressure Kathmandu to return some of the recently acquired territories to its original owners.[14] Pratap Singh ordered his troops further east into Sikkim, angering the Tibetans.[15]

The British had come to see the route to Tibet through Bhutan more promising and the Bhutanese more amenable to Company interests, especially after their military rout.[16] Yet fissures in the Gorkhali court – symbolized by Pratap Singh's decision to exile his younger brother, Bahadur Shah, to India, immediately upon ascending the throne – encouraged the Company to take a new look at Nepal. But Pratap Singh died unexpectedly in November 1777, leaving his infant son, Rana Bahadur, on the throne.

Upon becoming regent, Rajendra Lakshmi, the new king's mother, recalled Bahadur from exile. The in-laws ruled jointly until their priorities clashed, particularly over stepping up territorial conquests. Bahadur briefly succeeded in imprisoning Rajendra Lakshmi before she mobilized loyalists to regain power and exile her brother-in-law once again. The deepening factionalism in Kathmandu only seemed to intensify the Company's eagerness to reopen the valley's trade routes. The British sought four trading posts in Nepal to cover eastern, middle and western Tibet, even as they continued efforts to open a direct route to Lhasa through Bhutan.

Opposition from Lhasa and Beijing

Vexed by Kathmandu's desire to monopolize Tibetan trade, the Company now confronted the Tibetans' growing ambivalence. The Panchen Lama, who had cordially received Bogle, denied another British officer entry into Tashilhunpo, citing opposition from both Lhasa and Beijing.[17] Following the Panchen Lama's contacts with the British, the Chinese emperor had repeatedly invited the Tibetan leader to Beijing. As the latest invitation coincided with Qianlong's seventieth birthday celebrations in 1779, the Panchen Lama decided to go. Before leaving, he wrote to Nepal on the importance of reopening the trade routes.

Encouraged by Bogle's mission, Hastings viewed the Tibetan leader as a possible mediator with Beijing. He believed Bogle had failed to obtain a trade agreement with Shigatse in 1775 primarily because of Qing opposition. But Hastings, who planned to send Bogle to the Chinese capital during the Panchen Lama's visit, had to abandon the effort because of the lama's mysterious death in Beijing in 1780. Bogle himself died in Calcutta six months later.

Hastings sent Lieutenant Samuel Turner, a relative serving in the Company army, to attend the installation of the new Panchen Lama in 1783. But Turner quickly discovered that power had shifted to Lhasa, where he was not allowed to proceed. He, too, counseled Hastings to focus on the Kuti route. Gorkhali suspicions of possible British support to the western states, coupled with instability in the court, discouraged foreign traders from traveling through Nepal, a key provision of the 1775 treaty. The Tibetans started to look for alternatives through Sikkim and Bhutan, which Kathmandu considered a violation of the treaty.[18]

First Nepal–Tibet war

Rajendra Lakshmi's death in 1785, before King Rana Bahadur attained majority, paved the way for Bahadur Shah's return as regent. After the failure of Pratap Singh's initiatives, Tibetan affairs had receded to the background. With the military making new demands on the treasury, Bahadur focused once again on the trade and coinage issues. Another spur was the political situation in Tibet, where the Eighth Dalai Lama had assumed political authority, following Panchen Lama's death, and had begun joint rule with the Chinese ambans.[19] Sensing a hardening of Lhasa's stance, the Nepalese accused the Tibetans of mixing dust with its exported salt, and of imposing heavy taxes on flour. Bahadur's proposal for talks was rebuffed as the Tibetans indicated, according to Nepalese records, that "if the Goorkha wished for war, he was welcome to advance."[20]

The prospect of full-blown conflict grew as the Tenth Shamarpa Lama, a half-brother of the late Panchen Lama, arrived in Kathmandu in early 1788. A brother of the regent in Tashilhunpo, the Shamarpa was also related to the Dalai Lama's family, but represented a rival sect. Involved in a bitter dispute over the generous gifts Qianlong had bestowed on the third Panchen Lama, Shamarpa eventually received his share. The Dalai Lama's regent, however, placed him under house arrest on charges of embezzlement. Fearing suppression of the lamaist school he represented, the Shamarpa Lama fled Tibet through Sikkim. When he arrived in Kathmandu, Bahadur Shah appointed him advisor on Tibetan affairs, a decision that infuriated Lhasa. Seeking to use the Shamarpa's presence to resolve the long-running dispute with Tibet, Bahadur Shah threatened to occupy Kuti and Kerong.[21] Lhasa responded by closing the trade routes.

Nepal wrote to the Chinese emperor explaining the origins of the dispute and complaining about Tibet's failure to co-operate, but the ambans chose not to forward the missive to Beijing.[22] Bahadur mounted a two-pronged assault on the Tsang province in 1788. From the Kerong corridor, some 6,000 troops backed by 3,200 porters set out for Tashilhunpo, 640 km away. During one of the early battles, the Tibetans captured a Nepalese commander, prompting Kathmandu to send reinforcements that eventually freed him. On the eastern Kuti front, 11,000 soldiers and 3,000 porters marched ahead with greater ease.

Tashilhunpo sent pleas for help to both China and the East India Company. In his letter to the British, the regent for the Panchen Lama urged the governor-general, Charles Cornwallis, to maintain strict secrecy over the correspondence. The Dalai Lama, for his part, sought to step up pressure by encouraging the ruler of the principality of Jumla in western Nepal to renew its hostilities with the Gorkhalis. The ruler captured some Gorkhali fortresses before facing a counter-offensive that brought his land under Kathmandu's control for the first time. The Jumla ruler himself fled into exile in Tibet.

Cornwallis carefully weighed the economic and political costs of intervention. Despite having surrendered to George Washington's army at Yorktown a decade earlier, an act that set the stage for the loss of the American colonies, Cornwallis' military reputation in London was still sufficiently intact to warrant his current appointment. The new governor-general was disinclined to risk precipitate action at a time when his predecessor, Warren Hastings, was facing a grueling impeachment trial at Westminster, accused of poor military judgment, maladministration and bestowing undue patronage during his tenure in India. In the end, Cornwallis wrote to the Panchen Lama explaining the huge costs involved in sending an army to Shigatse and reminding him that the British had suffered no provocation or injury from the Nepalese. Furthermore, Cornwallis wrote, the Chinese emperor might be displeased with any British interference in Tibet that Beijing had not explicitly invited.

Pledging not to assist to Nepal, the governor-general refused to maintain the secrecy the Panchen Lama had sought with regard to the Company's extensive commercial relations with China.[23] The system of trade in Canton that had informally been in place since the seventeenth century, and was carried out through a handful of Beijing-selected merchants, had created regular disputes. This forced local authorities to issue edicts that British traders found increasingly restrictive. In an attempt to gain greater trade rights, they had lobbied for an audience with the emperor to make requests for better facilities, a process that was under way.

Hearing of the Nepalese invasion, Qianlong sent three senior officials to investigate. Most Tibetans wanted to repulse the Nepalese militarily, but the imperial officers leading 2,000 Chinese troops into Tibet seemed unsure of victory. Instead, they pressed the Tibetans to reach an early agreement with Nepal. As the Nepalese forces closed in on Tashilhunpo, the Tibetans agreed to open negotiations. In the east, Nepalese forces launched a simultaneous attack on Sikkim with a view to controlling the crucial Chumbi valley trade route. Lhasa, in Kathmandu's view, had opened that route in violation of their treaty. The Gorkhali forces drove the ruler of Sikkim into exile in Tibet and occupied all of western Sikkim.

In their report to Beijing, the Qing investigators blamed members of the Tibetan government and the ambans for the war.[24] They also informed the Nepalese that the dispute could be resolved if Kathmandu sent a high-level mission to the emperor with gifts. Expecting better terms with the Tibetans through Qing intercession, the Nepalese accepted. The result was the Kerong Treaty of 1789, which granted Kathmandu some territory and important commercial concessions. Tibet agreed to exchange one pure coin for two debased ones and to pay 50,000 rupees to Nepal each year. According to Nepalese sources, Kathmandu regained control of Kuti, while the Tibetans acknowledged the Gorkhali succession to the Mallas' authority over Kathmandu valley. In short, the Nepalese believed they had won the war.

The imperial mediators apparently did not take part in the negotiations or examine the treaty's contents. Anxious to avoid military action at all costs, they seemed satisfied with Kathmandu's readiness to send a mission to Beijing.[25] The imperial commanders reported to Beijing that they had driven out the Nepalese without the loss of a single Chinese soldier. The invaders had not only surrendered but would now be paying tribute to the Qing court, a view the Nepalese did not share. The chief imperial investigator did not inform Beijing of the terms of the Nepal–Tibet treaty and merely reported how he had obtained a Nepalese pledge never to attack Tibet again. He described Tibet's annual payments as "land rent" rather than a tribute.[26] From those reports, Beijing, too, had good reason to celebrate a resounding victory.

Nepal sent a 25-member mission to Beijing in September 1789 with a memorial and presents to Qianlong. Received with full honors by the Qing court, the delegation remained in the Chinese capital for a month and a half. Granting the delegates four audiences, the emperor presented far more valuable gifts to the Nepalese monarch. Qianlong also bestowed the Chinese title of "Ertini Wang" (Brilliant King) on Rana Bahadur Shah. Bahadur Shah received the title of "Kung" (Duke).[27]

The Tibetans had willingly paid the first installment to secure the Nepalese withdrawal. The Dalai Lama now sought a reduction in payments, insisting the treaty contained a payment reduction provision on condition that a senior Tibetan official visited Nepal and made a formal request to this effect. But the Tibetans felt they had legitimate grounds to cease payment altogether, since Nepal had become a Qing tributary following the king's acceptance of the Chinese feudatory title.[28]

Second Nepal–Tibet war

Accusing Lhasa of bad faith, Kathmandu stepped up its threats. Tibet proposed talks in Kuti in August, and Nepal sent the Shamarpa Lama as a delegate. The Tibetans insisted the Nepalese had come prepared for a fight, while the Nepalese accused the Tibetans of trying to arrest the Shamarpa Lama and force a war.[29] An 18,000-strong Nepalese army marched to Tashilhunpo from Kerong, Kuti and Kharta, in far eastern Nepal, meeting virtually no resistance. The regent fled with the infant Panchen Lama to Lhasa, as the Tibetans sent pleas for assistance to Beijing.

Hearing of the second Nepalese invasion, Qianlong summoned the chief Qing official he had sent to investigate the first attack, but according to Chinese annals he had since committed suicide.[30] Punishing the commanders of the first campaign, Qianlong sought new military leaders for a decisive operation against the Nepalese, as more bad news came from Shigatse. The Nepalese commanders had demanded 120 kg of gold and 100,000 rupees from the lamas in money owed under the peace treaty. Rebuffed, the Nepalese then sacked the Tashilhunpo monastery. Mindful of the threat to Beijing's regional influence a Tibetan rout would represent, Qianlong also believed the lamas might have appealed for British aid.[31]

The man Qianlong chose to lead the punitive expedition was Fukangan, a nephew of the empress, considered an able but unscrupulous military commander. The general had distinguished himself by suppressing rebellions in the western Chinese provinces of Sichuan and Gansu, and he had been responsible for pacifying unrest in the recently occupied island of Taiwan. Some 10,000 troops were withdrawn from the Eight Banners, the force that had led the conquest of China, from the Army of the Green Standard, an exclusively Chinese force, and from military colonies in the border areas. The army marched into Tibet from Qinghai during the winter of 1791–1792, crossing high mountain passes in deep snow. During the long advance to Tibet, local officials gave logistical support to the expedition.[32]

To buy time the emperor offered the Nepalese the prospect of a diplomatic resolution. Dispatching an emissary to Kathmandu, Qianlong demanded the restitution of the Tashilhunpo plunder and the surrender of the Shamarpa Lama. Privately, the Chinese also encouraged the Newar traders in Tibet to incite their brethren in Kathmandu Valley against the Gorkhalis.[33] Bahadur Shah seemed to discount the likelihood of a costly and arduous trans-Himalayan Qing expedition in defense of Tibet, but was cautious enough to make preparations.

Arriving in Kathmandu in January 1792, the Chinese envoy discovered that a British delegate had just preceded him on a trade mission. Bahadur Shah believed he could win political and military support from the British if he signed a commercial treaty, a perception the Company assiduously encouraged. The regent mustered enough support, in a court traditionally suspicious of the Company, to sign the treaty on March 1, 1792. By this time the Chinese envoy had recorded his annoyance with Bahadur's indifference.[34]

Nepalese forces arrested a Newar trader trying to cross the border and sent him to Kathmandu, where Bahadur Shah personally interrogated him. Learning of Fukangan's arrival in Tibet, Bahadur released the trader and sent him to the Chinese general with a letter citing Nepal's grievances. He also hinted that Nepal had reined in the British who had long harbored designs on Tibet. Abandoning the Qing strategy of secrecy, Fukangan wrote to the British about his plan to invade Nepal and sought the support of all neighboring powers.[35] He also experienced a resurgence of the old Tibetan fears of an avowedly Hindu neighbor. "I am a monk [so] I must not encourage armies to advance and injure living beings," Chinese annals record the Dalai Lama as telling him.

> But the Gorkhas do not believe in Buddhism. Their will is to ridicule us. Therefore, I would like to emphasize the use of military force to solve disturbances in the border areas. If we could do so, the Yellow Hat sect will be protected.[36]

Sino-Nepalese war

By the time the main Chinese force arrived in central Tibet in the summer of 1792, the Nepalese had evacuated Tashilhunpo and retreated some 250 km to the Dingri Plains. In preparation for the Chinese offensive, the Nepalese court had appointed Damodar Pande as overall commander.[37] On the Kuti front, the battles started with small confrontations. The Nepalese had maintained strong defensive positions, but they were swiftly pushed back. The Chinese marched through Kerong amid a heavy loss of life on both sides, forcing the Nepalese to retreat further.

After another series of battles, the Nepalese pulled back almost 85 km from the border, securing defensive positions along the Betrawati River. Reaching a deadlock 32 km from Kathmandu, Bahadur Shah appealed for British military aid.[38] Cornwallis also received a letter from the Dalai Lama informing him that the Chinese army had defeated the Nepalese and urging him not to interfere on their behalf.[39] Echoing his missive to the Tibetans, the governor-general declined Bahadur's request, citing as his reason the Company's extensive commercial relations with the Chinese.[40]

The British situation, however, was becoming more dire. A Chinese force, in the words of a chronicler, now had "a distant view of the valley of the Ganges, and of the richest of the East India Company's possessions."[41] If Chinese troops were to subdue Nepal and maintain a permanent presence, it was felt that the border disputes which would almost inevitably follow would impair commercial relations between the Company and China in Canton. The first British embassy of 1788 was called off after the sudden death its leader. A second was quickly organized under Lord George Macartney, who was in China at the time. Military intervention on behalf of Nepal would have threatened Chinese–British relations, and British military aid to Nepal would have required a direct departure from the policy laid down for the Company's general guidance by Parliament. The practical challenges of deploying a force over harsh terrain were an added disincentive to intervening on Nepal's behalf.

Making the best of the situation, Cornwallis offered to send an envoy to mediate between China and Nepal.[42] Behind the veneer of neutrality, Calcutta believed it could establish direct contacts with Fukangan and collect intelligence on Nepal while Kathmandu and Beijing confronted each other. The Nepalese account of the war spoke of significant Chinese losses in a series of subsequent battles and floods. The overextended Chinese dropped their insistence to negotiate only after capturing Nuwakot. The Nepalese, for their part, failed to negotiate a settlement while still in control of Tibetan territory and put too much faith in the prospect of British assistance.

After a major battle on October 5, 1792, the Nepalese recognized that prolonged conflict would endanger not only their military reputation but also their independence. Putting a positive face on the events, a Nepalese chronicle noted: "[T]he Chinese emperor, thinking it better to live in friendship with the Gorkhalis, made peace with them."[43] The Chinese were equally keen to negotiate. Faced with overstretched lines of communication and the risk of losing supplies, Fukangan hoped to cross the pass back into Tibet before the advent of winter. He negotiated peace terms that were later approved by the emperor.[44]

Under the terms of the Treaty of Betrawati, the Nepalese agreed to restore all their plunder, to pay an annual tribute to the emperor of China and to send an embassy to Beijing once every five years. The Nepalese had to withdraw entirely from Tibet and renounce any trans-Himalayan ambitions, while China undertook to assist Nepal if it was ever invaded by a foreign power. Although no text of the treaty was ever formalized, its provisions were detailed in secondary sources.[45] Nepal promptly sent a mission to China in October 1792 carrying a special letter and gifts from Rana Bahadur to Qianlong.[46]

Embittered by what it considered Britain's betrayal, Kathmandu saw little justification for the Kirkpatrick mission, which had been tasked with inducing the Nepalese to abide by the 1792 commercial treaty, and especially to encourage the wool trade with Tibet through Nepal. Kirkpatrick was also instructed to press upon the Nepalese the urgency of establishing a resident British officer to protect the trade and improve relations.[47] After some delay, the mission was allowed to travel to Kathmandu, but it was viewed from the start with utmost suspicion. Bahadur Shah conveyed to Kirkpatrick his disappointment at Britain's failure to provide military assistance in Nepal's hour of need.[48] Sensing the futility of the enterprise, Kirkpatrick shortly afterward returned to Bengal.

Last of Qianlong's "ten glorious military campaigns"

For Qianlong, the Treaty of Betrawati marked the last of the ten glorious military campaigns of his reign. But the war had not been devastating for the Nepalese. An original Chinese objective had been the return of Nepal to the original native tribes, an objective Beijing had to abandon once its troops got bogged down.[49] Although they lost Kerong and Kuti, the Nepalese retained all of the territories to the south of the Himalayas as well as their commercial privileges in Tibet. No Chinese imperial high commissioner was nominated for Nepal. Nor were any Chinese troops left in the kingdom. Kathmandu was not obliged to adopt the Chinese coinage; nor were Nepalese recruits ever conscripted to fight under the Chinese banner.[50]

By breaching the formidable natural defensive barrier between the Indian subcontinent and Central Asia, the Qing had displayed their military might. But the invasion of Nepal taxed Qing supply lines to the limit and the imperial force had been disoriented by the rapid shift from mountain to jungle fighting.[51] The campaign proved extremely expensive for the Qing, and much of the money spent on the campaign was never accounted for satisfactorily.[52] The total cost of the second Gorkha campaign alone, according to Chinese sources, amounted to more than ten million taels, which represented about a quarter of Qing tax income for that year.[53]

Although the British strove to exhibit a posture of strict neutrality, China was not entirely mollified by their refusal to aid Nepal or Tibet. Conceding that Cornwallis' letter had impelled Nepal to submit to the emperor, Fukangan nevertheless gave a very unfavorable account of the conduct of the English, even suspecting that British troops were fighting in the Nepalese army.[54] Lord Macartney, King George III's emissary to the Qing court, blamed the failure of his mission on Manchu suspicions that the British had backed Nepal.[55] The Chinese closed all passes into Tibet to Indian natives, forcing the Company to spend considerable time and resources on studying the possible impact of Sino-Nepalese relations upon British interests in the region.[56]

Victory proved to be an illusion for the Tibetans. The ease with which the Nepalese mounted two successive invasions forced the Chinese to strengthen their control of Tibet's domestic and foreign affairs. Blaming the Nepalese for the conflict, Qianlong also cited abuses by the Tibetan Buddhist monastic establishment. While Lhasa virtually abolished the line of the Shamarpa Lama and made recognition and enthronement of any future incarnate a punishable offense,[57] Qianlong moved to control the process by which all top lamas were chosen. He decreed that a golden urn be sent from Beijing to Lhasa and carry the names of the candidates for the Dalai and Panchen Lamas, from which the amban would draw selections in token consultation with the monastic establishment.[58]

The war proved particularly ruinous for the Nepalese regent, whom most courtiers blamed for the war. King Rana Bahadur, who had turned 18 shortly after the war, was anxious to gain full powers. The rupture in the Kathmandu court was widening fast, turning into a full-blown conflict between Bahadur Shah and his nephew. In 1794 Bahadur was forced to leave the palace, effectively surrendering his political role. When Rana Bahadur decided to marry a Brahmin widow, Bahadur joined the conservative Hindu elite in voicing opposition. Infuriated, the king placed Bahadur under house arrest and went ahead with the marriage. Bahadur Shah, writing to inform the ambans that Rana Bahadur now held the reins of administration, enclosed a letter addressed to the emperor.

Instead of forwarding it to Beijing, the ambans advised Bahadur Shah and Rana Bahadur to live in amity.

The next Nepalese mission to China was not due until 1797, but the court decided to dispatch it two years early. This was because Qianlong, considering it improper to rule longer than the 61-year reign of his grandfather, Kangxi, had abdicated in favor of his son, Jiajing. The Chinese had wanted Nepal to send a special mission to the new emperor, but the Nepalese proposed a single one that would serve both purposes, which Beijing accepted. Although Bahadur had been relieved of all offices, he still sent presents to the emperor. The Chinese politely declined, saying it was against the custom of the Qing court to accept gifts from anyone not holding power.[59] During their 35-day stay in Beijing, the members of the mission held audiences with the emperor on no fewer than 25 occasions.[60] Overall, Sino-Nepalese relations seemed to have grown closer, though largely on Beijing's terms. Among Qianlong's last instructions to his successor were not to interfere unnecessarily in "Goorkha affairs".[61]

Bahadur Shah now wrote to the ambans of his desire to visit China to pay his respects to the new emperor.[62] Instead, they forwarded the missive to Rana Bahadur to ascertain whether the request had the king's approval. Accusing his uncle of plotting a coup with Chinese assistance, the king imprisoned him at the end of February 1797.[63] In late June, Bahadur Shah died amid claims that he was murdered on the orders of his nephew.

In nine years, Bahadur Shah had conquered the whole of western Nepal and Kumaon in an exercise in imperial expansion never before witnessed in the Himalayan region.[64] It was during his regency that, in the words of a leading Nepalese historian: "Nepal passed definitely from the status of an insignificant state to that of a power in the Indian subcontinent."[65] Yet he met a tragic end amid allegations of submission to both the British and the Chinese – the ultimate violation of his father's founding precept.

Conclusion

Any hope Britain or Tibet might have entertained for a revival of the trans-Himalayan trading system after the Gorkhali conquest of Kathmandu valley was frustrated by Prithvi Narayan Shah's determination to impose his own terms, a course of action followed by his immediate successors. The Gorkhali expansion eastward had begun to worry the hitherto aloof Chinese because of the threat it posed to Sikkim and Bhutan, which shared close religious links with the Qing's own protectorate, Tibet. Once the Gorkhalis took advantage of factional quarrels in Tibet to invade the territory, the Qing considered it a challenge to their own prestige. A massive Chinese punitive expedition pushed the Nepalese military back to the outskirts of Kathmandu, forcing it to sue for peace, but not before Beijing had begun counting the high cost of intervention to its side.

Despite their troubled relations with Nepal, the British did not want the kingdom to be defeated, for fear of one day having to confront the Chinese directly. The British did not want to help Nepal either, for that would have affected their extensive commercial interests with China. Their abortive attempt to mediate between Nepal and China ended up alienating both. In seeking to keep both the Nepalese and the British at bay, the Tibetans ended up with tighter Chinese control. The Nepalese, although not fully aware of the implications of the tributary relationship that came as the price for peace, considered the 1792 treaty an opportunity to open direct political links with the Qing court. Despite their impressive military feat, the Chinese were wary of new involvement across the Himalayas given the material and human cost of the war, something neither the Nepalese nor the British understood at the time. Accordingly Nepal and the British East India Company would spend considerable time weighing China's motives and intentions south of the Himalayas.

3 Containment and carnage

Bahadur Shah's death did not consolidate King Rana Bahadur's position, particularly since the late regent's supporters still controlled the influential army. Damodar Pande, the leading commander in the war with the Tibetans, emerged as a rival to Rana Bahadur. Hostility to the monarch grew when he excluded his eldest son from succession in favor of his infant offspring by the controversial Brahmin consort. Unsure of his courtiers' loyalty to the new heir-apparent, Rana Bahadur abdicated in March 1799, placing the infant Girban Yuddha on the throne, and requesting the Chinese grant him royal rank. The Jiajing emperor, who had just assumed independent control after the death of his father, Qianlong, consented – but with a proviso. Since the new ruler was only two years old, his father's name should appear jointly in correspondence.[1]

Satisfied, Rana Bahadur retired to what was officially described as a life of religious meditation on the outskirts of Kathmandu, during which he cared for his smallpox-stricken consort, Kantabati. When she died, Rana Bahadur began desecrating the temples he had sought to propitiate on her behalf. Taking the infant king to the safety of Nuwakot, key courtiers reaffirmed their allegiance to Girban. The former king moved to reassert his authority before realizing he lacked support among important military commanders. In May 1800 Rana Bahadur went into exile in the north Indian pilgrimage of Benares with his senior queen, Rajrajeswari, and a retinue of loyalists, leaving junior queen Subarnaprabha as regent.

Rana Bahadur's departure did little to calm his rivals, who recognized he could rally exiled dissidents and negotiate directly with the British to mount a comeback. As the former king deftly fanned those fears, the British, too, felt they could play off the competing Nepalese factions to win the best terms. The Company was intent on reviving the 1792 commercial treaty and establishing a residency in Kathmandu. Although the Himalayan war had closed Tibet to British India, the Company had used 'native' agents who returned with reports of lucrative trading opportunities. To ward off the British, Damodar Pande and his allies sought Chinese support. In a letter to the ambans, they claimed the ex-king had gone into exile to regain power through British help. The Chinese curtly advised the courtiers to persuade Rana Bahadur to return.[2]

British exploit Nepalese divisions

The third tribute mission to Beijing was due in 1800, but considering the political turmoil in Nepal, the ambans permitted a year's delay.[3] As the situation deteriorated, the ambans allowed a senior Nepalese official to come up to the Tibetan border with the tribute, promising to forward it to Beijing. In this delicate situation, Damodar Pande recognized that any concession to the British, while undermining the threat Rana Bahadur posed, would alienate the Nepalese. But he eventually went along with the British, who, by the end of 1800, saw fewer benefits in wooing Rana Bahadur. Governor-General Richard Wellesley, after vanquishing Mysore's meddlesome Tipu Sultan the previous summer, had drawn the larger lesson from the episode: independent and well-armed native states remained potential allies against the Raj.[4] Although he had greater leverage over Rana Bahadur, Wellesley recognized the uncertainties inherent in restoring the exiled king over the objections of powerful courtiers. That could require him to send an expeditionary force to Nepal, infuriating its people and possibly China.

For Nepal, the most controversial provision of the new commercial treaty was the establishment of a British residency, which Captain W.D. Knox, a member of the ill-fated Kirkpatrick mission, would now head. The main function of the resident, according to the treaty, was to regularize relations between the two governments, but Knox was given secret instructions to obtain information about the government, the military and Nepal's connections with other states, particularly China.[5] As to trade specifically, Knox was told to "direct your attention as to the means of opening a beneficial trade with the countries of Bootan and Tibet either directly with the Company's Provinces, or through the medium of the merchants of Nepal."[6] Wellesley instructed Knox to exercise utmost secrecy in his conduct in Nepal, as the treaty, in the governor-general's words, was based, "not on a desire for an alliance with the British, but on a fear that the British might assist Rana Bahadur to regain the throne in Kathmandu."[7]

Nepal saw the establishment of the residency as a prelude to loss of independence, a signature British legacy in the neighborhood. Holding Damodar Pande responsible for an unpopular treaty, supporters deserted him in large numbers to join Rana Bahadur. Exasperated by the court's antipathy, Knox returned to India in March 1803. Wellesley abrogated the treaty the following year, adding that he had no reason for keeping Rana Bahadur in India against his own will.[8] This set the stage for Rana Bahadur's return home in February 1804. Damodar Pande, who attempted to organize a final resistance, was arrested and executed. The ex-king went on to assume full powers in the name of his son. The Chinese, while interested in these developments, maintained a hands-off policy.[9]

Anticipating greater Company assertiveness after its victory over the Marathas in northern and central India, Rana Bahadur focused on strengthening his army. He occupied the western principality of Palpa, whose ruler he felt had been collaborating with the Company.[10] Rana Bahadur's crackdown on rivals culminated in his assassination in April 1806 by his half-brother, Sher Bahadur

Shah, an act that set off an orgy of violence in the capital. From the carnage rose Bhimsen Thapa, a confidante of Rana Bahadur, who carried the infant king to safety and mounted a bloody purge of the Pandes and other rivals. The two senior queens were forced onto Rana Bahadur's funeral pyre, in accordance with the Hindu practice of *sati*, as the third, Lalita Tripurasundari, became regent.

A "very vigorous rash man"

The British carefully appraised the man one chronicler would call a "very vigorous rash young man who viewed the Company with contempt partly out of hope of protection from the Chinese."[11] One of Bhimsen's first acts was to step up the military campaign in the west beyond Kumaon. The hill territory up to the Sutlej River was either conquered or brought into an alliance with the Gorkha dynasty, giving it firm control over every practical route into Tibet. As the Company had grown into a political entity that now emphasized the sanctity of borders, it gradually abandoned Warren Hastings' policy of appeasing Nepal for trade.

The Chinese, too, were grappling with new challenges. During much of the tumult surrounding Rana Bahadur's abdication, exile and return, the Qing had faced an open rebellion by the White Lotus Society, a secret religious organization that advocated restoration of the Ming Dynasty and promised personal salvation to followers. The uprising may have been one of the consequences of the 1792 war with Nepal. As the Qing demobilized military personnel without giving them the assurance of alternative means of support, many were believed to have joined the rebellion.[12] By the time Bhimsen took power the Qing had suppressed the rebels, but their eight-year uprising had shattered the myth of Manchu invincibility. Wary of new instability, the Chinese keenly watched developments in Nepal. Although the political situation had improved, Kathmandu pleaded that it could send a mission only to Tibet, citing the king's minority as the reason. The request was granted and the mission left in 1807 to hand over the presents and petition to the ambans.[13]

By 1808, the Sikh ruler Ranjit Singh was growing apprehensive of a Nepalese-led hill state in the territory to the north of his domain, particularly one that might compete for control of the strategic Kashmir region.[14] He intervened in support of the state of Kangra, driving the Nepalese invaders back across the Sutlej. But Ranjit Singh, who saw the British as a perennial threat to his dominion, also considered the Nepalese potential allies. Nepal's conquests in the west had provoked disputes with the British. Claiming all territories of the vanquished kings, including those in the plains, Kathmandu had occupied them by 1810. Colonel David Ochterlony, the British commander in the area, instructed the Nepalese general, Amar Singh Thapa, to confine himself to the hills. Unprepared for hostilities with the British, Kathmandu withdrew from the disputed areas. Yet, having seen one native state after another fall into British subsidiary alliances, Bhimsen was growing apprehensive of the Company's motives.

When time came for the fifth tribute mission to China, Nepal again sought permission to send a delegation to the Tibet border, pleading the king's minority.

Suspecting a ploy to abandon the tribute system altogether, the ambans insisted on a fully-fledged mission to Beijing.[15] The compilation of the tribute calendar was exclusively an imperial privilege, formally promulgated and disseminated throughout the empire every year. To receive it was to admit one's tributary status; to refuse it was to place oneself in open insurrection.[16] In general, the imperial court reserved the right to fix the nature of the tribute, but the Nepalese seemed to exercise latitude in the determining of the list.[17]

The Chinese were more particular about the frequency and route of missions from various tributaries, in keeping with the definition of the relationship. The five-yearly Nepalese tribute mission was instructed to arrive by way of Tibet through Chengdu, the capital of Sichuan. The accompanying letters were required to be in the 'petitionary' form used by Chinese officials in addressing the throne.[18] But the Nepalese enjoyed the freedom to draft the letters, allowing the ambans to make the needed changes.[19] The court ritual required that whoever approached the throne perform the kowtow, i.e., kneel three times, and at each kneeling bow three times until his head touched the floor, signifying that the emperor was a god.[20]

The Nepalese mission of 1812 became the first to go all the way to Beijing since 1795. Kathmandu used the opportunity to make a strong appeal for Chinese assistance in the event of war with the British, but received an exhortation to live in harmony. Undaunted, Kathmandu sought out alliances with the rulers of Holkar, Gwalior, Bharatpur, Rampur, Lucknow, Lahore and other Indian states resentful of the British. When an Anglo-Nepalese commission investigating the territorial disputes issued a report in favor of the Company, Bhimsen Thapa decided to challenge it.

Anglo-Nepalese war

During the early nineteenth century, largely for fear of antagonizing China, the Company had carefully avoided war with Nepal. That sensitivity also extended from British military preoccupations in central India and Punjab as well as in Europe. In London there was a growing fear that the Company was becoming dangerously overstretched and that the expanding Indian empire was becoming a state within a state. Gradually, however, most Nepal experts in the British administration seemed to discount the impact war with Nepal would have on London's relations with China.[21]

In the spring of 1814, Governor-General Francis Rawdon-Hastings demanded that Nepal evacuate the disputed territories.[22] When the Company reoccupied the districts in April, Nepal offered no resistance. British forces were withdrawn at the start of the monsoon season, paving the way for the deployment of native police. In early May, Nepalese troops raided the territory, killing several police officers. The Company issued an ultimatum for a settlement, which Nepal rebuffed. Sensing an imminent British invasion, Kathmandu pleaded for Chinese assistance, invoking the 1792 treaty. In a communication to the ambans, the Nepalese claimed the British were planning ultimately to force their way into Tibet.

The skeptical ambans rejected Nepal's request but forwarded a summary of the situation to Beijing. The king of Sikkim, apprehensive of Nepalese expansion, sided with the Company, while the Bhutanese, wary of the British, sympathized with Nepal. The Panchen Lama and some Lhasa officials urged China to assist Nepal. The regent of the Dalai Lama wrote to the heads of Tibetan monasteries to pray for Nepal's military success, but ultimately advised Kathmandu to settle the dispute on the best terms possible.[23]

The governor-general declared war on November 1, 1814, dividing his forces into four separate armies from west to east. The British met with several early disasters attributed to ignorance of the country and of the enemy.[24] Of these four thrusts, only one, led by David Ochterlony in the west, was successful. He was operating on the left bank of the Sutlej River, facing General Amar Singh Thapa and some 3,000 Nepalese troops. Hastings appeared to have genuinely feared that the Chinese might come to the aid of Nepal and issued orders to British commanders not to fire upon Chinese troops unless it was certain that they were hostile. The Company also considered the eventuality of defeated Nepalese forces taking refuge in Tibet.[25]

Nepal sent several more letters to Lhasa in the winter of 1814–1815, describing the seriousness of British aggression and soliciting financial assistance. The situation in the western hills and the Terai was becoming critical. Although the Nepalese soldiers made great use of the terrain, Ochterlony was able to use his superior artillery to blast his way into the fortresses. The British commander also found that he could outmaneuver the Nepalese, thanks to superior logistics. By early 1815 Kathmandu considered suing for peace, but Amar Singh Thapa warned that under the pretence of a settlement, the British would militarily subjugate Nepal.[26] For the British there was much more at stake than teaching the Nepalese a lesson. "To be foiled by the Gurkhas, or to make a discreditable accommodation with them, would have led to incalculable mischief," Hastings would tell the War Office in London.[27] By May, as Kumaon and territories further west fell to the British, General Amar Singh surrendered to Ochterlony. Nepal was required to cede a third of its territory and accept the residency as the price of peace.

In a letter to the ambans, Bhimsen complained that Beijing's continued indifference might force Nepal to give up its traditional relationship with China and become a vassal of the British.[28] The annexation of Kumaon gave British India a common border with Tibet for the first time.[29] Rumors of Asiatic Russian merchants in Tibet had already led the British to view Kumaon and Garhwal as a productive route for direct commerce with Tibet. With the annexation of those territories, and with the Simla hill countries confirmed as Indian protectorates, British hopes of breaking through Tibet's isolation were raised.[30] There was a feeling within the Company that China would not object to its conquest of territories in the western Himalayas. Since the Nepalese had acquired them after 1792, they were not held to form part of the kingdom as understood in the Sino-Nepalese peace terms.[31]

Still, the British did not want to antagonize China at a time when they were simultaneously seeking commercial concessions there through a mission headed by Lord Amherst. British interests in China outweighed any advantages to be gained from war with Nepal. Hastings had warned Lord Amherst that he might be questioned about the situation in the Himalayas.[32] In an effort to win Chinese confidence the British sought to promote relations with Sikkim – a traditional ally of Tibet – by promising to restore territory lost to the Nepalese. The ambans, who had ignored previous Nepalese pleas, now seemed sufficiently alarmed. Hastings had sent letters to China and all the neighboring powers cautioning them against aiding the enemies of British rule. The Chinese resident forwarded the Nepalese and British missives to Beijing.[33] Still declining to assist Nepal, the emperor instructed the ambans to tighten security on the border.

Growing Sikh and Maratha assertiveness encouraged the Nepalese to procrastinate and eventually refuse to ratify Amar Singh's terms.[34] Ochterlony warned the Nepalese that all other points of the treaty were more or less open to subsequent discussion, but that "they must take either the resident or war."[35] At the end of January 1816, the British made a second thrust, this time aiming for Kathmandu. After a heroic but hopeless resistance, the Nepalese ratified what became known as the Treaty of Sugauli – named after the Indian city it was signed in – on March 4, 1816.

Despite rebuffing the last Nepalese appeal, the Jiajing emperor decided to send a small military force to Tibet to ascertain the state of affairs. As General Saichunga, the Chinese commander in Sichuan province, proceeded to Lhasa, a Nepalese messenger gave him news that a peace treaty had been signed. The general went on to Lhasa and wrote to Hastings in May 1816 about the Nepalese allegation that the Company had demanded "free passage" to Tibet and had ordered Kathmandu to become a British vassal. The governor-general wrote back, blaming Nepal for the war. The Chinese commander had also written to Kathmandu in May, expressing the emperor's displeasure with the allegations in the letter. He warned that China would punish the Nepalese if the accusations turned out to be falsehoods. In response, Kathmandu emphasized the importance of Nepal to the defense of Tibet, but the Chinese commander, now writing jointly with the ambans, became more critical of Kathmandu. Virtually accusing the Nepalese of exaggerating the British threat to Tibet, he warned of a fully-fledged invasion if Kathmandu failed to send the tribute mission on schedule. The Chinese had planned to move troops to the border with Nepal before the Panchen Lama and other Tibetan officials persuaded the Chinese commander to wait for a Nepalese mission.[36]

Nepal advances "China threat"

Nepal now hoped to exploit the Company's apprehensions over the presence of the Chinese army in Tibet to evict the British residency and restore part or all of the territory lost in the Sugauli Treaty. At this point, Hastings, too, seemed prepared for major concessions on Nepal in order to appease China; even the withdrawal of the residency as a last resort.[37] But he was skeptical of Kathmandu's reading of Chinese sentiments, and wrote directly to the Chinese commander in Tibet. Meanwhile, receiving the Nepalese delegation at Shigatse, the Chinese commander scolded them for having brought on the war.[38]

When the Nepalese sought Beijing's help to secure the withdrawal of the residency, the Chinese commander referred to the British explanation that Kathmandu had consented to its establishment in the first place.[39] But Saichunga did request Calcutta withdraw the resident in consideration of the "ties of friendship" between China and India.[40] Hastings deftly said he could do so if China were to station an agent in Kathmandu to prevent the recurrence of disputes. The Chinese refused, thus tacitly accepting the British presence. The extent of the Qing court's reluctance to get involved in the Anglo-Nepalese conflict would be underscored when it scolded Saichunga for issuing an official document counseling both sides to pursue peace.[41]

The British were not unanimous in claiming victory, either. The first foray into Nepal in 1814–1815 had troubled the Duke of York, the Commander-in-Chief of the British army, who wondered why "it was ever necessary." Even after the triumph the government and the directors were not always convinced of the necessity of that war, and there was some reluctance to grant the campaign's hero, now Major-General Ochterlony, a £1,000 annuity.[42] By the end of 1816, the Company decided to return to Nepal part of the Terai land it had seized during the war. Judging from the timings of correspondence between Nepal, India and China it seems likely this decision was the result of the Saichunga mission, and in particular Britain's eagerness to demonstrate to the Chinese that they had no intention of annexing Nepal.[43]

Greater clarity in trans-Himalayan triangle

After the Sugauli Treaty, British India's relations with China vis-à-vis Nepal seemed to have acquired greater clarity. Beijing saw Tibet as an integral part of its frontier-security system, and China would respond to any threat there. As to Nepal, China considered it free to act in domestic and foreign affairs as long as it dispatched periodic missions to Beijing.

Shortly after the war, King Girban Yuddha attained majority and was growing vexed by Bhimsen's refusal to turn over full powers. But Girban Yuddha contracted smallpox and died, leaving the throne to his three-year-old son, Rajendra Bikram.[44] The senior queen, Rajendra's mother, became a *sati*, while two weeks later, the junior queen died, purportedly of smallpox. As another spate of conspiracy theories swirled, Lalita Tripurasundari, now the queen grandmother, again stepped into the regency. The prime minister, whose position was secured, was still personally held responsible for Nepal's defeat in the war. He saw an opportunity to bolster his nationalist credentials. In announcing Girban Yuddha's death to the Chinese emperor, Bhimsen made an appeal for support in future hostilities with the British. Beijing instructed the infant monarch to "remain on good terms with his neighbors and attend to all matters with the utmost diligence."[45]

Bhimsen then pursued a dual-track approach. He adhered to the terms of the Sugauli Treaty and projected himself to the British as the best guarantor of peace. By maintaining a large standing army, he presented himself to his compatriots as the bulwark against further British intervention. Kathmandu continued restrictions on Indian traders and tightly controlled access to the British resident.[46] He would seek to widen his room for maneuver at the first indication of an alteration in the balance of power.

Considering Britain's preoccupation with renewed wars in central India, Bhimsen instructed the 1817 tribute mission to make a personal appeal for assistance to the emperor. The delegation leader was told to maintain friendly relations with Calcutta.[47] Bhimsen now tried to re-establish contacts with key Indian states and apparently contemplated renewing hostilities with the British. But the reverses the Marathas suffered in November 1817 dashed Kathmandu's hopes. Still, Bhimsen continued with the reorganization and expansion of the Nepalese military.

The death of the Jiajing emperor in 1820 required the dispatch of a special Nepalese mission to congratulate his successor, Daoguang. Kathmandu sought permission to send a single mission with usual five-yearly presents and special presents for the new emperor, which the ambans granted. As the delegation left for Beijing in 1822, Bhimsen made yet another appeal for Chinese assistance against the British, to little avail.[48] However, Beijing was eager to confer ceremonialism on the relationship. Daoguang granted Bhimsen the right to wear the double-eyed peacock's feather, a highly prized and distinguished decoration granted to dignitaries immediately below imperial ranks.[49] Five years later, Daoguang granted the leader of the mission 17 audiences,[50] but that translated into little tangible support for Bhimsen.

Although the prime minister had benefited from the succession of two minors to the throne, his power rested with his ability to manage the court factions.[51] Bhimsen would shortly face a double blow: the death of Queen Regent Lalita in 1832 followed by Rajendra's attainment of majority the following year. Brian Hodgson, the new resident, began demanding meetings with Rajendra directly so that he could better acquaint the court with the real intention of the British and free the residency from Bhimsen's machinations.[52] The prime minister made no effort to seek Chinese support through the tribute mission due that year, probably dissuaded by Beijing's failure to aid Burma, another Qing tributary, in its war with Britain.

Although China had not deliberately surrendered its dominance in Nepal to Britain, the effect was unmistakable. Thus, for Bhimsen, accommodation with the Company on the best possible terms became the only realistic alternative. By 1834, he had granted the resident direct access to the king and dispatched Mathabar Singh – a nephew and confidant – to Calcutta with instructions to proceed to England with professions of good faith. Britain, which had initially favored the overture, refused to issue Mathabar formal papers to proceed from Calcutta to London in a shift some attributed to Hodgson's desire to undermine the Thapas.[53] The residency shifted its support to the rival Pande family, but, unbeknownst to Hodgson, Rana Jang Pande, the faction's leader, was assuring the Chinese emperor that "even now we can defeat them [the British] if the emperor orders this to be done, if aid is given and we are restored to our forefathers' posts."[54]

Growing factionalism in the Nepalese court

As King Rajendra moved to assert his authority, the senior queen, Samrajya Lakshmi, joined court Brahmins in undermining the prime minister. For the British, the monarchy posed its own problems, with Hodgson reporting that Rajendra had reached a secret understanding with Punjab's Ranjit Singh.[55] Fresh Nepalese troop deployments along the southern frontier, amid rumors that Russia was contemplating an invasion of India, raised British suspicions. Bhimsen's fortunes suffered another blow in 1837 when Rajendra took away his authority to appoint the leader of the mission to China.[56]

The mission leader, Pushkar Shah, a distant relation of the royal family, carried a letter to the emperor in which Rajendra described Bhimsen as a pro-British courtier. The king requested either troops or a subsidy of 20 million rupees to oppose the British, which Beijing rebuffed. As the power equations were being reset, the youngest son of the senior queen suddenly died. The Pande clan spread rumors of Bhimsen's involvement, ensuring his imprisonment. Under pressure from the senior queen, Rajendra appointed Rana Jang as prime minister.

As the opposition split into factions, Rajendra dismissed Pande three months later and appointed his chief preceptor, Ranganath Poudyal, as prime minister. In March 1838, the charges against Bhimsen Thapa were withdrawn and he was permitted to retire to his ancestral home in Gorkha. Poudyal, who steadily lost popularity, was replaced by Pushkar Shah, who had just returned from Beijing. Hodgson now wrote of a perceptible anti-British tilt in Kathmandu as the court sent emissaries to Burma, China, Lahore and Gwalior with letters from Rajendra. Agreeing that Nepal was the most dangerous enemy the British faced in India, Governor-General Auckland put on a show of strength by sending an "army of observation" to the border. Lord Auckland advised Hodgson, however, that the army would not be used against Nepal because the campaign just begun in Afghanistan "renders it inexpedient that we should seek to force on a crisis, at this time, on our relations with Kathmandoo."[57]

In an effort to pacify the governor-general, Rajendra recalled Bhimsen from Gorkha, an act that drove the Pandes to resurrect the poison charge and throw him back in prison. Rana Jang returned as prime minister in April and oversaw Bhimsen's trial, during which he now stood accused of poisoning both Girban Yuddha and his widow. In July, the old general committed suicide in prison.[58]

The imbroglio in Afghanistan and the triumph of anti-British forces in Burma prompted Kathmandu to dispatch diplomatic missions in 1839. Clearly, Hodgson's calculations in supporting Rajendra had failed. The resident threatened war if the palace did not mend its ways, and shifted support instead to Ranganath

Poudyal, who became premier. Rajendra promised to "totally cease all secret intrigues whatever by messengers or letters" and "to have no further intercourse with dependent allies of the Company" without British permission.[59]

The Opium War

Tensions were growing between Britain and the Qing, who were pressing for stronger measures to suppress the growing opium trade they blamed for undermining the social relationships so essential to Confucian society.[60] Yet the fact remained that the British conquest of India was largely sustained by the fast-growing net revenue from opium sold in China.[61] The Anglo-Chinese crisis raised Nepal's hopes of gaining assistance from Beijing. Rana Jang Pande, by now acknowledged as the most anti-British courtier, was appointed prime minister in February 1840 and Kathmandu sent a letter to the Qing emperor offering to attack the British in India.[62] The ambans refused to forward it to Beijing, reminding Kathmandu that the Chinese were perfectly capable of handling the British threat to Canton.

China hardly wanted trouble with the British on a distant section of the frontier when it already faced a major challenge on the mainland. This was a conclusion Calcutta was quick to act on. Governor-General Auckland instructed Hodgson to press the palace to dismiss Rana Jang Pande and appoint a government consisting of pro-British courtiers.[63] The so-called "peace party," consisting of junior Queen Rajya Lakshmi and Ranganath Poudyal, was led by Fatteh Jang Shah as prime minister in November. The rival faction responded by dispatching envoys to the rulers of Punjab and Gwalior with instructions to give verbal messages highlighting the need for resistance to British designs. But individual rulers had their own considerations. The ruler of Gwalior, in his eagerness to ingratiate himself with the British, forwarded the Nepalese message to the British.[64]

In the wake of Chinese reverses in the Opium War, Kathmandu believed Beijing might become more receptive to a military alliance. Rajendra appointed Jagat Bam Pande, a member of the anti-British camp, as leader of the tribute mission. The envoy left Kathmandu in July 1942 with a letter to the emperor asking for troops or financial assistance to cope with an alleged British threat to invade Nepal if it refused to allow the transit of a British army to Tibet.[65] By the time Jagat Bam reached Beijing, the Opium War had been settled through the Treaty of Nanking. Beijing rejected Nepal's request for assistance, saying it was not China's policy "to send troops to protect the countries of the foreign barbarians."[66]

Although the British had inflicted a decisive defeat on the Qing, they had a lingering fear of China's future motives and ambitions in Nepal. At this point one leading Chinese diplomat, reviewing his country's defeat in the Opium War, had Nepal in mind while perfecting his version of the "let barbarians fight barbarians" doctrine. He envisaged a two-pronged Nepalese and Russian attack on India complementing a French–American sea attack.[67] British apprehensions were exacerbated by the debacle in Afghanistan in 1842, one of the worst military setbacks the Company had faced. The new British Governor-General, Lord Ellenborough, ordered the residency in Kathmandu to desist from interfering in the court's politics.[68]

By 1842 factionalism had deepened to the point where most of the nobles – backed by the military – organized a "national movement." The senior queen, Samrajya Lakshmi, had died the previous year and Crown Prince Surendra's erratic behavior had begun to worry the nobles. They demanded that Rajendra restrain the crown prince and grant authority to the junior queen, Rajya Lakshmi.[69] Mathabar Singh Thapa was invited to return from exile in India and assume the premiership the following year. Mathabar's effort to play off the three court factions against each other tragically backfired on him. Summoned to the palace for urgent consultations late one night in May 1845 the prime minister was shot from behind a screen in the royal chamber. Although first reports suggested that Rajendra himself had opened fire, it was generally believed Jang Bahadur Kunwar, a nephew of Mathabar, had committed the murder on royal orders. After three months of squabbling, a coalition government was formed in September 1845, again headed by Fateh Jang Shah.

The outbreak of the Anglo-Sikh war at the end of the year raised hopes in Nepal that the Company would not be able to outlast the fighting spirit of the Sikhs. Kathmandu yet again turned to Beijing for assistance against the British, but the ambans' reply followed what had become established pattern. The Gorkhas were instructed to "maintain as much as possible good relations with [Calcutta] and have no misunderstanding with them."[70] The Sikhs' defeat forced Kathmandu to ponder its future in the midst of intensifying factionalism.

By autumn 1846, Jang Bahadur was rapidly rising in the army ranks and in the court, while the dominant faction was led by Gagan Singh, a confidant of the queen. On the night of September 14, Gagan Singh was murdered while in prayer at his private chapel. Upon receiving the news, the agitated queen summoned the leading nobles to the palace courtyard in the middle of the night, demanding to know the murderer's identity. As factional finger-pointing escalated into a full-scale war of accusations, Jang's loyalists – the only group that had arrived at the palace fully armed – went on the offensive. In the ensuing massacre, 32 leading nobles and more than 100 others were butchered. Once the fighting subsided, the Kunwar brothers emerged as the sole surviving faction. The queen appointed Jang Bahadur prime minister and commander-in-chief.

Conclusion

Reined in in the north by the Chinese, Nepal stepped up its campaign for territorial expansion in the south, east and west, where another power had become formidable. During the early nineteenth century, the East India Company had been baffled by the nature of the China–Nepal relationship, an ambiguity Nepal shrewdly fostered to its advantage. Territorial disputes along the ill-defined border exacerbated lingering differences over trade, and precipitated full-scale war between British India and Nepal in 1814. Disappointed by Beijing's refusal to offer the military and political support it believed the 1792 peace treaty guaranteed, Kathmandu sought peace with the British at the cost of ceding a third of its territory, hoping to reclaim it another day.

Enduring doubts over the status of Nepal–China relations in British minds helped Nepal limit the damage and even win some concessions from the East India Company. Maintaining relations with the Qing court through the imperial representative in Lhasa, the faction-ridden Nepalese court strove to strengthen its commercial privileges in Tibet, alternately wooing the Chinese and British for the best political terms. But the British, initially wary of Chinese intervention on Nepal's behalf, steadily grew in confidence and were able to adopt a more aggressive stance as China proved itself reluctant to become involved at anything other than a diplomatic level. By the middle of the nineteenth century the last group of contenders in the Nepalese court to survive the cycles of factional bloodshed realized that it was not only China that had seemingly abandoned them: all of Nepal's potential allies against the Company in India had come under Britain's sway.

4 Crowns and empires

If Jang Bahadur comprehended the recklessness of persisting with an anti-British policy, he also understood the benefits of retaining the traditional relationship with China. With disparate remnants of the opposition on British Indian soil, the East India Company still had the capacity to undermine the new government, especially when Jang's personal position was far from secure. Once Queen Rajya Lakshmi realized she lacked Jang's support in her quest to appoint her own son as crown prince, she began plotting against him. Discovering the conspiracy, Jang arrested and executed the key players, stripped the queen of all powers and ordered her exiled to Benares. Citing his own remorse at the massive bloodletting, King Rajendra accompanied her, leaving Crown Prince Surendra at the helm.

Jang had allowed Rajendra to leave on the undertaking that he would forfeit the throne if he failed to return within a stipulated time. From exile, however, the king sent loyalists to Kathmandu to sound out the possibility of regaining powers from Jang. Accusing the monarch of plotting to assassinate him, Jang ousted Rajendra and enthroned Surendra. Undaunted, the deposed king raised an army and headed back into Nepalese territory to regain his throne. But Rajendra's forces were routed, and Jang's soldiers brought the former king to Kathmandu where he would live out his life under guard.

Still uncertain of his legitimacy, Jang reached out for external recognition. Sensing that Governor-General Harding was in no hurry to recognize the new regime, Jang turned his attention northward.[1] The ambans normally reminded Kathmandu when the tribute mission was next due. Since no missive had arrived this time, Jang made his own inquiry.[2] In June 1847, a delegation departed with the traditional gifts and petition to the emperor. Learning of the mission's arrival in Lhasa, the emperor instructed the ambans to recognize the new Nepalese ruler.[3] Thus Jang was able to win formal recognition of his rule from China before Britain.[4] Meanwhile inconsistencies in Jang's policies toward the British started to emerge. In 1848 he offered the British resident the services of eight Nepalese regiments in the war against the Sikhs, which Calcutta declined. The following year Jang granted the queen regent of Lahore asylum in Nepal.[5] The fall of the Sikh kingdom eventually forced him to recognize the importance of maintaining relations with the British.

Across the "black seas"

More confident of his position, Jang decided to visit England. To be received by the Queen as a representative of the Nepalese sovereign, he believed, would strengthen his position back home.[6] Jang also hoped to establish direct contact with the Court of Directors, the Court of Proprietors and Members of Parliament in London, who he believed could give him a stronger hand in negotiations with Calcutta. In early 1850, Jang Bahadur set out on a journey across the "black seas," taboo under Hindu tradition, accompanied by two brothers and several advisers.

Arriving in England in late May, Jang met with Queen Victoria, senior British politicians and top Company officials and visited some key mining and manu-facturing districts, but failed to establish direct correspondence with London. He insisted on visiting France on his way back home, despite British opposition, and arrived in Paris in late August where Prince Louis Napoleon, President of the Republic and the future Emperor Napoleon III, received him.[7] As Jang returned to Kathmandu in February 1851 to great public fanfare, traditionalists resented his sacrilege. In collusion with the palace, they plotted a coup, which Jang easily foiled.

Jang Bahadur continued to pay attention to developments and opportunities across the Himalayas. Hearing of the outbreak of the Taiping Rebellion, Jang offered the emperor the services of 10,000 soldiers, an offer Beijing politely declined.[8] When he sent the next tribute mission to China in August 1852 the circumstances proved politically unpropitious. The British residency reported a rumor that the new Chinese emperor, Xianfeng, had refused to accept the Nepa-lese presents, offended that Jang himself had gone to London to pay respect to the British queen.[9] The emperor was said to have threatened war, although both claims subsequently turned out to be false. However, the enterprise proved eco-nomically novel. The 1852 mission marked the first time Kathmandu allowed members to carry commodities for trading purposes, including opium – under diplomatic privilege – which aroused considerable suspicion among the Chinese.[10]

Nepal's third war with Tibet

The head of the Nepalese mission and his deputy both died in Beijing and the leadership passed to a junior officer. The Taiping Rebellion forced the Nepalese mission to take an alternative route back to Tibet from Beijing, and its return home was delayed by alleged harassment by Tibetan authorities, who now viewed Nepal–China ties with growing wariness.[11] When the sole surviving member reported this back, Jang resolved to go to war against Tibet. China's preoccupation with the rebellion, and British involvement in the Crimean War, made the timing propitious, as did the fragile situation in Tibet, where the Panchen and Dalai Lama had died in quick succession. Jang drew up a longer list of grievances that now included the maltreatment of Newar traders, expulsion of the Nepalese representative from Lhasa, a boundary dispute in the Kuti area, and the imposition of higher customs duties on Nepalese imports.[12]

In response to Jang's ultimatum Lhasa sent representatives to Kathmandu, where the Nepalese insisted on a payment of ten million rupees and the ceding of the Kerong and Kuti passes. Tibet refused and Jang declared war in March 1855, sending soldiers to four fronts under the command of his brothers. After much difficulty the Nepalese did occupy the strategic fortress of Jhunga and the passes of Kuti and Kerong, but the first phase of the war was inconclusive. Peace talks with the Tibetans failed and negotiations with the Chinese fared no better. The Nepalese mounted a second series of surprise attacks, with Jang at one point taking personal command at the front. The Tibetans sued for peace at a time when Kathmandu itself was anxious for a settlement: the war was proving expensive and was universally unpopular.[13] A series of negotiations produced the Treaty of Thapathali in March 1856, that widened commercial opportunities for Nepal and granted certain extraterritorial rights to its traders.

Under the terms of the agreement, which pledged a mutual policy of non-aggression, Nepal would appoint as envoy in Lhasa a senior civilian or military government official instead of a representative of the trading community. Nepal agreed to assist Tibet in the event of foreign aggression, which Lhasa hoped also meant the ambans and Qing troops. The ambans, however, inserted a preamble in which Kathmandu and Lhasa agreed to regard the Chinese emperor with respect. The Chinese reworded the relevant treaty clause to ensure its exclusion from the category of foreign aggressors Nepal might be called upon to assist the Tibetans against.[14] The treaty also stipulated that Tibet would make an annual cash payment to Nepal.[15] But Kathmandu won no territory, did not regain coinage rights in Tibet, and received no compensation for either war expenses or the abuses that had precipitated the conflict.

Four months later, Jang Bahadur resigned as premier and advised the monarch to appoint his brother, Bam Bahadur, as his successor. King Surendra gave Jang the title of Maharaja of Kaski and Lamjung, two former principalities in the west neighboring Gorkha, the seat of the Shah Dynasty. Jang obtained special powers to impose or commute capital punishment, to appoint or dismiss government officials, to declare war or make peace with Tibet, China, Britain or other foreign powers, to dispense justice and punishment to criminals, and to formulate new laws and repeal or modify old laws pertaining to the judicial and military departments of the government. Jang devised a roll of succession intended to preserve power within his extended family of brothers, sons and nephews. However, the British resident reiterated Calcutta's longstanding refusal to recognize anyone but the king as the sovereign.

The Sepoy Mutiny

Where once there had been mutual suspicion, British–Nepalese relations now assumed a degree of stability, which Calcutta attributed in part to Jang's understanding of Britain's power and resources.[16] The other reason was China, whose weakness became clear to Jang during the Tibet war. Beijing's inability to prevent the conflict or to influence its outcome in Tibet's favor stood in sharp contrast to the Qing role during the 1788–1789 war. If a tilt toward the British became a necessity for Jang, the timing, too, was favorable. As a wide-scale mutiny among native troops in northern and central India in 1856–1857 threatened British rule, Jang returned to the premiership after his brother's death. He ordered 4,000 troops to India before personally leading a contingent of another 8,000 men to help the Company recapture Gorakhpur and Lucknow and suppress the mutineers. As the British paid for the troops and compensated the wounded and relatives of those killed, Queen Victoria made Jang a Knight Grand Cross of the Order of the Bath. In 1860, the British restored a vital tract of territory in the western plains that Nepal had previously ceded after the 1816 war.

The Chinese, too, had begun diplomatic overtures to Nepal. In August 1858 a Qing delegation arrived in Kathmandu with ceremonial robes of honor and presents for the king and prime minister as a token of their satisfaction at the ending of hostilities with Tibet. In Lhasa, meanwhile, rivalries between the Dalai Lama's regent and a leading minister led to rioting. Fearing an escalation of violence the ambans, who had only 500 troops to protect their mission, sought and received Nepalese help.[17] When the time came for the next tribute mission, the emperor, via the ambans, instructed Nepal to send only the *arji*, or petition, instead of men with lavish presents. This assertion of traditional Qing authority and benevolence came amid a weakening of the imperial regime. Britain's insistence on greater commercial and political rights met with Chinese resistance, provoking the Second Opium War. A defeated China ratified the Treaty of Tianjin in October 1960 that, among other things, allowed Britain, France, and Russia and the United States to station legations in Beijing and, in effect, legalized the opium trade.

The Tibetans, too, had begun re-evaluating their prospects vis-à-vis China and Britain. Despite the growth of Han Chinese populations in adjacent areas, Beijing had hardly interfered in Tibet's domestic affairs. The emperor patronized Buddhism and generously donated to the monasteries. For Tibet, the commercial advantages flowing from its status as a Qing dependency were becoming conspicuous, and it did not want to trade that for British domination. Thus, some Tibetans began constructing the image of a protective Qing that was intent on preventing the British from dealing directly with Lhasa.

The Tibetan aristocracy, which had hitherto welcomed trade with Nepal, became wary of the extraterritorial privileges of Nepalese merchants. More importantly, they saw the Nepalese as an extension of British aggression. Tensions escalated in 1862 when a Newar trader was killed in violence in the Tibetan capital. As Kathmandu threatened Lhasa with invasion, the ambans stepped in to mediate, prompting Jang to halt military preparations. Endemic border disputes caused a crisis in relations between Bhutan and the British and in December 1863 the British occupied the mountain passes in southern Bhutan. The Bhutanese sought Nepalese mediation or assistance, but Jang was not inclined to endanger his relations with the British.

Britain's entrenchment at the doorstep of southern Tibet forced the Qing to move closer to Kathmandu. Between August and October 1864 several Chinese officials visited Nepal, ostensibly for consultations on the situation in Bhutan as well as on British policy toward India's northern border. After a lapse of more than 14 years, Nepal sent a tribute mission to China in 1866, but the circumstances were far from favorable. Citing the Muslim Panthay rebellion raging in western China, the ambans barred the delegation from proceeding onward to Beijing. Operating on firm instructions from Kathmandu to continue toward their destination, the mission members waited for nearly two years at Tachien-lu, on the border with Sichuan, for Chinese permission, before turning back.[18]

Still, the Chinese stepped up efforts to build closer relations with Nepal and Jang, in exchange, began seeking more prestigious Chinese honors.[19] In April 1871 a Qing mission arrived in the Nepalese capital to confer upon Jang Bahadur the insignia of *thong-lin-pimma-kokang-wang-shang* – transliterated as "Truly valiant prince, commander-in-chief of the army" – accompanied by the Double-Eyed Peacock Feather and the Sable Coat.[20] The following year, Nepal intimated to the ambans that it would send the next tribute mission only if it would be allowed to reach Beijing, an assurance the ambans could not make. As the Nepalese persisted, the two sides agreed to cancel the mission.[21]

Renewed tensions with Tibet

Nepalese–Tibetan relations came under renewed strain at this time, as Kathmandu accused Lhasa of ignoring the maltreatment of Nepalese merchants. The Tibetans seemed to have been convinced that the Chinese, with Bhutanese and Nepalese assistance, were plotting to reinforce their hold on Tibet.[22] After an increase in attacks on Nepalese traders, Jang Bahadur delivered a strong protest to the Tibetans and sought the ambans' mediation. Discovering that the ambans were instead helping the Tibetans prepare fortifications along the Nepalese border, Jang Bahadur withdrew his resident, broke relations and closed his frontiers to Tibetan traders. The Tibetans, who believed the British were behind Jang's belligerence, stopped all trade on the Sikkim border.

Calcutta's relations with Kathmandu, in the words of a contemporary chronicler, had become so "frank and cordial that no better understanding is left to be wished for."[23] Yet many still suspected Jang of using the latest crisis as an excuse to purchase British arms to modernize his army. As the crisis with Tibet escalated, Jang Bahadur ordered a partial Nepalese mobilization, but by 1875, through Chinese mediation, the situation had improved and the Nepalese envoy returned to Lhasa. What brought Kathmandu, Beijing and Lhasa closer was a road the British had completed through Sikkim up to a pass leading into the vital Chumbi valley. Jang informed the ambans of his intention to dispatch the next tribute mission to Beijing in the summer of 1877. He died in February that year.

Jang's brothers against Jang's sons

Ranoddip Singh, Jang's oldest surviving brother, succeeded to the premiership, but real power lay in the hands of his more ambitious younger brother, Dhir. The new premier faced strong opposition from the sons of Jang Bahadur, who questioned the legality of his simultaneous accession to the prerogatives and powers of the maharaja of Kaski and Lamjung as well. They had expected the latter title to go to Jang's direct descendents. Despite the cordiality surrounding Nepalese–British relations, Ranoddip recognized the potential for mischief, especially at a time when the palace was anxious to regain its powers. To fortify himself, Ranoddip sought to strengthen relations with Beijing, possibly even securing a Chinese title equivalent to that bestowed on Jang.

In 1877 Ranoddip dispatched the five-yearly mission to Beijing, but it got off to an inauspicious start. Stopped at Tachien-lu, the mission leader was ordered to surrender gifts for the emperor and return home. He refused. In the interim, a Chinese envoy arrived in Kathmandu in January 1878 to confer upon Ranoddip the *thong-lin-pimma-kokang-wang-shang*. While the mission was eventually allowed to proceed to Beijing, ill will persisted. The Chinese, suspecting some mission members were spying for the British and perhaps were even Englishmen in disguise, isolated the delegation from foreigners.[24] While these developments seemed to underscore China's ambivalence towards Nepal, Beijing was also sensitive to the kingdom's role in its own security.[25]

Tensions between Nepal and Tibet resurfaced in 1883 when a group of Tibetans looted some 84 Nepalese-owned shops in Lhasa following a dispute between a Newar merchant and two Tibetan women. Kathmandu suspected the three main Lhasa monasteries had secretly encouraged the mob, while many Tibetans saw the growing ties between China and Nepal as a threat to their autonomy.[26] Kathmandu and Lhasa eventually reached a settlement under which the merchants were compensated for their losses. Upon hearing of a French attack on China in 1884, Ranoddip offered military assistance to Beijing,[27] for which the Qing court thanked Nepal in traditional style: China did not want to trouble its friend.

Ranoddip was careful to exhibit some tactical evenhandedness. In 1885 he sent a mission to the British viceroy, Lord Dufferin, offering 15,000 Nepalese troops for immediate use in the event of a Russian advance through Afghanistan.[28] Although Lord Dufferin politely declined the offer, he sought Kathmandu's help in obtaining recruits for the Gurkha regiments in the Indian Army. Despite the thorniness of the issue, Ranoddip recognized the advantages to both countries of an understanding being reached. A general permission to enlist in the Gurkha regiments of the Indian Army was published in Kathmandu.[29] Anxious to proceed cautiously with British, Ranoddip now informed the ambans of his desire to send the next mission. But his internal position had been undermined the previous year by the death of Dhir. By entering into a rapprochement with Jang's sons, Ranoddip served to alienate Dhir's sons.

The Shamsher coup

On the night of November 21, 1885, Ranoddip's nephews made their way to his private chambers claiming they were carrying an urgent letter from the British residency. As the prime minister lay resting on the bed, one opened fire at close range, killing him. The Shamsher brothers, using soldiers under the command of the eldest, Bir, went after Jang's family members and supporters, blaming them for Ranoddip's assassination. The ensuing carnage claimed dozens of lives, including that of Jang's son, Jagat. Many Shamsher opponents, including some royals, sought and received refuge in the British residency.

Bir Shamsher easily secured his appointment as maharaja and prime minister, since King Prithvi Bir was an infant and the queen mother ever more pliant after the horrors just perpetrated. Palace imprimatur ensured the loyalty of the army. Calcutta offered de jure acknowledgment of the new regime, but held back on formal recognition. The delay was partly rooted in deliberations over whether Calcutta could gain any specific advantages in terms of Gurkha recruitment and loosening restrictions on the resident's movements. Bir strove to assure Calcutta that his government was not anti-British and, despite the circumstances of its rise, enjoyed the full backing of the Nepalese. He also promised to fulfill all commitments made by previous governments. After Lord Dufferin gave formal British recognition to Bir's government on January 30, 1886, Bir helped the British recruit Gurkhas for three more regiments.[30]

But Bir still perceived a threat from Calcutta. The residency had offered safe passage to the refugees to Indian territory where they joined descendants of the nobility Jang Bahadur had displaced. The prime minister thus reached out to China. The court had already addressed a letter to the ambans justifying the assassination of Ranoddip Singh and requesting the emperor "as in former cases, to bestow upon [Bir] the title of 'Valiant Prince,' together with official robes."[31] In 1886 Bir Shamsher again wrote to the Chinese requesting that the tribute mission be allowed to proceed to Beijing, and received permission. It remained in China and Tibet for five years rather than the two years mission members normally spent.[32]

The extended stay raised apprehensions in Calcutta in view of its own negotiations with Beijing on the matters of Burma, Sikkim and Tibet. When a Chinese envoy arrived in Kathmandu with the official letter of patent and appropriate robes, rumors began circulating in India that the Nepalese had concluded a secret treaty with China. While the British attached much significance to the Chinese mission's extended stay, opinion seemed divided between those who did and did not consider Nepal to be a menace.[33] In 1891, Lord Lansdowne, the new viceroy, counseled a policy of conciliation and compromise.

Kathmandu dispatched another tribute mission to Beijing in June 1894, but the letter that the Nepalese mission carried to the emperor set off a hectic correspondence between Calcutta and Kathmandu. The first version of the letter that the British saw was a translation of the Chinese text as published in the *Beijing Gazette*. Calcutta considered the terminology used to address the emperor as "excessively submissive" and raised the matter with the Nepalese government. Bir Shamsher responded by saying there had been no alteration in the customary form of address to the emperor in the letter. He provided the resident with the Nepalese version of the letter, which was strikingly different in tone from the text that appeared in the *Beijing Gazette*. In the Nepalese version, the emperor was addressed respectfully, but essentially as an equal. In the published account, the Nepalese king appeared as a humble petitioner before the emperor.

The explanation lay in the ambans' office. During earlier missions, the ambans drafted the letter of tribute, which used the extravagant honorific forms considered appropriate by his emperor. While Nepal subsequently gained some leeway over the text, the ambans retained influence over the final text.[34] Once this became clear Calcutta instructed the British minister in Beijing to inform the Foreign Office that "the submissive expressions in the Nepalese letters are not regarded by Her Majesty's Government as an acknowledgement of vassalage, or indeed as anything more than a purely formal and complimentary style of address."[35]

Certainly, Nepal did not consider its freedom constrained by China. In 1890 Bir had escorted Prince Albert Victor, the grandson of Queen Victoria and second in the line of succession to the throne, during a hunting expedition in the Terai. Three years later, Archduke Franz Ferdinand of Austria, whose assassination nearly two decades later would trigger World War I, arrived for the sport. Now Bir himself wanted to visit Great Britain, but another crisis with Tibet intervened.

Tensions anew with Tibet

The 1884 treaty had failed to generate much goodwill in the first place. Now a dispute erupted when Tibetan border officers intercepted a consignment of tea that Kathmandu had sent to its envoy's office in Lhasa for delivery to the Dalai Lama and other Tibetan leaders as presents. China enjoyed sole rights to trade tea in Tibet, and the ambans returned the consignment and the traders back to Nepal with a formal reprimand in February 1891. The Nepalese took exception to what they considered the letter's derogatory language.[36] About this time the Tibetans, who had been supplying salt to Nepal in exchange for rice, revised the terms of barter. The Nepalese protested and threatened to import the product from India. When the Tibetans rejected the protests Nepal stopped salt imports from Tibet and curtailed rice exports.

Tensions escalated in September 1893 when a border incident claimed three Nepalese lives. Bir Shamsher sent three army regiments to the border, though he later recalled them after receiving a Tibetan apology. The rancor did not go away. The outbreak of the Sino-Japanese war in 1894 fuelled rumors that Nepal was about to attack Tibet, taking advantage of Beijing's preoccupation. The crisis with Tibet was only dissipated when Kathmandu accepted Lhasa's proposal for a fluctuating exchange rate between salt and rice based on supply and quality.[37]

In 1896, Lord Elgin, the new viceroy, supported Bir's desire to visit London. But Bir wished to be treated as ambassador plenipotentiary, complete with a 19-gun salute. The India Office in London balked, fearing Kathmandu might use the elevated recognition to establish contact with 'another power'. Bir later dropped the idea, citing domestic preoccupations.[38] That other power was looming larger. Russia had established ties with Tibet through its own trans-Baikal Buddhist communities, most notably the Buriats, who saw Lhasa as home for their branch of the faith. In the 1860s, Agvan Dorzhiev, a Buriat theology student, attended the Drepung Monastery in Lhasa, winning the highest award for a Buddhist scholar. In the mid-1880s, he was named as one of the new Thirteenth Dalai Lama's teachers, and as his spiritual adviser. The young and ambitious Tibetan leader – or at least a powerful section around him – tended to see the Russians as Buddhists who were unlikely to interfere with their traditions. Dorzhiev also had close contacts in the Tsar's inner circle. The information he brought to St. Petersburg from Lhasa served to strengthen Russian suspicions of their British rivals' motives in Asia.

Russia sees Nepal as threat

Influential factions at the Tsar's court were already envisaging Russian influence over all of inner Asia as far south as the Himalayas. By 1895 the Russians had occupied Samarkand, Bokhara and Khokand. As Russia's influential finance minister Count Sergei Yulyevich Witte urged the tsar to do everything possible to counteract the extension of British influence over Tibet, an influential Russian newspaper reported that Nepal was threatening the Dalai Lama with invasion.[39]

George Nathaniel Curzon, appointed viceroy of India in the autumn of 1898, saw Asian domination as the ultimate ambition of the Russians. Based on his extensive travels to Central Asia and Russia a decade earlier, Curzon had been arguing in favor of an anti-Russian policy in the region. As viceroy he sought to open direct negotiations with Tibet, even at the cost of infuriating Beijing, the traditional intermediary. Dorzhiev was already advocating Tibet turn to Russia to seek protection from Britain and China, and in December 1898 he was granted an audience with Tsar Nicholas II.

Lord Curzon focused on the possibility of forging closer ties with Nepal but the Boxer Rebellion complicated relations because of Calcutta's decision to include a Gurkha Rifles unit in the Indian army detachment sent to China. Dorzhiev, meanwhile, returned to Russia in 1900 as the head of an official Tibetan embassy to seek the intercession of Russia for Tibet, "which is menaced by England, mainly from Nepal."[40] Although Curzon initially appeared to discount the importance of Dorzhiev's trips to Russia, he attempted once again to woo Nepal, intimating that he would be pleased to accept an earlier invitation to take part in a shooting party in the Terai.[41] Bir agreed, but noted that due to ill health he would not be able to accompany the viceroy.

On March 5, 1901, before the visit, Bir Shamsher died. His successor, Dev Shamsher, also declined to escort Curzon and deputed his younger brother,

Chandra. Two months after his return from the Terai, Chandra staged a coup. Dev Shamsher was banished into internal exile and eventually allowed to settle in India, where he would spend the remainder of his life.

Conclusion

The rise of a new aristocracy in 1846 inaugurated a new era of cordiality between British India and Nepal, but it was by no means trouble free. This shift was spurred in large part by China's diminishing ability to influence developments in Nepal. Still, maintaining the tributary relationship with China served Nepal's political purpose of preventing its formal absorption into the British Empire. The decline of imperial China also emboldened Nepal to revive its territorial and commercial claims on Tibet. During Nepal's third war with Tibet the British were apprehensive that China might misconstrue Jang's ambition as part of a British-inspired imperialistic design, and ultimately affect Anglo-Chinese commercial interests. The Chinese became increasingly keen to keep Nepal quiet and avoid any confrontation with the British in the kingdom. A formal peace treaty did little to address the underlying tensions.

The Shamsher Ranas came under greater pressure from Britain, which was eager to secure greater concessions on the recruitment of Gurkhas. But they could not shield themselves from new developments across the Himalayas, where the young and dynamic Thirteenth Dalai Lama assumed full spiritual and temporal powers in Tibet in 1894. As the weakened Qing remained silent spectators of trans-Himalayan politics it increased the scope for greater Nepalese maneuverability in the management its foreign affairs, and the growth of general political distrust in the region.

5   Games great and small

When King Prithvi Bir sent official notifications to the British and Chinese governments of Chandra Shamsher's appointment as prime minister in June 1901, Lord Curzon extended immediate recognition. This deepened suspicions in Nepal that the viceroy might have struck some kind of a deal with Chandra during the hunting expedition in the Terai that was immediately followed by his successful coup. To the Chinese, the Nepalese monarch requested that the traditional honor and robes meant for Dev Shamsher now be transferred to his successor. Chandra had an immediate task: the 1894 mission to Beijing had returned home long after the next one was due. The ambans permitted Kathmandu to postpone the mission, citing the famine in Shanxi province.[1]

Britain's worries grew as Avgan Dorzhiev made another visit to Russia in 1901. This time he had passed through Kathmandu on his way to St. Petersberg, visiting monasteries and offering powdered gold and saffron at the Bauddha Nath stupa.[2] The Buriat, who had enjoyed previous audiences with Tsar Nicholas II but had made only oral requests for assistance on behalf of Tibet, now carried a written appeal from the Potala.[3] Curzon strongly suspected tsarist collusion. With Qing rule disintegrating he felt it would be up to Britain to pre-empt suspected Russian moves to capitalize on Tibet's political vacuum.[4]

Curzon's need for more information from inside Tibet encouraged him to shed more of his suspicions of the Nepalese. Chandra sent the viceroy a report of a conversation between the Nepalese envoy and a senior Tibetan official, who denied any ulterior motives behind the Dalai Lama–Dorzhiev connection. Six months later, during another conversation, the same Tibetan official complained to the Nepalese envoy that the British were needlessly spreading rumors of Russian influence.[5]

Contending with the Russians

By mid-1902 the British minister in Beijing reported that Tibet and Russia had reached some kind of agreement. If this were indeed the case, Curzon stated in a report to London, he would put a British army into Lhasa without the slightest delay. Since a Russian protectorate over Tibet would be a threat to India and even more so to Nepal, a British ally, it must be prevented at all costs, he added.[6]

While Chandra was no less apprehensive of Russian intentions, he believed that British–Russian rivalry would also offer Nepal opportunities to expand its influence in Tibet.

Curzon got an opportunity to personally size up Chandra on the Tibet issue in January 1903 on the occasion of festivities held in Delhi to celebrate the coronation of King Edward VII as emperor of India. During private talks subsequently described as catalytic in making up Curzon's mind, Chandra sought to impress upon the viceroy the urgency of quick action in Tibet to forestall the Russians. In his letter to London recommending an expedition to Tibet, Curzon counseled "acting in complete unison with the Nepalese Darbar [and] even invite them, if thought advisable, to take part in our mission."[7] He contemplated the Nepalese might be encouraged to send a separate column accompanied by British officers, by an independent route to Tibet. The viceroy attached a note of his talks with Chandra as proof of Nepalese cordiality.[8]

Chandra returned home with China uppermost on his mind for an additional reason. After several reminders to the ambans the prime minister received word that a special Chinese delegation would arrive in Kathmandu to confer on him the *thong-lin-pimma-kokang-wang-shang*. Accepting the honor at a special ceremony in April, Chandra expressed gratitude to the emperor, but, in private, was far from pleased. He felt the formal attire accompanying the title was of a rank lesser to that conferred upon his predecessors.[9] Once Kathmandu pointed out the lapse Beijing sent the appropriate robes.

Curzon's proposal for an expedition to Tibet had put London in a dilemma. The British had just begun discussions with the Russians regarding Central Asia and felt an expedition to Tibet might endanger that process. There was another predicament. A forward policy on Tibet would require a public statement regarding China's claim to sovereignty in Tibet, something the British wanted to avoid. Although some in the India Office in London wanted Nepal to intervene directly, Curzon feared that greater latitude might provide an opportunity for the Nepalese to escape British control, especially under a less friendly leader.[10]

Complaining of Tibetan violation of treaty obligations and injury to trade, Britain decided to send a mission consisting of 200 rifles under the command of Colonel Francis Younghusband: sufficient to dissuade the defiant Tibetans. Chandra urged the Dalai Lama to make peace with the British, citing the advantages Nepal had derived from its alliance since 1816. Should Lhasa persist with its defiance, Chandra said he would not come to Tibet's assistance.[11] The Dalai Lama's government snubbed the Younghusband mission, sending subordinates who refused to receive the British unless they withdrew from Khambadzong into Indian territory. Younghusband refused and fortified his camp before returning to report to the viceroy. With London finally having given its assent, Curzon now raised a larger force. The Tibetans, determined to fight, distributed large quantities of rifles and put soldiers on alert.[12]

Nepal redefines obligations to Tibet

Citing intelligence that the Dalai Lama had received a bishop's robe from the tsar along with a large supply of arms and ammunition, Kathmandu demanded an explanation from Lhasa. If the reports were true, Chandra warned, Nepal would oppose this apparent growth in Russian involvement in Tibet, through war if necessary.[13] In effect, Chandra interpreted Nepal's obligations under the 1856 treaty as consisting of a duty to extend advice and counsel rather than armed assistance in case of aggression against Tibet by a foreign power. Curzon declined Chandra's offer of troops but accepted the loan of several thousand yaks and porters for transportation. Chandra forwarded to Calcutta the Nepalese envoy's reports from Lhasa, which served as the single most important source of information on the attitude of the Tibetan authorities.[14]

Younghusband marched into Lhasa on August 3, 1904, inflicting a massive loss of life on the Tibetan army. But he found no sign of Russian agents or munitions. The Dalai Lama, who had escaped before Younghusband's arrival, took refuge in Mongolia and appealed to the tsar to "assume protection" over Tibet.[15] Beijing opposed the British advance but also refused the ambans' effort to expand their personal guard. The ambans then asked Nepal for 2,000 armed troops, promising full compensation. But Kathmandu refused saying it would antagonize the Tibetans.[16]

Tibetan officials reluctantly agreed to Younghusband's terms to gain the withdrawal of British troops. Through the Anglo-Tibet Convention of 1904, which the ambans refused to sign, Tibet accepted Britain's protectorate over Sikkim and gave the British the right to establish trade marts in three Tibetan towns. In a clause ambiguous enough to exclude China and Russia, the agreement forbade any other foreign power from exercising political influence in Tibet. An indemnity of £562,500 was levied and British troops were to occupy the Chumbi Valley, Tibetan territory contiguous with Sikkim, until this was paid. The British trade agent was authorized to visit the Tibetan capital to discuss issues flowing from the treaty. In other words, British India virtually converted Tibet into another of its "native state" protectorates.[17] The Nepalese envoy, along with a representative of the Bhutanese government, figured prominently in the Anglo-Tibetan negotiations. For his "valuable support" in this enterprise, and in the recruitment of Gurkha regiments in the British Indian army, Chandra would be made a Knight Grand Commander of the Star of India, the senior order of chivalry associated with the Empire of India.

Externally, too, the Lhasa Convention proved highly unpopular from the outset. Britain's influence to the north of the Himalayas served to strain its relations with Russia and China. St. Petersburg saw the agreement as a prelude to an unwarranted extension of British influence in Central Asia. The Qing government, which rejected the Tibetans' right to negotiate with a foreign power, also formally rejected it.[18] Beijing did, however, indicate that it was prepared to ratify the convention if the British would in return recognize China's sovereignty in Tibet. But London would acknowledge only China's suzerainty. From

Mongolia, the Dalai Lama, who rejected the treaty, established direct contacts with Russian officials. In London, as photographs were published of British soldiers mowing down poorly armed Tibetans, public opinion turned against the military action and the government censured Younghusband for acting not in accordance with his instructions and diluted the terms of the treaty.

At the end of 1905 the new Liberal government, according greater priority to relations with China and Russia, agreed to recognize Chinese "suzerainty" over Tibet and to admit that Beijing was excluded from the term "foreign power" as used in the Lhasa Convention. Beijing was further placated by London's undertaking "not to annex Tibetan territory or to interfere in the administration of Tibet." In exchange, Beijing confirmed the 1904 Lhasa Convention in an amended form, guaranteeing "not to permit any other foreign state to interfere with the territory or internal administration of Tibet." In 1907 Britain and Russia recognized Chinese suzerainty over Tibet and pledged not to interfere in the region's internal matters. Both sides also agreed not to post any representatives to Lhasa, although British special trade interests were recognized. Nepal, whose monopoly on trade with Tibet had been broken as a result of the opening of a direct route from India, now saw an erosion of its political influence over its neighbor.[19]

China's forward policy

Seeking to reverse some of the damage done by what it considered the ambitious and rash policies of the Thirteenth Dalai Lama, China embarked on its own forward policy. In the autumn of 1906, Beijing dispatched a special commissioner, Zhang Yintang, to the region, who moved to dilute British influence by purging Tibetan officials who had negotiated with Younghusband. The powers of the ambans were increased as Chinese troops in Lhasa were strengthened. But Qing attempts to impose control over Tibetan regions that bordered China led to serious resistance. Beijing responded by appointing General Zhao Erfeng as imperial commissioner, and sent him to pacify the frontier districts. The ambans and General Zhang sought to woo Nepal by lauding the "able statesmanship" of Prime Minister Chandra and commiserating over the damage done to Nepalese trade by the opening of the Chumbi Valley. During a meeting with the Nepalese envoy in January 1907, the senior amban was reported to have stated: "China, Nepal, Tibet, Bhutan and Sikkim might be compared to the five colours, viz, yellow, red, blue, black and green. A skilful painter may so arrange the colours as to produce a number of beautiful designs or effects."[20] General Zhang, praising the quality and strength of the Nepalese army, instructed the Tibetan regent to send military officers to Kathmandu for training, and even suggested a defensive alliance. If the proposal deepened suspicions in Lhasa, it met with a lukewarm response in Kathmandu. After the Lhasa Convention, Nepal supported a strengthening of China's position in Tibet, in order to forestall what it considered an assertive Dalai Lama from declaring independence. A militarily weak Tibet under Chinese suzerainty would help Kathmandu maintain its influence. Yet

Beijing's overt and stern assertions of power had produced tensions in Lhasa, which Nepal considered no less detrimental to its interests. The Nepalese envoy attempted a careful balancing act, urging the Tibetans not to alienate the ambans and persuading the Chinese not to push the Tibetans too hard.[21]

Detecting an added opportunity, Chandra persuaded the king to write to the Chinese that Tibet had been angered by Nepal's denial of military support. Beijing's failure to recognize Nepal's support would undermine Kathmandu's credibility.[22] In 1906 the king dispatched what would be the final tribute mission, making Nepal the last ever country to pay tribute to the Middle Kingdom.[23] But Chinese skepticism persisted, prompting Chandra to move closer to Britain.[24]

Like his uncle half a century earlier, Chandra recognized the virtues of acquiring a thorough personal knowledge of western civilization. He felt he could best discuss crucial bilateral issues in London directly, thereby affirming the status of Nepal as an independent and sovereign state. Chandra also sought a dependable supply of arms and ammunition, industrial and scientific machinery.[25] In the summer of 1908, Chandra visited England where, although not treated as an ambassador of an independent country, he received a 19-gun salute. King Edward VII honored him with the Order of the Knight Grand Cross of the Bath, the fourth most senior of the British Orders of Chivalry.[26]

As the Dalai Lama grew more anxious to leave Mongolia, British and Chinese officials, although eager to get him away from Russian influence, did not want him to return to Lhasa. Seeking to reach an understanding with the Qing court directly, the Dalai Lama traveled to Beijing in September 1908. The Dowager Empress Cixi had already announced plans for constitutional and administrative reforms and the Tibetan leader hoped to modify the *cho-yon* relationship the Fifth Dalai Lama had established with the Shunzhi emperor. But he found himself mired in the elaborate rituals and protocols of the court, and although he met the emperor and the empress dowager separately, the Qing refused his request to petition the throne directly. The following month the emperor and dowager empress died a day apart, and the Dalai Lama conducted religious services. In late 1909 he returned to Lhasa unaware that Qing forces were just behind him. Even in the midst of collapse, the Qing moved vigorously to reclaim its frontiers and convert Tibet into an obedient province of China.[27]

Lhasa's urgent pleas for assistance were rebuffed by Britain, Russia, France and Japan. The *kashag*, the governing council of Tibet loosely equivalent to a cabinet, now turned to Nepal, citing the 1856 treaty obligations. When Kathmandu refused military support, the Tibetans requested the Nepalese envoy to use his good offices to prevent the arrival of Chinese troops.[28] British, Tibetan and Nepalese accounts paint a fairly consistent picture of what happened next. The Nepalese envoy brought the Tibetan ministers and the senior amban to the conference table in Potala, but the amban insisted that since the troops were coming at the emperor's orders, they could not be stopped.

As the situation deteriorated, Kathmandu arranged a meeting between the Dalai Lama and the ambans during which both sides appeared ready for a compromise. The ambans gave assurances that the Chinese army was intended merely to police the trade marts. It would be dispersed as soon as it reached Lhasa and would not interfere in the internal affairs of Tibet. But on February 12, 1910, the Chinese army marched into Lhasa, overthrew the Tibetan government, and forced the Dalai Lama to flee to India. The Qing announced the Dalai Lama had been deposed, and a search for a successor began.[29]

The Tibetans renewed calls for military assistance from Nepal, which insisted on the return of the Dalai Lama to stabilize the situation. The Chinese, too, realizing the impossibility of governing Tibet without the co-operation of the Dalai Lama, sought the help of the Nepalese envoy to secure his return and acceptance of a spiritual role. Chandra Shamsher ordered the envoy to refuse the task, insisting that the senior amban himself travel to Darjeeling to negotiate with the Dalai Lama, who in turn was trying in vain to enlist British support to expel the Qing.[30]

Buoyed by Beijing's success, the junior amban had written to his superiors on the urgency of strengthening relations with Nepal. British policy by this time consisted of allowing Chinese control over Tibet but resisting any attempt by Beijing to interfere south of the Himalayas. London sent a note to Beijing conveying this message. In reply the Chinese referred to Nepal as a "feudatory" of China and maintained that Bhutan and Sikkim were both states in friendly relations with China. That missive began to shift British attitudes. For the first time imperial China had formally asserted its claim of suzerainty over Nepal.

Nepal, which had hitherto encouraged a nebulous relationship with China as a means of asserting its political independence from India, now dismissed the Chinese claims as an "unwarranted fiction" and a "damaging reflection on our national honor and independence."[31] Chandra used the Chinese claims to extract concessions from the British, including the granting to him of the rank of ambassador during his visits to India and London and the deletion of the reference to Nepal as a "native state" in the official *Imperial Gazetteer of India*. Such moves would convince Beijing of Nepal's independent status and discourage Chinese assertions of suzerain rights, the prime minister insisted. Chandra also renewed his call for a new treaty that would recognize more specifically Nepal's independence, and allow it to obtain more arms to counter the alleged threat from China. The British were prepared to make some minor concessions on the importation of arms and to reassure Kathmandu regarding its Tibetan interests, but rejected Chandra's specific requests.[32]

In late 1910, as Beijing was considering sending a mission to confer a new title on Chandra Shamsher, the prime minister instructed his representative in Lhasa to discourage the ambans from doing so, ostensibly on the grounds that he did not want to incur any new obligations to China. When the senior amban suggested that the next Nepalese tribute mission leave for China in 1912, the British resident informed Chandra Shamsher that this should be done only after consultation with the Government of India.[33] The mission was first postponed and then cancelled, in effect severing diplomatic relations between Nepal and China.

In November 1911 the shockwaves of the revolution that would ultimately topple the Manchu reached Tibet when a section of the Chinese garrison based there, mutinied. Chinese troops in Lhasa faced a lack of reinforcements and a shortage of food and sought a rapprochement with Tibetan leaders through the Nepalese envoy. Nepal felt its rights and privileges under the 1856 treaty were being flouted. The ambans had enlisted Nepalese subjects in unpaid labor and exacted money from Nepalese traders for the upkeep of the Chinese army. Soon the Chinese refused to recognize Nepalese passports, levied taxes on Nepalese shopkeepers and arrested those who refused to comply. Kathmandu lodged repeated protests but the ambans asserted that the treaty was not binding upon China. Moreover, in their view, Nepalese rights could not stand in the way of the maintenance of law and order. At one point they even asserted the right to dismiss the Nepalese envoy.[34] But Chandra Shamsher, who had recently hosted King George V on a hunting expedition in the Terai, stood firm. Kathmandu saw the return of the Dalai Lama as the best way of stabilizing the situation and put its military on high alert.

Republican China's reassertion

In February 1912 the Qing court announced the abdication of the last emperor, six-year-old Puyi, which brought to a close more than 2,000 years of imperial Chinese history. The republican government argued that the Chinese territories the Manchu emperors had subjugated, including Tibet, were part of their republic. Sun Yat-sen, the father of the revolution, had called for the creation of a strong Chinese state that would expel the Japanese from Manchuria, the Russians from Mongolia, and the British from Tibet. One of the urgent goals of the Chinese revolution was to restore China to its former greatness by regaining control of Tibet. In April President Yuan Shikai issued an edict that declared Tibet, Mongolia and Xinjiang to be on an equal footing with the main Chinese provinces and as integral parts of the republic.[35] This manifestation of Chinese nationalism pushed the British closer to the Dalai Lama. From exile, he now organized a military force to regain power. The Panchen Lama, who had headed a pro-Manchu group, also joined the Dalai Lama.

The Tibetans would soon expel all Chinese officials and troops. But victory, once again, seemed illusory. The Dalai Lama, who was back on Tibetan territory but had not yet reached the capital, received a "reinstatement" telegram from President Yuan. He replied that he had not asked for his former rank from the Chinese government and that he intended to exercise both temporal and ecclesiastic rule in Tibet. Any relationship between Tibet and China had been premised on the patron–priest relationship. Since the revolution had overthrown the emperor, that relationship no longer existed. He triumphantly returned to Lhasa in January 1913 and issued a proclamation considered the equivalent of a declaration of independence.[36]

The Nepalese representative in Lhasa functioned as mediator in the negotiations that led to the withdrawal of the Chinese forces. Although no territorial or commercial gains accrued to Nepal, it had assisted Tibet in ridding itself of the Chinese without at the same time antagonizing the latter.[37] As British India sought neutrality in the Sino-Tibetan dispute, Nepal saw the possibility of itself emerging as Tibet's protector. But that was not how the Chinese saw these developments. General Zhang Yintang, the Chinese commander, proposed a "union of Nepal with the five Affiliated Races of China," and suggested the deputation of a special delegation to Beijing for orders and advice. Chandra Shamsher replied politely to this incredible invitation, but stated: "Nepal is an ancient Hindu Kingdom, desirous of preserving her independence and her separate existence, [and] she cannot entertain the idea of such a union."[38]

Simla Convention

During 1913, there were intermittent hostilities on the Tibet–Sichuan frontier as China refused to recognize Tibet's independence. Growing Chinese influence and the possibility of Nepalese military action forced Britain to contemplate once again a permanent resident in Lhasa. Since that would have contravened earlier agreements, the British government sought an alternative. It eventually proposed a tripartite conference to settle the terms of relationship between Tibet and China as well as to delimit the boundary between Tibet and India. Lhasa agreed almost immediately, and Beijing after some delay. Under British pressure President Yuan declared autonomy for Tibet. London then extended diplomatic recognition to Yuan's regime. Representatives of the three governments inaugurated a series of meetings at the northwestern Indian city of Simla in October 1913. The major points at issue were those concerning Sino-Tibetan relations. There was an opportunity for the British representative, A.H. McMahon, to negotiate the entire Tibetan border. The 1890 convention had outlined Tibet's border with Sikkim. But the frontiers with Nepal and Bhutan, between the eastern and western ends of British India's borders with Tibet, had not been satisfactorily defined. Each contained its own complications and would have required the presence of representatives of both countries at Simla. McMahon did not want to widen the scope of the discussions when the immediate objective of securing British India's northern borders was complicated enough.[39]

His apprehensions were not misplaced. The positions taken by China and Tibet were so far apart that four months of negotiations failed to provide a solution. McMahon proposed a compromise under which Tibet would be divided into inner and outer zones. Outer, or central, Tibet would enjoy complete autonomy, while the inner region (most of the area to the east of the upper Yangtze) would continue to be administered by China. Outer Tibet would recognize China's suzerainty. Despite having reservations the Tibetans accepted. The Chinese, who signed the agreement, later refused to ratify it. The clauses that solely concerned Tibet and India were ratified. Those affecting China, including British and Tibetan recognition of Chinese suzerainty in Tibet, were "suspended" pending Beijing's ratification. The Chinese claimed that their non-ratification invalidated the entire Convention, an assertion that would leave a wider impact in the region.

Although politically independent, Nepal had become an informal part of the British Empire under indirect control mechanisms such as military and trade.

During World War I Kathmandu loaned the Government of India ten battalions of the Nepalese state army and facilitated recruitment for the Gurkha battalions in the British Indian Army. Some 55,000 Nepalese were recruited into those units during The Great War, many serving in the European or the Middle Eastern theater as well as in the 1919 Waziristan campaign in Afghanistan. They served with great distinction and suffered heavy casualties. Thousands more volunteered for other units that included the Assam and Burma Military Police, the Dacca Police Battalion, the Army Bearer Corps, and the Labor Corps.

After the war, Kathmandu and London agreed that the British owed a debt of gratitude to Nepal. The character of the gesture became the subject of delicate and prolonged discussions between the two governments. Chandra was made an honorary general in the British Army and an Honorary Knight Grand Cross of St. Michael and St. George, and was thereafter addressed as "His Highness" by the British. The prime minister proposed in 1919 the restoration of those sections of the Terai that had been ceded to the British in 1816 and had not been restored in 1858. The viceroy said that a territorial reward could not be sanctioned, and instead offered an annual "gift" to Nepal of one million rupees. In a further effort to appease Nepalese opinion, the resident was renamed British envoy and the residency turned into legation in June 1920. The government of India declared that "this decision is intended to emphasize the unrestricted independence of the Kingdom of the Gorkhas, which is on an entirely different footing from that of the protected States of India."[40] Encouraged by this shift, Chandra Shamsher renewed his proposal for a new treaty during the visit of the Prince of Wales in 1921 on a hunting expedition to the Terai. Although the British were sympathetic this time, it took nearly two years of negotiations "and the weighing of literally every single word" to produce a draft agreement.[41]

In the treaty signed on December 21, 1923, at Sugauli – where the treaty ending the 1814–1816 war had been concluded – Nepal finally obtained an unequivocal recognition of its independence. Both governments agreed "mutually to acknowledge and respect each other's independence both internal and external." The scope of Nepal's independence, however, was circumscribed by a clause that obligated each government "to exert its good offices" to remove causes of "any serious friction or misunderstanding with neighboring states whose frontiers adjoin theirs." Although defined in terms of mutual obligation, this meant that Kathmandu would continue to consult the government of India on relations with Tibet, Sikkim, Bhutan and China. Nepal gained the right to import arms and ammunition without prior approval from the government of India as long as "the intentions of the Nepal Government are friendly and that there is no immediate danger to India from such importations."[42] With the independence movement gathering strength, that provision was critical for the British.

Britain's willingness to accord greater respect for Nepal's sovereignty and independence was now attributed to London's desire to emphasize its formal separateness from India and thereby prevent a rise in sympathy for the freedom struggle. Events were moving rapidly in China, too, where young nationalists, outraged by the Versailles Treaty's granting of German concessions to Japan, launched in 1919 what would be known as the May 4 Movement. Two years later, young revolutionaries formed the Chinese Communist Party and gave another ideological dimension to the resentment over the humiliation inflicted by foreigners. The signs were becoming ominous for Kathmandu by 1924, when Sun Yat-sen, grand marshal of the Kuomintang military government that asserted authority over southern China, listed Nepal as one of the territories "lost" by China.[43] But the Nationalists were to be gripped by internal matters, when the death of Sun the following year precipitated a power struggle between the right wing, led by Chiang Kai-shek, and the leftist and Communist faction.

Inside Tibet the failure of the Simla Conference forced some to contemplate the possibility of hostilities with China. A group of young Tibetan aristocratic officials pressed for the creation of a strong military as part of a broader reform campaign. But the reformers were pitted against formidable opponents in the aristocratic elites and the monastic leadership, and by the mid-1920s, the Dalai Lama backtracked.[44] The reformers continued their quest for independence by sounding out international allies. Buddhist leaders in the Soviet Union tried to accommodate their faith to Communism by showing similarities between the two. In 1927 Dorzhiev sent a letter to the Thirteenth Dalai Lama praising Soviet policy toward its minority nationalities, attempting to use his influence to convince the Dalai Lama to turn to the Russians. As Josef Stalin consolidated his control, he began his collectivization and anti-religious program in 1929, extending it to his Buddhist population. Dorzhiev now advised the Dalai Lama against trusting the Soviets.

The total number of Nepalese in Tibet around this time comprised about 600–700 Newars and more than 1,000 of mixed parentage.[45] As Nepalese traders and merchants in Lhasa, Kuti, and some other towns complained of harassment and Tibetan violations of its treaty obligations, the Nepalese representative reported of difficulties in dealing with these problems with Lhasa officials. By the late 1920s Chandra was contemplating an invasion of Tibet and sounding out the British government for military aid. London acknowledged its obligation under Treaty of 1923 to supply arms to Nepal but refused to provide military aid and offered mediation instead. Disappointed, but undaunted, Chandra drew 25 million rupees from the state treasury and ordered general preparations. He died on November 25, 1929.

War with Tibet averted

Amid the prolonged dispute London was coming under pressure to supply arms (and in so doing reassure the Nepalese of its determination to uphold its treaty obligations) and demonstrate moral support for the new prime minister, Bhim Shamsher. When Kathmandu accepted an apology offered by the Tibetans, the British, who had worked strenuously behind the scenes, were particularly relieved at the turn of events.[46] Still, Bhim seemed vexed by Lhasa's ability to influence Nepal–China relations, having declared at one point: "Tibet has blocked our way to China."[47] If Kathmandu considered Tibet partially responsible for the break in Sino-Nepalese relations after the fall of the Qing dynasty, it was not going to let Lhasa continue to stand in the way.

The Chiang Kai-shek government seemed keen to renew relations with Nepal. In May 1930 it dispatched a mission to Kathmandu carrying letters and presents to King Tribhuvan, and the prime minister. During their six-week stay the Chinese delegates held several meetings with Bhim concerning political and other issues. Yet the extent of Chinese enthusiasm also piqued the Nepalese. In his letter to King Tribhuvan, Chiang offered "to assume responsibility" to settle the boundary dispute between Nepal and Tibet. In response, Bhim "repudiated in toto any claim of the Chinese Government to interfere in any question of this nature."[48] From Kathmandu's perspective China had no role whatsoever to play in Nepal–Tibet relations after 1911. That assertion was rooted more in Kathmandu's desire to ward off any Chinese ambitions than in acknowledging Tibetan independence.

In January 1932 Bhim returned to Kathmandu after what he considered had been a fruitful and cordial exchange of views with the new viceroy, the Earl of Willingdon. But he had to address internal challenges. By revising the order of succession to the advantage of his offspring, Bhim had widened rivalries within the larger Rana family. Opponents had begun secretly organizing the overthrow of Rana rule, with support from the royal palace.[49] The population of Kathmandu, fearful of government reprisals, showed little overt support for the opposition. The tight control of the Ranas ensured that news of the opposition did not get outside Nepal. International actors were busy wooing the Ranas and would have had little time for its critics. Leading opponents of the Ranas in exile would try to build support among constituents of the Indian freedom movement. But that promised few results, as the British would be increasingly drawn against the growing freedom movement. Mahatma Gandhi, who had formally demanded independence in 1930, was arrested in January 1932. The Indian National Congress was declared illegal, a move that raised the specter of further unrest. In February the Chinese government sent a special mission to Nepal to bestow Chinese titles upon Bhim Shamsher in recognition of his friendly attitude and the goodwill of the Nepalese government towards China.[50] This time the Chinese were careful not to ruffle Nepalese feathers.

As China witnessed an intensification of the Nationalist–Communist conflict amid a tightening of the Japanese hold on the northeast, the Thirteenth Dalai Lama died in Lhasa in December 1933. The departure of one of the few recent Dalai Lamas who had lived to maturity raised considerable uncertainty in itself. Exacerbating the general sense of apprehension was the fact that, shortly before his death, the Thirteenth Dalai Lama had predicted, among other things, that the communist onslaught that had consumed Mongolia might advance to Tibet, erasing the names of the Dalai and Panchen Lamas, destroying monasteries and killing and chasing away monks and nuns.[51]

With Bhim Shamsher's death the previous year, Nepal, too, had a new ruler. Juddha Shamsher was preoccupied, first, with relief and recovery after a massive earthquake, and then a challenge to his personal rule. As he consolidated power,

Nepal gained further recognition of its independent status. The British government agreed to the establishment of a Nepalese legation in London, and designated its representative in Kathmandu envoy extraordinary and minister plenipotentiary. China, too, began engaging Nepal more actively. Tibet had allowed a condolence mission sent by the Chiang government to visit Lhasa, a mission sent to investigate whether Tibet was now willing to join the Chinese Republic. Declining the offer, Tibet reasserted its independence but permitted the mission to open an office to facilitate negotiations aimed at resolving the question. Although the talks proved futile, the Chinese expanded their gaze across the Himalayas.

In June 1934 Chiang sent a goodwill mission to bestow Chinese titles upon the new prime minister.[52] Explaining to the delegates that Nepal had established a legation in London on an experimental basis, Juddha said Kathmandu might open its second mission in the Chinese nationalist capital of Nanjing.[53] Back home the delegation members urged their government to help Nepal do just this. But internal matters would preoccupy the Chiang government. Mao's Red Army began its year-long Long March, Chiang declared war on Japan a year later, and forged a unity with Mao against its old enemy.

Nepal's relationship with Britain would also take precedence because of internal developments in India. Since the time of Chandra Shamsher, Kathmandu had co-operated with the British authorities in checking so-called "subversive elements," i.e., Indians who sought refuge in Nepal. They were kept under surveillance and occasionally arrested and extradited in exchange for similar British-imposed restrictions on Nepalese oppositions groups in India. But the rise to power of the Indian National Congress, with its modernist, democratic and anti-feudal proclivities, was inspiring the growth of similar opposition to the Ranas' rule. To check the growth of such opposition Juddha needed to bolster co-operation with the British at a time when another rising power had its sights on the region.

Hitler's men come calling

A German delegation arrived in Kathmandu in 1937 to confer upon Juddha Shamsher the Order of the Star of the German Red Cross with Sash, in recognition of his reconstruction efforts after the devastating earthquake. Juddha praised the "wonderful qualities of head and heart displayed by your great leader, Adolf Hitler, and of his inspiring re-creation of the German nation."[54] The German delegation leader stated that his country had no political interest in the subcontinent and stressed the importance of peaceful co-operation in the spheres of trade and spiritual understanding. In January 1939 a delegation of five scientists from Germany arrived in the Tibetan capital, where they were received by the regent. The mission leader Ernst Schäffer, who had already been on two previous missions to Tibet, and other members persuaded the regent to correspond with Adolf Hitler. Some Nazi militarists were already viewing Tibet as a potential base for attacking British India.[55] The mission, which had entered Tibet through Sikkim, sought to return by way of Nepal, but the British persuaded Kathmandu to block the team.[56]

Months after the Schäffer Expedition, Germany invaded Poland. World War II began at about the same time as Japan was defeated in Mongolia. Having made little headway in conquering the rest of China, Japan turned its attention to Indochina and the Pacific. While Tibet maintained neutrality during the war, Japanese interest in the region grew after its invasion of Burma at the start of 1942 and as the scope of its Greater East Asia Co-Prosperity Sphere expanded.[57] But the Tibetans had already discovered that neither Japan nor Germany could be a reliable defense against the Soviets.

At the outbreak of the war, Nepal had immediately declared support for Britain, which had already recognized that the sturdy Nepalese offered "a cheaper version of Europeans whose equal they were in courage and fidelity."[58] Through friendship with the British, the Rana regime could protect itself from external enemies without compromising its autonomy over internal matters. But Nepal continued to assert its independence in familiar ways. When Chiang visited India in February 1942, mainly to try to rally British support against Japan, he met the Nepalese envoy to India and discussed the possibility of renewing relations. Kathmandu donated $10,000 to the Chinese Red Cross Fund as a friendly gesture.[59] The war and political turmoil in China itself would impede progress. And a new power entered the Himalayan region in the summer of 1942.

When Japan severed the Allies' Burma Road supply artery to China, planes were flown over the Himalayan mountains. But their payloads were too small and too many planes crashed: the Allies were now desperate for a land route that would reconnect China and India. That search fell to two Americans of the Office of Strategic Services (OSS), the forerunner of the Central Intelligence Agency. Concluding that one viable land route would require traversing Tibet, the OSS team made its way to Lhasa. Once in the Tibetan capital, however, the team leader, in deference to his hosts' sentiments, apparently abandoned the effort.[60]

The Tibetans' reluctance to co-operate with the Allies had angered Chiang. The establishment of a Foreign Affairs Bureau in Lhasa, a move widely perceived as an infringement upon China's territorial integrity and sovereignty, served to harden Nationalist opinion.[61] Yet Chiang had to weigh that against the fact that a recalcitrant Tibet still served as buffer zone against potential threats from the Indian subcontinent, providing the last line of defense for southwest China.[62]

The Quit India Movement launched by Mahatma Gandhi later in the year raised fears of a Japanese front on Burma. For Nepal, Gandhi's campaign had an ominous immediacy. Thousands of Nepalese living in India participated in the movement and built contacts with the nationalist movement there. The experience served only to energize them toward breaking free of the shackles in their own country. Juddha, who had cracked down on dissent by ordering the execution of four prominent opponents, continued to face a challenge as King

Tribhuvan initiated secret contacts with the opposition. The aftermath of war brought new pressures.

Nepal's contribution to the Allied war effort would far exceed that made during World War I.[63] The end of World War II in 1945 posed the challenge of rehabilitating 200,000 veterans the British had demobilized with minimal financial assistance. Many had been exposed to the Indian nationalist movement and thus were deemed potentially subversive. In late November Juddha Shamsher resigned from all offices, handing over power to his nephew Padma. With the departure of the British from the subcontinent only a matter of time, the third generation of Rana rulers desperately needed new external allies. While the Chinese re-emerged as a possibility, there was another candidate.

Although Rana envoys had visited the United States earlier, the first official Nepalese delegation arrived in Washington in July 1946. The three-member team spent several weeks there as guests of the State and War Departments and met with President Harry S. Truman. In November 1946, after a gap of 12 years, the Chinese Nationalist Government sent a goodwill mission to Nepal under the leadership of Chiang's private secretary.[64] Kathmandu also enthusiastically accepted the Indian invitation to the Asian Relations Conference in New Delhi in March 1947, viewing participation as a worldwide demonstration of its sovereign status as well as an opportunity to interact with other independent Asian governments.

Nepal and the Truman Doctrine

Although the OSS mission had failed in its original purpose to open the route across Tibet, it succeeded in its objective "to move across Tibet ... observing attitudes of the people of Tibet; to seek allies and discover enemies; locate strategic targets and survey the territory as a possible field for future activity."[65] That would prove important for future U.S. administrations as the Cold War dynamics shifted priorities. President Truman pledged to "support free peoples who are resisting attempted subjugation by armed minorities or by outside pressure." The Ranas hoped to employ the Truman Doctrine, which primarily enshrined containment of communism as a principal pivot of American foreign policy, to pre-empt any threat from independent India's leaders. In April 1947 President Truman dispatched a special representative to present a letter to King Tribhuvan in which the United States recognized the independence of Nepal. Under an Agreement of Commerce and Friendship, signed in Kathmandu, the two countries established diplomatic and consular relations. To the disappointment of the Ranas, however, Washington decided not to establish embassies in the respective capitals.

Buoyed by the Chinese mission to Kathmandu the previous year, Nepal dispatched a goodwill mission to Nanjing in May 1947, its first mission to China in 41 years. Chiang invested the leader of the mission with the First Class Order of Cloud and Banner and placed his own plane at the disposal of the Nepalese general for his return journey to India.[66] But there was little tangible outcome, as

Chiang had begun to lose momentum against his Communist rivals. In any case, Nepal's southern neighbor was growing in influence.

As India prepared for independence, it inherited the mutually advantageous "special relationship" with Nepal from the departing British. The advent of a democratically elected leadership in India goaded the Ranas toward another survival gambit. Prime Minister Padma Shamsher announced in May 1947 that he would institute basic constitutional reforms aimed at democratizing the regime, and a team of Indian constitutional experts arrived in Kathmandu to advise him. To their chagrin, Nehru urged anti-Rana Nepalese groups not to press the rulers too hard for concessions.[67]

On August 9, 1947, one week before independence, a tripartite agreement was concluded between the British, Indians and Nepalese under which the existing Gurkha regiments were divided between Britain and India. Kathmandu and New Delhi concluded a "standstill agreement" under which India's status as the successor-power to the British was recognized, and the terms of relationship between Nepal and India as they existed prior to independence were retained, pending new arrangements. India's acceptance of the 1923 treaty (also known as the Second Sugauli Treaty) between Britain and Nepal, served to allay Kathmandu's fears that it would be treated as another of the Indian native states that were coerced into accession to the Indian Union.[68] The constitution promulgated by

Figure 5.1 Prime Ministers Jawaharlal Nehru and Mohan Shamsher Jang Bahadur Rana (second and third from left), flanked by aides at a reception in New Delhi in February 1950 (photo: author's collection).

Padma Shamsher in January 1948, while supported by New Delhi, faced an immediate challenge from a powerful faction within the Ranas. Padma Shamsher was forced to resign three months later and the new prime minister, Mohan Shamsher, quietly shelved the reforms.

Nehru's "middle way"

Prime Minister Nehru and most other Indian leaders were convinced that limited political reform in Nepal was essential if an upheaval was to be avoided. Negotiations between Kathmandu and New Delhi began in the middle of 1949 and drafts of a new treaty were exchanged. But Kathmandu, which had applied for admission to the United Nations earlier in the year, demurred. The ascendancy of the hard-line Rana faction pushed Nepalese opposition groups toward a more extreme program in alliance with disgruntled members of the Rana family.

Independent India accepted China as the suzerain power in Tibet and the pronouncements of the new Indian leaders suggested that they envisaged the Dalai Lama's government wielding broad autonomous powers approximating independence.[69] When the Nationalist Government of China fell in 1949, Lhasa sought to move further in asserting its freedom. After expelling the Chinese mission in place in the capital since 1934, the Dalai Lama decided to dispatch political missions to the United States, Britain, India and Nepal. None was actually sent, not least because Washington and London made it clear that they would have refused to receive them. Chinese communist leaders, who had asserted their intention to liberate Tibet, now saw this as the next objective of the new People's Republic. India, which struggled to craft a response in consultation with the two western capitals, became clearer on its own policy toward Nepal.

As Mohan Shamsher visited the Indian capital for talks, Nehru told parliament "it is not possible for the Indian Government to tolerate any invasion of Nepal from anywhere, even though there is no military alliance between the two countries. Any possible invasion of Nepal ... would inevitably involve the safety of India."[70] Mohan Shamsher, however, sought to win Indian support for his regime by projecting the Rana system as a bulwark against communist subversion from the north.[71] After follow-up talks, New Delhi and Kathmandu formalized their new relationship on July 31, 1950 by signing treaties of peace and friendship as well as trade and commerce.[72]

Conclusion

With the turn of the century, as new players like Russia, Japan and Germany emerged in the region, the British sought to use Sino-Nepalese contacts to further their own interests. Nepal, however, was intent on using its political influence in Tibet to bolster its regional profile and mediated between the British and the Tibetans and later between the Tibetans and the Chinese. Stymied by his home government's broader geo-strategic considerations, Lord Curzon's aggressive policies created ambiguities that only the Chinese could exploit. They undertook to bring Tibet under Beijing's provincial framework by playing up the rivalry of the European powers and asserting their claims to Nepal and all the other sub-Himalayan states. Under pressure from the British, Nepal abandoned the tributary relationship with China. Yet Britain saw acknowledgment of Chinese suzerainty over Tibet as an instrument that would not only deprive Beijing of effective control but also keep out rival powers.

The British scrupulously avoided interfering in Nepal's domestic affairs and gradually accepted its formal independence. Despite calling the five-yearly missions to an end the Ranas never completely discounted China's importance. They maintained and glorified the myth of Nepal's historical contacts with the Middle Kingdom. After the fall of the Qing, Republican China continued to send ceremonial robes and titles to new Nepalese leaders, who gladly accepted them. Two world wars, the Chinese civil war, India's freedom movement and the British withdrawal from the subcontinent had shifted the ground under the Rana oligarchy. The leaders of independent India, like their British forerunners, saw Nepal an integral part of the Indian security system on the vital Himalayan frontier. Reluctant to support Nepal's democratic opposition, New Delhi devised the 1950 Peace and Friendship Treaty as an instrument to affirm the requisite political and security relationship in keeping with the realities of the time.

6   Cold War contortions

On October 7, 1950, Chinese communist troops attacked the Tibetan garrison at Chamdo, the strategic administrative center adjacent to the provinces of Sichuan, Yunnan and Qinghai. Although there was no immediate advance toward central Tibet, Beijing Radio announced that the whole of Tibet would be "liberated" soon. The central tenet of the China policy Prime Minister Jawaharlal Nehru had inherited from the British – the maintenance of Tibet as an autonomous buffer between the two Asian giants – had now come apart.

The Nehru government, like its counterpart in London, did not believe Beijing would invade Tibet at the same time it was involved in Korea. Mao Zedong, for his part, believed hostile forces supported by Britain, India, and the United States were turning the region into an anti-Beijing front.[1] The Chinese Communist Party (CCP) believed the international environment was conducive to military action. Despite Tibet's de facto independent status from 1911 to 1950, the international community had never formally recognized it as an independent state. The Korean War and the harsh Tibetan terrain, however, forced Mao to moderate his initial policy of an exclusively "military liberation."[2]

Nepal had had no direct official contact with China since the fall of the Qing. Relations with Tibet, however, were governed by the 1856 treaty, and its mutual-defense provision was still in force. Stung by past disappointments, Lhasa did not request military help from Nepal against the Chinese. India, Britain, the United States and the wider international community ignored Tibetan appeals for political and diplomatic support. In fact, Nehru now conceded that China's sovereignty – as opposed to suzerainty – in Tibet would have to be recognized. Through quiet diplomacy he hoped to secure two broad objectives: to enable the Dalai Lama's government to retain a broad degree of autonomy, and to protect India's privileged position on trade and official representation.

Nehru had accepted the separate status of the Himalayan border states in exchange for recognition of India's special interests there. Nepal emerged with the fewest restrictions on its sovereignty, obligated only to consult with India on certain foreign policy questions. Through the 1950 Treaty of Peace and Friendship, India, in effect, had accepted the legitimacy of the Rana regime. As events in Tibet forced New Delhi to reconsider that approach, the internal political situation reached a tipping point. The Nepali Congress, disenchanted by what it considered Nehru's soft line on the Ranas, abandoned its non-violent campaign in favor of an armed struggle. Concluding that the Rana regime had become vulnerable to communist subversion from the north, India contemplated a more representative political system.

The spur came a month after the Chinese moved into Tibet. On November 6, King Tribhuvan and almost the entire royal family left the palace for what was officially scheduled as a hunting trip. Instead, they drove into the Indian Embassy and requested asylum. The stunned Ranas deposed Tribhuvan the following day and enthroned his toddler grandson, Gyanendra, the only male in the line of succession left behind.[3] Nepal urged India, Britain and the United States – the three countries with which it had diplomatic relations – to recognize the new king, as Tribhuvan requested political asylum in India. Under pressure from Nehru, Prime Minister Mohan Shamsher allowed the royal family to fly to the Indian capital. At Delhi airport, Nehru accorded Tribhuvan the full honors due the head of a sovereign state. The Nepali Congress established bases on Indian territory and mounted a series of attacks inside Nepal.

Shortly after the People's Liberation Army moved into Tibet, Yang Shang-kun, chief of the General Office of the Chinese Communist Party and a future president of the People's Republic of China, had said in a message: "After the liberation of Tibet, the Chinese people and Nepalese people will be united in close solidarity for the sake of defending Asia and preserving world peace."[4] Speaking in parliament on December 6, Nehru made the strongest statement yet on his government's views:

> From time immemorial, the Himalayas have provided us with magnificent frontiers....We cannot allow that barrier to be penetrated because it is also the principal barrier to India. Therefore, much as we appreciate the independence of Nepal, we cannot allow anything to go wrong in Nepal or permit that barrier to be crossed or weakened, because that would be a risk to our own security.[5]

India would continue to recognize Tribhuvan as king, New Delhi declared, and urged the great powers to make every effort to solve the tangle peacefully. London initially sought to mobilize the Americans to put pressure on Nehru, but in the end, both followed New Delhi.[6] The result was the "Delhi Compromise" of February 7, 1951, under which King Tribhuvan, the Ranas and the Nepali Congress agreed to form a coalition cabinet under the general supervision of the monarch. King Tribhuvan returned to Kathmandu on February 15 to a tumultuous public reception, and appointed the coalition cabinet three days later. For the first time since 1846, a monarch had exercised sovereign powers at his own discretion.

Democracy from abroad

The revolution had indigenous roots, but its outcome was designed by India. The 104-year-old Rana period had officially ended, but Mohan Shamsher Rana remained as prime minister, albeit as a commoner. Many in the Nepali Congress complained that the revolution was incomplete, but they could do little. Since India had implicitly assumed responsibility for the implementation of the deal, all three political players had become dependent on New Delhi, a situation that would play into the hands of the Nepalese nationalists and communists. India became openly involved in Nepalese affairs, largely aided by local leaders' eagerness for New Delhi's guidance. Burdened by its own contradiction, the Rana-Congress coalition collapsed in November.

The development led to further rancor, as King Tribhuvan appointed as prime minister Matrika Prasad Koirala, who was reportedly India's preference.[7] The growing influence of the Indian ambassador began to irritate the Kathmandu elite, but their attention would be diverted toward China. In late January there was an open revolt in the Raksha Dal, a paramilitary organization consisting of former anti-Rana insurgents. The rebels freed from detention Dr. K.I. Singh, a leading commander of the insurgency who had become a bitter critic of the Delhi Compromise, and named him their leader. Prime Minister Koirala pleaded for Indian military assistance to put down the rebellion, over the objections of his defense minister.[8]

K.I. Singh demanded the formation of an all-party government, including the communists but excluding the pro-Rana Gorkha Parishad. He wanted Nepal to establish diplomatic relations with other countries based on equality, and to renounce special ties with any particular country, a thinly veiled reference to India.[9] As the Nepalese army moved in to subdue the rebels, Singh and 37 followers slipped away into Tibet. The abortive coup led to the proscription of the Communist Party and another organization representing members of ethnic communities inhabiting the northern border, decisions later disclosed as having come at the behest of India.[10] Nepal now stepped onto the wider front against China as the United States weighed the political, economic and psychological consequences of the loss of south Asia to communism.[11]

The Chinese had begun to modify their regional policies. Shortly after occupying Tibet, Beijing had warned the Dalai Lama against sending missions to other countries and cautioned other governments against receiving them. But they looked the other way for three years when Lhasa continued sending annual tribute missions to Nepal.[12] The flight of K.I. Singh complicated Nepal's position vis-à-vis its giant neighbors. Refusing Kathmandu's extradition request, Lhasa granted Dr. Singh and his group asylum.[13] Under the 17-point Agreement signed the previous May, Lhasa had conceded control of its foreign relations and surrendered its treaty-making powers to the People's Republic of China in return for a promise that Tibet's cultural and religious autonomy would be respected.

Nepal felt the impact of that treaty in other ways. The Chinese began to curb the activities of Nepalese traders, imposed restrictions on Nepalese pilgrims, and pressured the Tibetans to stop the tribute missions. Beijing offered to establish diplomatic ties and sign a non-aggression or mutual defense pact with Nepal, but the kingdom declined in deference to Indian sensitivities. Fears were expressed in Nepal, India and the West that the Chinese might use K.I. Singh to mount a communist guerrilla war in Nepal.[14] Rolling out the red carpet to Singh in Beijing, Chinese officials called him the "potential leader of a Free Nepal."[15]

Nepalese leaders, on Indian advice, continued to regard China as a potential threat. Military reforms and laws were introduced to combat Chinese propaganda and subversion amid ominous signs of growing communist interest in Nepal. Some Chinese maps depicted parts of Nepal as falling within Tibet and documents found on Nepalese communists arrested in the border region of northwest Nepal showed they had established contacts with Tibetan and Chinese Communists. The Nepalese Communists stepped up their claim that Nepal had become a satellite colony of India and the 'Anglo-American imperialists' who were using the country as a strategic base for an attack against China.[16] An Indian military mission, originally scheduled to complete its task in a year, stayed on indefinitely. The deployment of Indian military personnel in northern border posts on the access routes between Nepal and Tibet sparked public criticism. Indian economic aid programs, along with efforts to modernize the Nepalese bureaucracy, had already become controversial.

Riven by dissensions in the Nepali Congress, the M.P. Koirala government collapsed in August 1952. New Delhi, by then, had concluded that the monarchy was the only institution capable of achieving some degree of political stability and economic progress in Nepal. Yet it was becoming drawn more closely into Nepalese affairs. Prominent Nepalese leaders began demanding the establishment of diplomatic relations with China as a counterbalance, but New Delhi's opposition precluded any significant initiative. Chinese Premier Zhou Enlai had suggested a tripartite conference of China, India and Nepal to discuss the question of Tibet, which India rebuffed.[17] Yet there was skepticism over China's motives in Nepal, especially in view of Beijing's past claims of suzerainty over Nepal and considering that it had intervened in Tibet to assert its historical claim to the region.

Nepal recognized India's own dilemma over China. Nehru tended to view Beijing's ambitions as being limited to Tibet, and his position on Korea reflected his desire to engage with China. But many colleagues and opposition politicians alike attributed a more sinister motive to the Chinese push.[18] When Nepal appeared to make conflicting responses to China's intervention in Tibet, Nehru even upbraided Kathmandu.[19] New Delhi wanted Kathmandu to come out with an unambiguous position recognizing Chinese sovereignty over Tibet.

Sino-Indian agreement on Tibet

Beijing and New Delhi signed an agreement on April 29, 1954, regulating trade and pilgrim traffic between India and Tibet and fixing the number and location of trade agencies each government was to be permitted to establish in the territory of the other. The preamble of the treaty also included the first exposition of what became known as the *pancha shila*, or the "five principles of peaceful coexistence." All unilateral privileges India had enjoyed in what was referred to as the "Tibet region of China," ended. The Indian military escort had to be withdrawn, all Indian government buildings and postal, telegraph and telephone installations were to be handed over to the Chinese. In return for trade facilities in Tibet, Delhi had to grant the Chinese similar facilities in India.

An elated Nehru told the Indian Parliament: "We have done no better thing than this [agreeing that Tibet belongs to China] since we became independent."[20] Two days after the agreement, King Tribhuvan and his foreign minister flew to New Delhi, where they were advised to conform Nepal's relations with Tibet to the terms of the Sino-Indian treaty. India, however, had no intention of sharing its influence over Nepal with China. Nehru was specific when he told parliament that he had reiterated to King Tribhuvan that Nepal should "coordinate its foreign policy with India."[21]

The People's Republic of China was anxious for more vigorous action. Premier Zhou Enlai announced at the first National People's Congress in China in the fall of 1954 that contacts with Nepal had been made to establish "normal relations."[22] In late September, Kathmandu welcomed Zhou's statement in a shift that may have been linked to progress on the ground in Tibet.[23] Earlier that month Chairman Mao had met the Dalai Lama in Beijing, and the spiritual leader began to hope that Tibet might be able to coexist peacefully between Chinese claims of sovereignty and Tibetans' right to preserve their cultural and religious identity.

Nepal–China relations figured during discussions between Nehru and Zhou during the Indian Prime Minister's state visit to China in October 1954.[24] Prime Minister Koirala met Nehru in Calcutta before and after the Indian premier's visit to China. At a news conference at New Delhi shortly after his return, Nehru strongly implied that Beijing had recognized Nepal as an exclusive Indian sphere of influence, something Beijing never chose to confirm or deny.[25] On the question of diplomatic relations between Nepal and China, Nehru said: "That is a matter which the Nepalese government no doubt will deal with in its own way."[26] Negotiations between the Chinese and Nepalese ambassadors in New Delhi started the following month.

While India remained Nepal's dominant external partner, the kingdom continued to explore its broader international options. Washington had steadily developed an interest in the tiny Himalayan outpost now that the rise of communism in China opened up a new front for the Americans' policy of containment. Nehru resented this move and was unabashed in conveying his sentiment.[27] The Eisenhower administration was decidedly more hawkish than its predecessor in its pursuit of U.S. interests in south Asia, as its cementing of a strategic partnership with Pakistan would go on to underline. King Tribhuvan was preparing to pay a visit to the United States, but deteriorating health forced him to undergo prolonged medical treatment in Europe.[28] He died in Switzerland on March 13, 1955, after suffering a massive heart attack.

New king, new outlook

Under Tribhuvan, New Delhi had defined the principles and the conditions under which Kathmandu interacted with the rest of the world. The new monarch,

Mahendra, was more assertive about Nepal's independent place in the international community. As crown prince, Mahendra had been disenchanted by the preponderance of Indian advisers in the palace. However, his skepticism was said to have been rooted deeper during the months of exile in New Delhi where he saw the 1951 Delhi Compromise evolve in its final form as purely an Indian response to ensure its primacy in Nepal.[29] As he was being drawn more actively into the affairs of state during his father's illness, Mahendra had come to view an increasingly assertive China as counterweight to Indian influence in Nepal.[30]

The two major foreign policy achievements during the first year of Mahendra's reign were the culmination of processes that had begun earlier. Nepal, which had applied for U.N. membership in 1949, was finally admitted after the Soviet Union agreed to a package deal allowing 16 new members into the world body. The second event was spurred by Nepal's assessment of its options amid shifts in regional dynamics. Talks between the Nepalese and Chinese ambassadors in New Delhi had led to a basic agreement on establishing diplomatic relations, but little tangible progress had been made. The Conference of Asian and African nations in the Indonesian city of Bandung in April 1955 provided a major spur. The leader of the Nepalese delegation, acting on personal instructions from King Mahendra, met with Premier Zhou, who reiterated assurances of peaceful Chinese intentions.[31] From the Nepalese perspective, the Bandung Conference provided an opportunity for Kathmandu, New Delhi and Beijing to recalibrate their relations with greater independence of one another.

While India had been advising Nepal on opening diplomatic ties with China, Kathmandu would keep the details very closely guarded. In late July, the Chinese ambassador in India, General Yuan Chung-hsien, arrived in Kathmandu and rigorous behind-the-scenes negotiations produced an agreement that called for diplomatic relations based upon the *pancha shila*. The Chinese ambassador to India was appointed to serve at the same time as ambassador to Nepal, but from his base in New Delhi: in conformity with Indian wishes. A resident embassy was not immediately established in Kathmandu. The fact that the leader of the Chinese delegation that came to negotiate the agreement was almost immediately accredited as ambassador designate suggested the urgency with which the new king approached the subject.[32] Now K.I. Singh's presence in China became an embarrassment.

In Beijing the previous year Nehru had held discussions with Zhou on Singh's presence and, most likely, on his return. The Chinese had always planned to send him back, and said as much to a Nepalese youth delegation visiting Peking in 1953. But no timetable had been set. While some of their initial fears had subsided, many in Nepal, India and the West still saw Singh as a Chinese asset Beijing could deploy in the future. In the spring of 1955 as China and Nepal set out to establish diplomatic relations, Singh and his colleagues were on their way from Beijing to Kathmandu.[33] At the end of August, weeks after Mahendra had accepted the credentials of the Chinese envoy, Singh and some 30 followers reached the border, seeking permission to enter Nepal. After Singh gave the palace assurances of his peaceful intentions, Mahendra granted him a pardon.

Once in Kathmandu, Singh said he had not come to propagate communism and that the monarchy was still a necessity in Nepal. In a surprising turnaround, Singh began advocating closer ties with India, a country which, in his words, was not to be feared because it had no malevolent intentions toward its neighbors.[34]

In early 1956, as opposition to his direct rule mounted, Mahendra named as premier Tanka Prasad Acharya. Known for his skepticism regarding India, Acharya had been among the earliest advocates of diplomatic relations with the People's Republic of China. During his first news conference Acharya pledged to modify Nepal's "special relations" with India in the direction of "equal friendship" with all countries.[35] When the king lifted the ban on the Communist Party in April, imposed for its support of the K.I. Singh uprising, it created cracks in the organization, the first in a series that would splinter Nepal's communist movement.[36] The international press corps that arrived to cover King Mahendra's coronation ceremony in May was intrigued equally by the trappings of tradition as well as Chinese motives in Nepal and how the Indians might react.[37]

Vice Premier Ulanfu, who represented Beijing at the coronation, expressed China's "sympathy" with Nepal's efforts toward economic development, and signaled Beijing's willingness to join the community of aid donors.[38] Actively involved in China's efforts to integrate Tibet, Ulanfu also prepared the way for Sino-Nepalese talks on Tibet. They assumed added significance amid a serious boundary dispute between India and China along the western Himalayan border, near the Nepal–Tibet–India tri-juncture. The outbreak of a massive rebellion against Chinese communist rule among the Khampas of eastern Tibet exacerbated tensions.

In September Kathmandu and Beijing signed an agreement reaffirming the *pancha shila* as the basis of relations. The Chinese communists now formally renounced those claims to Nepal they had once joined the Qing and the Nationalists in asserting. The treaty abrogated all past agreements between Nepal and Tibet and allowed Kathmandu to establish trade agencies at Lhasa, Shigatse, Kerong and Kuti in Tibet. Beijing was accorded the right to establish an equal number of trade agencies in Nepal at locations to be determined later. Pilgrimage by Nepalese and Tibetans in each other's territory would continue according to "religious custom" and local trade in the border regions would continue. Nepalese residents in Tibet lost all the extraterritorial rights and special privileges that they had enjoyed under the 1856 treaty.

Unable to criticize a sovereign and independent nation's decision to conduct its own foreign policy, New Delhi instead cited the possibility of Chinese communist agents streaming over the Himalayas to carry out espionage. In response Nepalese officials stated they could not reject China's advances indefinitely given the 1,400 km border with Tibet.[39]

Nepal–China relations went on the upswing immediately. The following month, Prime Minister Acharya led a 12-member official delegation on a ten day tour of China, the first Nepalese prime minister to visit a country other than India for nearly half a century. Beijing organized an enthusiastic reception, promised

20 million rupees in cash and 40 million rupees worth of machinery, equipment, materials and other commodities. Acharya lauded the new ties.[40] The Chinese agreed not to dispatch technical personnel in connection with the aid, thereby allowing them to disclaim any intention of establishing an aid program office in Kathmandu, a situation the Nepalese compared favorably to both American and Indian aid models. The outright grant of currency without restrictions on use was perceived in Kathmandu as China's recognition of Nepal's own capacity to administer development programs. At this time Nepal had begun exercising greater independence in external relations. At the U.N. General Assembly on the Hungarian question in 1956, Nepal voted with the West against the Soviet bloc, a first demonstration of Kathmandu's breaking of ranks with New Delhi.

Zhou Enlai affirms "blood ties"

China's unwillingness to recognize Nepal as an Indian sphere of influence became perceptible during Premier Zhou's visit to Kathmandu in February 1957. Acharya hailed Zhou as a "soldier and statesman who is an intimate trans-Himalayan friend" while the Chinese premier brought the first installment of the aid grant as an assurance of friendship. Although Zhou was careful to laud the state of Sino-Indian relationship, he also referred to the "blood ties" between Nepal and China.[41] This apparent reference to Nepalese ethnic groups of Mongoloid origin was an implicit challenge to India's traditional assertion of special relations with Nepal. Acharya might have been expected to take new initiatives on China after Zhou's visit, but facing growing political and popular pressure, he grew intemperate in his public comments. In mid-July, Mahendra dismissed Acharya and his cabinet, springing up a surprise two weeks later by asking Dr. K.I. Singh to form the new government.

"Special relations" with India had become the dominant theme of Dr. Singh's foreign policy pronouncements after his return from China. As prime minister he announced that China and the Soviet Union would not be allowed to establish embassies in Kathmandu. Nor would Nepal immediately seek to establish diplomatic relations with other countries. Since these assertions contradicted King Mahendra's general foreign policy orientation they fueled speculation that Dr. Singh was mounting a challenge to the palace. The rival school held that the prime minister was merely reflecting the palace's effort to assuage some of India's concerns, after the pro-China tilt of the Acharya government. Regardless, the Singh government was embroiled in conflicts on multiple political fronts, prompting Mahendra to dismiss it in mid-November.

The monarch introduced a period of direct rule that emphasized the extension of Nepal's international engagement beyond its immediate neighbors. Mahendra believed he could secure Nepal's place in the world better by involving as many countries as possible. In early 1958 Nepal and the United States established embassies in their respective capitals, which paved the way for the setting up of Chinese and Soviet embassies. In April he renewed an agreement with Britain on the recruitment of Gurkha soldiers and terminated the Indian military mission later in the year.

Mahendra paid a state visit to the Soviet Union in June amid early indications that Moscow and Beijing had been drifting apart. The Soviet Union would embark on an aid program in Nepal, hailing ties as an example of Moscow's diplomatic successes in nations with diverse social systems. The growing alienation of the two communist behemoths was giving shape to a quadrangular jockeying in Nepal involving New Delhi, Beijing, Washington and Moscow.

Flight of the Dalai Lama

After the 1949 communist takeover of the mainland, Washington saw the Tibetan resistance not only as a key lever against Beijing but also against international communism. As early as 1951, the Americans had wanted the Dalai Lama to go into exile, in either India or Sri Lanka, and remain the symbol of the Tibetan resistance. In meetings with the Dalai Lama's brother Gyalo Thondup, U.S. officials promised military aid, to the extent possible. The Dalai Lama apparently felt his duty was to stay home and preserve his people's freedom by negotiating with Beijing.[42]

Despite having accepted the 17-point Agreement affirming China's sovereignty over Tibet, the Dalai Lama continued sending tribute missions to Nepal. Having ratified the agreement above the objections of key political advisers, the Dalai Lama's support was grudging at best. Continuing the missions to Nepal became a way of asserting claims of independence. Unsure of the terms of their relations with India on Tibet, the Chinese looked the other way until 1953 when the last Tibetan mission arrived in Kathmandu. The Dalai Lama's cautious expectations of Beijing seemed to have been dashed during his final encounter with Mao on the eve of his return to Lhasa in 1955, and he found the chairman adopting a harder posture on religion.[43]

By late December, declassified files revealed, President Eisenhower had signed a secret presidential directive ordering the CIA to step up covert activities against communist regimes on a global basis. The growing resistance in eastern Tibet represented the kind of "troublesome problems for international communism" that the directive was intended to exploit.[44] Despite the Dalai Lama's public opposition to violence, by 1957–1958, the CIA had run operations to provide support to the Tibetan resistance. Tibetans were brought to Colorado in the United States and given training in high-altitude communications and guerrilla warfare techniques. They were then dropped back into Tibet. The idea was to train Tibetan fighters in the use of weapons the Americans would supply. But the Tibetan rebels, who fought conventional battles, were quickly decimated.

In March 1959 Beijing brutally quashed a full-scale uprising in Lhasa which left the Dalai Lama feeling he was "standing between two volcanoes, each likely to erupt at any moment."[45] Rumors began swirling in and around Lhasa that Beijing was planning to abduct the Dalai Lama. At the end of March the Dalai Lama fled to India, where he repudiated the 17-point Agreement and would go on to set up a government in exile. Nepal figured on Nehru's decision to offer asylum to the Dalai Lama in an interesting way. During his 1954 visit to Beijing, Nehru stated he had raised the issue of China's asylum to Dr. K.I. Singh. Zhou had assured Nehru that it had only been a matter of international protocol. Moreover, Zhou also said that in 1950 when the Dalai Lama had nearly sought asylum in India, China would have considered it as accepted international behavior if New Delhi had granted him refuge. Nehru thus expected the Chinese to accept India's asylum to the Dalai Lama as conforming to international protocol and not as an unfriendly act.[46] That would be far from the case.

The fall of Tibet took on added significance for Nepal, which was in the midst of its first nationwide democratic elections. The 1951 Delhi Compromise had envisaged elections to an assembly that would write a democratic constitution for Nepal. Political instability and the palace's desire to consolidate its position had resulted in repeated delays. Amid the posturing the Nepali Congress abandoned its demand for elections to a constituent assembly in favor of parliamentary elections; in effect, conceding to the palace the right to grant the constitution. International power politics, too, had played a part in the imbroglio. During his visit to Moscow the previous year, King Mahendra was reportedly advised not to abandon personal rule and risk the chaos of anything even faintly resembling Western parliamentarianism. Similar advice was given to him in France. Mahendra returned to Kathmandu in September disposed to postpone the elections. But sensing the monarchy's need to find a broader and more stable basis for the regime, he decided to take the risk.[47] Accordingly, a palace-appointed panel made up of key politicians drafted a constitution with the assistance of a leading British constitutional expert. Nepal's first democratic elections were staggered over more than a month.

The Nepali Congress, the party most closely identified with the 1950 revolution, won an overwhelming victory, gaining two-thirds of the seats in the lower house of parliament. Mahendra was said to share his father's reluctance to see the outspoken, assertive and rash B.P. Koirala as premier, and many attributed this sentiment to the delay in the monarch's invitation to the Nepali Congress to form the government.[48] B.P. Koirala, fearing a pre-emptive coup by the palace, at one point reportedly sought arms from the Americans for his protection, but the United States did not want to become involved.[49]

Once it became clear that Koirala would indeed become prime minister, China emerged as a test of his commitment to exercising an independent foreign policy. Yet Koirala saw the kingdom's place firmly south of the Himalayas. The Nepali Congress had issued a hard-hitting statement against China on Tibet after the election, though this had come before the Koirala government had taken power.[50] The tenor of the condemnation raised questions about the foreign policy of the Nepali Congress government, which Koirala sought to clarify in mid-April, stating it was "absurd to suggest that recent Tibetan developments will affect our traditional relations with our great neighbor China." But he also reiterated the view that recent events in Tibet had affected the people of Nepal deeply.[51] Mahendra, for his part, met with Nehru in a border town to discuss

Tibet. The Communist Party of Nepal was the only organization that supported the Chinese action, condemning the rebellion as one "engineered by a handful of Tibetan reactionaries with the aid of imperialists."[52]

Two weeks later the Nepali Congress adopted a resolution on Tibet which went even further in characterizing Chinese action in Tibet as within the "19th century imperialist tradition" and asserted that "it would be a reactionary step if China tries to establish its sovereignty over Tibet on the basis of old standards." The Nepali Congress, with origins rooted in its Indian exile during the anti-Rana movement and whose ideological and policy orientation ever since had placed it closer to India, was skeptical of Chinese motives. Stating that China's breach of its promise of autonomy had caused the Tibetans to rise in a national revolt, the party said: "It is the duty of China to satisfy them by giving them what they want."[53] Koirala told the party's legislators that his government's foreign policy would continue to be based on neutrality and non-alignment, but repeated that "China must unequivocally allow Tibet to exercise full autonomy within the 1951 Sino-Tibetan agreement."[54]

The Nepali Congress was rattled by the developments in Tibet when it formally took office on May 27, 1959. According to official sources in Kathmandu at least eight Nepalese citizens were taken into custody for their alleged complicity in the revolt, and denied the right to meet the consul-general. Trade had diminished amid the deepening unrest. Now Beijing's announcement that the Chinese currency would be the only legal currency in Tibet threatened the finances of Nepalese traders. Reports of new Chinese restrictions on Nepalese traders raised fears of mass eviction. Some of the refugees pouring into Nepal were armed and thus posed new internal security challenges.[55] Calibrating its response with that of the Indian government became the prudent course for the Koirala government.

Nehru's arrival in June offered the Nepalese an insight into the evolution of India's views on China. At a public meeting Nehru appeared to mock the *pancha shila* approach to foreign policy that he had once celebrated, claiming no one observed it anymore.[56] In separate talks with Mahendra and Koirala, Nehru discussed the Tibet situation and ways of strengthening Nepal's northern border posts, if necessary with Indian assistance. A joint communiqué by the two prime ministers referred only obliquely to the Tibet situation but spoke of an "identity of views" between Kathmandu and New Delhi, prompting Koirala critics to denounce what they described as abandonment of Nepalese neutrality. While Koirala strenuously denied the charge, his government, based on Indian promises of financial and material support, announced a 100 percent increase in defense expenditures primarily aimed at strengthening the northern border.

The deterioration in Sino-Indian relations set the stage for a new Chinese approach on Nepal. In late August Chinese troops fired on and drove out Indian patrols from Longju in the eastern sector of their disputed border. In September, Zhou, replying to Nehru's letter, appeared to challenge the entire Sino-Indian border and question New Delhi's influence in the Himalayan border kingdoms. At the same time Beijing began to reassure Kathmandu by emphasizing its peaceful intentions. The authorities in Tibet held a conference with Nepalese representatives in Lhasa to discuss the difficulties that had arisen in the border trade. Nepalese citizens arrested during the disturbances were released and most of the travel restrictions were lifted. Announcing that the Nepalese could now exchange the illegal Tibetan currency at face value for Chinese currency, Beijing proposed talks on a new trade treaty. In October, Chinese Ambassador Pan Zili arrived in Kathmandu for a second time since the Lhasa uprising for talks on economic assistance. Kathmandu, too, had made overtures. The Koirala government continued to support Beijing's right to the seat reserved for China at the United Nations and pressed to separate the membership question from the Tibet issue. It abstained from a resolution condemning China's behavior in Tibet.

But Koirala was caught deeper in the regional vortex. In November, Nehru declared in parliament in New Delhi that any aggression on Nepal and Bhutan would be treated as an aggression on India and would be accordingly dealt with.[57] Koirala's critics seized upon those comments. As protests mounted, Koirala explained that Nehru had merely suggested India would send help if it were sought, and had not implied unilateral action. In another statement to parliament Nehru affirmed he agreed entirely with Koirala's interpretation of this position. But he went on to make public for the first time the contemporaneous exchange of letters with the 1950 Treaty that said: "Neither Government should tolerate any threat to the security of the other by a foreign aggressor. To deal with any such threat, the two Governments shall consult with each other and devise effective countermeasures."[58] Subtly but calculatedly, Nehru only reinforced his government's interpretation of the security relationship with Kathmandu.

By early December, there were persistent rumors of Chinese troop movements into three important sections of Jumla district in northwestern Nepal.[59] Two senior Nepali Congress legislators accused China of having started active infiltration in Nepal.[60] It would emerge later that Kathmandu had invited People's Liberation Army forces to expel Tibetan insurgents camping there.[61] Some voices in the West now began describing Nepal as potentially a part of the American defense perimeter.[62]

During a visit to India in January 1960 Prime Minister Koirala rejected a joint defense arrangement between Nepal and India and urged New Delhi and Beijing to settle their differences peacefully. Koirala traveled to China in March where in one public statement he made a veiled criticism of Beijing's policy toward New Delhi.[63] The Chinese, who did not appear provoked in public, worked to assuage Nepal's concerns by establishing a joint committee to demarcate the 1,400 km frontier, and proposing the withdrawal of troops and military patrols to a 20 km distance of either side.[64] Announcing a $21 million grant, Beijing decided to set up residential embassies in Kathmandu and Beijing. The Chinese were also keen to sign a non-aggression pact, but the Nepalese, in ostensible deference to Indian sensitivities, declined. Then Beijing proposed a treaty of peace and friendship, which Koirala asked to be delayed for further consultations. In marked contrast to Acharya's visit in 1956, the Chinese made no public references to India in connection with Beijing–Kathmandu relations.

Mao Zedong on Mount Everest

There were interesting moments during Koirala's talks. Responding to his request for economic assistance, Zhou carefully suggested that his government did not consider it prudent to equal Indian aid. Nor would Kathmandu benefit from any perception that China was in any kind of rivalry with India over the kingdom.[65] During a hastily arranged late-night meeting with the Nepalese prime minister Mao said he had been briefed on Koirala's talks with Zhou. Mao broached the issue of Mount Everest, suggesting that it be placed under joint ownership and renamed Friendship Peak.[66] Koirala rejected this, pointing out that the mountain belonged to Nepal. Mao questioned that claim saying Nepal did not even have a name for the peak, while the Chinese called it Qomolongma. Correcting Mao, Koirala said the Nepalese called it Sagarmatha, and politely reminded the chairman that Qomolongma was a Tibetan name. To this, Mao responded that Tibet was part of China.[67] The two leaders broke up without reaching a decision.

Back in Kathmandu Koirala revealed that the Chinese had laid claims to Mount Everest, but that he had rejected any encroachment on traditional territory.[68] Kathmandu witnessed the first anti-Chinese demonstration in its history. When Zhou arrived in New Delhi in April Indian reporters asked him about the

Figure 6.1 Prime Minister Jawaharlal Nehru speaking at a state banquet given in his honor by King Mahendra and Queen Ratna in Kathmandu in June 1959. Prime Minister B.P. Koirala is on the extreme right (photo: author's collection).

Everest controversy. The Chinese premier stated that it was under discussion between the prime ministers of the two countries, a discussion that he did not intend to disclose.[69] But he had a specific proposal for India: reciprocal acceptance of existing realities in both sectors. In other words China would abandon its territorial claim in the east in return for India abandoning its claims in the west. But the public mood in India had soured amid a groundswell of sympathy for Tibet and growing perceptions of Chinese hostile intent, and Nehru rejected Zhou's proposal.

When Zhou arrived in Kathmandu on April 26, on his second visit to Nepal in three years, the Everest controversy continued to echo. In public Zhou extolled the state of bilateral relations and pledged China's respect for Nepal's independent policy of neutrality. During private discussions Zhou once again raised the issue of a non-aggression treaty with Nepal.[70] Recognizing that such an accord would virtually undercut the 1950 Treaty with India, Nepal declined. However, the two governments signed a Treaty of Peace and Friendship. Speaking to Nepalese traders Zhou endorsed the proposal for a Kathmandu–Tibet highway, which the Koirala government rebuffed as economically unviable. Zhou told reporters that China was prepared to share sovereignty of Mount Everest and would recognize official Nepalese maps showing the peak on the Nepal–Tibet border. Koirala declared that the Everest peak belonged to Nepal, but conceded Chinese control of the northern face. By the time Zhou left Kathmandu relations seemed to have become cordial.

But the euphoria was short-lived. In early May rumors that a Chinese mountaineering team was poised for an assault on Everest swept through Kathmandu. Beijing initially denied the story even though, according to subsequent Chinese reports, the team conquered the peak. The Nepalese government had not been informed, much less consulted, about the expedition. It protested Beijing's description of Everest as "the highest peak in the Chinese fatherland." Tensions escalated in June after Chinese troops killed a Nepalese officer and captured 16 unarmed soldiers operating on the frontier with Tibet. Koirala told parliament that a protest note had been sent to China. Initially voicing surprise at the Nepalese claim, China later acknowledged the attack and sent an apology.[71] Reports that Chinese troops had entered a Nepalese village and shifted a boundary pillar prompted Koirala to accuse Beijing of violating the border agreement. China said it had withdrawn the troops from the 20 km demilitarized zone on the border. Zhou suggested that both countries establish embassies in each other's capital to avoid such incidents in the future, but Koirala was non-committal.

Mustang warriors

Subsequently declassified documents reveal a far more complex picture, as Nepal was drawn directly into the next stage of the Americans' involvement with the Tibetan resistance. After the Lhasa uprising the Chinese had launched a major air campaign that killed many insurgents and dispersed the others. President Eisenhower sought advice on whether continuing the resistance might not provoke even harsher reprisals by the Chinese. Secretary of State Christian Herter urged that the operations be continued, arguing that "not only would continued successful resistance by the Tibetans prove to be a serious harassment to the Chinese Communists but it would serve to keep the spark alive in the entire area."[72] That sentiment was said to have been shared by most of Eisenhower's advisers.

In early 1960, Tibetan resistance leaders had approached the CIA with a proposal to revive the resistance movement in western Tibet from a safe haven in Mustang, a semi-autonomous kingdom within Nepal that protruded across the Himalayas. Despite the latest setbacks neither the Tibetans nor the Americans were willing to give up the struggle. Washington could not, however, agree to establish a base in Nepal without seeking the permission of the Nepalese government, a step that was ruled out for political and security reasons. The Americans and the Tibetans worked out a plan under which 2,100 former fighters would be infiltrated in increments of three hundred to Mustang. They would then move across the border into Tibet to locate safe areas in which they could receive shipments of arms and operate as guerrillas. Only after the first group had established itself would the next increment be sent into Mustang and onward into Tibet. The CIA's Tibetan activities comprised a program of political, propaganda, and intelligence operations aimed at impairing the international influence of Communist China by maintaining the concept of an autonomous Tibet. The existence of a free Tibet in exile would also help to expose the hollowness of Communist China's pretensions to sponsoring "national liberation" movements around the world.[73]

Some indications of Nepal's descent into the Cold War whirlpool were available then. Prime Minister Koirala told a news conference that the authorities had captured Tibetan refugees with arms, ammunition and walkie-talkies and that he would not tolerate Nepal being used as a base for military operations against China.[74] The overall secrecy surrounding the incident bolstered Koirala's critics on the left as well as the right; they censured the government for espousing a pro-Indian orientation that threatened Nepal's national integrity. In an effort to repair ties the Koirala government allowed China to open its embassy in Kathmandu in August 1960. The joint boundary commission met the following month to begin discussions on the demarcation of the Nepal–Tibet border.

In September Koirala led the Nepalese delegation to the United Nations General Assembly. On the sidelines he met President Eisenhower. The American leader was particularly struck by Koirala's explanation of how the Communist Chinese were far more reasonable in negotiating their border disputes with Nepal than they were with India.[75] Eisenhower, however, had a more somber message. He said that King Mahendra, during a visit to the United States earlier in the year, had voiced dissatisfaction with Koirala. Eisenhower urged Koirala to patch up relations with the king in the interests of democratic stability.[76]

The prospects for that seemed to be receding. King Mahendra had been publicly reminding the government that he would be forced to act to defend the nation if the Nepali Congress failed to do so. Violence in the western district of

Gorkha, the seat of the Shah dynasty, underlined a potentially serious law and order problem. But the opposition used it to step up pressure on the government.[77] As rumors of a royal takeover swirled, Koirala acknowledged there was little he could do against a monarch who had the full backing of the army.

On December 16, 1960, King Mahendra went on national radio to announce he had used his emergency powers to dismiss the Koirala cabinet and take over the administration. He claimed the Nepali Congress had fostered corruption, promoted the party above the nation's interest, failed to maintain law and order and encouraged "anti-national elements."[78] Earlier in the day, Koirala and most of his ministers, along with many politicians of other parties, had been arrested and imprisoned by the army. Those who avoided the royal dragnet slipped across the southern border and sought refuge in India.

Conclusion

Nepal's experiment with democracy had begun and then collapsed in the wake of watershed events in Tibet. The Chinese invasion and occupation in late 1950 had precipitated an Indian-led effort to oust the century-long Rana oligarchy, empower the monarchy and political parties, and liberalize the body-politic – the aim being to counter what was considered to be the very real threat of communist subversion. India ended up micro-managing Nepalese domestic and foreign policies – often with the help of a pliant local political elite – fueling resentment among nationalists and communists and the growing educated classes.

Nine years later, after the flight of the Fourteenth Dalai Lama to India following an abortive anti-Beijing uprising, Tibet set in motion a chain of events that would consume Nepalese democracy and position the kingdom firmly as a key – if obscure – arena of the Cold War. The Chinese invasion had brought India down squarely on the side of the monarchy, while the Dalai Lama's escape pushed New Delhi and the palace in opposite directions, which widened the room for new players and new alignments.

7 Perilous pragmatism

King Mahendra's coup drew token opposition from ordinary Nepalese, and virtually no reaction from China. Although more restrained than other Nepali Congressmen in his comments on China's policies in Tibet, Prime Minister Koirala had become more candid in articulating them. Beijing, on the other hand, had been familiar with Koirala's strong anti-communist record as well as his party's strong ties to India. Koirala himself would later dismiss suggestions that the Chinese were somehow behind his overthrow.[1] The western democracies were open – if somewhat subdued – in their criticism of the royal coup.

During a state visit to the United States the previous year, Mahendra had highlighted Nepal's geo-political vulnerabilities during an address to the U.S. Congress. Moreover, he had returned from a state visit to Britain – the first by a Nepalese monarch – only weeks before his takeover. Amid the emergence of right wing authoritarian regimes in Asia, Africa and Latin America – usually with western governments' tacit backing – it was not difficult for many Nepalese to see the political changes at home as part of that disturbing global trend.

It was India's position that would prove to be the most clamorous – and controversial. There was speculation that Prime Minister Jawaharlal Nehru had some prior knowledge of Mahendra's move.[2] The Indian army chief, a confidante of Nehru, was on a visit to Nepal during the time and had held consultations with the monarch. Furthermore, it was no secret that Nehru's own relations with Koirala had become troubled, especially after their spat over interpretation of the 1950 Treaty vis-à-vis the threat from China. However, the subsequent public posture of India gave no indication of any prior knowledge. Nehru called the royal intervention a "setback to democracy"[3] while other Indian politicians and the media were more strident in their criticism.

The palace received a major boost when Queen Elizabeth arrived on a four-day state visit in February, despite objections from the Labour opposition. Projecting the monarchy as the pre-eminent symbol of national unity and social values, the royal regime branded its domestic adversaries, many of whom had taken shelter in India, as "anti-national elements." Critics considered the king's use of nationalism as a tool to bolster his power.

The Chinese maintained a business-as-usual posture in public as a second session of the border commission reconvened in Beijing in early 1961 to examine the survey reports. A month later the two governments reached an agreement that affirmed a series of border points, and border teams were sent to demarcate the boundary. Another session of the joint commission opened in Kathmandu in late July to finalize the terms of a formal treaty. China and Nepal reached a draft treaty on the border in August and prepared a provisional map delineating the border in all but three places.

During the third session of the commission, China for the first time made public its claims in the Everest area, proposing joint sovereignty over the peak and making the crest the boundary line. This was a reiteration of Mao Zedong's formula that Koirala had rejected during his visit to China.[4] Spurning the offer again, King Mahendra publicly reiterated Nepal's claim to the peak. Both governments decided to keep the issue out of the joint commission and focus on a search for a mutually acceptable compromise.

The conspicuous upswing in Sino-Nepalese relations coincided with growing coverage in the Western media on how the once-isolated kingdom now held an importance far beyond its size.[5] Documents made public years later would underscore the extent of that reality. Soon after assuming office in January 1961, President John F. Kennedy's administration decided to concentrate the CIA-backed Tibetan guerrilla forces in Mustang, one of three Nepalese districts abutting beyond the Himalayas into Tibet.[6] The ruler of Mustang was of Tibetan ancestry sympathetic to the cause, while the Dhaulagiri and Annapurna mountain ranges formed natural boundaries that protected on several flanks. Lo Mantang, the capital, was just 32 km from the Tibet border, while Lhasa lay 560 km further.[7]

For Kathmandu and Beijing, addressing what would become known as a key front of the Khampa insurgency in private seemed to be the prudent course.[8] Their focus shifted to consolidating economic relations. In the spring of 1961 China sent a delegation to discuss aid projects. Beijing subsequently agreed to give Nepal a hard currency equivalent to ten million Indian rupees and commodities worth 25 million rupees as a gift. The money would be used to provide the local currency required for Chinese-aided paper, cement and shoe factories, all enterprises aimed at bolstering the kingdom's self-reliance.

King Mahendra visits China

In late September, less than a year after his takeover, Mahendra set off on a state visit to China. He held official talks with the head of state, Liu Shaoqi, and Premier Zhou Enlai, while paying a courtesy call on Chairman Mao Zedong. In a rare gesture Mao paid a return call on the king. The king and queen joined the Chinese leadership in public ceremonies marking the anniversary of the founding of the People's Republic of China. The highlight of the royal visit was the border treaty Mahendra signed with Liu, which set up a joint commission on questions relating to the alignment, location, and maintenance of the 79 demarcation markers. Rival claims to Mount Everest's peak had been settled based on existing maps, which showed the peak to be on the border.

Figure 7.1 Chairman Mao receiving King Mahendra and Queen Ratna during their state visit to China in October 1961 (photo courtesy: Niranjan Bhattarai/Anoop Bhattarai).

On his return to Kathmandu Mahendra reported that China had ceded 480 square kilometers of territory to Nepal. The king asserted that Everest continued to belong to Nepal "as usual." A communiqué issued simultaneously in both capitals said China would give Nepal more economic aid and would provide $9.8 million for a road linking Kathmandu with Tibet. The visit seemed to fit into the wider expectations of the Chinese leadership, for whom security of national borders was a paramount objective. Aid, which was extended almost simultaneously with all border treaties, emerged as a means of preserving the balance of power on the subcontinent.[9] New Delhi officially welcomed the Sino-Nepalese border treaty, stating that the same principles could facilitate a solution to its border disputes with Beijing. The unofficial view was more skeptical. Some saw the treaty as a Chinese tool to isolate India as a recalcitrant neighbor unwilling to reach a settlement on boundary issues.[10]

In public, Kathmandu and Beijing hailed the road agreement as another step in the consolidation of bilateral ties. The circumstances leading up to the treaty fueled some controversy. During the king's meetings in Beijing, according to one account, neither side had raised the matter. On the day before his departure, however, the Chinese presented a draft road agreement to Mahendra. Beijing seemed to imply that the implementation of the border treaty depended upon Kathmandu's positive response on the road question.[11] At a broader level the Chinese perhaps saw the Nepalese government needed a Chinese counterweight, and extracted a strategic price.[12] When Dr. Tulsi Giri, who was part of the royal entourage, signed the treaty on Nepal's behalf, the move was interpreted as an indication of Mahendra's displeasure with the Chinese pressure tactics. The alternative interpretation held that the road agreement had been planned all along, but that Kathmandu and Beijing intended to use last-minute adjustments and the use of lower-level signatories as a way of muffling India's reaction.[13]

What really happened was hard to tell, but the dissemination of both versions would eventually work to Nepal's advantage, maintaining the creative ambiguity that had become a hallmark of Nepalese diplomatic tradition. Under the terms of the agreement China promised $9.8 million in aid for construction work in Nepalese territory, together with the necessary technical expertise and equipment. Kathmandu insisted on and secured an undertaking that Chinese assistance should be provided only at its request.[14] Clearly Beijing had grown anxious to promote the project, despite the severe financial crunch the disastrous Great Leap Forward had left behind. When the Tanka Prasad Acharya government had raised the road project, Beijing had turned it down and Zhou had raised the offer unsuccessfully with B.P. Koirala.[15]

But now the matter had become urgent, especially given Beijing's difficulties in supplying its military in Tibet. The roads into Tibet from the east and northeast traversed harsh terrain. They were expensive to maintain and were becoming more susceptible to sabotage by Tibetan rebels. The road from the northwest was easier and safer, but it crossed the Aksai Chin plateau, then in bitter dispute between India and China. Beijing's problems were compounded by the ban New Delhi imposed in 1960 on trade in strategic goods with Tibet, eliminating what had been China's primary source of supply for many commodities. Since India's blockade did not apply to Nepal, Beijing saw the Kathmandu–Tibet road as potentially more valuable.

In the midst of worsening relations with India, Mahendra, who was increasingly apprehensive that Nehru might attempt another 1950-like intervention in Nepal, viewed the road agreement as a vital bargaining chip. To assuage New Delhi, Kathmandu publicly discounted the political and strategic significance of the road and stressed instead its economic importance. This reasoning did not impress New Delhi and the Indian media was almost unanimously opposed to the agreement. Officially, the Nehru government maintained that Kathmandu had not violated the letter of the 1950 Treaty by its failure to consult with New Delhi prior to signing the agreement. Still, Nehru told parliament, he was "not satisfied" that India's interests were unaffected by the road.[16] Dismissing suggestions that the Chinese military might use the road to enter the kingdom, Mahendra said communism would not enter Nepal "in a taxi cab."[17] Mao Zedong would summarize more graphically Beijing's thinking a few years later in a meeting with a visiting Nepalese delegation. Discussing the possibility of building more roads into Nepal, Mao said: "Once these roads are open, India may be a bit more respectful toward you."[18]

Resistance to the royal regime, which had begun in the early fall of 1961, grew after Mahendra returned from China, as the Nepali Congress launched a wide-scale armed campaign. The palace, which had become more strident in its criticism of India, at the same time also appeared sympathetic to New Delhi's claim that the road would undermine the Indian blockade of Chinese forces in Tibet. In early December Kathmandu imposed a limited ban on the export of strategic goods – including iron products, cement, petrol, kerosene and coal – to Tibet.[19]

The Kennedy administration considered Beijing likely to continue active competition with India for influence in Nepal and saw the tendency of Nepal to try to play off one side against the other as likely to continue to cause problems in Sino-Indian relations.[20] The White House was thus caught between continuing efforts to influence the king to reach an accommodation with the Nepali Congress, and supporting a rebellion intended to destroy the king's power and to establish a new government. In view of the inevitable chaos that would be exploited by the Communists as well as the Nepali Congress' presumed inability to establish a viable government, Kennedy advisers continued reconciliation efforts.[21]

Despite a failed assassination attempt on Mahendra in January 1962 that Nepal claimed was plotted on Indian soil, both governments recognized the urgency of high-level dialogue. In late January a spokesman for the Nepalese Foreign Ministry announced that "unidentified aircraft" were dropping arms to Tibetan rebels in the Mustang area. The Nepalese army was incapable of handling the well-armed Khampas on its own, he declared, and if the Chinese should feel threatened by the rebels and should demand the right to send troops into Nepal to bring the Tibetans under control, there was little Kathmandu could do but comply with the request. New Delhi reiterated its promise to come to Nepal's assistance in meeting external aggression.[22] King Mahendra arrived in New Delhi in mid-April, emphasizing the necessity for states to abide by the *pancha shila* principles "not only by words but also by deeds."[23] When he insisted that Nepal's internal troubles were solely the handiwork of rebels based in India, Nehru reiterated that fundamental economic and political factors were at the root of the disturbances. He proposed another "middle way" compromise between the royal regime and the Nepali Congress, which the palace spurned.

Squeezed between increasingly assertive giant neighbors, Nepal viewed the competition between the two as ultimately beneficial to its own economic development – but only if the kingdom could strike the right balance. But in a hardening of its stance, New Delhi imposed an unofficial economic blockade of Nepal, citing a number of minor incidents on the border. The flow of essential commodities into Nepal was halted, although no formal ban was announced. The palace now seemed to have run out of options.

Sino-Indian war

On October 5, 1962, Chinese Foreign Minister Chen Yi made a remark at a banquet in Beijing to celebrate the first anniversary of the Nepalese–Chinese boundary treaty that continues to resonate in the Nepalese psyche: "In case any foreign army makes a foolhardy attempt to attack Nepal ... China will side with the Nepalese people."[24] A close ally of Mao Zedong and one of China's ten marshals, Chen had accompanied Zhou on his trip to Nepal two years earlier. Later in the month Chinese military forces moved across the Indian border at the extreme eastern and western ends of the frontier. The Indian forces in North Eastern Frontier Agency were badly mauled, while in the west the Chinese seized virtually the entire area on the Ladakh–Tibet border that was in dispute. Having attained their major objectives the Chinese imposed a unilateral ceasefire, which the battered Indian forces also respected. By mid-December a tenuous peace had been restored.

Precariously positioned between the belligerents, Nepal did not become directly involved. But the war would strongly influence its political development. Mahendra refused to take sides. "Mr. Nehru's hair has grown grey striving for peace ... and I know the Chinese Premier has faith in *pancha shila*," he had stated at one point.[25] For New Delhi, Mahendra's assertion of neutrality amounted to a brazen repudiation of the 1950 Peace and Friendship Treaty. But Nehru, who now needed a friendly buffer between him and China, also recognized his limits. According to U.S. intelligence experts the Chinese offensive of October 1962 reflected Beijing's desire "to consolidate its control over Tibet and to safeguard it against infiltration and subversion." China's longer-range goal sprang from "its expansionist ambitions south of the Himalayas" where it hoped "eventually to detach Nepal, Sikkim, and Bhutan from India's influence and make them satellites of China."[26] The White House sought to bolster Nepal – as well as Sikkim and Bhutan – to counter Communist efforts to bring them into the Chinese orbit. It was prepared for a re-examination of the U.S. policy of trying to fix firmly the major responsibility for these areas on India.[27] Nepal had become one of the first countries where the Kennedy administration deployed its new Peace Corps.

As New Delhi toned down criticism of the palace, the stridency in the Indian media, too, lost some of its sting. Nepali Congress leader Subarna Shamsher Rana suspended the anti-palace insurgency, fearing a "false step" during the Chinese attack on India.[28] The unofficial economic blockade was lifted, and trade began to flow across the border again. Shortly thereafter, the Nepali Congress, under Indian pressure, formally ended its insurgency.

The palace, having condemned the parliamentary system as incompatible with Nepalese values and requirements, came up with an alternative model: a partyless system of hierarchical councils rooted in Hindu tradition, suitably modified to affirm the king as the source and wielder of power. A key plank of the nationalist platform was a policy of widening Nepal's external contacts. China inevitably came to be seen as a heavier counterweight to India. Yet Nepal was cautious to reassert its independence and warned that it would not submit to aggression from any state. The king welcomed New Delhi's offer of a rapprochement and Kathmandu abated its anti-India stridency, while Indian officials stopped making statements implying that Nepal fell under their sphere of influence.

Nepal took another significant step in affirming China's sovereignty in Tibet in 1962, by designating its envoy at Lhasa as consul-general. The office was not under the jurisdiction of the Nepalese embassy in Beijing but was directly administered by Kathmandu. The number of Nepalese in Tibet had dwindled considerably as, over the generations, an increasing number had descended from both parents born in Tibet. More and more people who claimed to be Nepalese citizens spoke only Tibetan and had never visited Nepal. Partly because of Nepalese property laws that discriminated against those with mixed parentage, many such people chose to accept Chinese rather than Nepalese citizenship when they were given the choice for the first time between 1960 and 1962. Chinese officials gave equal opportunities for trade transactions of both types of Nepalese, regardless of whether they were born in Nepal of Nepalese mothers or born in Tibet of Tibetan mothers.[29]

While the Nepalese people for the first time were formally aligned on both sides of the northern frontier, the other cross-border problem had grown serious. King Mahendra had shown considerable courage in accepting refugees from Tibet, considering the potential for reprisals from the Chinese. He granted asylum to poor farmers and high lamas alike and built refugee relief camps along the many mountain passes. Many of these Tibetans recalled Mahendra's visits to their camp and some even claimed support from the king for their cause.[30] But another group of Tibetans was turning Mustang into a potential trouble zone. Some of the men the CIA had trained in the U.S. joined other resistance leaders recruited in India and headed to Mustang. Chinese control of all the territory inside Tibet deprived the resistance of a safe haven in which to regroup before taking on the People's Liberation Army in classic guerilla style, forcing them instead into direct battles.[31]

In Mustang the fighters could now establish camps from which they could periodically sneak across the border into Tibet, raiding army camps, dynamiting roads, stealing animals, and collecting information and transmitting it by radio to the United States. One of their methods was to ambush People's Liberation Army convoys, kill the soldiers, and confiscate all their weapons, supplies, and materials.[32] The rebels would go on to capture documents describing Beijing's plans to move many more troops into Tibet, documents that also provided the first concrete evidence of the Sino-Soviet rift and other important insights into China's early efforts to develop a nuclear weapons capability.[33]

Nepal publicly denied the existence of the bases, while the Chinese continued to press the palace for action in private. Kathmandu's reliance on economic and political support encouraged it toward undeclared co-operation with the United States. Beijing, which now appeared to treat Nepal in the wider context of conflict with India, carefully avoided a public rupture with Kathmandu.

Chinese foreign aid

China initially extended aid only to nations on its borders with which it once carried on tributary relations. While Korea, Vietnam and Mongolia were the first to receive aid, and in the largest quantities, Cambodia, Burma and Nepal soon joined the list. It made little difference whether recipients were communist or not.[34] Growing Sino-Nepalese economic engagement over the years brought its own problems. The purpose of Chinese aid was to bolster Nepalese constituencies that saw Beijing as a counterweight to New Delhi.[35] However, this also precipitated American, British, and Soviet aid strategies that were designed to offset Chinese successes. Kathmandu felt Beijing had ungraciously dropped two of its four projects, forcing it to question for the first time the efficacy and value of Chinese aid, inquiries traditionally reserved for Indian and American programs. Beijing, too, appeared to be weighing the benefits of its engagement, and began speaking of friendship and support for the Nepalese people rather than for the government. The rift between the communist giants also came into play. The pro-China wing of the Nepal Communist Party was in exile in India espousing revolutionary tactics against the palace, while the pro-Soviet wing of the party was tacitly supporting the king.[36]

As the Kathmandu–Tibet road opened to one-way traffic in December 1964, a Chinese technician defected and somehow made his way to Taiwan, where he charged that the road was intended for aggressive purposes. Specifically, he alleged that bridges on the road were being constructed of sufficient strength to carry tanks, in violation of the agreement, a charge the Soviet media in particular played up. Kathmandu began encouraging efforts to involve as many countries as possible in Nepal's development as the best guarantee of the nation's sovereignty and independence.[37] The same year, Kathmandu rejected a Chinese proposal to build a road connecting the Kathmandu–Tibet highway with a point in the eastern plains. Beijing was said to have made angry objections in private concerning Kathmandu's rejection of the road proposal, but made no public denunciation.[38] Foreign Minister Chen Yi, during a visit to Kathmandu in March 1965, extolled Nepal as a good neighbor and praised Mahendra as an "outstanding statesman."[39]

After a third CIA air-drop of arms, ammunition and food supplies to the Mustang rebels in 1965,[40] the Chinese once again pressed the palace for action. Around this time several Khampas were arrested in Kathmandu with arms and radios after anonymous phone calls to the city's newspapers led to the seizure of several caches of arms. It was discovered that the arms came from the United States Embassy, resulting in the expulsion of an American diplomat. U.S. aid workers were also forbidden from using the private plane, helicopters and airstrip that belonged to the U.S. Agency for International Development.[41] Beijing, while appreciative, considered the response insufficient. The Chinese, who formally established the Tibet Autonomous Region in September 1965, were reportedly beginning to wonder whether their intensive courtship of the royal regime in Nepal was worth the trouble and expense.[42]

Mahendra did not seem to want to lean too heavily toward Beijing, either. Nepal, after all, received more aid from India than any other country and 95 percent of its trade was still with its southern neighbor. Moreover, the international climate was changing dramatically. The split in the communist edifice was becoming increasingly apparent closer to home. Mahendra, who had sought to secure his place between the two ideological blocs, now confronted the same balancing act between the two communist behemoths.

With India, Nepal continued to observe the basic provisions of the 1950 Treaty. In secret letters exchanged in January 1965, India agreed to provide military material to Nepal on a gratis basis. It also acknowledged Nepal's freedom to import from or through the territory of India, arms, ammunition or warlike materials necessary for its security under procedures that were to be worked out by the two governments acting in consultation. Any shortfalls in supply were to be met by the United States or Britain, with details to be co-ordinated at a suitable time. The secret 1965 agreement showed Nepal's respect for Indian security concerns, and while New Delhi reciprocated by extending more aid and better trade conditions, its suspicions persisted. As the Tibet–Kathmandhu road neared completion, India proposed an agreement under which India and Nepal would undertake joint defense against China, which Kathmandu declined.[43]

Mahendra flew to Delhi in late November 1965, just weeks after India held on to the Valley of Kashmir in its second war with Pakistan. Kathmandu had given Beijing approval to build another road from the capital to Pokhara 175 km to the northwest. The prospect of Chinese technicians and personnel working in the heart of the territory from where many of the Gurkha soldiers in the Indian and British armies came raised some concern. The implication that the Chinese might also be working to soften any hostility to future People's Liberation Army incursions through the Himalayas would gain resonance in the coming years.

By this time, in a throwback to the days of the Raj, Indian opinion on Chinese motives in Nepal seemed divided. China, one of school of thought in India held, was satisfied with a friendly Nepal and did not intend to create a satellite. Accordingly, Chinese aid and trade were limited and had demonstrative value. If Beijing were truly determined to exclude India from Nepal its efforts would have been on a much larger scale and it would not have depended primarily on Mahendra's goodwill.[44] Another group saw China's long-term intent as creating a federation of the Himalayan states of Nepal, Bhutan and Sikkim under its overlordship.[45] Amid all this uncertainty the Indian government saw an opening. During a visit to Nepal in October 1966, Indira Gandhi – who had become prime minister early in the year – renamed the Indian Aid Mission as the Indian Co-operation Mission, ostensibly to foster a greater sense of partnership. While Nepalese sensitivities over India's domineering attitude seemed to have drawn Gandhi's attention, she also used the visit to assure the palace of New Delhi's recognition of its supremacy and to deliver an undertaking that India would not insist on the restoration of parliamentary democracy. Such messages had an influential and immediate effect on the king, and in early 1967 he amended the constitution to enshrine partylessness as the defining character of the system.

Cultural Revolution chills

Sino-Nepalese relations were relatively undisturbed by the early convulsions of the Cultural Revolution Mao Zedong had unleashed in 1966. Even when the tumult spread into Tibet, Beijing and Kathmandu continued to praise each other's policy of peaceful coexistence. But China's relations with India began to deteriorate markedly. When an armed peasant struggle against landlords broke out in the Darjeeling area of West Bengal, the Chinese media hailed it as the opening of an Indian revolution of a type envisaged by Mao Zedong.[46] It was against this somber background that the Kathmandu–Tibet road was opened to traffic in May 1967. Promising little immediate economic or commercial value to the Nepalese, the road was not a viable alternative to the transit route to Calcutta, either. However it was of great strategic importance, establishing direct links between two major Chinese army bases in Tibet and Kathmandu, and from there to the Indian border. The Indians thus felt their northern states vulnerable to a rapid Chinese thrust.[47]

The road opened on the eve of what was to be the worst phase of Sino-Nepalese relations. The discord began when the official *Beijing Review* reported that Nepalese attending the inauguration of the road by King Mahendra had shouted: "The great leader Chairman Mao is the red sun which shines most brightly in the hearts of the people of the whole world."[48] According to one Nepalese journal, however, nobody else heard the Nepalese present on the occasion praising Mao in that way.[49] The expulsion of two Chinese diplomats by India two weeks later intensified tensions in Kathmandu. On June 17 some 200 Chinese Embassy officials and project technicians, led by the ambassador, Yang Gongsu, gathered at Kathmandu airport to welcome two Chinese diplomats they had been told were on their way. Discovering that the duo were not on the flight from New Delhi, the crowd shouted anti-Indian and pro-Cultural Revolution slogans. As New Delhi lodged a strong protest, Nepalese Foreign Ministry officials met with Chinese Embassy staff to express their dissatisfaction with events.[50]

Recriminations escalated later in the month at the annual exhibition held to celebrate the king's birthday, when the Chinese sought to put up a portrait in their stand of Mao beside one of Mahendra. Nepal refused, saying its laws did not permit foreign missions to put up portraits of anybody except the head of state. Although he had fallen out of favor, Liu Shaoqi was still China's head of state. When the Chinese insisted on their right to put up Mao's portrait, a group of Nepalese students attacked the stand on July 1. The demonstrators then moved toward the center of the city, where they stoned a Chinese Embassy vehicle and attacked the Nepal–China Friendship Association library. The official Chinese media accused U.S. "imperialists," Soviet "revisionists" and Indian "reactionaries" of having instigated the Nepalese "hooligans" who had perpetrated "this vile anti-China outrage."[51] It also directly accused the Nepalese authorities of having approved of and supported the protests, prompting the Nepalese foreign secretary to protest against what he called the "false and baseless reports."[52]

Nepal believed the Chinese Embassy and Foreign Ministry in Beijing had sought to resolve the new tensions privately before they were overruled by the radicals.[53] Publicly accusing the Nepalese government of complicity, a commentary on Beijing Radio insisted that Kathmandu "must promptly annul all measures discriminating against China and stop all anti-Chinese utterances and deeds on Nepalese territory."[54] Ambassador Yang, like most of his colleagues posted around the world would soon be, had been recalled to Beijing amid the Cultural Revolution's tumult. Weeks later, however, the Chinese charge d'affaires carried a letter to King Mahendra from Premier Zhou, who, writing with the assent of Mao, stated that, in the interests of "friendship," Beijing would take no retaliatory actions against Kathmandu for the anti-Chinese incidents. Still, Nepal grew more suspicious of China and established a committee in its Foreign Ministry to evaluate security reports on the activities of Chinese, as well as Soviet, officials in Nepal.[55] The Chinese, too, appeared to have recognized the imperative of mollifying Kathmandu in order to prevent New Delhi from reasserting its influence in the kingdom. By the late summer of 1967, Foreign Minister Chen Yi invited his counterpart, Kirti Nidhi Bista, to pay a visit.

In September 1967 fighting broke out between Indian and Chinese troops on the Sikkim–Tibet border, marking the most serious incident since 1962, at a time of growing apprehensions in Kathmandu. The United States had not sought formal permission from the Nepalese government for the Mustang base.[56] As the initiative gathered pace the palace had certainly looked the other way. From Kathmandu's perspective this was a way of involving the United States more deeply in Nepal's affairs, and a round about way of gaining protection in the event of any future conflict between Nepal's two giant neighbors.[57] Growing U.S. involvement in southeast Asia now resulted in the diminution of the CIA support to the Mustang base. Washington chose to spend time, energy, and resources on other areas where returns were promising. Yet Kathmandu recognized that American interest in the Khampas as a tool against international communism was by no means over. A lessening of American ardor, Nepal felt, would leave it increasingly vulnerable to Chinese pressure. In conversations with American diplomats palace and government officials continued to voice their discomfort with the Khampa presence and the threat it posed to Nepal's policy of non-alignment.[58]

King Mahendra himself raised the issue with President Lyndon Johnson during a state visit to the United States in November 1967. The raids by Tibetan fighters continued sporadically, although the tightening of Chinese border patrols made them exceedingly difficult after 1967. The anti-Beijing resistance reached a peak of intensity during 1968. The new geo-political pressures appeared to create a new mood of compromise in the palace. The Nepali Congress' Subarna Shamsher Rana issued a statement pledging co-operation with the king and returned to Nepal. After some delay, the palace freed Koirala and his principal associate, Ganesh Man Singh, from an eight-year prison sentence. While New Delhi and Washington welcomed the move, Beijing did not react. As the prospects of a rapprochement receded, Koirala and Singh went into exile in India and stepped up their tirades against the royal regime. Mahendra now sought out new venues to promote Nepal's international profile. The kingdom's election to a two-year term on the United Nations Security Council in 1968 was considered the crowning achievement of its drive to play an independent role in the international arena. But, as Kathmandu soon discovered, key challenges remained closer to home.

In March 1969, a group of Indian Parliament members led by one of India's respected leaders, Jaya Prakash Narayan, urged their government to make a fresh appraisal of its policy toward Tibet. They cited Tibet's strategic importance to the national security of several Asian countries, including India. "Independent Tibet is vital not only to the national interest of India but also to that of the Soviet Republics of Central Asia, of Mongolia, of Pakistan, of Nepal, Bhutan, Sikkim and of Burma," they said in a statement.[59] Kathmandu was vexed by what it considered a calculated effort on the part of India to constrain its foreign policy options. But more unpleasantness was in store.

During a visit to Kathmandu three months later, Indian Foreign Minister Dinesh Singh reaffirmed that Nepal and India shared special relations. Prime Minister Bista, in an interview with the Nepalese government media, said the principle of special relations, except for geographical, social and economic realities, did not fit with the modern advancement of Nepal's foreign relations.[60] He went on to demand the withdrawal of Indian military checkpoints along the Nepal–China border, insisting that Nepalese troops were available and capable of defending it. Stating that the Indian military liaison team stationed in Kathmandu had completed its work, Bista demanded its withdrawal as well.[61] In response to a question on the 1950 Treaty, Prime Minister Bista said: "Since India did not inform Nepal before purchasing weapons from the Soviet Union and the United States of America during the Indo-Pak and the Indo-China wars, it is no more necessary for Nepal to exchange views regarding the same."[62] Kathmandu, seeking major changes in the security relationship, apparently considered neither the 1965 letters nor the 1950 Treaty binding. China, denouncing India as "expansionist," commended Bista for his statement.[63] The fact that Kathmandu's assertiveness came three weeks after Bista's return from a visit to China was not lost on India. Chinese Vice-Premier Li Xiannian had praised Nepal for its "marked success in safeguarding state sovereignty, opposing imperialism and expansionism and adhering to a foreign policy of peace, neutrality and independence."[64] Resentful of Nepal's behavior, New Delhi nevertheless proceeded to meet those demands.

Tibetans refugees in Nepal

Around this time the Nepalese population in Tibet faced further legal restrictions on their movement and residence. Changes in Nepal's law of inheritance led to a further decrease of the Nepalese community in Tibet. Children born of the same father were now entitled to equal property rights regardless of their mother's status, leading many people of mixed heritage to return to Nepal. The focus now fell on the Tibetans in Nepal, especially since it became apparent that their presence would be far from temporary. In the early 1960s the Nepalese government had arranged to provide the first wave of Tibetan refugees with land. It established four "temporary" settlements in an arrangement that enabled the Nepalese government to disavow any direct support for the refugees in order to avoid jeopardizing relations with China. In August 1964 the Nepalese government allowed the United Nations High Commissioner for Refugees (UNHCR) to open an office in Kathmandu to serve as a liaison between the Tibetan community and the government. The Swiss government, the U.S. Agency for International Development, the U.N. Children's Fund, the World Health Organization, and various non-governmental agencies all provided aid in the form of medical care, primary school education, construction of housing, and food rations. The Dalai Lama's government-in-exile appointed representatives to administer the settlements.

Over time each Tibetan settlement began to establish industries to sustain itself, which were then converted into private companies managed, although not owned, by the Tibetan refugees. Some Tibetans also established shops, hotels, and restaurants. This also brought growing complaints from the Chinese that many of these businesses also served as fronts for the Tibetan resistance, and pressure on Kathmandu to act increased.

Split in Mustang rebel leadership

The Mustang rebel leadership suffered a split in 1969. The Dalai Lama's brother, Gyalo Thondup, replaced base leader Baba Yeshi, already battling allegations of embezzlement, with Gyatho Wangdu, one of the original CIA trainees. Refusing to take on his new job as deputy head of security at Dharamsala Yeshi returned to Mustang, organized his few remaining loyalists, and defected to make a deal with the Nepalese authorities. In return for leading the Royal Nepalese Army to the Khampas, the defectors would receive plots of land. As CIA money dried up, the Indians placed their entire Tibet operation under the umbrella of the Research and Analysis Wing of the Intelligence Bureau, supervising it from the Prime Minister's Office. They established the Indo-Tibetan Border Police and recruited Tibetans as part of the Indian Army.

In early 1970 Nepal's hopes of building its diplomatic stature dissipated as Premiers Zhou and Gandhi failed to attend Crown Prince Birendra's wedding.[65] While Gandhi cited domestic preoccupations, Zhou, as the world would soon discover, was busy with Mao contemplating ways of reopening some form of dialogue with the United States. The United States, too, in early 1970, expressed its readiness to send a representative to Beijing. As Dwight D. Eisenhower's vice-president Richard Nixon had been committed to continuing the CIA's backing for Tibetan resistance. But by the time he won the presidency in 1968, Nixon had become an ardent advocate of what was to be his crowning accomplishment: the opening to China. The CIA's Tibet project, in any case, had withered. The prime factor driving Sino-American negotiations was their mutual fear of the U.S.S.R. But that precipitated an opposing pull, culminating in the 1971 Indo-Soviet Treaty of Peace, Friendship and Co-operation.

The dismemberment of Pakistan and the creation of Bangladesh in the east, an act enabled via Indian intervention supported by a Soviet veto at the U.N.

Security Council, created a palpable sense of vulnerability in Nepal. India had deployed some members of the Indo-Tibetan Border Police in the Bangladesh war, while the Nepali Congress had provided arms to the Bangladeshi freedom fighters. Washington and Beijing were now alarmed by the inroads the Soviets were making in southern Asia through their Indian alliance. In talks with Chinese officials in New York, following the destruction of the Pakistani army in the east in December, U.S. National Security Adviser Henry Kissinger stressed the objective of preventing an attack on West Pakistan by India, saying: "We are afraid that if nothing is done to stop it, East Pakistan will become a Bhutan and West Pakistan will become a Nepal. And India with Soviet help would be free to turn its energies elsewhere."[66]

The intensification of Sino-Soviet tensions in 1971 raised Chinese fears of a Soviet-supported Indian advance into Tibet. Having dealt successfully with the Pakistani threat by supporting "Bangladeshi national liberation," India, the Chinese feared, might look north at Tibet. The convulsions of the Cultural Revolution and the fallout from Lin Biao's attempted coup d'état against Mao made the People's Republic of China's leadership particularly vulnerable. China appeared fully convinced that Nepal would not allow its territory to be used as a springboard for subversive activities in Tibet.[67] But that was more a result of Beijing's rapprochement with Washington than any surge of confidence in Nepal's ability to deter any further destabilization.

For Kathmandu, Beijing's failure to come to the rescue of its West Pakistan ally in the Indo-Pakistani war of late 1971 exposed the limited economic, diplomatic and military capability of China south of the Himalayas. The emergence of Bangladesh as an independent state in the face of Beijing's determined – if only vocal – opposition, was indicative of China's inability to challenge India's status as the hegemonic power in south Asia. At this time, reports were circulating in Nepal that Prime Minister Indira Gandhi had devised a plan to mobilize Nepalese ethnic communities against the palace and the traditional elite.[68] In an effort to cushion his regime against possible Indian maneuvering, Mahendra was contemplating political reforms, possibly including a rapprochement with Koirala.[69] An announcement was expected after the monarch's return from the royal retreat in southern Nepal. Instead, state media reported early on the morning of January 31, 1972 that Mahendra had died of a massive heart attack.

Conclusion

Sino-Nepalese relations had matured significantly under King Mahendra, but, in reality, lacked the intimacy many in India and the West tended to attribute to them. Mahendra had traveled abroad extensively during a reign of nearly 17 years, but he never visited China again after his maiden 1961 trip. Nor had any senior Chinese leader visited Nepal during Mahendra's supreme leadership of the Panchayat system. Domestically, Mahendra had dominated the political scene, in the words of a close associate, "through a pragmatic use of tradition, experimentation, and manipulation [and] exuded both internally and externally an atmosphere of stability."[70]

In its global struggle against communism Tibet had become an invaluable pawn for Washington. After the war in 1962 shattered the bonhomie between China and India, New Delhi, too, saw the political value of the Tibetan exiles. But India avoided full co-ordination with Washington, which it continued to distrust on account of its courting of rival Pakistan. Nepal hosted Tibetan refugees and CIA-backed rebels, while at the same time affirming Chinese sovereignty over the region. As Washington courted Beijing, Moscow and New Delhi cemented a military relationship that emboldened India to help dismember Pakistan and create Bangladesh, while China largely stood by. The fact that Mahendra's sudden death came in the midst of fundamental change in the scale and character of China's and India's respective roles in the region brought new apprehensions at home and abroad.

8 Reforms and recriminations

Less than a month after Birendra's enthronement, U.S. President Richard Nixon made his landmark trip to China. For Nepal, the "week that changed the world" underscored the erosion of its importance as an arena for Washington and Beijing to counter each other's influence in the region. Kathmandu, which had attracted American interest as "a listening post" on China, and in particular Tibet (second in importance only to Hong Kong[1]) now remained wary of the potential of the growing Indo-Soviet alliance.

Birendra brought with him an image that was perceptibly distinct from that of his father, attributable largely to his exposure to western liberal thought. The first Nepalese monarch to have received a formal education, he had undergone diverse academic experiences in India, Britain, the United States and Japan. As public dissatisfaction with the Panchayat system's inability to accelerate national development grew, many expected Birendra to use his familiarity with the open and liberal political dynamics of the outside world to reset the initiative. While the new monarch's early emphasis fell on political discipline, administrative efficiency, and economic development, in some areas of foreign policy Birendra appeared more resolute than his father in defining Nepal's independent national identity. In an interview with an American news magazine, he said Nepal was not a part of the subcontinent but rather a part of Asia that touched both India and China.[2]

At a conference of non-aligned nations in Algeria in September 1973, Birendra voiced Nepal's desire to live as a zone of peace between the Asian giants. New Delhi quietly indicated its displeasure with Birendra's effort to redefine geo-politics during his first visit to India as king the following month. Prime Minister Indira Gandhi's government continued to refuse to provide encouragement to exiled anti-monarchy forces, but expected Kathmandu to acknowledge and honor India's interests in the kingdom. Specifically, New Delhi reminded landlocked Nepal that the economic benefits it extended depended on reciprocity. Palace advisers sensed that Gandhi possessed a capacity to act far more ruthlessly and decisively to get what she wanted for India than did her late father, Jawaharlal Nehru, a sentiment Birendra was believed to share.[3]

In December Birendra carried his new foreign policy outlook to Beijing, where he held extensive talks with Chairman Mao Zedong. Sympathetic to the royal message, Mao broached the potential of a Beijing–Lhasa train service that might ultimately be extended to the Nepalese border to link the two countries economically and physically.[4] However, Mao told Birendra, the Khampa rebels were posing a major obstacle to better relations.[5] Although American support to the Tibetan rebels had dried up, the Chinese leader had continuing reason for concern. The Soviets had been in touch with Tibetan refugees in Nepal and in India and had stepped up their propaganda war against the Chinese occupation.[6]

During his talks with Birendra, Premier Zhou Enlai publicly reaffirmed China's support for the Nepalese "in their struggle against foreign interference." But Zhou had become a target of the radicals, who accused him of taking a soft line with the Americans. In the official Chinese media's picture of Mao's meeting with the Nepalese king and queen, Zhou was seen seated in a chair normally reserved for a junior interpreter.[7] While the Chinese would be able to suppress full public knowledge of their internal problems for some time yet, their shrewd emphasis on reciprocity with Nepal yielded results.

In early 1974 Kathmandu declared the entire northwestern region around Mustang a restricted zone and began deploying thousands of troops. In March the government sent emissaries to Gyatho Wangdu, the Khampa rebel commander, offering a trade-off. It would provide almost half a million dollars in rehabilitation assistance as well as rights to land and buildings already developed there, in exchange for a full surrender and the disbanding of the camps. When the Khampas refused, Kathmandu gave the resistance an ultimatum to surrender by July.[8] The UNHCR had discontinued its assistance program for Tibetan refugees and had closed its Kathmandu office the previous year, concluding that Nepal was well on its way to achieving a durable solution to the problem through local integration. Having won recognition of its record on the humanitarian side, Kathmandu felt emboldened to deal with the menacing political dimension. Events across Nepal's eastern frontier in another Himalayan state historically linked to Tibet heightened Nepalese anxieties.

As India became directly involved in the growing political turmoil in Sikkim, many Nepalese felt New Delhi had fomented the unrest it was now offering to help end. Sikkim's king, or *chogyal*, had asked Indian troops to help control demonstrators threatening to storm his palace. The riots stemmed from a controversy over the nation's electoral procedures – a system that inadequately represented the settlers from Nepal, who made up 75 percent of Sikkim's 210,000 population. India subdued the demonstrators, but there was a clear perception in Kathmandu that it may have incited them in the first place. The *chogyal*, who had headed the 1949 team that negotiated a treaty with India making Sikkim an Indian protectorate, made plans to seek greater independence from India. He envisioned a Sikkim that would conduct its own foreign and military affairs and one day enter the United Nations as a fully independent state. New Delhi then pressured the *chogyal* into accepting an agreement that stripped him of all power. In elections supervised by India in April 1974 candidates from the anti-*chogyal*, pro-India Sikkim National Congress party won 30 of the 32 seats. The new assembly's first act was to strip the *chogyal* of his powers and table a resolution calling for closer ties with New Delhi, a move widely interpreted as a prelude to the merger of the state with India.

Chinese media emphasized that Nepal might be India's next target.[9] The only other country to offer a stinging rebuke to New Delhi was Pakistan. New Delhi did not appreciate Nepal having sided with its two major adversaries and regarded it as an indirect challenge to India's newly acquired sense of importance as a mini-super power (as demonstrated by military victory over Pakistan and the recent explosion of a nuclear device). In September, as the Indian parliament passed the bill to absorb the state, protesters in Kathmandu attacked the Indian embassy and cultural center, and Indian shops. New Delhi, insisting it was merely acting in accordance with the wishes of the Sikkimese people, retorted that the "vulgar" demonstrations in Kathmandu had official backing.

Crackdown in Mustang

When the Khampa rebels in Mustang failed to surrender before the July deadline passed, Nepalese troops launched a major operation in the autumn of 1974 to ferret out the remaining guerrillas. The Indian government pressed the Dalai Lama to act, insisting that the Chinese and the Nepalese would blame him should war break out in Mustang.[10] Hoping to avoid needless bloodshed the Dalai Lama sent a representative with a message urging the rebels to lay down their arms. As a tape recording of his appeal was played, many fighters complained they could not surrender to the Nepalese when they had not done so to the Chinese. In the end, most complied. Among those who did not was the resistance leader, Wangdu, who had pleaded unsuccessfully with the CIA to continue supporting the Mustang operations.[11] Although he had pressed many rebels to lay down their arms in order to ensure the well-being of the thousands of refugees living in Nepal, Wangdu himself sought to arrange an orderly surrender. The Nepalese army suspected a ploy and continued to advance. At this point the Khampas realized that they were caught between the Chinese as well as Nepalese armies. Wangdu and forty of his men ran for a month, venturing into Tibet and then retreating. Wangdu's remaining option was to escape to India, where he believed he could organize a peaceful surrender from India.[12]

At the Tinker Pass in Jumla, once an independent principality that had been closely allied with Tibet until the late eighteenth century, the Khampas and the Nepalese army were engaged in a fierce fire-fight. Assisted by elements of the anti-Wangdu faction the Nepalese troops eventually killed the resistance leader and four of his men, while the remainder surrendered. The Royal Nepalese Army then began clean-up operations. Baba Yeshi, the rebel leader who had broken from Wangdu, was brought by Nepalese army helicopter to identify Wangdu's body.[13] Predictably, Beijing applauded Kathmandu's action. New Delhi, equally predictably, was not impressed. The Tibetan resistance was one of India's principal leverages in negotiations with China on their Himalayan border. If the Khampas were to be brought under control, the Indians preferred to do this in exchange for a concession, such as the termination of Chinese support for Naga and Mizo rebels in northeastern India.[14]

Shortly after Nepalese military disarmed the Tibetan rebels Beijing offered to build a $75 million highway from the tourist resort of Pokhara to the midwestern regional headquarters of Surkhet. The previous year China had completed a road from Kathmandu to Pokhara, installed an electric trolley-bus system in a busy Kathmandu district, and constructed a ring road on the outer perimeter of the Kathmandu valley. The new road would extend the transport link from the Kodari Pass and Kathmandu more than 300>km west through rugged hills. Emboldened by Chinese aid, Kathmandu sought greater recognition of its political independence.

King Birendra's Zone of Peace proposal

In an address to dignitaries attending his coronation in February 1975, Birendra formally proposed that Nepal be declared a Zone of Peace (ZOP) where military competition would be off-limits, a theme that would go on to define the kingdom's foreign policy for the duration of his direct rule.[15] The proposal stemmed from Kathmandu's growing concerns over India's intrigues in Sikkim, the growth of left-wing extremism in eastern Nepal drawing support from India, New Delhi's successful nuclear tests, and India's perceived collusion with the Soviets in the overthrow of the monarchy in Afghanistan. New Delhi saw the ZOP proposal as a brazen attempt to circumvent the "special relations" between the two countries it believed the 1950 Treaty had enshrined.[16] Cold War power politics surfaced in the reaction to the proposal. Kathmandu had appeared satisfied that American interests in the kingdom had become independent of India, while New Delhi perceived Washington's activities in Kathmandu as specifically aimed at undermining India's role in the region.[17] The Soviets, who initially welcomed the proposal, backtracked after appeals from India, while Chinese leaders extended enthusiastic support.

Sikkim's *chogyal* had attended Birendra's coronation and met with Chinese and Pakistani diplomats, raising concerns in New Delhi that he was lobbying support for Sikkimese independence. In public comments the *chogyal* was critical of India's efforts to stymie Sikkim's desire to build its international stature. After he returned home in April events moved swiftly. Indian troops surrounded the *chogyal's* palace and put him under house arrest. In a hastily organized referendum in April, the people of Sikkim voted to relinquish their sovereignty and the Indian parliament overwhelmingly formalized the merger. Prime Minister Gandhi's declaration of a state of emergency in India in June provided the opportunity for Beijing to ratchet up the propaganda war on New Delhi's regional policy.[18]

The erosion of freedoms in the world's most populous democracy energized hard-line elements within the Panchayat system and by the end of the year King Birendra announced constitutional changes that battered his image as a reformer. The partyless system turned into a de facto one-party state with the creation of quasi-judicial organizations to vet and monitor politicians.[19] Nonetheless Nepal figured highly on the Sino-American agenda. During President Gerald Ford's talks with Deng Xiaoping in Beijing in December, Ford specifically asked Deng, whom Mao had now rehabilitated, whether he saw any threat of an Indian invasion of Nepal. Acknowledging that Nepal felt such a threat, Deng said he saw no indications of India making open military moves.

Asserting that China was doing all it could to help Nepal, Deng conceded that there were limits to its actions. "Perhaps things will get better when our railroad to Tibet is accomplished," he added, urging Washington to do more with Nepal. Ford said he was sending a friend as ambassador. Secretary of State Henry Kissinger interjected: "This shows the significance we attach to Nepal." Deng added: "It is necessary to help Nepal. They are a nation that can fight. Nepal isn't Sikkim or Bhutan."[20]

That was precisely the image King Birendra was anxious to project. He actively sought international recognition that Nepal no longer lived under India's economic or defensive umbrella. At international conferences Kathmandu continued to lobby for international guarantees of unrestricted transit rights to and from the ocean for landlocked states such as itself. China, Pakistan and Bangladesh became the most vociferous supporters of the ZOP proposal.

Air bridge across the Himalayas

In June Birendra became the first foreign head of state to visit Tibet, flying over the Himalayas. Prime Minister Hua Guofeng – whom Mao had appointed to the job after Zhou Enlai's death earlier in the year – and Foreign Minister Qiao Guanhua came from Beijing to Chengdu in Sichuan to welcome the monarch and to emphasize that Nepal's relations with China were also "special."[21] At an official banquet, Hua described the ZOP proposal as reflecting "the strong desire of the people of Nepal to safeguard national independence and state sovereignty ... and the Chinese government firmly supported this just proposition."[22] Birendra, alluding to both the Khampas in Nepal and Nepali Congress politicians in India, declared: "We will not allow the use of our soil for any activity hostile to any country and we expect reciprocity in this matter." The king then flew off to Lhasa, the first foreign head of state to be allowed by the Chinese to visit Tibet. Conspicuously absent on the royal itinerary was Beijing, where Chairman Mao was said to be gravely ill. Presumably both sides had agreed in advance to avoid the possible embarrassment of Birendra visiting the capital without being able to schedule a meeting with Mao.[23] The public display of sturdiness in the Sino-Nepalese partnership continued as Kathmandu backed the expulsion of Taiwan from the International Monetary Fund.[24]

Differences over the political nature of Nepal's relationship with India grew as negotiations dragged on past the Trade and Transit Treaty's expiration date. When India refused to add a more specific freedom of transit clause in the new treaty, Kathmandu spurned New Delhi's draft. Nepalese hopes of more vigorous Chinese support were dashed, as this was a period of internal flux in post-Mao China.

Still, Beijing had gone out of its way to support the ZOP proposal. Speaking at a banquet in honor of Prime Minister Zulfiqar Ali Bhutto in Beijing in late May, Hua had said: "We firmly support the just stand taken by His Majesty the King of Nepal in declaring a zone of peace. We are ready to assume appropriate commitments arising therefrom."[25] In a statement at the United Nations General Assembly in October, Chinese Foreign Minister Qiao Guanhua reiterated China's firm support to the proposal.[26] By 1976–1977 Chinese aid to Nepal had reached a record high of $2 million a year, nearly equaling for the first time Indian aid to Nepal. Public reaffirmations of support for the ZOP helped Beijing maintain a business-as-usual posture on Nepal.

The critical response for Nepal, of course, was that of India. Although New Delhi officially had kept the proposal under active consideration, the Indira Gandhi government made it clear that it would not accede to the ZOP in any form, shape, or definition. In what would go on to represent India's virtual rejection of the proposal, New Delhi wanted south Asia declared a zone of peace. Moreover, India considered the 1950 Indo-Nepalese Treaty to still be in force in all its aspects, without need of revision or abrogation.

Kathmandu cautiously welcomed the defeat of Indira Gandhi and her Congress party in the March 1977 election. This contrasted sharply with the stance of Beijing, which welcomed the development as a setback for Soviet hegemony in south Asia and noted the new directions of Indian foreign policy under the Janata Party-led coalition government.[27] Kathmandu, which hoped the new era of coalition politics would keep New Delhi internally preoccupied, also had new worries. While Mrs. Gandhi had adopted an increasingly hard line on political and economic relations with Nepal, she had also dissociated her government from the Nepalese opposition forces based there, and had applied ever sharper restrictions on their operations.

The situation had become so difficult for the Nepalese exiles that former prime minister Koirala – the international face of the Nepalese opposition – decided to return to Nepal in December 1976 without having extracted any concessions from the royal regime, which promptly imprisoned him again. The Janata Party government included a number of old socialist party leaders who had enjoyed a long relationship with Koirala and other Nepalese opposition leaders. Some of these leaders had also been vocal supporters of Tibetan independence. This raised concern in Kathmandu about the policy of the new Indian government not only toward the royal regime but also over Nepal's role in any potential trouble in Tibet.

The Janata government moved to reassure Kathmandu. In early 1978 Morarji Desai, the new prime minister, admitted that Indira Gandhi's government should not have annexed Sikkim.[28] He said he regretted an act whose colonial overtones had not only troubled many Indians but had also raised fears among other small nations bordering India that a similar fate might befall them. But, he said, it could not be undone. Although the statement scarcely had practical consequence, some in Kathmandu still saw it as an overture. The Janata government moved to assuage Kathmandu in other ways, but with limited success.

During his visit to Kathmandu in December 1977, Desai had agreed to sign separate trade and transit treaties, but his government continued to ignore the Zone of Peace proposal. The rebuff did not prevent Kathmandu from stepping up its international campaign to promote the proposal. Some Indians saw Chinese encouragement. The rival school, however, saw the post-Mao Chinese leadership demonstrating greater flexibility toward India. According to this view, Beijing was not ready to extend unqualified support to the royal regime. Under Deng, they noted, the anti-Indian content of Chinese propaganda in Nepal declined rapidly and they expected Chinese aid to continue in a less contentious fashion.

Deng Xiaoping visits Nepal

Amid these competing assumptions, Chinese Vice-Premier Deng Xiaoping arrived in Kathmandu in February 1978. The fact that Nepal formed part of his first foreign tour since his return to power assumed considerable importance in both countries.[29] Applauding the state of bilateral relations, Deng also reiterated China's support for Nepal's peace zone proposal. In his speeches in Kathmandu Deng urged the countries of south Asia to join against foreign hegemony, which he said "has caused long-term instability in this region, seriously threatening the independence and security of countries in this region, and has encountered the opposition and condemnation of the peoples of South Asia."[30] Beijing extended a fair amount of economic and technical aid, and even encouraged border trade in a limited way, yet quietly shelved the road building project previously discussed.[31] Broader aid talks foundered on conflicting priorities: Beijing sought to develop joint ventures while Kathmandu wanted traditional grant-based projects.[32]

In late August, Nepal and China signed an agreement on the much-anticipated "trans-Himalayan air route" under which Royal Nepal Airlines would operate a regular air service to Beijing, which could be extended to Tokyo via Shanghai. A country which until recently China had considered a conduit for the outside world to infiltrate Tibet was now being used by Beijing to reach out. The following month, Hua and Deng welcomed Prime Minister Bista in Beijing. One major outcome was an agreement for Chinese assistance in the establishment of sugar and paper factories, costing $40 million.

The visit turned out to be less propitious internally for Bista. In Beijing he welcomed the new Sino-Japanese Treaty of Peace and Friendship. Bista had commented that the treaty would be a contributing factor to "stability" in the southeast Asian region. In view of Soviet opposition to the signing of the treaty, observers noted a "tilt" in Nepal's foreign policy toward China vis-à-vis the Soviet Union. Those concerns emerged amid a wider perception of a cooling of relations with Moscow, which prompted a rebuttal from the Soviet ambassador.[33]

By April 1979, as disaffection with the Panchayat system grew, student protests snowballed into a fully-fledged movement against the partyless system.

Figure 8.1 Chinese Vice-Premier Deng Xiaoping donning a Nepalese cap at a public function in Kathmandu in 1978 (photo: author's collection).

King Birendra announced he would hold a national referendum to determine whether the Nepalese people wanted a return to multiparty democracy or to continue with a reformed partyless system. The implications of a reversion to a pre-Panchayat order was not lost on Beijing, especially considering that the dominant political parties such as the Nepali Congress and the communist factions shared close ties with India. During a brief visit to China in August, King Birendra assured Beijing that whatever the outcome of the referendum the basic structure of Nepalese foreign policy would not be changed.[34]

On his way back home after an extended international tour, Birendra arrived in New Delhi with a stern message. If India did not prevent the activities of the Russian-supported elements on the Indo-Nepalese border, the monarch told his hosts, Beijing would not keep quiet.[35] This admonition came amid a widespread rumor that four officials from the Soviet embassy in Kathmandu had been asked to leave Nepal because their activities were objectionable to the Nepalese government. Birendra now urged the Nepalese to be vigilant of "colonialism with attractive slogans" and a "cold-war like situation in the South Asian Sub-continent."[36]

When Chinese Foreign Minister Huang Hua visited Nepal in November to sign the second Sino-Nepalese border protocol, he seemed satisfied by Nepal's support for the Chinese position on the Kampuchean issue. The Nepalese side expressed satisfaction over Chinese support for the ZOP proposal. As Sino-Soviet relations deteriorated once again, Moscow hinted that it might adopt a more assertive approach toward Tibet. In a United Nations debate over the China–Vietnam war, the Soviet representative raised the question of Tibet and implicitly condemned its occupation by China in 1950 by comparing that move to China's 1979 attack on Vietnam. Then in June the Dalai Lama made his first visit to the U.S.S.R., followed by a visit to the Mongolian People's Republic.[37]

The return of pro-Soviet Indira Gandhi to power in early 1980 brought about a new dynamic. Gandhi had criticized the Janata government for needless concessions in the neighborhood. Kathmandu expected New Delhi to be stricter in asserting its role and sought to bolster its international position. The royal regime was helped by the narrow victory the partyless system won in May 1980 and Birendra sought to institute constitutional reforms that would introduce a more representative and responsible system through direct elections to the legislature.

New hope for peace in Tibet

China now made a key policy shift on Tibet. During a visit to the region in mid-May, Hu Yaobang, the new Chinese Communist Party general secretary, conceded Beijing had made mistakes in the past. He promised Tibetans that the central government would endeavor to rectify them and bring about the sort of political and economic reform that would significantly benefit the people. This rare candor emerged in the context of larger developments surrounding the rise of reformists under Deng, who sought a more substantial break from Mao. Although he dealt mainly with mainland issues as part of his Four Modernizations, launched in December 1978, Deng also confronted the key anomaly in Tibet. Moreover, he had been one of the three men who drew up the plan for the expedition into Tibet in 1950. As the political commissar of the Southwestern Military Region at the time, he was directly responsible for devising the Party's Tibet policy and knew the senior cadres and military officers serving there.[38]

Deng was believed to have been the author of the document that eventually became the basis for the 17-point Agreement.[39]

Over the decades Beijing had invested considerably in the region but believed it was not reaping commensurate political dividends. The Chinese had begun a process of rapprochement with the Dalai Lama's brother, Gyalo Thondup, who had visited China at Deng's invitation the previous year. Although the trip was not immediately publicized in the media, Deng was quoted as having told Gyalo during an earlier meeting that all matters except Tibetan independence could be discussed.[40] But fact-finding missions sent from Dharamsala to Tibet to ascertain the true state of affairs painted a grim picture.

As Deng gradually gained control over the Party, Hua was denounced for promoting policies that sought to perpetuate Mao's legacy and replaced by Zhao Ziyang as premier in September 1980. Hu Yaobang took over Hua's post as party chairman the following January. Both Zhao and Hu were Deng protégés dedicated to Chinese economic reform. The Dalai Lama wrote a letter to Deng in March 1981, stating the fact-finding teams had reported back to him that 90 percent of Tibetans were suffering both mentally and physically, and that the deplorable situation was not caused by natural calamities but by human actions.[41] Yet the prospects for dialogue had not ended, especially given the Dalai Lama's personal admiration for Hu Yaobang.[42]

In June, Chinese Premier Zhao Ziyang arrived in Kathmandu, the first Chinese head of government to arrive in Kathmandu in two decades.[43] Zhao reaffirmed Beijing's support for the ZOP proposal, seeking to underscore the stability inherent in Sino-Nepalese relations. In public Beijing stressed the importance of placing ties with New Delhi on a new footing. Zhou called for a "package solution" to the boundary question with India and added that the possibility of a "breakthrough" in Sino-Indian relations depended on the existence of sincerity on both sides.[44] Yet there were some misgivings in Kathmandu concerning Beijing's position. Speaking to a member of India's parliament the previous month, Deng Xiaoping had referred to India as the "elder brother" of south Asia. This was attributed to Deng's revival of the long-dormant proposal for an east-west swap solution to the territorial question.[45]

King Birendra's visit to China's Gansu province in July 1982 assumed importance amid reports of strains elsewhere on the foreign front. According to several newspapers in Kathmandu, customs authorities at Tribhuvan Airport allowed the Soviet embassy to bring in 17 truck loads of goods without the usual checking requirements. There were rumors in Kathmandu that the Soviets were supplying arms and cash to certain groups in Nepal. There were also suggestions that Prime Minister Surya Bahadur Thapa himself had unofficially granted unauthorized importations to accommodate the Soviets.[46] By July 1983 Thapa had been voted out as premier by the legislature in a move that he and his loyalists claimed the palace had orchestrated.

A tilt to the West

As Nepal's foreign policy pronouncements had become overtly pro-western, particularly on the issues of Afghanistan and Kampuchea, King Birendra left on a state visit to the United States in December. President Ronald Reagan supported the monarch's proposal to have Nepal accepted as a zone of peace, and the visit was acclaimed in Nepal as a triumph for its foreign policy. Earlier in the year French President François Mitterrand, who had become the first head of government of a major western power to visit Nepal, accepted the proposal. Both Washington and Paris, however, expressed the need for Nepal to work closely with its neighbors to make the proposal a reality.[47]

In March 1984 President Li Xiannian became the first Chinese head of state to visit the Himalayan kingdom. As deputy premier in the late 1960s, Li had praised Nepal's ability to withstand Indian pressure under King Mahendra. Now emerging as a key ally of Deng Xiaoping, Li was more restrained on Nepal's political and diplomatic affairs. A key source of Nepalese concern related to China's aid program, which, in world terms, had been in decline since 1976. By 1983 the Chinese government had taken a new direction in foreign aid policy. In an effort to extend foreign relations to as many potential aid recipients as possible, China increased the number of countries it targeted for aid donations.[48] Furthermore, China started to make significant aid funds through the United Nations and other international organizations.

During Li's visit China undertook to build a second major Tibet–Nepal highway, this one cutting through the Mustang region and linking Pokhara with the Xinjiang–Tibet highway. China also looked to promote political, trade, and cultural delegations between Nepal and China's Tibet region. China subsequently signed an agreement that would bring regular trading caravans into its western regions, from Nepal as well as Pakistan.

The assassination of Prime Minister Indira Gandhi in October 1984 brought uncertainty in the region as a whole. Rajiv Gandhi, Indira's son and the new prime minister, was an unknown quantity. Despite their periodic tensions with the monarchy, both Jawaharlal Nehru and Indira Gandhi had accorded respect to the palace's rule. Amid uncertainty over how Rajiv Gandhi and his group of younger Congress Party members would approach Nepal, Kathmandu and Beijing continued to promote economic engagement. In April 1985 they reached agreement to permit travel by foreigners through the mountain passes of the Himalayas into Tibet. Hitherto visitors to Tibet had had to make the long trip through China itself. These agreements, which marked the first relaxation of border controls in more than 30 years, came as talks between Dharamsala and Beijing stalled.

The opening of the border was expected to also help tourism in Nepal, but those hopes received a serious blow in June when the country suffered its worst terrorist attacks. Six people died in Kathmandu as a result. A shadowy republican outfit led by a Nepalese leader living in exile in India claimed responsibility for the attacks on the royal palace gate, the national legislature and a luxury hotel owned by the royal family. The Nepali Congress called off a national movement for the restoration of democracy it had recently launched, but the kingdom's image as a Shangri-La received a setback. The experiment in Tibet was a disappointment for China as well. Tourists complained of primitive conditions on the road between Tibet and Nepal, while Chinese officials imposed new limits on access to Tibet, citing dissatisfaction with foreign journalists' portrayals of the country in their reports.[49]

Under Rajiv Gandhi's government New Delhi reiterated its longstanding complaint that Nepal wanted economic advantages from India whilst at the same time eroding symbols of the two countries' "special" relationship. Of particular concern to New Delhi was the growing number of Chinese technicians involved in projects in Nepal. Beijing's reversion to a less India-deferring policy toward Nepal – underscored by its agreement the previous year to build a second trans-Himalayan highway – may have been related to India's failure to accept the east-west swap settlement of the boundary issue revived by Deng in 1980.[50] But New Delhi voiced its concern during King Birendra's visit to New Delhi in 1985. Distrust came to the fore again over Nepal's plans to construct a series of bridges linking the east-west highway across the southwestern part of the country. Indian sensitivity stemmed from the fact that the area fell near the western junction between Nepal, India, and China.

Nepal insisted the highway was a vital artery and would remain incomplete without the bridges. So it decided that the section would be constructed with international loans under the auspices of the World Bank. China made the lowest bid, which New Delhi opposed in a formal representation to Kathmandu. After Nepal cancelled the contract and compensated the Chinese contractor, India came forward with an offer of financial grants for the complete construction of the section.[51] Seeking to broaden its horizons, Nepal now became an active proponent of the South Asian Association for Regional Cooperation (SAARC) created to promote what was officially billed as the "collective self-reliance" of one-fifth of humanity. The leaders of India, Pakistan, Bangladesh, Sri Lanka, Bhutan, the Maldives and Nepal formally launched the organization at a summit in Dhaka in 1985. Kathmandu would go on to host the secretariat of the organization.

Nepal had won international acclaim for having taken in thousands of Tibetan refugees and affording them the possibility of becoming contributing members of the societies of their host country while at the same time preserving their own identity.[52] Nepal, too, owed much to the Tibetan refugees. By the mid-1980s the carpet industry that the early wave of asylum seekers had established had become the second-largest earner of foreign currency for Nepal. Kathmandu's approach toward new refugees from across the Himalayas began to tighten after August 1986, when Nepal and China executed a new treaty that significantly restricted the ability of Tibetans to travel through or into the kingdom. Then, in November, Tibet became the center of national controversy as Kathmandu hosted a major international Buddhist conference. There were reports that the sponsors had invited both the Dalai and Panchen Lamas, but were forced by the

Nepalese government to cancel the invitation to the Dalai Lama. In the past Kathmandu had allowed the Dalai Lama to visit Lumbini under carefully supervised circumstances.[53] But allowing him into the capital, the Nepalese government feared, would seriously undermine the kingdom's relations with China.

Under the new arrangement the Panchen Lama, who was also the vice-chairman of the Standing Committee of the National People's Congress of China, was invited to visit Nepal by the vice-chairman of the National Panchayat.[54] Beijing had taken a calculated risk in allowing the Panchen Lama to travel abroad, especially since he had recently been freed after years of house arrest. The decision to allow him to travel to Nepal must have come from Beijing's confidence in its ability to use him as a rival to the Dalai Lama, a ploy that had worked well for Beijing in the past. The Dalai Lama, for his part, embarked on another phase of conciliation. In 1987 he called for the establishment of Tibet as a zone of peace and said he continued to seek dialogue with Beijing with the aim of achieving genuine self-rule for Tibet within China. Stability in the region, at least from Beijing's point of view, now depended in large measure on forging links with Nepal. China and Nepal also agreed to inaugurate charter air flights between Lhasa and Kathmandu.

A flurry of international visitors throughout 1987, including West German Chancellor Helmut Kohl and Spain's King Juan Carlos, brought high-profile political as well as economic support to the kingdom. The leaders of the SAARC met in Kathmandu in early November and discussed the possibilities of enhancing regional co-operation. Yet the smaller countries had cause for concern as India became increasingly involved in the deteriorating situation in Sri Lanka. Kathmandu condemned New Delhi's unilateral action in air-dropping relief supplies in Jaffna Peninsula, although it understood India's desire to help the Sri Lankan Tamils on humanitarian grounds.[55] However, when India and Sri Lanka signed an agreement in late July to bring peace to the island nation, Kathmandu welcomed the accord, thereby recognizing India's security role in Sri Lanka.

Nepal's dilemma was similar to China's. After all, this was an agreement Colombo and New Delhi had concluded. Yet the move raised concerns in Kathmandu as well as Beijing about India's intentions toward its smaller neighbors in south Asia. Kathmandu in particular saw the Sri Lankan episode as just the beginning of India's effort to assert its military authority in the region. In September King Birendra visited China for talks with Deng and President Li. Privately China's leaders were very critical of the deployment of the Indian Peace-Keeping Force.[56] Birendra, for his part, sought to dispel China's misgivings about Nepal's political balance between its giant neighbors, especially in the aftermath of the road contract controversy.

The Dalai Lama now embarked on a course that would step up the internationalization of the Tibet issue. Addressing the U.S. Congressional Human Rights Caucus in Washington in mid-September, he put forth a "Five-Point Peace Plan," the most controversial element of which called for the transformation of the whole of Tibet (Inner and Outer) into a zone of peace. As he envisaged it, any peace zone in the Himalayas would require withdrawal of Chinese and Indian troops.[57] Official covert U.S. backing for anti-Beijing forces in the 1950s and 1960s had failed to make much headway amid China's vigorous military response and splits in the rebel leadership.

By the time Washington withdrew its support in response to its rapprochement with Beijing, the Free Tibet movement had succeeded in gaining supporters in the world of celebrity. Actors, musicians, authors, professors and lawyers joined hands to raise awareness as well as funds. Capitol Hill's involvement on the Tibetan issue now brought the related issue of Taiwan into focus, vexing the Chinese. Within Tibet the Dalai Lama's new international assertiveness energized followers, who began demonstrations against Beijing. By October communications with Tibet were cut and authorities moved to keep foreigners from entering the remote Himalayan region as it marked the 37th anniversary of Chinese Communist rule. As China reversed its policy of promoting the region for tourism, the Chinese Embassy in Kathmandu stopped issuing travel visas. As anti-Beijing protests swelled in Tibet, Chinese security forces began arresting dissidents.

Chinese arms, Indian arm-twisting

At this time India was recalibrating the framework of its own relations with China. Rajiv Gandhi decided to accept China's proposal that the two countries improve relations, even while continuing to disagree on the complex territorial issue. As Kathmandu stepped up efforts to reinforce its independence and sovereignty, through an exchange of high-level visits with other international capitals, Indian political circles began weighing Nepal's potential role in what they considered to be a highly troublesome area of the subcontinent.[58]

India's suspicions were fueled in March 1988 when Nepal sought to purchase $20 million worth of light arms, ammunition, boots and uniforms, and 16 anti-aircraft guns from China. In a coincidence harking back from the early 1960s, the banned Nepali Congress began campaigning for a restoration of multiparty democracy, taking advantage of the growing popular discontent against the partyless system. The palace and the government tended to see New Delhi as the prime instigator, a perception the Indian media did little to dispel. If India's objective was to prise Nepal away from China by tacitly backing the opposition, then the move backfired. The palace showed every indication of pressing ahead with the arms purchase.

From New Delhi's perspective the sale was a violation of its 1950 Treaty with Kathmandu, as well an infringement of an agreement signed in 1965. Kathmandu maintained that such agreements only covered munitions imports through India, not those via other countries. Reports of a secret Sino-Nepalese agreement in the fall of 1988 providing for the exchange of intelligence between the two governments further irritated India.[59] Insisting that it urgently needed to modernize its military, Kathmandu claimed China had offered for many years to sell arms but that it had declined, preferring to continue relying on New Delhi. However, the Nepalese complained, India did not always meet their requests.

In response to the claim that each country was obligated by the 1950 Treaty to consult the other over any misunderstanding that might cause any breach in friendly relations, Kathmandu reminded New Delhi that it had not initiated any consultation before going to war with China in 1962 or Pakistan in 1965 and 1971.[60]

Recognizing the fait accompli, New Delhi sought to recalibrate its stance. In July 1988, shortly after the first consignment of arms began arriving over the Kathmandu–Lhasa highway, Prime Minister Gandhi dispatched a special envoy to Birendra seeking assurances that Nepal would not again purchase arms from China and that the weapons already purchased would not be used against India.[61] Birendra refused, insisting on Nepal's sovereign right to purchase weapons it considered necessary for its defense. Stressing that the weapons were intended for internal security and antiterrorism, and did not constitute a threat to India, Birendra also told the envoy that Nepal planned to increase the size of its army by two divisions over the next decade, almost double its present size.[62]

This defiance heightened New Delhi's concerns over the possibility of Sino-Nepalese military ties that might evolve toward a Pakistan-like relationship with China. The Chinese government defended the sale, insisting that Nepal, as a sovereign independent country, was entitled to purchase any material it considered necessary for its defense. China, for its part, was free to sell them. Moreover, Beijing contended that the materials sold to Nepal could not be construed as constituting a threat to India.[63] But New Delhi was not assured of Beijing's wider position vis-à-vis India, a doubt that had begun with the process of Sino-Soviet rapprochement. Prime Minister Gandhi contemplated changes in the level and method of bilateral discussions. Specifically, he decided that talks should be raised from the vice-ministerial to the ministerial or even prime ministerial, level. Beijing, too, increasingly recognized the fact that Tibet could be used to put foreign pressure on China, especially after the Dalai Lama's Five Point Plan had gained considerable international attention.

In July 1988 came the Tibetan leader's Strasbourg proposal, granting major political concessions to China. Beijing could remain responsible for Tibet's foreign policy and defense. The right to maintain a restricted number of military installations in Tibet would be limited until a regional peace conference and international agreement decided otherwise. From Dharamsala's standpoint Strasbourg was a compromise on Tibetan independence. It envisaged local autonomy where Tibet would be a self-governing democratic political entity founded on law in association with the People's Republic of China.[64] But China saw the Strasbourg proposal as implying independence. Therefore it was in its interests to assuage India – the host of the Tibetan government in exile – by agreeing to the resumption of talks.

Gandhi formally conveyed the Indian shift on the level of method of bilateral discussions during his visit to Beijing in December 1988, the first such visit by an Indian premier since 1954. It also marked the first Sino-Indian summit meeting since Zhou Enlai's ill-fated mission to India in 1960. The Chinese in return obtained an affirmation from Rajiv Gandhi that India recognized Tibet as a part of China, and that India would not interfere in China's internal affairs, or allow Tibetans in India to conduct political activities.[65]

It was unclear whether the arms sales or the general thrust of Sino-Nepalese relations formed part of Gandhi's discussions in China. But after the Indian premier's return, New Delhi struck hard – and in a familiar way. It refused to extend the trade and transit treaties that had expired in March 1988. When those treaties finally lapsed – after two six-month extensions – in March 1989, the Indian government closed down 13 of the 15 border crossing points and instituted a series of other economic sanctions against Nepal.

Clearly New Delhi had been encouraged in taking such actions by Beijing's new preoccupations. In January 1989 the Tenth Panchen Lama died mysteriously, days after criticizing Beijing's policies in Tibet. In early March, on the eve of the 30th anniversary of the beginning of an abortive anti-Chinese uprising that resulted in the Dalai Lama's fleeing into exile in India, Chinese officials began a security crackdown and ordered foreigners out. That unrest would provide the backdrop to the massive student protests in Beijing that led up to the June 4 Tiananmen Square massacre. Already dealing with a rise in the number of refugees during the unrest two years earlier, Nepal now saw another surge. It decided to stop registering Tibetan refugees and no longer allowed new arrivals to remain in the country.[66]

Once the Indian sanctions started creating fuel shortages Beijing began ferrying some 300 tons of gasoline and kerosene into Kathmandu. But greatly increased transportation costs meant that Nepal ended up paying prices above world market prices for Chinese oil.[67] Several delegations traveled between Lhasa and Kathmandu in an effort to expand trade, as China gave a substantial amount of salt free of cost. A Chinese Foreign Ministry spokesman expressed concern about the "serious difficulties facing the Nepalese people" and called on Nepal and India to "iron out their differences ... and resume their normal trade at an early date." He also maintained that landlocked countries were entitled to transit through neighboring countries.

The Chinese media criticized India's actions, albeit obliquely. "The key [to the India–Nepal dispute] is that India wants its security interests to take priority in its relations with Nepal, while Nepal persists in keeping relations with India on the basis of mutual respect for sovereignty, equality and mutual benefit," the *Beijing Review* reported.[68] Clearly such bland statements of fact fell far short of the kind of support the palace had expected.

King Birendra and Rajiv Gandhi discussed their contentious bilateral issues at the ninth non-aligned summit in Belgrade in September. Birendra urged Gandhi not to link security to the trade and transit issues, but the Indian premier insisted on this as well as the necessity of reviewing the entire gamut of relations, including security perceptions and the 1950 treaty.[69] The palace once again focused on China, where the Tibet issue had come to the fore once again. After the Tiananmen Square crackdown the Dalai Lama had issued a statement criticizing the Chinese leadership's action. Deng Xiaoping, who was said to have taken the criticism as a personal affront, broke all further discussions with the Tibetans.

Four months later the Nobel Institute announced that the Dalai Lama had won the 1989 Nobel Peace Prize. Calling it a western plot to divide the country and restore feudalism in Tibet, China denounced the decision as "preposterous" interference in its domestic affairs.[70]

As that controversy raged, Premier Li Peng arrived in Kathmandu in November 1989 as part of a tour of smaller south Asian nations. Having emerged as Deng's personal choice to lead the Chinese Communist Party after Zhao Ziyang's purge, Li was still trying to consolidate his position. A foreign trip was selected as the best way of portraying to the international community the stability China had acquired in the post-Tiananmen months. During Li's visit China granted Nepal $13.6 million for new economic projects. Li assured his hosts in Kathmandu:

> It has always been China's steadfast policy to develop good-neighborly and friendly relations with every country in South Asia. No matter what happens in the international situation, China will always support Nepal and other South Asian countries in their efforts to safeguard independence and sovereignty.

Li also implied criticism of India, telling a press conference in Kathmandu that China was "concerned' about the situation in south Asia where "some factors" gave rise to "instability." In this regard China believed that "all countries, big or small, should be treated equally. Problems and disputes should be handled according to the *pancha shila* without resorting to force or other means."[71] Referring specifically to the Indian–Nepal confrontation, Li said that "as a major country in South Asia," India should be "more magnanimous and generous" in handling issues with Nepal. Li's mild statements and subdued support were in marked contrast to earlier Chinese pronouncements, reflecting Chinese recognition of the changed political climate in south Asia.[72] Li, in effect, advised Nepal to consolidate its relations with India.

That opportunity seemed to emerge in early December when V.P. Singh took over from Rajiv Gandhi as prime minister, following the Congress Party's electoral defeat. While members of the Singh-led coalition had strongly campaigned against Gandhi's mishandling of Sri Lanka and Nepal, Kathmandu also recognized that the new government consisted of parties traditionally sympathetic to the Nepalese opposition. In December the Nepalese government cancelled a Tibetan cultural festival and refused to permit Tibetans in Kathmandu to celebrate the Dalai Lama's receipt of the Nobel Peace Prize.[73] Accepting the peace prize in Oslo, the Dalai Lama reiterated his proposal that Tibet become a demilitarized "peace sanctuary." In a lecture the following day the Dalai Lama set forth a plan to create Tibet as the world's largest natural park or biosphere, where development would be strictly sustainable. But it all depended on China agreeing to stop its exploitive and aggressive development, ceasing nuclear weapons testing in eastern Tibet, stopping its policy of transferring Han Chinese settlers into the region, and accepting Tibet's right to self-determination.[74] Beijing once again rejected it as a thinly-disguised plan for independence.

Nepal failed to get much sympathy from the rest of the world despite continuing to portray itself as a small helpless nation at the mercy of a big power. Internally it was weakened by domestic criticism of its handling of the impasse. Even within the National Panchayat there was no consensus on the policy option taken by the government. The Nepali Congress announced its campaign to force the palace to legalize political parties, a cause Nepal's heavily splintered and squabbling communist factions rallied round to join. Leading Indian politicians representing almost the entire ideological spectrum attended the Nepali Congress conference to express their solidarity with the proposed movement.

The movement began on what was officially celebrated as Democracy Day in February, the 39th anniversary of the end of Rana rule. After the first few weeks, by most accounts, the protests seemed to have lost momentum. But toward the middle of March the movement gained strength, no doubt helped by the government's crackdown. As the Panchayat government arrested top leaders, less prominent ones evaded arrest to clandestinely lead the demonstrations. Soon members of Nepal's nascent but increasingly vocal civil society joined the protests. Doctors, engineers, lawyers, teachers, writers, artists – and later many government workers – joined the politicians to drive to movement.

At this point King Birendra apparently renewed efforts to seek assurances of Chinese support, reportedly sending a representative secretly to Beijing to solicit support. The emissary was received by President Yang Shangkun, who expressed China's complete support for the king's efforts to prevent "chaos" in Nepal. It was also reported that China had quietly deployed military forces to its border with Nepal.[75] But the Chinese Foreign Ministry described events in Nepal as an entirely internal affair.

A separate demonstration organized by an extremist faction of communists turned violent in front of the royal palace. At least 50 people were killed when the Royal Nepalese Army opened fire on demonstrators it feared were about to storm the palace, an act that prompted widespread international condemnation. At this point the American and European ambassadors pressed the palace to reach out to the opposition before the extremists took control of the streets. On the night of April 8, during a meeting with a delegation of senior opposition leaders, King Birendra announced he had lifted the ban on political parties. The monarch invited the Nepali Congress to lead an interim government in partnership with an alliance of communist parties.

Conclusion

As a result of its rapprochement with Beijing, Washington withdrew financial and political support to the anti-Chinese Tibetan resistance in the early 1970s. Yet the cause of Tibetan freedom had already begun to pick up momentum among international celebrities and, later, the wider public. The Indo-Soviet alliance and the dismemberment of Pakistan in the 1971 war with India raised new fears in Nepal, which sought solace in an emerging Sino-American convergence on south Asia. India's annexation of the former Himalayan kingdom of Sikkim later in the decade impelled Nepal to try to break out of the stifling embrace of India and veer toward a military relationship with China in the late 1980s. Unrest in Tibet morphed into the wider nationwide student protests that resulted in the Tiananmen Square crackdown.

International opprobrium and the imperative of improving its own relations with India dissuaded Beijing from supporting the palace more energetically. China also must have weighed the fact that the Nepalese communists had withdrawn support for the partyless political system and joined the Nepali Congress campaign to restore parliamentary democracy. Although under official government ban, key elements of the heavily splintered Nepalese communist movement had tacitly co-operated with the king, if only to confront the their principal adversary, the Nepali Congress. This was one reason why the partyless system lasted as long as it did. But with communism under assault in the rest of the world by 1989–1990, the besieged Nepalese communists chose to project themselves as democrats by allying with the Nepali Congress.

A prolonged crisis, from Beijing's perspective, could precipitate political and economic collapse, even possibly leading to the overthrow of the monarchy. In that event direct Indian military intervention in Nepal could not be ruled out.[76] The Nepalese monarchy was forced to cede power to the political parties, which were ideologically more compatible with India: bitter memories of China's refusal to help Nepal during the 1814–1816 Anglo-Nepalese war still resonated among some.

9 Realpolitik to regicide

Even before the democratic exhilaration caused by the tearing down of the Berlin Wall in November 1989, most Nepalese had deemed political reform at home inevitable. Although it was not immediately clear, King Birendra's decision to legalize political parties after a three-decade ban was also partly a response to growing Indian assertiveness vis-à-vis China in the kingdom. During the height of the pro-democracy protests in the spring of 1990, India had submitted to the palace a draft treaty that would have redefined Nepal's security relations more tightly within India's interpretation of the 1950 Peace and Friendship Treaty.

China, it subsequently emerged, had advised Nepal of the limits of the support it could offer. Beijing had informed Kathmandu that transportation difficulties, coupled with its own financial constraints, would preclude it from providing enough support to overcome the Indian trade and transit embargo.[1] Politically, the Chinese could have done more. Beijing was conspicuously reserved in its public criticism of India's muscle-flexing against a small landlocked neighbor. In cases where it did make pronouncements, the tone and tenor fell far short of what Beijing had employed in the early 1960s and what it would use after the mid-2000s. In the event King Birendra, according to the nationalist narrative that would catch on with remarkable swiftness across the political spectrum, saw compromise with his people as a way of fending off India. While the Chinese were certainly anxious to prevent any loss of ground during those weeks of tumult, it was unclear whether they had played any part in nudging the palace towards compromise with the opposition.

Among ordinary Nepalese the restoration of democracy raised expectations of a new approach to foreign policy. However, interim Prime Minister Krishna Prasad Bhattarai called for a return of "natural" ties with India, a striking assertion considering that the ruling coalition included communist factions traditionally skeptical of Nepal's southern neighbor. When Bhattarai took that message to New Delhi in June 1990, India reciprocated by reopening the critical border points. The new government, which had already repudiated King Birendra's Zone of Peace proposal as irrelevant in the new political context, reaffirmed the validity of the 1950 Treaty. Before leaving for India, Bhattarai had asked Beijing to withhold delivery of the last installment of the weapons shipment.[2] He explained to his hosts that the previous government purchased arms from China only because they were cheaper than those that could be supplied by India. The joint communiqué, issued after Bhattarai's visit, in essence sought to re-instate the relationship India and Nepal shared before the royal takeover three decades earlier.

Nepal and India pledged to co-operate in industrial development, in harnessing the waters of their common rivers, and in protecting the environment. The phrase "common rivers" unleashed a firestorm back home. Bhattarai explained he had used the words without considering their legal implications. Since most of the rivers from Tibet flowed into the Bay of Bengal through Nepal, the premier stated, he had merely suggested the possibility of tripartite co-operation in the future. For many Nepalese the term "common" contained a sinister ring. Communist members of the constitution-drafting commission, already wary of Indian motives, pushed harder for a provision requiring ratification by two-thirds of both houses in cases where treaties had long-term consequences.

New foreign policy trends

While this conspicuous reorientation in Nepalese foreign policy represented a setback to China, Bhattarai was sensitive to maintaining friendship with the kingdom's northern neighbor. There had been some uncertainty about how the new prime minister – and other democratic politicians – would view China's long support for the monarchy at the expense of both the democrats and communists. Shortly after his appointment Bhattarai had praised what he called China's neutrality during the pro-democracy movement, and subsequently asserted that bilateral relations would remain unaffected by their ties with other countries.[3] Bhattarai faced his first test on China in early 1991 after a local Buddhist organization invited the Dalai Lama on a week-long visit to Nepal.

Although the Nepali Congress and the communist front were careful to proclaim their intention to maintain continuity in relations with Beijing, both forces acknowledged the incongruity of a democratic system restricting the Tibetan exiles. The Chinese Embassy in Kathmandu issued a strong statement opposing the visit, claiming it had political motives pertaining to China's internal affairs.[4] The situation in Tibet itself had undergone some change. The previous May Beijing had lifted a 13-month state of martial law in Lhasa, signaling a potential easing of tensions. But the Dalai Lama's growing international profile was irritating the Chinese, who claimed the Tibetan leader was veering dangerously toward the idea of complete independence while counseling reconciliation. The Dalai Lama's office saved Bhattarai any further embarrassment by cancelling the visit.

Bhattarai, who had successfully overseen the promulgation of a democratic constitution and the first multiparty elections in more than three decades, failed to win a seat in parliament in May 1991, partly because of his perceived proximity to India. The Nepali Congress emerged with a majority in the lower house, with the communists a close second. Girija Prasad Koirala, the only senior member of the Nepali Congress elected to parliament, became prime minister, the third Koirala brother to do so. During decades in exile Koirala had worked actively to build the Nepali Congress organization as well as strengthen resistance to the Panchayat system. In that capacity he had built personal relationships with most prominent Indian leaders, prompting many Nepalese to consider him friendlier to India than Bhattarai had been. Much attention thus was focused on Koirala's visit to New Delhi in December, during which the two governments signed trade and transit treaties that formally healed the rupture. As India offered assistance to several development projects, Koirala assured his hosts that Nepal would not purchase arms from China again.[5]

While that assertion – particularly its implied restriction on Nepalese freedom of choice – would have been enough to rile Koirala's critics, the Communist Party of Nepal-Unified Marxist Leninists (CPN-UML) stepped up pressure by accusing the prime minister of signing secret agreements prejudicial to Nepalese interests. The most controversial was one in which Nepal apparently ceded land for the construction of part of a barrage on the Mahakali River on its western border. Koirala insisted that the Tanakpur Accord, named for the township concerned, was merely an understanding that did not require parliamentary ratification. The opposition contended otherwise, a stand the Supreme Court would subsequently uphold.

A week after Koirala's return, Li Peng arrived in India on the first visit by a Chinese premier in 32 years. The positive atmosphere Li's visit created led some in Nepal to conclude that Beijing had no immediate concerns about Kathmandu's growing friendship with New Delhi.[6] In statements to parliament Koirala affirmed his government's commitment to maintain cordial relations with China, a pledge that was put to the test in early 1992 when a group of armed Tibetans crossed into Nepal and attacked security officers. The police opened fire in self-defense, killing one Tibetan, an act that prompted an outcry from human rights organizations. Koirala defended the action, saying the police were merely preventing the Tibetans from unlawfully entering Nepal. The Dalai Lama urged Tibetans in Nepal to uphold the country's laws and maintain good relations with the Nepalese.

But Koirala's problems were only compounded on the eve of his departure for China, in what was to be the first visit by a Nepalese prime minister since the restoration of democracy. In March Tibetans in Kathmandu observed the 33rd anniversary of the uprising against Chinese rule and the Dalai Lama's flight into exile. Koirala prevented the Tibetans from marching on the Chinese Embassy, prompting another round of criticism from human rights organizations. In Beijing, Koirala and his host, Premier Li Peng, reviewed the state of bilateral relations in talks that were dominated by the Tibet issue.

Beijing's hopes of an easing of tensions in the territory had not materialized. During the Dalai Lama's visit to the United States the previous year, George H.W. Bush had become the first sitting American president to meet the Tibetan spiritual leader. The Dalai Lama was also received warmly by U.S. legislators on Capitol Hill. The Chinese government protested strongly against what it called interference in its internal affairs, to little apparent effect in the United States. Koirala assured his Chinese hosts that Nepal recognized Tibet as an autonomous region of China and would not allow anti-Chinese activities on Nepalese soil. Beijing pledged 410 million rupees in new economic and technical assistance. After Koirala's return Nepal and China stepped up efforts to promote economic relations, moving to ease procedures for trans-Himalayan trade and tourism.

These developments came amid a hardening of Nepalese public opinion against India, evidenced during a visit in October by Prime Minister P.V. Narasimha Rao. He faced black flags and other protests, reminiscent of the protests that had greeted Nehru in the 1950s. New Delhi seemed ready to offer some concessions on Tanakpur, but apparently only in exchange for Nepal's full cooperation in clamping down on anti-Indian terrorism.[7] Specifically, Rao was said to have sought the stationing of Indian security and intelligence agents along Nepal's northern border, where New Delhi suspected terrorist organizations had set up camps.[8]

Koirala now confronted what would become another foreign policy challenge in the form of the influx of refugees from Bhutan. After a census in the early 1990s, the Bhutanese government began expelling what it called illegal migrants, many of whom were Nepali speakers. The displaced Bhutanese claimed they were evicted as part of King Jigme Singhe Wangchuck's crackdown on the kingdom's democracy movement. In September–October 1991, thousands started crossing West Bengal into eastern Nepal. Since Nepal and Bhutan do not share a border, India was the first country of asylum for these people. Koirala sought the intervention of India, but India refused to mediate in negotiations between Nepal and Bhutan without Bhutan formally requesting it. Kathmandu could have internationalized the issue, but Koirala hardly was in a position to alienate New Delhi, Thimphu's principal external patron.

Yet New Delhi would become more deeply embroiled in Nepalese politics. The death of CPN-UML general secretary Madan Bhandari and another leading associate in a car accident in May 1993 intensified the nationalist opposition to Koirala. As a leading critic of the Tanakpur Agreement and the growing pro-Indian tilt of the government, the charismatic Bhandari's support base was growing outside his party. CPN-UML supporters took to the streets for days, often violently, accusing Koirala and India of involvement in the death.

A modicum of optimism was generated by a reopening of contacts in 1993 between the Dalai Lama's representative, his elder brother and troubleshooter, Gyalo Thondup, and Chinese authorities in Beijing. This was Thondup's eleventh visit, and one during which procedures for the selection of the new incarnation of the Panchen Lama appear to have been discussed. The Dalai Lama was informed that he would be welcome to raise any issue, barring independence, for discussion.[9] The Koirala government faced embarrassment in June when a visiting Indian leader and prominent China hawk, George Fernandes, slipped into the Tibetan township of Khasa apparently without informing the Nepalese government. Back in Kathmandu he insisted that Tibet's independence was central to India's national security, prompting the Nepalese Foreign Ministry to issue a formal statement describing the remarks as unfortunate.[10]

The Chinese continued to maintain close ties with the monarchy, which controlled the powerful army. On the eve of King Birendra's week-long state visit to China in September, the Chinese ambassador in Kathmandu described the restoration of democracy as an internal Nepalese matter that had no impact on bilateral relations. Noting that Nepal had significantly improved relations with India during the preceding two years, the Chinese ambassador said it was only "natural" and "appropriate" in view of their religious, cultural and social affinities. He said cordial relations between Nepal and India were important for the peace and stability of the entire region.[11]

During talks in Beijing King Birendra and President Jiang Zemin expressed satisfaction at the steady consolidation of bilateral ties. In private Chinese officials and academics continued to insist that as sovereign independent nations, China and its south Asian neighbors were free to establish any kind of relationship they desired based on *pancha shila*.[12] However, they muted public criticism of New Delhi's efforts to limit China's relations with south Asian countries to avoid fanning anti-Chinese sentiments in India. Beijing sought to cultivate India as a counterweight to the United States and the West. At a minimum it sought to preempt New Delhi from joining the other side.

Chinese satisfaction

Beijing seemed satisfied by Kathmandu's reaffirmations that the restoration of democracy did not diminish its commitment to curb anti-Chinese activities. Chinese confidence seemed to be bolstered in August 1993 when the Dalai Lama insisted at a news conference that he was struggling for Tibet's political autonomy, not independence. In late October Prime Minister Koirala made a private visit to Tibet. An increase in high-level Sino-Nepalese contacts did not seem to ruffle India, at least not in public. Worrying for New Delhi, however, was the rapidity with which it was being sucked deep into Nepalese politics as the controversy over the Tanakpur treaty deepened. The Supreme Court's order to the government to seek parliamentary ratification of the agreement had already struck a heavy blow on Koirala. The Nepali Congress was now gripped by an internal power struggle between Koirala and Bhattarai loyalists. Nepal's second elected government collapsed in July 1994 after nearly a third of Nepali Congress legislators failed to show up for a crucial vote. When Koirala dissolved parliament and ordered fresh elections the opposition challenged the move at the Supreme Court, claiming it could form a new government. Months later, the justices upheld the prime minister's dissolution order.

In the election campaign, the CPN-UML accused the Nepali Congress government of selling out to India on a variety of issues. Opposition leader Manmohan Adhikary claimed that Nepal would become another Sikkim if the Nepali Congress were returned to power.[13] The opposition strategy appeared to work: the CPN-UML won the largest number of seats in a hung parliament. The party drew its strength primarily from the influential Marxist-Leninist (M-L) faction of Nepal's heavily splintered communist movement. After joining hands with the Nepali

Congress to overthrow the Panchayat system, the M-L gradually gave up its ideological orthodoxy. Following the merger of the M-L and Marxist factions in 1991 the new CPN-UML espoused democratization and economic liberalization. Considerable attention also focused on the new prime minister, Manmohan Adhikary, who had begun his political career in India as a communist activist. In the 1950s he had spent several years in China receiving medical treatment, although his presence there did not carry the political connotations Dr. K.I. Singh's had.

In what had become an annual event after the restoration of democracy, the Dalai Lama's followers announced they would hold a peace march on Tibetan Uprising Day on March 10, 1995. This caused additional alarm both in Kathmandu and Beijing, especially since the Dalai Lama had suspended dialogue with China due to lack of progress. There was also apprehension that the protests could take a more belligerent turn. Again, the Dalai Lama eased the tension by urging the organizers to call off the march.[14]

Adhikary maintained what had become an unspoken diplomatic tradition by making India the destination of his first foreign visit as prime minister in mid-April. A vocal critic of Nepal's "unequal" treaties with India, the CPN-UML had vowed to review them if it came to power. In New Delhi, however, Adhikary made only a tepid assertion of Nepal's desire for more equal treatment. On the question of arms imports Adhikary departed significantly from his two predecessors, asserting Nepal's right to buy arms "wherever we can get them cheap." But he was careful to add that India, being a close neighbor, would be kept informed.[15]

A week later Adhikary landed in Beijing where Premier Li Peng described Sino-Nepalese ties as a model of state-to-state relations and thanked Kathmandu for its steadfast support on the issues of Tibet and Taiwan. In another sign of the shifting times Li told Adhikary that China appreciated the growing cordiality of relations between Nepal and India.[16] But Adhikary returned to confront the complexities of Nepal's Tibet challenge. Reports of a rise in forced return of Tibetan refugees to Chinese authorities prompted an outcry among local and international human rights organizations. The government, denying the existence of any new policy of returning asylum-seekers, instead blamed corrupt border guards.[17] Nepalese authorities permitted Tibetans who had sought refuge before December 31, 1989, and their descendants, to remain in Nepal. They were provided with a refugee identity certificate, which allowed them to remain in the country with certain limited civil rights and restricted freedom of movement within the country, and some degree of security.

After that date Tibetans that Nepalese police caught at the border were turned over to the Chinese. Those arrested inside Nepalese territory were turned over to the Department of Immigration, which then contacted UNHCR. These Tibetans benefited from the so-called 'Gentlemen's Agreement' between Nepal and the UNHCR that assured safe transit on their journey to India.[18]

The rancor over Tibet's future was about grow as the Dalai Lama in May 1995 named a six-year-old boy, Gedhun Choekyi Nyima, as the true reincarnation of the Panchen Lama. The Chinese authorities placed the boy under house arrest and designated another six-year-old boy, Gyancain Norbu, as their officially sanctioned Panchen Lama. Nepal's role as a conduit for subversive activities now resurfaced in Beijing's considerations.

By this time the Nepali Congress and the royalist Rastriya Prajatantra Party (RPP) had stepped up attacks on the CPN-UML government. In a preemptive action, Adhikary dissolved parliament and ordered fresh elections, expecting to return to power with an absolute majority. The Nepali Congress declared the dissolution unconstitutional and asked the Supreme Court to re-instate parliament. The court agreed and the Adhikary government collapsed in a subsequent no-confidence motion. Sher Bahadur Deuba of the Nepali Congress led a coalition government with the RPP and the Terai-based Nepal Sadbhavana Party (NSP). Nepal's turbulent politics now faced its first experiment in elected coalition government. The RPP, consisting predominantly of senior members of the partyless system, had emerged as the third largest political force. Many expected King Birendra to exert some moderating influence not only in the political sphere but also in striking a balance between the kingdom's giant neighbors. China, however, would be drawn into Nepal in an unflattering way.

Outbreak of Maoist insurgency

In February 1996 the Communist Party of Nepal (Maoist) launched an armed campaign against the monarchy and parliamentary democracy after the Deuba government ignored its 40-point charter of demands. The Maoists sought, among other things, the abrogation of unequal treaties with India at a time when Deuba was busy preparing for a visit to New Delhi to sign a high-profile treaty on joint development of the Mahakali River. At this time there was a spurt in high-level exchanges between Nepal and China. Two months after returning from New Delhi, Deuba paid an official visit to China where he signed agreements to promote trade and commerce, and set up joint-venture industries and exchange visits of academics and scholars.

Four months later King Birendra paid a week-long unofficial visit to China, during which President Jiang Zemin expressed appreciation for the monarch's "longstanding and clear" support for China's position on Tibet. The monarch reaffirmed that Nepal would never allow its territory to be used against China, a message he would subsequently reiterate in Tibet. Two months earlier the Dalai Lama had sworn in a new Tibetan government-in-exile, following elections. As Beijing was weighing the full implications of that move it had reason for satisfaction as far as Kathmandu was concerned. The Koirala, Adhikary and Deuba governments had essentially reiterated the China policy developed by the monarchy.

Jiang Zemin visits Nepal

President Jiang paid a state visit to Nepal in December as part of a south Asian journey, becoming the highest-ranking Chinese leader to arrive since the restoration of democracy. Jiang praised Nepal's historic position as a cultural and commercial centre linking south and central Asia and reiterated China's strong support for Nepal's independence, sovereignty and territorial integrity. While Beijing pledged 80 million yuan (500 million rupees) in new economic assistance, the circumstances surrounding Jiang's visit were revealing. His brief Kathmandu itinerary was reportedly finalized only at the last minute, when he was already in Islamabad, and came as a result of hectic lobbying by the palace. Although the Chinese president had arrived on a state visit, he stayed at the royal palace, creating a perception in Kathmandu that Beijing had resolved to build on its special relationship with the monarchy. This was interpreted as a display of Chinese disapproval of the way successive elected governments had conducted their China policy.[19]

The Nepalese political establishment had little time to weigh the import of the Chinese moves, as political wrangling deepened inside parliament and on the streets. The collapse of the Deuba government, through a no-confidence vote in parliament in mid-1997, led to a succession of coalitions and internal fissures within the major parties. Royalists Lokendra Bahadur Chand and Surya Bahadur Thapa of the RPP briefly headed coalitions with the support of the CPN-UML and the Nepali Congress respectively. The Chand and Thapa governments offered customary commitments to balancing Nepalese foreign policy but were preoccupied with their own survival. In March 1998 the CPN-UML split, largely over differences festering since the ratification of the controversial Mahakali Treaty with India.

At this point a legacy of the Sino-Indian war of 1962 had returned to mar Nepalese politics. National attention was focused on the Indian military posts on the Kalapani, a 35 square kilometer border area between northwest Nepal, India and Tibet. Under the terms of the 1816 Sugauli Treaty the Kali River marked the western border between India and Nepal. The pilgrim-cum-trade route there from India to Tibet runs for the most part on the west bank of the Kali, but at Kalapani it crosses briefly to the east bank. How Indian military units first occupied the area remains unclear and marred in controversy. India appears to have maintained its presence in the context of the build-up to the 1962 Sino-Indian war, considering its importance as a potential strategic route from Tibet into northern India. Although the area was spared conflict, Nepal was concerned enough about the Chinese threat after the war to apparently allow Indian troops to occupy some posts in its kingdom as a defensive measure. India had since withdrawn from all of them, except Kalapani.[20]

Over time the dispute grew amid differences in the maps each country possessed. India asserted that old British surveys and maps showed this section as part of India. But Nepal pointed to other maps and documents to support its claims. The Indian External Affairs Ministry opposed the withdrawal of troops, insisting that it would have an adverse bearing on national security, and claimed the issue had been needlessly exaggerated. The Indian government suggested a resolution through a joint working group, which meant drawn-out negotiations. Kathmandu and other parts of the country saw noisy demonstrations, organized primarily by the UML and radical communist groups. The prospect of drawing China into the dispute became attractive to a section of Nepalese communists

Figure 9.1 King Birendra and Prime Minister Atal Bihari Vajpayee during a meeting in New Delhi in January 1999 (photo courtesy: Press Information Bureau of the Government of India).

keen to batter both the Nepali Congress and the monarchy. But Beijing maintained that the Kalapani dispute was a bilateral issue Kathmandu and New Delhi would have to resolve.

The palace's relations with New Delhi seemed to have shed the inhibitions of the past, as King Birendra made several private and official visits to India. Enough trust had developed that, in the words of a former Indian ambassador to Nepal, "neither country was taken by surprise by developments in the other."[21] India had begun re-evaluating the palace's role in the face of the political instability multiparty democracy had bred. The rapprochement accelerated in 1998 after the election of the Hindu nationalist Bharatiya Janata Party government under Prime Minister Atal Behari Vajpayee, who had personal interest and sympathy for Nepal as the world's only officially Hindu state. In January 1999 the Vajpayee government invited King Birendra as the chief guest at India's traditional Republic Day parade, the first time a Nepalese leader had been accorded the honor. The gesture conveyed the impression that India may have finally recognized Nepal's full independence and sovereignty.[22]

As the Maoist rebels began making greater inroads into the rural hinterland in the western hills, Girija Prasad Koirala returned as premier in April 1999 in an uneasy coalition with rival communist factions. The following year, he took the Nepalese to their third election in eight years and Koirala's Nepali Congress returned to power with a majority largely resulting from his promise to hand over the premiership to his rival, Krishna Prasad Bhattarai.

Shifting regional dynamics

During much of the 1990s China had become candid in applauding Nepal's growing relations with India, prompting suggestions that Beijing had once again conceded Nepal as part of the Indian sphere of influence. This was a time when Beijing felt increasingly confident about its place in the world. The recovery in July 1997 of Hong Kong, improvements in relations with the U.S. after the Taiwan Strait crises, and its weathering of the Asian financial crisis without the need to devalue its currency, had bolstered its confidence. Almost all foreign economic sanctions imposed in the aftermath of the Tiananmen Square crackdown had been lifted. Human rights no longer appeared to be a major impediment to China's foreign economic relations.

Regional dynamics shifted sharply in May 1998 following India's nuclear tests, especially after New Delhi justified them by claiming the threat from China. Almost exactly a year later, U.S. aircraft "accidentally" bombed the Chinese Embassy in Belgrade. The Japanese Diet ratified the Revised Guidelines for Defense Cooperation with the United States, refusing to specify to Beijing's satisfaction whether Taiwan was included in the ambiguous phrase "areas surrounding Japan." The enunciation in June of the "Clinton Doctrine" led a new round of debate in China, where it was perceived as espousing the legitimacy of military interventions in sovereign nations for humanitarian purposes. Beijing considered the implications for Taiwan, Xinjiang and Tibet.

In the intervening months Beijing and New Delhi carefully moved to accentuate the compatibility of their broader national interests. During Indian Foreign Minister Jaswant Singh's visit to China in June 1999, both governments made public statements to the effect that neither considered the other a threat to its security. Singh's visit coincided with the Kargil conflict between India and Pakistan. New Delhi seemed satisfied that China's stand on Kashmir had now become more convergent with the international position. Many Chinese officials and analysts concluded that international security trends were now turning against Beijing's interests.

Beijing began to step up its strategic interest in Nepal. In September 1999 Chinese leader Li Peng told the visiting former Nepalese premier, Sher Bahadur Deuba, that China valued its friendship with Nepal not only as a neighbor but also from the security point of view.[23] Li's reference to the Himalayas as never being a barrier in promoting friendship and co-operation came at a time when Indian Foreign Minister Jaswant Singh was in Kathmandu for talks on boosting security co-operation.

China's "Go West" campaign

The geographic element of China's growing interest in Nepal came to the fore with Beijing's announcement of its "Go West" Campaign, as the Chinese leadership had become increasingly concerned by regional inequalities. While coastal Special Economic Zones and eastern urban centers flourished economically,

China's western and interior regions, comprising more than 23 percent of the population and more than half of China's total land area, lagged behind with high rates of poverty and lower levels of development. Many of China's 100 million ethnic minorities lived in this region and, especially in Xinjiang, economic disparities fuelled ethnic tensions. President Jiang Zemin declared that, "the development of the west is crucial to China's stability, the Communist Party's hold on power, and the revitalization of the Chinese people."[24]

With this convergence of Chinese internal and international imperatives, Nepal was drawn closer to Beijing's concept of comprehensive national security. From Beijing's perspective the wave of democratization in the kingdom, initiated in the early 1990s, was the result of external influences. But the shift in the power matrix did not appear to have been helpful in normalizing the national political life and saving a shattered economy.[25] Instability in Nepal ran counter to the Chinese imperative of strengthening national sovereignty and territorial integrity, continuing its economic and social development, and maintaining its international stature.

The Tibet issue took another rancorous turn in early 2000, when the 14-year-old Karmapa Lama, the third ranking spiritual leader in Tibet, secretly escaped to India through Nepal.[26] Although Kathmandu denied them, media reports provided precise details of his movements.[27] The Karmapa Lama became the highest-ranking religious leader to leave Tibet since the Dalai Lama had sought refuge in India.[28] Beijing initially said the Karmapa Lama had explained that he had gone to India only temporarily. However, Chinese concerns grew after India granted him political asylum. For Nepal this development came on the heels of the hijacking of an Indian Airlines flight from Kathmandu, leading to a ten day ordeal that ended in Kandahar, Afghanistan. The incident heightened regional tensions as India accused Pakistan of masterminding the crime. That event capped a series of developments that prompted the Vajpayee government to defer to the Indian bureaucracy's hard-line position on various issues. Amid growing rifts in the Nepali Congress, Koirala dislodged Bhattarai to become premier.

The deepening political and regional uncertainty helped the Maoist rebels make greater inroads outside their stronghold of the mid-western hills. Initially dismissed as a law and order problem, the insurgency escalated progressively. A gloomier fate for the entire country was predicted by a leading American research organization. With its accumulating problems Nepal was heading for a change in the political system, Stratfor said, pointing to the possibility of its becoming a Maoist state.[29] Regardless of the nature of the change, the organization concluded, China would gain an advantage at the expense of Indian interests in the geo-strategically invaluable nation. Koirala stepped up efforts to counter the Maoist insurgency but King Birendra refused to mobilize the army against Nepalese citizens. There was some speculation that the palace had initiated separate contacts with the Maoists regarding a peace settlement.[30] Although they did not rule out peace talks the insurgents became bolder and more lethal in their attacks on police stations, government offices and other state installations.

By the summer of 2000 Chinese attention was focused on the U.S. presidential election campaign, in which the George W. Bush team portrayed China as a "strategic competitor," not a "strategic partner." Washington strove to strengthen its military relations with Tokyo and had bolstered ties with India during the Clinton visit. Bush announced that he would move ahead vigorously with the National Missile Defense (NMD) program, perceived to be directed partially at China. This fitted neatly into the Chinese perception that American military strategy was shifting to Asia. The August 2000 visit to India by Japanese Prime Minister Yoshiro Mori underscored Tokyo's changing perception of India's growing profile. Prime Minister Mori went on to make a brief stopover in Kathmandu, becoming the first Japanese head of government to do so.

China steps up its profile

Chinese Defense Minister Chi Haotian arrived in Kathmandu in February 2001, inaugurating another exchange of high-profile visits between the two countries. Nepal was hastily added to Chi's itinerary, marking the first time a Chinese defense minister had paid an official visit to the kingdom. The fact that Nepal was part of an itinerary that also took him to Laos, Vietnam and Cambodia – a region Beijing traditionally held important from the economic, political, cultural and strategic points of view – was deemed additionally significant.[31]

During a state visit to China later in the month, King Birendra was the guest of honor of the Chinese government at the inaugural ceremony of the Boao Forum for Asia on the island of Hainan. Twenty-four Asian countries had come together to form a regional version of the World Economic Forum that met annually in the Swiss city of Davos. President Jiang, while meeting with King Birendra, described maintenance of good relations with Nepal as a matter of Chinese policy.[32] Premier Zhu Rongji called the king "a respected and well-known friend of the Chinese people," a man who had enjoyed a "deep friendship" with Chinese leaders over three generations and who had made a great contribution to the growth of Chinese–Nepalese relations.[33]

By this time Sino-American relations had plunged to one of their lowest ebbs. In early April the Chinese Air Force forced a U.S. spy plane to land on a Chinese island, then detained its crew for 11 days. The acknowledgment in some American quarters that the country that agreed to station its space-linked surveillance, intelligence and navigation systems in the Himalayas would get geo-strategic leverage over its neighboring Asian regions, had already found resonance in the Nepalese media.[34] It was not difficult for some Nepalese to see their country's potential value to the America's NMD program as well as to the myriad dimensions of an evolving space-based technology. Nor was it difficult to perceive the geo-strategic pressures building on Nepal, considering India's support for the NMD.[35] Foreign Minister Chakra Prasad Bastola indicated in a newspaper interview that Nepal risked being drawn into a new Cold War.[36]

In May Chinese Premier Zhu Rongji arrived on an official visit to Nepal with an agenda top-heavy with economic and commercial matters. Bilateral trade was valued at $220 million in 1999, representing a 200 percent growth over the previous year. The two countries were involved in some 20 joint ventures in Nepal, and the Nepalese business community remained hopeful of more. During Zhu's visit Kathmandu and Beijing signed six agreements to bolster ties, including one on the construction of the Syabrubesi–Rasuwagadi road to link up with Kerong and Lhasa in Tibet. While economic and commercial relations dominated the official coverage of the visit, Beijing conveyed its deep concern over the Maoist insurgency and sought to dispel suspicions of its involvement.

A week before Zhu's arrival the Chinese ambassador in Kathmandu had made the first official and exhaustive comment on the insurgency, criticizing, among other things, the rebels' dishonoring of Mao's name. The perception of Beijing being behind the Maoist insurgency was more widespread in the West. While Indian newspapers and magazines continued to make periodic references to the Maoists' purported links to China, there was no sign within Nepal that the rebels enjoyed sanctuary on Chinese territory or received arms from Beijing.

Zhu's delegation also sought reassurances from Nepal that it would curtail activities aimed against China primarily by groups such as the Free Tibet movement. While some Nepalese tended to see successive multiparty governments not doing enough to win China's confidence on the Tibet issue, leaders of political parties suggested that there was little that democratic governments could do to curtail free speech. Although political party leaders repeatedly pledged their commitment to the one China policy, Beijing seemed privately concerned that members of these same Nepalese parties were closely associated with Tibetan groups and perhaps the beneficiaries of political donations.[37]

King Birendra hosted a banquet for Zhu in the palace during which the premier lauded the achievements Nepal had made under the king's leadership. Birendra praised China for giving great understanding to Nepal's efforts in defending national sovereignty and safeguarding national dignity, and providing Nepal selfless help.[38] Zhu's visit was inevitably analyzed against the background of a perceptibly sharpening Sino-Indian-American tripolarity. After Zhu's departure an alliance of communist opposition parties organized strikes in Kathmandu and other cities, severely disrupting public life.

In the rural hinterland the Maoist rebels were growing increasingly lethal in their attacks on government officials and installations. Amid the domestic and regional instability there was speculation that King Birendra was contemplating drastic political intervention.[39] Some Nepalese sources suggested privately that greater economic integration with China would form part of an impending political change, something China's pre-eminent scholar on Nepal would affirm years later.[40] Instead, on June 2, 2001, Nepalese woke up to shocking news. The previous night King Birendra, Queen Aishwarya, and their three children, along with half a dozen other relatives, were killed within the walls of the heavily fortified palace.

International radio and television stations reported that a drunken Crown Prince Dipendra had gone on a murder spree after failing to win parental consent to marry the girl of his choice. Overcome by guilt, Dipendra then was said to have turned his gun on himself. Rumors swirled that no heir to the throne had survived the carnage. Armed Maoist rebels, who were reported to have seized Narayanhity Palace, were on the verge of declaring a People's Republic of Nepal. As the Nepalese state media persisted with a dose of dour funereal music, the government maintained a prolonged silence, which served only to fuel more rumors. When the State Council finally made a formal announcement concerning the death of Birendra late in the morning, it avoided any mention of the gory and perplexing details. In keeping with tradition, the council said, Crown Prince Dipendra had been named the new king. But he was "physically unable to discharge his responsibilities." Dipendra's uncle, Prince Gyanendra, who was out of the capital on a previously scheduled engagement, was proclaimed regent.

Conclusion

The restoration of multiparty democracy in 1990 had bolstered the position of India and the West in Nepal, as the Dalai Lama succeeded in internationalizing the Tibet question. This raised the anxiety of China, which was traditionally wary of the Nepalese political parties, but Beijing continued to influence Kathmandu's Tibet policy through its proximity to the monarchy, which controlled the powerful military. When Nepalese Maoists launched a violent insurgency against the monarchy and democracy in 1996, Beijing, under the pragmatism it had perfected into post-Mao foreign policy, shunned the rebels. As Nepal's tenuous balance was shattered in a mysterious palace massacre, China was not far from Nepalese minds.

During his near three decade reign, Birendra had visited China ten times. He was the first foreign leader the Chinese had invited to Tibet. From Mao Zedong and Zhou Enlai through Deng Xiaoping to Jiang Zemin, Birendra had maintained contacts with three generations of Chinese communist leaders. The last foreign country Birendra visited was China, where he was accorded special honor at the inaugural session of the region's premier economic forum Beijing had sponsored. The last foreign leader to visit Nepal during Birendra's reign was Chinese Premier Zhu Rongji. Speculation instantly grew that the murdered royal family were victims of a plot caused by Birendra's close relations with Beijing. But the Chinese, like much of the world, were worried by the fallout from the worst royal massacre since Russia's communist leader Vladimir Lenin ordered the murders of the deposed Romanovs in 1918.

10 Mao versus monarchy

The ghastly end of a popular monarch and his entire family within the heavily secured palace walls at a time of growing national turmoil was tragic enough for the ordinary Nepalese to comprehend. Kathmandu's probing tabloids had hardly associated Crown Prince Dipendra with even a minor indiscretion in recent years. His complicity in the horrific bloodbath was inexplicable. Compounding the confusion was Gyanendra's public image as a hardliner who purportedly had opposed Birendra's decision to restore multiparty democracy in 1990. The fact that Gyanendra was absent from the palace gathering, that his wife, Komal, sustained only minor injuries and that his notoriously wild son, Paras, escaped unhurt set off conspiracy theories. They meshed into the massive outpouring of grief during the extended royal funeral procession and cremations on the banks of the Bagmati River at the Pashupatinath Temple.

Two days later, with the Kathmandu valley still under curfew, the State Council announced that Dipendra had died of his self-inflicted gunshot wounds. Gyanendra was now crowned king – for the second time in four decades – as the body of Dipendra was rushed under military escort to Pashupati for a hasty funeral. The monarchy, which had created the modern Nepalese state, had survived, but barely. With the mainstream political parties discredited by their constant bickering and endless allegations of corruption, public attention now focused on the Maoists. Having driven out the state from the rural hinterland, the rebels had begun spreading their terror in urban centers. They seized upon the tragedy to project themselves as the only guarantors of stability.

The Maoists' ascension to power, from New Delhi's perspective, could provide greater leverage to China and Pakistan. Moreover, Maoist groups on both sides of the vast and unregulated border could join forces and create a very unstable northern Himalayan belt.[1] Beijing, on the other hand, had only recently criticized the Nepalese rebels for tarnishing the reputation of the Great Helmsman with their murder and terror. Nepalese Maoist leaders regularly condemned the current Chinese leaders as revisionists. A violent radical communist movement next door to Tibet at a time of growing regional economic imbalance within the mainland was something that worried Beijing.

Rejecting the official story blaming Dipendra for the carnage, the Maoists had already pointed to the possibility of a grand international conspiracy against

Birendra. Dr. Baburam Bhattarai, the rebels' chief idealogue, in a newspaper article suggested that the U.S. Central Intelligence Agency and India's Research and Analysis Wing had masterminded Birendra's assassination because the monarch had consistently refused to unleash the military against the Maoists and join the U.S.-led campaign to contain China. Claiming that the Maoists had struck an undeclared alliance with Birendra because of his liberal and nationalistic approach, Bhattarai equated the palace bloodbath to the 1846 Kot Massacre that brought Jang Bahadur Rana to power and urged the military not to recognize the new king.[2]

For much of the country – and the world – the badly bruised monarchy remained the best guarantee against a Maoist takeover, especially since the military was traditionally loyal to the king. As Gyanendra sought to consolidate his position, speculation grew that he might do away with the existing political structure. In India and the West there were suggestions that he might be pro-Chinese.[3] Some Chinese officials, however, privately tended to agree with the Maoists' version of events.

Gyanendra sought to allay the suspicions of the political parties by publicly pledging to follow the path of constitutional monarchy and the multiparty system adopted by his brother. The Maoists, however, urged the Nepalese people to institutionalize the "embryonic" republic that had emerged from the palace massacre and stepped up attacks on government installations. Prime Minister Girija Prasad Koirala, under fire from the opposition CPN-UML and the Maoists, now faced growing dissent within his own Nepali Congress. Maoist leader Prachanda raised the stakes by offering to hold peace talks only if Koirala stepped down.

The prime minister resigned in July after claiming he had failed to persuade Gyanendra to mobilize the army against Maoist rebels. His party rival, Sher Bahadur Deuba, returned as premier, pledging to start peace talks with the Maoists, an overture the rebels reciprocated by agreeing to a ceasefire. Shortly after the first round of peace talks in August, Royal Nepal Army chief General Prajwalla Rana stated, while hosting a Chinese military delegation, that the Nepalese military was equally concerned with the security interests of China.[4] The delegation leader assured Prime Minister Deuba that the People's Liberation Army would work with the Nepalese Army to maintain peace and stability in the bordering areas.[5]

War on terror comes home

After the 9/11 attacks on New York City and Washington D.C., Deuba offered the use of Nepalese airspace to the U.S. military for refueling as its contribution to the global war on terrorism. Washington reportedly offered ten bulletproof helicopters to the Nepalese army.[6] The Maoists began to suspect collusion between Kathmandu and Washington to bring the Nepalese insurgency within the ambit of the U.S.-led anti-terrorism campaign. After a third round of talks ended in a stalemate in November, the Maoists pulled out of the peace process and attacked the Royal Nepal Army for the first time. King Gyanendra, on

Deuba's recommendation, declared a state of emergency and mobilized the army against the rebels, winning much-needed international support.

The insurgency fed primarily on the frustration of the common people with the inability of the democratic system to fulfill their expectations. Poverty, socio-cultural and economic inequality, and the exclusionary tendencies of the state were the primary contributors. By 2001 the Maoists were able to adjust the principles of Marxism, Leninism and Maoism to the Nepalese context. While their attacks on the state grew deadlier, the Maoists in fact used selective violence, mobilizing popular fronts among students, women, and labourers to further their political goals. They also exploited contradictions and rivalries within and among political parties, between the palace and the parties and opted for negotiations for both tactical and strategic purposes.[7]

The growing lethality of the conflict hit the economy hard – particularly the lucrative tourism industry. Periodic demonstrations of anti-Indian sentiment discouraged visitors from India, who found new destinations in southeast Asia. When China designated Nepal as one of its most-favored tourist destinations, many Nepalese expected an influx of Chinese tourists to revive the economy.

In early 2002 the Deuba government had received a major diplomatic boost when U.S. Secretary of State Colin Powell arrived on an overnight visit to Kathmandu. Before landing in the Nepalese capital Powell had told reporters that the Maoist insurgency "really is the kind of thing we're fighting against throughout the world."[8] Although the first American secretary of state to visit Nepal since the establishment of diplomatic relations in 1947 did not make any aid or military commitments, he did discuss the country's needs with King Gyanendra, Prime Minister Deuba and senior Nepalese military officials. Powell's visit raised questions in the Nepalese and Indian media over Washington's increasing interest in south Asia and what it portended for India's "pre-eminent role in the region."[9] Beijing's anxiety grew over its wider regional concerns. The most obvious was the U.S.-led war in Afghanistan, right on the China's doorstep. Beijing viewed with apprehension the potential for refugees to stream across the border from Afghanistan and the potential for unrest in Xinjiang Province by non-Han Uighurs who opposed Chinese rule.

Eager to bolster Nepal's military capabilities in the anti-insurgency campaign, in mid-May Deuba left Kathmandu for Washington and London for meetings with President George W. Bush and Prime Minister Tony Blair. Deuba became the first Nepalese prime minister to be received in the Oval Office by an American president and Bush pledged $20 million in support of Nepalese forces. In London Blair pledged to support Nepal in its efforts to restore political stability. The Europeans placed greater hope on a negotiated settlement, an approach that would contrast sharply with the American position in the months ahead. Nepal had increased its visibility on western strategic maps, a development China increasingly viewed with concern.[10]

As the political arena turned more rancorous, King Gyanendra left for India in June on his first official visit abroad since ascending to the throne, with an agenda focusing on the Maoist insurgency. He sought to emphasize the frequency with which key rebel leaders slipped across the border and co-ordinated their activities from India, making it difficult for Nepal to crack down on their operations. Concern that India was losing the leverage it had enjoyed with the United States and Britain since Jawaharlal Nehru's premiership also found resonance in the Indian media.[11]

Two weeks later King Gyanendra paid a ten-day goodwill visit to China, during which President Jiang Zemin pledged his government's support for Nepal's crackdown on what he called "armed anti-government forces." The choice of words reflected China's deep dilemma. A Chinese Foreign Ministry spokesman said Beijing had never supported Nepal's Maoists, who he accused of soiling the memory of the Great Helmsman.[12] King Gyanendra assured Jiang that Nepal would never allow its territory to be used as a "venue for any activity undermining China's interests." The role of India and the United States vis-à-vis Nepal also emerged during the visit. A leading Chinese scholar played down suggestions of China's rivalry with India, saying relations between them had improved markedly since the end of the Cold War. More worrisome to Beijing, he noted, were the new pledges of military aid to Nepal by Britain and the United States.[13]

Beijing saw the use of the term "Maoist" as an insult to China's great leader Mao Zedong. China labeled the Communist Party of Nepal (Maoist) as an "anti-government outfit." Throughout the decade-long violence there was little evidence of Chinese support for the Maoist insurgency in Nepal.[14] Although reports of ultra-leftist Chinese communists' backing for the rebels persisted, these were never substantiated. Chinese officials had long maintained that while Mao Zedong was a great Chinese leader, his advocacy of "People's War" took place at a very different time and circumstance in China and could not be replicated. The visit of another People's Liberation Army delegation to Nepal underscored the growing importance Beijing accorded to stability in Nepal. Prime Minister Deuba vowed "to support China as ever at the international stage on all issues, including the issues of Tibet and human rights."[15]

Return of royal assertiveness

Facing strong opposition from his own Nepali Congress to an extension of emergency rule, Deuba dissolved parliament and ordered fresh elections. The Nepali Congress expelled the prime minister, who subsequently split the ruling party and registered his own faction to take part in the elections. But growing Maoist violence made those elections impossible. Deuba urged King Gyanendra to postpone the polls but the monarch, after consulting with politicians and constitutional experts, dismissed Deuba on October 4, 2002. New Delhi, like Washington and London, offered mild criticism of the monarch's move, while China described it as an internal matter. A week later, the king appointed Rastriya Prajatantra Party leader Lokendra Bahadur Chand to head a caretaker government, a move that infuriated the mainstream parties who had expected one of their own leaders to get the job. They united against what they called the return of "royal autocracy." The new foreign minister, Narendra Bikram Shah, told a visiting delegation from Tibet that Kathmandu wanted to enhance its "special relationship" with China,[16] using a term traditionally associated with Nepal's relations with its southern neighbor.

Early in the new year, behind-the-scenes initiatives by the new government produced another ceasefire with the Maoist rebels. Opposition parties, suspicious of a deal between the palace and the rebels to marginalize them, refused to take part. New Delhi, too, seemed displeased with Kathmandu's lack of consultation and reiterated its concern that the inflow of arms from the U.S. and other western nations could escalate growing violence of the conflict.[17] As Maoist negotiators arrived in Kathmandu for informal preparatory talks, the monarch left on a "pilgrimage" to India, his second visit in eight months. In New Delhi he met with all the key Indian political figures, prompting new speculation of a breakthrough. The Maoists' hopes of making gains were dashed when Washington placed the rebels in the State Department's "Other Terrorist Groups" listing.[18] Under the designation Washington ordered the freezing of all Maoist assets in the U.S. and banned most transactions and dealings with the organization.[19] The Maoists had no assets or transactions in the U.S. and were unlikely to be affected by the decision, but they recognized its political significance.

The Tibet issue brought the Sino-Indian-U.S. triangle into sharp focus in May 2003, when Nepal handed over to China 18 Tibetan refugees who it said had entered the kingdom illegally. The United States, Britain and the UNHCR criticized the move as a violation of Nepal's obligations under international law, while Beijing publicly defended Kathmandu's stand. A statement from the Chinese embassy said the deported Tibetans were not refugees but Chinese nationals who had violated the immigration laws of Nepal and China. Beijing mounted the kind of vigorous defense of the action that the Nepalese government could not have.

Since the refugees would have traveled onward to India it was assumed that the Nepalese handed them to the Chinese with India's approval.[20] The deportation was seen as a joint effort by Beijing and New Delhi to demonstrate mounting displeasure with growing Western involvement in Nepal on the eve of Indian Prime Minister Atal Behari Vajpayee's trip to China. In a joint communiqué after the visit, New Delhi explicitly referred to Tibet as part of China and pledged to discourage anti-Chinese activities on Indian soil. In return for India's commitment, Beijing for the first time referred to Sikkim as a part of India in a separate agreement on expanding border trade.[21]

As New Delhi and Beijing agreed to open a trade route through Sikkim, the Indian media explained how Nepal could stand to gain.[22] But the kingdom was veering more deeply into instability. Amid faltering peace talks and stepped-up pressure from the opposition, Prime Minister Chand resigned and Surya Bahadur Thapa was nominated to succeed him on June 5. Continuing the groundwork laid earlier, a third round of negotiations were held with the new government team. The talks broke down on August 27 after the government refused demands for a constituent assembly and the Maoists accused the army of massacring over a dozen party members. As the rebels intensified attacks, Beijing – as well as New Delhi – strongly condemned them.

India's concerns now seemed to be more focused on the U.S., which continued to insist that Nepal's limited government finances, weak border controls and poor security made it a convenient transit point for international terrorists.[23] New Delhi saw a contradiction between Washington's stepped-up military assistance to Kathmandu amid its insistence on a peaceful solution to end the insurgency. While U.S. diplomats argued that military aid was modest and intended merely to help the government force the Maoists back to the negotiating table, New Delhi viewed such aid as fueling the insurgency. In the view of one Indian analyst, the U.S. wanted to take advantage of Nepalese political instability to keep a vigil on China and India by bolstering its presence in Nepal.[24]

In the face of mounting opposition pressure Prime Minister Thapa resigned in early May 2004 and Beijing now began emphasizing that Nepal must resolve its problems alone.[25] A significant change in China's position was set out by its ambassador, Sun Heping, during a public address in late May. Implicitly repudiating his predecessor's assertion two years earlier that the Maoist revolutionaries were "terrorists," he explained that calling them "anti-government forces" was not the same thing as the "terrorist" tag used by India and the U.S. He emphasized that hostile activities by Tibetan separatists was China's major concern in Nepal.

Sun's comments came after elections in India unexpectedly turned out the Bharatiya Janata Party (BJP) government and brought to power a Congress-led government. This subtle shift in Chinese policy was a thinly veiled warning to the new Indian government about its policy on Kathmandu. Beijing had not forgotten the Congress' history of heavy-handedness on Nepal. Beijing also expressed interest in joining the South Asian Association for Regional Cooperation and contributing to the economic development of the region. As King Gyanendra surprised many by recalling Sher Bahadur Deuba as premier, he sent Parasu Narayan Chaudhari, the chairman of the State Council, to China for talks with Premier Wen Jiabao. With parliament dissolved and most political parties on the streets, the council had assumed a key advisory role.

Amid indications of a new Chinese thrust, Indian Foreign Minister K. Natwar Singh arrived in Kathmandu in early June. Prime Minister Manmohan Singh's coalition government saw the political crisis in Nepal as a challenge that could assume dangerous dimensions for India. After tightening their control in Nepal's rural areas the Maoists had stepped up attacks in Kathmandu. Spiraling violence and the near-total breakdown of law and order raised Indian fears of a large-scale refugee influx from Nepal through the open border. The Indian media, reflecting a growing view of official opinion, urged New Delhi to prepare for a situation similar to that in 1971 when Indira Gandhi was forced to intervene in what was to become Bangladesh.[26]

China, too, was feeling the growing impact of the Maoist insurgency, which forced a Chinese firm to pull out of a section of road project in a remote western region on the border. Nepal's new army chief General Pyar Jung Thapa, on a visit to Beijing, sought China's help to fight the Maoists. The imperative was growing on Beijing to act. As the army stepped up land and air attacks on the Maoists, Crown Prince Paras visited China in August and held talks with President Hu Jintao. The following month, Prime Minister Deuba, on an official visit to India, received assurances of greater military assistance against the insurgency.[27]

King Gyanendra postponed an official visit to India in December, hours before he was to have boarded the aircraft, because of the death of former Indian Prime Minister P.V. Narasimha Rao. As New Delhi and Kathmandu sought to work out a new schedule, speculation grew that the two governments disagreed on the agenda.[28] The monarch reportedly sought India's support for taking a more direct role in fighting the Maoists. New Delhi, for its part, wanted the king to appoint an India-friendly politician from the mainstream parties as premier in exchange for supporting his direct role. Maoist leader Prachanda declared that he would talk only with the palace, since it held the actual reins of power.

In the face of mounting pressure from China, Prime Minister Deuba ordered the closure of the Office of the Dalai Lama's Representative and the Tibetan Refugee Welfare Office. As Maoist attacks grew deadlier and challenged urban centers, King Gyanendra dismissed the Deuba government and took direct control of the government on the morning of February 1, 2005. Appointing himself head of government, King Gyanendra named a cabinet of avowed royalists and technocrats, pledging to restore multiparty democracy within three years of restoring peace and security.

A pro-Chinese coup?

Washington and London joined the United Nations and the European Union in condemning as "undemocratic" the monarch's dismissal of Prime Minister Deuba's multiparty cabinet and his decision to directly rule the country. The most stinging rebuke came from India, which called the move a "setback to democracy." If Gyanendra's move was reminiscent of his father's takeover four decades earlier, New Delhi, too, chose the precise words Prime Minister Jawaharlal Nehru had employed then. New Delhi pulled out of a scheduled south Asian summit in Bangladesh, clearly anxious to avoid legitimizing the king.

China, by contrast, described the royal takeover as "an internal affair of Nepal."[29] While the response conformed to Beijing's official non-interventionist foreign policy, preceding developments seemed to suggest a quid pro quo. Although the Tibetan offices in Kathmandu had been ordered to close by the Deuba government, this order was believed to have come on royal instructions.[30] China's traditional support for the monarchy over the political parties certainly added to the perception that it was behind Gyanendra.

As Indian, American and British ambassadors left Kathmandu for consultations back home, King Gyanendra appointed as his deputies two former prime ministers who had remained consistently loyal to the palace. Dr. Tulsi Giri, who had just returned from nearly two decades of self-exile in Sri Lanka and India, was known for his nationalist rhetoric as King Mahendra's chief adviser during the early 1960s. Kirti Nidhi Bista, who had largely withdrawn from politics since 1990, was the only prime minister during the palace-led Panchayat decades to have visited China.

When Pakistan and, later, Russia, issued official statements echoing China's stand, the international battle lines seemed visible. To some analysts this marked a shift in the geo-political environment in southwestern Asia against the backdrop of tension between the United States and China and rivalry between Japan and China.[31] The latter assumed new prominence in Nepal. As Beijing marked 50 years of friendship with Kathmandu, Japan announced that it would extend Nepal a $17 million grant for food and development assistance. This came amid the virtual embargo Japan's western allies had imposed on the royal regime.

Was China now grooming another Tibet? That was a question raised in the U.S., particularly among ruling conservative circles. India and the United States were urged to make every attempt to prevent further destabilization in Nepal and deter further Chinese influence, which would only serve to agitate an already unstable regional security situation.[32] Another American analyst maintained that Nepal had slipped into a category of "zombie" countries, to which China provided just enough political, diplomatic, and security support for the ruler to survive sanctions and domestic popular revolts, while gaining a dependent state. Nepal, in other words, had joined the pariah nations of Myanmar (formerly Burma) and Zimbabwe.[33]

King Gyanendra's domestic critics did not envisage Nepal in that way. Representatives of political parties that had managed to evade the security agencies slipped into India, formed an alliance to restore democracy and pledged to restructure the state by bringing marginalized groups into the national mainstream. With one swift blow the palace had pushed the mainstream opposition closer to the Maoists, who had appeared to be mired by serious rifts. The Maoists denied allegations that the party's chief ideologue, Baburam Bhattarai, had been expelled from the organization, but rebel leader Prachanda subsequently issued a statement listing his grievances with his deputy.[34]

Chinese Premier Wen Jiabao skipped Nepal during his south Asia tour, which New Delhi interpreted as being in deference to its sensitivities.[35] However, Beijing signaled its intention to deal directly with Nepal by sending Foreign Minister Li Zhaoxing to Kathmandu in late March as part of celebrations marking the 50th anniversary of the establishment of diplomatic relations. Li met with King Gyanendra and delivered an invitation from President Hu Jintao to attend the Boao regional economic forum. There had been speculation that China would step into the breach after India, the United States and Britain suspended sales of weapons to Nepal. However, in a pre-departure news conference, Li said he had not discussed security matters with Nepalese officials.[36]

Shortly after Li's departure the government freed Nepali Congress President Girija Prasad Koirala and 200 political activists from detention, in a move seen as an effort to placate India.[37] In mid-April King Gyanendra appeared to make some progress in negotiations with India when, on the sidelines of an Afro–Asian summit in Bandung, Indonesia, the monarch met with Indian Prime

Minister Singh. New Delhi, the monarch told the media, had decided to resume military assistance to his government, prompting an outcry from the communist factions supporting the Singh coalition, which in turn forced the government to backtrack. By this time the monarch was in China attending the Boao Forum, where he received assurances of Beijing's full support and friendship. In a pointed comment, Vice Foreign Minister Wu Dawei urged the international community to "respect the choice made by the Nepalese people."[38]

China, backed by Pakistan and Russia, worked to prevent the U.N. Human Rights Commission in Geneva from proposing tough measures against Nepal for its deteriorating human rights situation. New Delhi, which appeared concerned that taking too hard a line with the king would push him closer to Beijing, joined the effort in Geneva. When King Gyanendra lifted the three-month-old state of emergency, some Indian analysts read the move as an acknowledgment by the monarch that his "China card" had failed.[39]

India, however, found itself in the middle of the Maoist rift and in the process revealed its own dilemma. In May the Nepalese army made public an audio tape said to contain a statement by Prachanda suggesting that New Delhi wanted Dr. Bhattarai reinstated.[40] Infuriated by the implication that New Delhi was in contact with the Maoist rebels, the Indian Embassy questioned the authenticity of the tape.[41] Yet one Indian newspaper revealed that Indian intelligence agencies were quietly chaperoning Dr. Bhattarai around New Delhi for talks.[42] Speculation that New Delhi was keen to use Indian communist parties' influence over the Maoists to get them to join the Seven Party Alliance (SPA) injected a new dimension to the debate, while indicating a rift in the UPA government on how to deal with Nepal.

In preliminary talks with the SPA the Maoists reaffirmed their objective of a democratic, multiparty republic, although they now appeared ready to leave the issue of the monarchy to the people to decide. The royal government vowed to declare political leaders terrorists if they joined hands with the Maoists. The SPA ruled out reconciliation with the king before democracy and full freedoms were restored. India, Britain and the European Union publicly supported the SPA agenda. The United States still seemed to support the palace's military solution. In an effort to intensify pressure on the palace, the Nepali Congress and the UML removed references to constitutional monarchy from their party statutes. The UML went a step further by adopting a democratic republic as its platform.

In August Foreign Minister Ramesh Nath Pandey visited Beijing, where he met with President Hu and held talks with senior Chinese officials. The Chinese government pledged additional aid of $12.3 million.[43] Beijing also agreed to allow Nepal use of Tibetan highways to transport supplies to regions suffering food shortages. An Indian magazine reported that Pandey had signed a deal under which Beijing would sell to Nepal arms worth 1.6 billion rupees.[44] Alarmed by this development India stepped up initiatives on a strategy to unite political parties in Nepal and mount international pressure on the king to restore democracy.[45]

As Gyanendra prepared to address the United Nations General Assembly in September and appeal to member states to help Nepal fight terrorism, the SPA wrote to Secretary-General Kofi Annan asking him to prevent the monarch from speaking. In a surprise move the Maoists declared a three-month unilateral ceasefire and appealed to the United Nations for assistance in bringing an end to the armed conflict, forcing the king to cancel his visit to New York.[46] The Maoist ceasefire drew praise from the political parties and the people, but the government refused to reciprocate and the army continued its offensive.

In October the king announced that parliamentary elections would be held in April 2007, but the opposition alliance, which viewed this move as an attempt by the king to legitimize his regime, said it would boycott all polls.[47] Army chief Pyar Jung Thapa traveled to Beijing, where Chinese Defense Minister Cao Gangchuan vowed to promote military co-operation.[48] China pledged almost $1 million in military assistance to Nepal's army. New Delhi voiced concern over the announcement, which coincided with an offer by China's ambassador in India to help to New Delhi crush its own Maoist guerrillas.[49]

At a summit of the South Asian Association for Regional Cooperation in Bangladesh in November, King Gyanendra led a successful campaign linking Afghanistan's full membership with China's inclusion as an observer. This move came as a surprise to India, which initially insisted there was no precedent for an observer or a dialogue partner, and suggested that a memorandum for co-operation be reached with China.[50] Prominent Indian thinkers had been advocating Beijing's inclusion, saying it would greatly enhance Sino-India ties and benefit the region. With Pakistan, Bangladesh and Sri Lanka supporting Nepal's proposal, India relented. While the Indian government made muted comments about Nepal's role during the summit, newspapers openly criticized the monarch for flashing the "China card." One editorial urged New Delhi "to find ways to squeeze [the monarch] further … to meet the Indian demand for an early end to his unconstitutional personal rule."[51]

From Dhaka, the king traveled on to Africa for three weeks. During this period Nepali Congress and UML leaders made several visits to India. Clearly, New Delhi had sanctioned – if not entirely facilitated – the SPA–Maoist meetings.[52] While Indian intelligence agencies were believed to be in contact with elements of the Nepalese Maoist leadership, the wider establishment was still distrustful of their motives. Moreover, the precise links between Nepalese Maoists and their Indian counterparts were nebulous. Even in the absence of overt links, a complete Maoist takeover of Nepal would provide significant ideological inspiration to the Indian Maoists. By pressuring them into mainstream politics, one group of Nepalese policymakers in India hoped to dilute the rebels' radicalism. There also seemed to be an expectation that the Maoists would have to be content with a secondary role behind the Nepali Congress and CPN-UML in open and competitive elections. This reasoning would have to overcome opposition in the ruling Congress party and in the Indian armed forces, where support for the monarchy was considerable.[53]

Any hesitation the Singh government may have had in pressuring the palace seemed to evaporate after King Gyanendra's Dhaka challenge. Negotiations in

Delhi resulted in a 12-point agreement which brought the rebels into the political mainstream and ended the decade-long insurrection. The SPA and Maoists agreed to hold constitutional assembly elections to draft a new constitution and to let the Nepalese people decide on the monarchy's future. The Maoists also pledged to fully abide by the results of constituent assembly elections. The United Nations and European Union welcomed the accord, while the U.S. remained cautious. After returning home, King Gyanendra reiterated his intention to follow his three-year roadmap.

Weeks after General Thapa returned from Beijing, China began delivering truck loads of military supplies to Nepal. Indian interest in Nepal's "China card" now grew into a serious inquiry into Beijing's motives in south Asia. Some Indian analysts appeared ready to tolerate a one-off Chinese replenishment of Nepal's armory.[54] Leading Indian newspapers, however, carried editorials urging New Delhi to use all possible means to teach the recalcitrant royal regime a fitting lesson.[55] Clearly India seemed to have reached a point of no return vis-à-vis the palace.

In December Chen Hao-su, the head of the Chinese People's Association for Friendship with Foreign Countries, arrived on visit to Nepal. At a conference, he affirmed as still valid the statement made over four decades earlier by Marshal Chen Yi that China would support Nepal if it were to be invaded by another country.[56] The statement was considered important not only because the official was the son of Chen Yi, but also because of his current position. The association provided significant policy input to the Chinese Foreign Ministry.

After returning from a visit to Pakistan Army chief Pyar Jung Thapa hosted a Chinese military delegation in Kathmandu. This prompted Indian Foreign Minister Pranab Mukherjee to express concern over Nepal's growing military ties with India's two traditional rivals.[57] The situation in Nepal figured during the second round of strategic dialogue in Beijing between Foreign Secretary Shyam Saran and Chinese Vice Foreign Minister for Asian Affairs, Wu Dawei. Saran, who also met Chinese State Councillor Tang Jiaxuan, Foreign Minister Li Zhaoxing and Executive Vice Foreign Minister Dai Bingguo, said he used the meeting to present Beijing with India's assessment of the situation in Nepal.[58]

Although a major army offensive in the Maoist stronghold of Rolpa led the rebels to end the truce, the Maoists said they would abide by the 12-point agreement with the SPA. As the government pressed ahead with its plan to hold local elections the Maoists launched attacks, killing a mayoral candidate. Meanwhile opposition parties urged people not to vote. On the first anniversary of the royal takeover the Maoists mounted a devastating attack on the western township of Palpa. Rebuffing national and international criticism, the government organized municipal elections, as planned, on February 8, under the protection of a massive security clampdown. With all the major parties boycotting the elections voter turnout was a dismal 21 percent. More than half of the available positions remained vacant due to a lack of candidates. The government, elated by the fact that it managed to conduct the elections at all, announced preparations for parliamentary elections. But trouble seemed to be brewing on a crucial front.

Beijing steps back

When a delegation led by Chinese State Councillor Tang Jiaxuan postponed its visit to Kathmandu by a month, there was instant speculation that Beijing was rethinking its Nepal policy.[59] Tang, as foreign minister, had accompanied Premier Zhu Rongji during his visit five years earlier. Beijing explained that the trip had to be rescheduled because of Chinese preoccupation with the party congress. But it gave rise to speculation nonetheless, no doubt happily fanned by the palace's opponents. But their jubilation was shortlived as U.S. Ambassador James Moriarty, in a public speech in mid-February, strongly criticized the SPA–Maoist agreement. He said he did not see a future for Nepal if the parties vowed to go ahead with the accord.[60] The fact that he waited three months to make his first direct criticism of the accord was significant. Describing the year-old royal rule a failure, Moriarty reiterated his call for reconciliation between the SPA and the palace. Despite his criticism of the palace, many saw Moriarty's speech as a prop for the king. Had Beijing's re-evaluation encouraged Washington to embark on its own?

Frustrated as it seemed to be with the palace's inability to stabilize the situation, Beijing was also apprehensive of the "color-coded" revolutions being waged around the world. An imposed recipe of democracy for Nepal, in Beijing's view, would open the door to India or western governments, especially the United States, to launch a campaign of intervention and coercion.[61] So it embarked on a mission of its own. In March, Tang became the highest-ranking foreign official to travel to Nepal since the king took power. Tang, holding the rank of deputy premier, met with King Gyanendra, senior ministers as well as opposition leaders. At the end of his three-day visit Tang stressed the importance of reconciliation between the king and the political parties. Based on fresh assessments by its embassy, China was now thought to have favored reconciliation between the palace and the political parties.[62] Beijing was presumably reluctant to take the hands-off approach it had adopted in 1989–1990, following which it had had to spend almost a decade regaining its influence.

In public comments Tang emphasized his country's approach of non-intervention towards Nepal's internal affairs, fully respecting any model of national development that the Nepalese people chose. Beijing now seemed to suggest that it could support political forces other than the monarchy. Clearly China was growing impatient that the royal regime had not moved closer to reaching consensus with the domestic forces. Privately, Chinese officials were disturbed by the incessant effort by some in the royal regime to flaunt China's support. Tang explicitly conveyed Beijing's concern of the kingdom becoming increasingly vulnerable to unexpected foreign involvements by articulating the need to preserve its independence, sovereignty and territorial integrity.[63]

The SPA announced a campaign to mount what it called the penultimate assault on royal authority. The Maoists, having announced another unilateral ceasefire, vowed to support the peaceful protests. The royal government made every effort to thwart the SPA's planned mass protests during the four-day general strike. Tens of thousands of people defied the ban and protested in various parts of the city. The government, citing rebel infiltration of the SPA protests, promised tougher measures. As pro-democracy protests swelled across Nepal, international pressure mounted on the palace to reach out to the political parties.

China consistently opposed third-party intervention in Nepal, while India considered itself the most qualified intermediary. Prime Minister Manmohan Singh sent Karan Singh, a senior member of his Congress Party and the son of Kashmir's last maharajah, as a special envoy to the palace. The primary purpose obviously was to persuade the monarch to reach an accommodation with parties and an agreed plan to restore democracy. New Delhi also seemed to have formed the opinion that the monarchy would be needed in any future settlement to provide a balance to Nepal's political system. Specifically, continuing doubts about the sincerity of the Maoists' willingness to accept multi-party democracy increased India's interest in the retention of monarchy with the support of the Royal Nepal Army.[64] Karan Singh, related to the Nepalese royal family through marriage, emerged from a meeting with King Gyanendra satisfied but non-committal.[65] Yet the choice of Karan Singh created suspicion in the opposition politicians from the outset. The streets continued to swell with angry protesters, in defiance of curfews.

On April 20 the monarch went on radio and television to invite the SPA to name a prime minister. China, like the United States, India, Canada and the European Union welcomed the proclamation, and urged the parties to work out a framework to form a new government. At home the royal proclamation triggered larger protests. The SPA, under strong pressure from cadres and supporters not to capitulate, declined the king's invitation to form a government. Anxious to avoid a bloody showdown foreign diplomats in Kathmandu unleashed another flurry of initiatives, primarily pressing the palace to accept the SPA's demands. King Gyanendra then issued another proclamation to the nation that, among other things, re-instated the House of Representatives. The SPA, which called off the protests, unanimously nominated Nepali Congress President Girija Prasad Koirala as prime minister.

Conclusion

In seeking to deploy China as a counterweight to India, King Gyanendra had gone further in public than his father and brother. Towards the end of his direct rule, the Chinese reined in their traditional support for the palace in a manner that was both unprecedented and conspicuous. This turn of events resulted from a mixture of Nepalese and Chinese realities that underscored the shift in regional and international dynamics. From 2000 to early 2006, Beijing had courted India with regular exchanges of high-level visits and modest concessions on outstanding issues. Yet Delhi – in Beijing's view – continued to move closer to Washington. Having concluded by late 2005 that its generosity was being interpreted as weakness, Beijing moved toward a tougher approach to New Delhi.[66]

Nepal might have been a key arena for the Chinese to challenge India, but things were slipping fast in the kingdom. Having chosen to back the monarchy and largely rebuffed the other political forces all these decades, the growing unpopularity of the king put Beijing at a disadvantage. Moreover, the Chinese were wary of the negotiations the palace was conducting separately with Washington and Delhi.[67] Once the mainstream parties launched protests against royal rule with support from the Maoist rebels, China recognized the extent to which the ground had shifted. India had played a crucial role in facilitating the alliance between the Seven Party Alliance and the Maoist rebels. The Chinese, having observed the degeneration of the post-1990 political process, had reason to fear that growing external involvement might create far greater instability in Nepal. This in turn could have grave implications for its own restive regions like Tibet and Xinjiang. Distancing itself from the monarchy became politically prudent.

11   Scramble for new allies

Anxious to preserve its position after the collapse of royal rule, China confronted the wariness displayed toward it by the new Nepalese political players. The mainstream parties had seen successive generations of the Chinese communist leadership maintain close ties with the palace during periods of both active royal rule and those when the kingdom had functioning elected governments. Fresh in the minds of the Maoist rebels was the fact that China had not only politically repudiated the Nepalese adherents of the Great Helmsman, but had also armed the royal regime against an insurgency they viewed as being in support of the poor and dispossessed.

The day after King Gyanendra restored parliament Beijing sent a top Foreign Ministry official to meet Prime Minister Girija Prasad Koirala and other senior political leaders.[1] But the country's attention was focused on the re-instated legislature where members moved swiftly to curtail the powers of the king, and more specifically the removal of his control of the army. Members also turned Nepal away from being the world's only Hindu state, changing it instead into a secular one, a decision influenced as much by the rise of minority voices as by the parties' disenchantment with what they considered the palace's blatant use of Hinduism as a political tool.

China found some of its apprehensions addressed early on, with the new government deciding to proceed with construction of a second Beijing-funded highway linking Nepal with Tibet.[2] Instead, India, the prime mover of the political events, found itself at the center of a fresh controversy. As Prime Minister Koirala prepared for an official visit to New Delhi, both the CPN-UML and the Maoists grew suspicious at the haste with which he had announced his travel plans. The visit served to bolster fears that New Delhi, in a throwback to the 1950s, was seeking to micro-manage the peace process. Prime Minister Manmohan Singh, breaking with tradition, traveled to the airport to welcome Koirala, where he described the Nepalese premier as south Asia's greatest leader. The enthusiastic reception Koirala received from across the political spectrum and the Indian government's promises of a "Himalayan Marshall Plan" did little to quell Nepalese suspicions.

The distrust did not stand in the way of the first high-level official talks between the Seven Party Alliance and the Maoists in mid-June. Flown in secretly from the tourist resort of Pokhara, Maoist supremo Prachanda held talks with Koirala and the other leaders of the alliance. The two sides announced an eight-point agreement on forming an interim government that would include the rebels. Making his first public appearance in the capital, Prachanda assured the country of his organization's commitment to peace, adding that the people would decide whether Nepal would retain a titular monarchy or become a democratic republic.

International reaction was mixed. India, along with the United Nations and Britain, enthusiastically welcomed the pact, while the United States insisted that the rebels disarm before joining the government. The Maoists refused to do so before the constituent assembly elections, apprehensive of the now-renamed Nepal Army's traditional ties with the monarchy. But they agreed to place their weapons under United Nations supervision.

China began expressing an old concern – U.S. plans to resettle more Tibetan refugees – with uncharacteristic candor. It virtually accused Nepal of issuing refugee identification cards to "illegal migrants," and described the move as a serious bilateral issue.[3] It would subsequently emerge that the royal regime had been negotiating in early 2006 with Washington on resettling 5,000 Tibetans from Nepal, a proposal the Bush administration had made the previous year. Although there was no official information on how the individuals would be chosen, word had spread that Tibetan veterans of the Mustang campaign would have priority for resettlement in the United States.[4] Caught between pressure from China to reject the American plan and the suspension of critical U.S. military aid, the royal regime was still negotiating a tradeoff at the time of its collapse.[5] Beijing was anxiously discouraging the new democratic government from approving the Bush administration's program. Tensions flared when Chinese border troops opened fire on a group of 70 Tibetans trying to cross into Nepal, killing at least two.[6]

As the Maoists and the government agreed to confine arms to one set of camps and restrict government troops to their barracks, hopes for peace brightened. Shortly after midnight on November 8, the SPA and the Maoists signed a six-point agreement ending the decade-long conflict and committing them to restoring lasting peace. Later in the month Maoist leader Prachanda made his first public visit to New Delhi. The Indian government publicly distanced itself from the visit and no senior government official or ruling Congress party leader met the Maoist chairman. A recurrent theme of Prachanda's public comments in New Delhi, on the eve of President Hu Jintao's visit, was that the Maoists would never allow Nepal to become a part of a western plot to pit the Asian giants against each other.

Uneasy peace between unlikely allies

After much wrangling the SPA and the Maoists signed a Comprehensive Peace Accord that formally ended the decade-long "people's war." The United Nations was invited to manage the arms of the national and Maoist armies, while the monarch was deprived of all political rights. Welcoming the agreement, India released senior Maoist leaders Chandra Prakash Gajurel and Mohan Baidya from prison. It was hard to avoid an impression of a quid pro quo, considering that the two men were among the leading critics of India in the organization. The peace process received another major boost in mid-December when the SPA and the Maoists approved an interim constitution that, in effect, suspended the monarchy and appointed the prime minister as provisional head of state. Early in 2007 the Maoists joined the interim legislature parliament, formally becoming part of the mainstream.

Although fears of growing external involvement in Nepal had partly led China to distance itself from the monarchy, Beijing saw the inevitability of some degree of internationalization and chose to become part of that process. The United Nations Security Council unanimously created a 12-month political mission to monitor the arms and armies of both the Maoists and the Nepalese Army. The United Nations Political Mission in Nepal, or UNMIN, would also help organize the constituent assembly elections. While the creation of the U.N. mission was widely hailed in Nepal, there were reports that China had insisted during closed-door consultations that the mission's duration should, as with other U.N. missions, be only six-months.[7] Beijing was also reportedly displeased with U.N. officials for their lack of consultation on the peace process.

After the Maoists joined the interim parliament Prachanda demanded the immediate abolition of the monarchy, claiming royalists were stoking ethnic tensions. Prime Minister Koirala urged the former rebels to wait until after the constituent assembly elections for the formal abolition of the monarchy. But with other ethnic groups now having launched protests, the future of the elections was becoming uncertain. Tensions were intensifying in the southern plains along the border with India, where the madhesis (Nepalese citizens native to the area), complained that the SPA and Maoists had perpetuated the community's traditional underrepresentation in Nepal's power structures. Two breakaway Maoist factions began sporadic armed attacks as a way of voicing local grievances, while a new organization, the Madhesi Janadhikar Forum (MJF), announced peaceful protests against the interim constitution.

Completing the first stage of registering Maoist arms and fighters, the United Nations noted a striking discrepancy between the number of weapons registered and the number of combatants, but added that it could not make a definitive judgment.[8] The government, which was in a position to make such a judgement, was torn between those who considered the disparity a serious threat and those who were reluctant to let it undermine the peace process. The Maoists, reiterating their demand for immediate abolition of the monarchy, stepped up consultations with the ruling alliance on the forming of an interim government, but these talks foundered over matters concerning who would get which political appointments.

In early March parliament amended the interim constitution to include a commitment to federalism, an increase in the number of constituencies in the Terai region and proportional representation for different ethnic groups and women within the administration. But the country was rocked by the worst violence since the peace process began. Some 29 people were killed and scores more injured in the southern district of Rautahat following a clash between MJF and Maoist activists, with almost all of the dead Maoists. Prachanda accused Hindu fundamentalists from India of orchestrating the attack as a way of subverting the election.[9]

Since the palace's capitulation Prachanda and other Maoist leaders had strongly backed the aging and ailing Koirala. Now a senior Maoist leader accused the prime minister of representing an alliance of Nepalese and Indians campaigning to save the monarchy.[10] From the other end of the ideological spectrum came calls for the creation of a Hindu republic by delinking the religion from the monarchy. After weeks of bluster and bargaining, as ordinary Nepalese had begun to doubt the prospects of free and fair elections, an interim government comprising the SPA and the Maoists was formed on April 1.

Continued Sino-Nepalese engagement

In the midst of political wrangling the Koirala government made a vivid display of its eagerness to engage with China. At the summit of the South Asian Association for Regional Cooperation in New Delhi in April, Nepal made a strong case for China's inclusion as a full member of the eight-nation organization. Beijing, along with South Korea, Japan, the United States and the European Union were invited for the first time as summit observers.[11] Although China's full membership enjoyed support among sections of Indian academia keen on accelerating economic co-operation, New Delhi's strategic anxieties about Beijing's ultimate motives in the region had restrained its official posture. That Koirala would so openly support China's full membership was significant, considering the widespread displeasure King Gyanendra had prompted from New Delhi when he had pushed for Beijing's inclusion as a mere observer the previous year.

Later in the month Beijing made a powerful public demonstration of its support for the political changes in Nepal. China's new ambassador, Zheng Xianglin, became the first foreign representative to present his credentials to Prime Minister Koirala, whom the interim constitution had additionally granted the powers and responsibilities of head of state following the virtual suspension of the monarchy. Beijing also moved swiftly to build ties with the Maoists. Sections of the Chinese media had already begun offering glowing tributes to the rebellion they had only recently condemned.[12] A leading Chinese academic claimed that the 2001 royal palace massacre was the result of a conspiracy of foreign elements anxious to prevent King Birendra from forging greater Sino-Nepalese ties.[13] Having maintained total silence on that horrific incident, the first significant reaction from China seemed to approximate that of the Nepalese Maoists in its immediate aftermath.

The SPA grew increasingly critical of the Maoists' failure to restore confiscated lands to the rightful owners, their continued extraction of "donations" from the public, and their frequent disruption of opponents' political activities. The

Maoists, on the other hand, were split between hard-liners and soft-liners, as rumors persisted of deepening differences between Prachanda and Dr. Baburam Bhattarai. Resentment was building among former rebel soldiers who increasingly felt the Maoists had abandoned their revolutionary ardor for an ambiguous place in the mainstream. Dissatisfaction mounted with the living conditions for People's Liberation Army fighters in holding camps and the lack of progress toward integrating them into the national army. Key generals of the national army began contending that politically indoctrinated cadres could not be included en masse or without meeting the regular rules and qualifications.

As each side accused the other of plotting to delay elections, the Maoists pulled out of the government. Prime Minister Koirala had hoped to retain a "ceremonial monarchy" but finally bowed to rising republican sentiment within his party. After months of protracted negotiations the Nepali Congress joined the other parties in immediately declaring Nepal a "federal democratic republic," the formal implementation of which would be made by the first session of the constituent assembly. The Maoists rejoined the government on December 31, officially putting the peace process back on track.

With the advent of the new year, as Beijing hosted junior Maoist functionaries, Prime Minister Koirala virtually blamed India for the troubles in the Terai. When India's oil monopoly blocked fuel supplies to Nepal, citing payment failures as the reason, Koirala publicly urged Beijing for assistance, specifically calling for expediting the extension of the Qinghai–Tibet railway to the Nepalese border.[14] As the prime minister's rhetoric against India grew, the military, too, began growing increasingly assertive. Shortly after paying a visit to India, Nepal's new army chief, General Rukmangad Katuwal headed for China in early January. Amid fresh reports of the arrival of arms from China and the United States,[15] India began voicing concern over the proliferation of China Study Centers in Nepal.[16] China, for its part, began expressing concern over the deterioration of the situation in the Terai. While the government remained circumspect on specifics, Chinese academics closely linked to the government began voicing Mao-era warnings that Beijing would not allow Nepal to become another Bhutan or Sikkim.

Tibet erupts again

Anti-Chinese protests broke out in Tibet on March 10 on the 49th anniversary of the abortive uprising against Chinese rule. The scale and seriousness of the protests surprised Beijing. In Kathmandu, Tibetans began staging daily protests in front of the Chinese Embassy, though Nepalese security forces beat them back. Chinese ambassador Zheng held a news conference to praise Nepalese police and denounce external forces for instigating violent activities against China. Beijing said "the Dalai Lama clique" was misusing the porous border between Nepal and India, and sending troublemakers from Dharamsala.

As Maoist leader Prachanda backed China's crackdown on the "separatist violence" in Tibet,[17] reports of Chinese plainclothes security agents directing the

Nepalese suppression emerged. International human rights watchdogs accused the Nepalese government of appeasing China.[18] The fact that the very same leaders who had opposed the royal regime's suppression were now ordering similar actions against the Tibetans was shocking to many Nepalese. More immediately the constituent assembly elections, delayed twice as a result of internal political rifts, stood threatened by the new instability. After much behind-the-scenes negotiation, the Tibetans suspended their protests in order to allow the crucial elections to go ahead.

Defying pundits and pollsters the Maoists won the largest share of seats in the April 10 elections, garnering 220 out of the 575 seats in the Constituent Assembly, compared to 110 seats for the Nepali Congress and 103 seats for the CPN-UML. The Maoists' triumph was widely attributed to their excellent publicity machine and grassroots efficiency, although critics complained of massive irregularities and voter intimidation. International poll monitors, including former U.S. president Jimmy Carter, were largely satisfied with the conduct of the elections, an endorsement that largely silenced the criticism.

With the Maoists poised to take the helm, expectations of an improvement in Sino-Nepalese relations grew. A high-level Chinese delegation visiting the country announced that Beijing planned within five years to link Tibet with Nepal by extending a railway line from Lhasa to Khasa on the China–Nepal.[19] An influential Chinese newspaper described the Maoists' victory as "a historic sea change." Noting that India and the U.S. both had designated the Maoists a "terrorist organization," Beijing also sought to draw a favorable contrast by suggesting it had only called the group anti-government rebels.[20]

Yet Beijing had more immediate worries, as Tibetan exiles resumed their protests. This time China expressed unhappiness over the Nepalese government's lackluster efforts to control the demonstrations. Chinese ambassador Zheng publicly urged Nepal to take sterner action against the Tibetan protesters.[21] He described the demonstrators as "separatists" who were being supported by United Nations offices and human rights groups. As Nepal began its harshest ever crackdown on Tibetan refugees, arresting the top three leaders in Kathmandu, international human rights organizations reacted angrily.[22]

Despite their impressive electoral performance the Maoists had not recorded an unqualified triumph. Bruised but unbeaten, the Nepali Congress and the UML were locked in a fierce conflict over the presidential election and the formation of the new government. As deposed king Gyanendra vacated the palace to live a life as a commoner now that his role had been formally abolished by the legislature, the Maoists insisted they should hold the posts of both president and prime minister. The Nepali Congress said Prime Minister Koirala should be the first president in recognition of his contributions to peace and democracy. The CPN-UML pushed the candidacy of its former general secretary Madhav Kumar Nepal, despite the fact that he had lost elections in both of the constituencies in which he was a candidate.

It was now that three Madhesi parties sought to establish an autonomous region in the Terai, a move that the larger parties blocked. After protracted negotiations Ram Baran Yadav, general secretary of the Nepali Congress, was elected Nepal's first president. With the first elected head of state hailing from the Terai, the Nepalese expected the process of reconciliation to become smoother. But the wrangling over the presidency would turn out to be a prelude to fiercer political struggles.

With the emergence of a new alliance in the assembly, Prachanda was elected prime minister, heading a coalition with the CPN-UML and the MJF. The Maoists, anxious to play down suggestions of an impending pro-Chinese tilt, insisted Nepal would maintain a foreign policy of equidistance with its two neighbors, while Prachanda acknowledged the country's deep "civilizational and cultural ties" with India.[23]

Rise and fall of the Maoist government

Pushpa Kamal Dahal – as the Maoist leader now preferred to be called – was sworn in as prime minister on August 18. Before the full domestic implications of a government led by the once-feared rebels could be gauged, Nepal was caught in a geo-political predicament. Days after taking the oath, Dahal flew to Beijing to attend the closing ceremony of the Olympic Games. A senior Indian politician had publicly urged Dahal not to make the trip, saying it would send a negative message to India, but the prime minister claimed Beijing would have

Figure 11.1 President Hu Jintao meeting Prime Minister Pushpa Kamal Dahal in Beijing in August 2008 (photo courtesy: Ministry of Foreign Affairs of the People's Republic of China).

greater cause for offense if he did not attend.[24] New Delhi saw the visit as a violation of an unwritten tradition which held that a new Nepalese leader always visited India first.[25]

In the Chinese capital Dahal held talks with Chinese President Hu Jintao and Premier Wen Jiabao during a visit that seemed to have all the trappings of an official affair. Technically, however, Dahal did uphold his predecessors' tradition weeks later. In his first formal visit abroad, he arrived in India carrying assurances of continued friendship and goodwill. During a trip that gained wide media coverage, Dahal sought to woo Indian investors and win over more skeptical elements such as the Bharatiya Janata Party. But any optimism that might have been generated was short-lived. Days after Dahal's return, Defense Minister Ram Bahadur Thapa departed for China, where he signed a military cooperation agreement.

Following the waves of anti-Chinese demonstrations by Tibetans, Beijing replaced its ambassador in Kathmandu, ostensibly over the embarrassing Tibetan protests.[26] That was a prelude to a wider jockeying for influence in the triangular relationship. Deputy Prime Minister Gautam urged China to help Nepal resolve its long-running dispute with India over the territory of Kalapani. Indian Foreign Minister Pranab Mukherjee, signaling India's displeasure, did not meet with Gautam during his visit a few days later. Shortly after Mukherjee's departure Chinese Foreign Minister Yang Jiechi arrived in Kathmandu undertaking to develop bilateral relations based on "real equality" so that it could become a "role model" for relationships between big and small countries.

At an official dinner Yang pledged that China would help Nepalese efforts to strengthen its sovereignty and independence. The statement prompted questions in the legislature as to whether the offer was made in response to any request Dahal might have made. Former king Gyanendra was quoted in an interview as saying that his policy of moving closer to China had brought about his downfall, clearly indicating that such a policy had angered India.[27]

A discomfited Chinese Ambassador Qiu Guohong praised the monarchy's contributions to fostering bilateral relations, while adding that Beijing respected the choice of the Nepalese people. But he was evasive when pressed by the deputy prime minister for Beijing's help in resolving the Kalapani dispute. That scarcely mollified India, which was concerned by a flurry of visits by senior Chinese military officials to Kathmandu. New Delhi felt Beijing might be seeking greater influence in the Nepalese Army, perhaps even attempting to install a Maoist commander as the top general of an integrated force.[28]

How far the Chinese would step in politically to support the Maoists remained unclear, given the ease with which they abandoned the monarchy. But Beijing did seem intent on making the most of the new camaraderie. A special envoy arrived in late February 2009 with the draft of new Peace and Friendship Treaty that reflected the changed political context.[29] Beijing expected to sign the treaty, which pledged greater Chinese political and economic support in exchange for firmer Nepalese actions against Tibetans, during Dahal's visit to China in early May.

Before the full implications of the new Chinese move could be gaged, the domestic political environment was vitiated by a deepening row over army chief General Rukmangad Katuwal's alleged insubordination to the elected government. Dahal, having long accused General Katuwal of defying government orders by making political statements and continuing recruitment, eventually fired him. The crisis took an ominous turn when President Yadav re-instated the general. An infuriated Dahal went on national television to announce his resignation, promising to fight for civilian supremacy and to free Nepal from the clutches of "foreign masters." Privately, Maoist leaders complained they had garnered broad political support for the move before Indian pressure forced the other parties to change their minds. India believed it shared special ties with the Nepal Army, as the chiefs also served as honorary generals in each other's forces. It seemed more worried about Chinese inroads into Nepal.[30]

In interviews with the Indian media Dahal claimed he was deposed in a concerted conspiracy by the Indian bureaucratic establishment at a time when the Indian politicians who drove the anti-palace alliance were busy on the electoral campaign trail. He told Indian journalists that the string of Chinese delegations visiting Nepal had not arrived at the Maoists' invitation.[31] Speculation over the precise circumstances surrounding Dahal's resignation, particularly New Delhi's alleged role, broadened into anxiety over the inordinate delay in forming the new government. After weeks of political wrangling, CPN-UML leader Madhav Kumar Nepal was appointed prime minister. The Maoists accused India of catapulting him to power, a protest that carried little credibility among ordinary Nepalese since the former rebels had brought him into parliament despite his electoral defeat.

Attention now focused on how Beijing would view the new premier. During one point in the anti-palace agitation, Madhav Nepal had strongly criticized China for arming the royal regime against the people. His accusation was considered doubly stinging since he had made it during a visit to India. Among the new premier's early affirmations was that Nepal did not intend to play China off against India and sought instead to pursue a balanced relationship. But other sections of the political establishment were not so constrained.

A group of Nepalese legislators traveled to Dharamsala in late June for a meeting with the Dalai Lama. Although the meeting was said to have been arranged by a private foundation, the legislators raised the stakes by inviting the Tibetan leader to visit Nepal. The Dalai Lama conceded that despite his long-standing desire to visit the country, successive Nepalese governments were not in a position to invite him because of sustained Chinese pressure.[32]

Days after that meeting Beijing sent a senior member of the Chinese Communist Party to register his government's concern at the fresh eruption of Free Tibet activities. China's urgency had been heightened by fresh clashes in the Xinjiang autonomous region involving ethnic Uighurs and Han Chinese, clashes which left over 150 dead and triggered an outcry from human rights organizations and exiled Uighur groups. Beijing feared the possibility of wider instability in the region bordering Tibet. The government announced a ban on anti-Chinese protests but clarified that the Dalai Lama was free to visit the country as long as he did not pursue a political agenda.

As Prime Minister Madhav Nepal traveled to India on a goodwill visit, Nepalese security and law enforcement officials held talks in Lhasa with their Chinese counterparts about securing the border and cracking down on anti-Tibet activities. Beijing characterized demands for a separate autonomous northern region in eastern Nepal, demands pursued by ethnic activists, as a western-funded effort to promote anti-Tibet activities.[33] Of the 14 Nepalese districts bordering Tibet, China considered eight sensitive and sought tougher measures from local authorities.

In September Zhang Gaoli, a member of the politburo of the Chinese Communist Party Central Committee, arrived on a five-day visit to Kathmandu at the invitation of the government. During the visit, the highest level of its kind since the post-2006 political changes, Zhang met with President Ram Baran Yadav, Prime Minister Madhav Nepal, and the leaders of the major political parties.

In a key speech in Kathmandu, Zhang – acknowledged by a leading Nepalese analyst as China's most senior "fifth generation leader" and a leading candidate to succeed the successor of President Hu Jintao – observed that "we have always treated our relations with Nepal from a strategic high and with a long-term view."[34] He thanked the government and people of Nepal for their sympathy and understanding on the issues of Tibet, Xinjiang and other matters of vital importance to China. Yet in his private meetings, he, too, was reported to have sought greater action from Nepal on curbing anti-China activities. Zhang was also reported to have advised the Maoists and the CPN-UML to forge unity to "match the forces that were inimical to China."[35]

Kathmandu sought to address some of Beijing's concerns by announcing it would soon deploy thousands of armed police along the Himalayan border, carefully asserting that it was not acting under pressure from China.[36] But the urgency on the part of the Chinese was unmistakable. The biennial defense white paper for 2008 for the first time listed "separatists ... working for the independence of Tibet" as a national security threat.[37] Some 2,500 Tibetans used to make the dangerous trip from Tibet to Nepal every year on their way to India to join the Dalai Lama. Activists claimed this number had fallen sharply since China mobilized its military in Tibet in March 2008. Official Nepalese reaffirmations of its "one China" policy had become repetitive since the abolition of the monarchy, but Beijing continued to put pressure on Kathmandu. Were the Chinese using the Tibet issue to pursue a broader agenda in Nepal?

Maoist leader Dahal helped deflect that question by claiming that India and the United States had been plotting serious anti-China activities from Nepal. This could even include an attack on China, an assertion that prompted ridicule from New Delhi.[38] Still, the allegation came amid a flurry of visits by western and Chinese ambassadors to Mustang, the one-time base of the Khampa rebellion. Rumors that Tibetan leaders from India had also visited the northwestern Nepalese region added an ominous chord to the discourse.

Dahal visited Hong Kong for what the Maoists officially described as a meeting with Nepalese supporters in the Chinese territory. The Nepalese media reported in substantial detail how the Maoist leader was whisked away from the airport for a secret meeting with unnamed Chinese officials who had flown in from Beijing. In October the Maoist leader visited China again, this time heading an eight member delegation of his party. It held four rounds of talks with Chinese Communist Party members. President Hu Jintao hosted Dahal as guest of honor at the country's 11th National Games in Shandong and met with him privately for 25 minutes. Chinese sources insisted that Hu and Dahal had met as leaders of their countries' respective communist parties to inaugurate the kind of inter-party ties that had not been possible during Dahal's previous visit as prime minister.[39]

The Dalai Lama's visit to the northeastern Indian state of Arunachal Pradesh in November prompted a strong denunciation from Beijing, which claims the region as southern Tibet. By raising tensions in the disputed region, according to one Chinese analyst, New Delhi hoped to force Beijing to resolve the issue on its terms.[40] Weeks earlier, Beijing had lodged a strong protest when Prime Minister Manmohan Singh visited the state during an election campaign.

After Dahal's return from China the Maoists ratcheted up their rhetorical campaign against India. In one public speech Dahal virtually accused New Delhi of masterminding the murders of King Birendra and the CPN-UML's charismatic general secretary Madan Bhandari. While such allegations were nothing new in Nepal's tiresome political discourse, this was the first time such a senior political leader had made them.[41]

During his visit to China in late December, Prime Minister Madhav Nepal reaffirmed Nepal's traditional "one China" policy. In an ostensible effort to underscore his commitment, the premier had begun the visit from Tibet. Beijing, which now considered Kathmandu's Tibet policy a litmus test of its professions of friendship,[42] was appreciative of the gesture. Over the next few weeks, Chinese analysts would emphasize the importance to China's security matters concerning the small border states adjoining both it and India. One asserted that the struggle between pro-India and pro-China forces in Nepal had reached a critical stage and that China needed to pay more attention to its interests there.[43]

The United States, which had largely followed India's lead during the second term of President Bush and first year of the Obama administration, now seemed to chart a middle ground. During his confirmation hearings in the Senate, the American ambassador-designate, Scott DeLisi, acknowledged China as a stakeholder in Nepal on a par with India, an assertion he repeated after assuming his responsibilities in Kathmandu. Washington and Beijing also held sub-regional consultations on south Asia in the Chinese capital. This appeared to bring them closer to the European point of view that the Maoists could no longer be isolated from power if Nepal were to achieve lasting peace and stability. While some Indians sulked at the loss of their initiative in Nepal, others were mindful of the negative fallout from any precipitate overt action. But the window of opportunity was narrowing. The threat of a serious political crisis loomed large as the assembly appeared certain to miss the deadline for drafting the new constitution.

After much last minute posturing the Maoists voted in favor of extending the constituent assembly for a year, after receiving what they believed was an assurance from Prime Minister Madhav Nepal that he would resign immediately. Hopes that the political parties had finally succeeded in creating space to sort out their difficulties faltered, however, as the Maoists accused the ruling coalition of betrayal. Prime Minister Madhav Nepal, backed by the Nepali Congress, refused to resign until the Maoists demonstrated their commitment to turn into a fully disarmed and transparent political party.

Growing Chinese involvement

When Premier Madhav Nepal did finally resign at the end of June, the parties failed to agree on a new government, despite successive rounds of voting for the prime minister in parliament. As the principal political parties continued to bicker over leadership of the next government, international stakeholders began a new round of consultations on how to prevent Nepal from slipping into deeper instability. While the Maoists continued to accuse India of pressuring legislators against voting for a government led by their party, the former rebels and China were caught up in salacious allegations of horse-trading. Nepalese and Indian media broadcast an audio tape purportedly showing a top Nepalese Maoist leader and a Chinese intermediary negotiating the funds necessary to buy some 50 legislators. Although both sides strenuously denied the allegations, they cast new questions over the Maoists' commitment to nationalism and Beijing's vaunted policy of non-interference. The Chinese Embassy in Kathmandu, for the first time in decades, witnessed demonstrations that were not linked to Tibet. The government's own commitment to democracy suffered a sharp blow when, reportedly responding to Chinese pressure, it prevented the estimated 20,000 Tibetans in exile in Nepal from voting for a new political head of the exiled Tibetan community.

When Maoist leader Dahal struck a secret deal with CPN-UML chairman Jhal Nath Khanal in February 2011, clearing the way for the formation of a new government, Kathmandu was rife with speculation that Beijing had crafted the "nationalist" alliance it had been calling for. While China refused to comment, Dahal insisted that the new government was a product of Nepalese genius, an apparent rebuke to India. Weeks later, General Chen Bingde, chief of the People's Liberation Army, arrived in Kathmandu with a large delegation and pledging $19 million in military assistance. Chen's visit was the highest level military delegation from China to visit in ten years. He signed agreements that included funds for infrastructure and equipment for the Nepalese army. Describing Chinese–Nepalese relations as important to "world peace and the Asia-Pacific region," Chen urged Nepalese political parties to ensure political stability.

Chen's visit came in the aftermath of the Dalai Lama's decision to step down as the political leader of the Tibetan government-in-exile. The withdrawal of the Dalai Lama from a political role raised concerns about a rise in militancy among

Tibetan exiles in India and Nepal, particularly among those who disagree with his acceptance of Tibetan autonomy within China rather than full independence. Days after Chen's departure Beijing recalled its ambassador, Qiu Guohong, before his three-year term expired, following what was said to be rifts within the embassy over the handling of the issue of Tibetans in Nepal. This was Beijing's second successive ambassadorial recall from Kathmandu over the Tibet question.

Weeks later the Chinese announced the appointment of Yang Houlan, then the ambassador for Korean Peninsular Affairs and someone ostensibly quite senior in the Chinese diplomatic service and presumably with stronger credentials within the Chinese Communist Party. Educated in the United States, Yang had served as his country's ambassador to Afghanistan, another chronically unstable country on China's periphery. The appointment of a seasoned diplomat with such a clear security affairs background was seen in Kathmandu as an outcome of Beijing's understandable anxiety to ensure that instability and turmoil in Nepal did not spill over into Tibet and beyond.[44]

Chinese distrust of Maoists

While China became more candid in emphasizing its desire to build a new strategic partnership with Nepal, a reliable partner seemed to have become all the more elusive. Beijing saw the Maoists as the best organized political force in Nepal and therefore best placed to unite a broader swathe of "nationalists."[45] But Beijing also seemed to have concerns about the ex-rebels. Despite their public denunciations of the Chinese leadership as revisionist, the Maoists had sought to build links with Beijing in the past. Some Chinese sources insisted that Beijing rebuffed them because of their commitment to engage with the legitimate government in Kathmandu, while other Chinese sources concluded the rebels were being supported by enemies of China.[46]

While China has avoided taking sides in Nepal's political disarray, seeking instead to build ties with all parties, it seems to distrust those sections of the Maoist leadership,which spent years in exile in India. The Chinese may have used the Maoists to convey some of their own negative views about India, but Dahal's penchant for including Beijing in some of his more ribald comments must have raised Beijing's skepticism. The skepticism of the Chinese, who in the words of a leading Nepalese analyst are following a policy of "never appear too hostile, never appear too friendly" vis-à-vis the Nepalese Maoists,[47] deepened amid the internal disputes within the party.

The Maoists' internal rifts

The dispute between Dahal and Bhattarai has been widely perceived as one between hard-liners and moderates in the party. By entering mainstream politics, many believed the Maoists had moderated their stated aim to establish a peasant-led revolutionary communist regime, notwithstanding their continuing rhetorical toughness. But the two factions have been speaking with different voices for far too long. The hard-liners, led by Mohan Baidya "Kiran," have not abandoned the path of revolution, while Bhattarai and his loyalists have sought to position the party more closely within the democratic mainstream. Dahal succeeded in straddling both camps before seeming to side with Bhattarai in mid-2011. Instead of isolating the hard-liners, Dahal seemed to have impelled the opposite reaction, a fact illustrated when Bhattarai and Dahal emerged together with a list of complaints against the chairman's leadership style. At the lower level a deepening sense of frustration has set in. After ousting the monarchy many Maoist cadres and former combatants expected to overwhelm, if not entirely edge out, the Nepali Congress and the CPN-UML. But the other two parties, also weakened by internal rifts, have bolstered their overall position by veering closer to the military. The Maoists' internal rifts were also perceived to be taking place against a backdrop of regional politics in which Bhattarai is believed to enjoy closer ties with India, while Baidya leads the "nationalists" anxiously courting China.

Beijing is reportedly keen to facilitate the integration of the former Maoist combatants into the Nepalese Army. That stands in contrast to the stand of India and, to a lesser degree, the United States and Britain, both traditional supporters of the Nepalese military. New Delhi, Washington and London are against wholesale entry of former Maoists into the army, a view shared by the Nepalese generals. They want a limited number of qualified former combatants to join a new paramilitary force charged with internal security responsibilities. But the acceptable number of such former Maoists remains the bone of contention.

There has been a serious formal commitment expressed in various instruments and representations regarding the integration of eligible armed combatants. Yet the process has run into serious trouble, both in terms of disagreement with the principle of integration, and dispute over the scale and nature of that integration from within the army itself. The issue of the reconfiguration of the Nepalese Army into one that truly represents a multi-ethnic people's democracy has also posed serious challenges. Senior army officers have been clear in public and private that integration would threaten the integrity, honesty and professionalism of the force. The army has proposed various options, the latest of which envisages a separate security force of 12,000 personnel, half of whom would be drawn from the People's Liberation Army.

The last-minute agreement in mid-May 2011 by the three principal parties to extend the tenure of the constituent assembly merely reflected their desire to avoid pushing Nepal into a vacuum, with basic tenets of a new constitution still the subject of bitter disagreement. Although Dahal appeared to have overcome an immediate challenge to his leadership the original conflicts within the Maoists over ideology and personality have not been resolved. Prime Minister Jhal Nath Khanal's resignation in mid-August, in the midst of deep divisions within both the CPN-UML and the Nepali Congress, came days before the arrival of President Hu Jintao's special envoy in Kathmandu. Zhou Yongkang, a member of the Chinese Communist Party's powerful nine-member Politburo Standing

Committee and the country's top security official, led a large delegation with an agenda primarily aimed at boosting security co-operation along the Nepal–Tibet border. Nepal's deepening instability appears to have united Beijing and New Delhi behind the Nepalese military, with the aim being to provide the basic steadiness they seek to continue their rivalry.

Conclusion

The failure of Nepalese democratic parties and the Maoists to formalize a post-monarchical constitution within the stipulated time frame has precipitated active external lobbying, which in turn has deepened the country's political turmoil. Fear of a return to violence led by a dissenting faction of the Nepalese Maoists grips China and India, both of which seek stability in the strategic doorstep buffer zone as part of their global rise. The United States, for its part, is wary of the prospect of having to take sides between the Asian giants in the event of a serious crisis.

Chinese experts have argued that Beijing supported the monarchy because it was patriotic and followed a "correct" foreign policy. Today they would be likely to adapt to the evolving situation in Nepal in keeping with pragmatic self-interest. It increasingly appears that Beijing is seeking to build a wider – and more durable – nationalist alliance comprising Maoists, former royalists, sections of the CPN-UML and elements of the Terai-based parties. But in its quest for a new role in Nepal, China must overcome renewed skepticism among its people and confront the complex external dynamics its political intrusions have energized.

12 Beyond Tibet

China's quest to secure its place in Nepal has been intensified by the pace with which its concerns have gone beyond the issue of Tibet there. Historically Nepal was viewed a "near barbarian" nation that needed to be kept in check as a means of stabilizing the periphery; today it has become for the Chinese a conduit to south Asia in the broadest sense of the term. A prominent Chinese expert on south Asia recently contended that India itself was prompting Beijing to reassess its policy in the region. Arguing that New Delhi had failed to address the "strategic autonomy" of other south Asian nations, he described the resultant discordance as a threat to Chinese interests. If India is anxious to lead south Asia by virtue of its size and strength, he contended, then it must only do so with the consent of its smaller neighbors.[1]

New Delhi dismisses such talk as part of a Chinese plot to pit India against the rest of south Asia. A growing and increasingly vociferous school of thought in India believes China's new assertiveness in Myanmar, Bangladesh, Sri Lanka and Pakistan have given it maritime security in the form of a "string of pearls" around India. This group sees a supportive – even if not entirely compliant – Nepal, providing Beijing direct land access to the Indian heartland through Nepal's long and unregulated border with India.[2] China's military build-up in Tibet thus becomes an inseparable dimension of India's perceptions of China's transportation and infrastructural connections with Nepal.

While India is unlikely to accede to Chinese pre-eminence in Nepal, it may have few alternatives, at least in the near term. Despite India's sustained support for Nepal's democratic aspirations, and generous economic assistance, Nepalese public opinion has hardened against the motives and intentions of New Delhi.[3] Indian security forces may already be stretched by insurgencies within its own boundaries, but pre-emptive military action by the Chinese in Nepal's hostile terrain would be unviable. Indian maneuvering in Nepalese politics is likely to continue, but only at the cost of further opprobrium from the Nepalese. As for soft power, India already wields much of it in Nepal. India could seek to use the growing pressure China has been exerting on successive Nepalese governments to crack down on the political activities of Tibetan exiles, thereby contrasting itself as more benign and concerned neighbor.

History suggests that Beijing's new assertiveness in Nepal could easily defer to that quintessentially Chinese pragmatism, thereby recognizing India's primacy in the Himalayan state. But history alone may not be a reliable pointer. China lost its long-standing ally, the Nepalese monarchy, at a time of growing challenges in Tibet. The issue of Tibetan freedom has assumed a momentum of its own in the West, which allows governments to disclaim involvement and attribute action to popular pressure. Having invested so much by way of military–security operations and development efforts through its "Go West" campaign, China has realized that internal stabilization efforts alone would not succeed in settling the issue of Tibet's status. Continued political instability in Nepal creates new vulnerabilities for Tibet and potentially also for the neighboring region of Xinjiang. Nepalese tolerance for the exercise of Tibetan democracy among exiles runs counter to Chinese interests. Beijing's much-vaunted claim of non-interference in the domestic affairs of other states faces a serious challenge with regard to Nepal. Yet Nepal's deepening instability, fueled by long-term latent grievances and the proliferation of external players, makes China remaining aloof less likely.

Complex dynamics

Chinese assertiveness in Nepal is likely to grow as part of its growing profile in south Asia and beyond. In pursuing its new-found activism, however, China faces a far more complex set of regional and international dynamics. The quality and content of Sino-Indian relations – centered in large measure on the Tibet issue – will be influenced by contextual, perceptual, institutional and generational factors. Moreover, there is a growing variety and volatility of the external variables that could affect bilateral relations. Chief among them has been the United States' own relations with China and with India. And then there are the less prominent players like the European Union, Pakistan, Japan and Russia that have the potential – if not already the power – to affect China's options and responses in Nepal.

Officially Sino-Indian relations have been improving. Trade between the south Asian giants, which stood at $2 billion in 2000–2001, reached an estimated $60 billion in 2010 and is expected to rise to $100 billion by 2015. In public Chinese and Indian leaders take every opportunity to extol their burgeoning economic relationship and to promise political and diplomatic progress. Behind the official good will, however, there has been a rising stridency in the media and academic circles in both countries. Some Chinese commentators have been warning India not to forget the "lesson" of 1962, with at least one calling for the dismemberment of India with the help of its smaller neighbors.[4] The public mood, too, seems to be hardening. One Chinese online survey in 2009 revealed that 90 percent of the respondents viewed India as a threat to their country.[5]

India, too, has seen a surge of vociferous academic and expert opinion on the nature, scope and content of the China threat. Some have been writing of war, on some scale, and soon, with one going as far as specifying a date: 2012.[6] Progress will depend on how China and India manage and overcome old and new challenges as they continue to rise in power and influence. The boundary dispute, Tibet, the economic content of the relationship, and China's role in the wider south Asian region are among the key issues. With Nepal figuring in each of them in one way or another, the nation is bound to experience any direct fallout.

The 1962 war essentially maintained the status quo along the 4,057 km border. Border talks have been proceeding slowly, fueling perceptions among some Indians that Beijing is merely lulling them into complacency and buying time to boost its comprehensive power. By appearing to suggest – or at least allowing Kathmandu to perceive – that it may have a role in resolving its territorial dispute with India over Kalapani, Beijing, in New Delhi's view, is demonstrating bad faith. While there has been no Chinese reaction to Nepal's small but vociferous movement campaigning to recover lands the British annexed through the 1816 Sugauli Treaty and which became part of independent India, Nepalese nationalists could seek to step up efforts to enlist Beijing's support.[7]

The People's Liberation Army's official history of the 1962 Sino-Indian War identifies Indian ambitions in Tibet as the root cause of the conflict. Mao once told a visiting Nepalese delegation that, in the opinion of the Indian government, Tibet belongs to India.[8] Although India has recognized Tibet as part of China, Beijing is not persuaded. The Dalai Lama, from Beijing's perspective, is not only a spiritual leader but also head of the unlawful government-in-exile. Without the active co-operation and tacit approval of the Indian government, he would not have been able to travel abroad for political activities.

The 2008 protests in Tibet, on the eve of the Beijing Olympics, were the most significant since 1959. With the three external powers most active on the Tibet issue – India, the United States and the European Union – increasingly involved in Nepal's peace process, Beijing's concerns about destabilization from that volatile frontier have grown. The inevitable passing of the Fourteenth Dalai Lama and ensuing succession politics are certain to energize an increasingly restless exile community in Nepal and those living across the porous border in India.

The Chinese passed regulations in 2007 that, in effect, ensured their final say in the selection of the new Dalai Lama. Tenzin Gyatso, the current Dalai Lama who in March 2011 announced his retirement from active day-to-day leadership, has said in the past that he might break with tradition and name a successor and that his successor might not even be reincarnated inside Tibet.[9] In an effort to forestall potential unrest inside Tibet, Beijing has begun adopting a number of measures. Substantial levels of aid have been pledged for the estimated six and a half million Tibetans living in what Beijing has designated as the Tibet Autonomous Region as well as in the neighboring provinces of Sichuan, Gansu and Qinghai.[10]

Many Indians believe that a resolution of the Tibet issue holds the key to a durable settlement with China. Hard-liners in India are becoming more forthright in their assertion that New Delhi should exploit what they consider China's Achilles heel. To secure progress on the border question, or on Kashmir, they feel India should remind the Chinese that by stepping up political, diplomatic and even military support for the Dalai Lama India should make it harder for its neighbor to maintain control over Tibet.[11] That confidence, however, is negated somewhat by Indian suspicions that the Karmapa Lama, whom many see as at least a transitional leader after the Dalai Lama's death and whom the Tibetan spiritual leader has espoused, might be a Chinese plant.[12]

Power-hungry giants

A new security crisis in Tibet would create a substantial flow of refugees into Nepal, increasing its geo-strategic vulnerabilities at a time when the Himalayan state is increasingly feeling squeezed by two of the world's fastest-growing energy consumers. China sees a link between Nepal's vast hydropower generation potential and Beijing's energy needs for furthering the development of its own western regions. Beijing insists its companies enjoy a reputation for the highest efficiencies and lowest cost and that they could resolve such issues as guarantees on market stability, security and contracts through regular dialogue.[13]

China's growing interest in hydroelectricity projects in Nepal as a means of fueling Tibet's development would raise the stakes for India, which has traditionally seen Nepal's water resources as falling exclusively within its zone of control. Many Nepalese have long-suspected that New Delhi is less interested in the development of the country's hydropower potential and more interested in controlling Nepal's water resources.[14] With China's emergence as a potential investor – and importer – the geo-political risks are certain to increase. Topography would continue to favor India, where all the Nepalese rivers flow. But that would provide small comfort. China is poised to enter as a direct stakeholder in Nepal's water resources at a time when New Delhi is already wary of Beijing's plans to divert the rivers of Tibet for irrigation, a move which could leave parts of India parched.[15]

Although Beijing has replaced Washington as New Delhi's top trading partner, India is a secondary source of commerce for China. Moreover, the trading relationship is profoundly unbalanced – with a reported $10 billion deficit in 2008. Indian exports to China are limited in their variety, and consist mostly of vast quantities of iron ore. The Chinese, on the other hand, have swamped the Indian market with manufactured goods.[16] New Delhi accuses Kathmandu of aiding the smuggling of Chinese consumer goods, which are popular throughout India. Such tensions are bound to grow as the Chinese bolster trade and transport links with Nepal.

As a matter of principle the Asian giants say they will not allow differences in any area to impede co-operation, where possible. This idealism could create too many points of potential conflict. The challenge is compounded by the perceptions that prevail in each country about the other. The people's values, attitudes, needs and expectations, institutional and generational, all point to external variables that can be mutually supportive or antagonistic at short notice. Although south Asia has traditionally ranked relatively low in Beijing's foreign policy agenda, some Chinese scholars insist their country has developed a more serious policy toward New Delhi and now acknowledge that India is becoming a major Asian power.[17] New Delhi, however, believes Beijing does not perceive India as an equal, a sentiment that plays into the hands of hard-liners.

Perceptions are heavily influenced by structural and institutional divergences gripping the partnership. With democracy institutionalized in India, it becomes tempting to bring in the factor of a future Chinese political system as an imponderable. Yet the question transcends the nature of the Chinese political system. Even if China were to move toward a more open and democratic system, would popularly elected leaders be any less sensitive about issues such as sovereignty and defense modernization? Specifically, they would have to move cautiously in negotiating a solution to the border dispute with India, given the potential for backlash among any number of constituencies.

Institutionally, experts have identified the People's Liberation Army as being far more hawkish in its attitude toward India and more suspicious of New Delhi's foreign policy objectives than the ruling civilian policy makers. In India, on the other hand, the military is seen as exerting a moderating influence on foreign policy toward China.[18] That seems to be changing, as the comments of the Indian army chief in late 2009 showed.[19] Even though in theory China's military is subservient to the Chinese Communist Party, the People's Liberation Army has been gaining substantial weight within the foreign policy-making process.[20] The candor with which the People's Liberation Army chief commented on Nepalese political affairs and his insistence on dealing directly with the Nepalese Army suggests that the military has gained a disproportionate influence over China's Nepal policy.

Should reforms in Indian civil–military relations allow senior officers a greater say in the defense policy-making process, that would change the parameters of the debate. Generational dynamics are also coming into play, as the new crop of leaders in India has come out of the 1962 "malaise" of defeat, and seems less deferential toward China. On the other hand, do China's new generation of leaders – lacking the personality of a Mao or a Deng – possess the credibility and stature to seek to change Beijing's basic orientation toward New Delhi?

US and India: unnatural allies

Despite these potential flashpoints it is hard to see New Delhi as a natural ally in a Washington-led effort to contain Beijing. The U.S. and India, to be sure, have come closer in remarkable ways in recent years. Having largely surmounted their Cold War era antagonisms, the world's two largest democracies have embarked on a truly unprecedented strategic partnership. The civil nuclear deal continues to be touted in both countries as a landmark development that has the potential to redesign the global security architecture. President George W. Bush, in essence, welcomed India to the nuclear club and played midwife to the birth of a new world power. Historians may eventually judge that act as a move of great strategic importance comparable to Nixon's opening to China.[21]

From the Indian viewpoint, matters are less sanguine. While playing the China card in India, some Indians conclude, Washington has tried to use the nuclear deal to not only draw New Delhi into the non-proliferation net but also block India from emerging as a fully-fledged nuclear weapons state. The effect of that, in the words of a leading Indian strategic analyst, would be to thwart India's rise as a true strategic peer to China.[22]

Indian skepticism of the United States runs deeper, rooted in its recognition of Washington's penchant for dictating to allies. Many Indians feel the United States endeavors to seize strategic and commercial opportunities in India without the readiness to make the necessary commitment that a long-term partnership entails, including being sensitive to each other's legitimate security concerns and interests.[23] President Barack Obama, like his predecessor, has sought to build strategic partnerships with both India and Pakistan to fight terrorism and advance democracy, which New Delhi considers inherently untenable.

Despite periodic public displays of a downturn in Washington–Beijing ties, there is still a feeling in New Delhi that China has become more important to the United States, at present, than India.[24] There is recognition that Washington would not want India to kowtow to a China seeking to supplant the United States as the leading force in Asia. But many Indians also acknowledge that the Americans also would not want to see the rise of a combative India. They see America's interest in Asia lying in hedging its own future options while balancing the various powers.[25]

While influential quarters in the U.S. have been candid in asserting their desire to build India as a counterweight to China, they also recognize the limits of that quest. The past continues to cast a shadow on the American view of India. India's espousal of non-alignment and subsequent proximity to the Soviet Union, coupled with American perceptions of Indian sanctimony on foreign policy, led to an estrangement between the world's two largest democracies.

Advocates of rapprochement on each side have different expectations. While the American motives sound idealistic, New Delhi appears to have made pragmatic calculations. In the words of one prominent Indian analyst, India "will never become another U.S. ally in the mould of the United Kingdom or Japan. But nor will it be an Asian France, seeking tactical independence within the framework of a formal alliance."[26] Even in the midst of their skepticism, Indian leaders can be expected to pursue the benefits of favorable U.S. ties, partly, too, as a hedge against any development of hostile ties with China. At a minimum, New Delhi would use its strategic ties with Washington to bolster its position in dealing with Beijing.[27]

Even where U.S. and Indian interests coincide, co-ordination is likely to be hampered by India's insistence on strategic autonomy. Accompanying a broad strategic convergence is an acknowledgment of a division of labor between them concerning Asian priorities. However, in south Asia, India certainly will seek to strengthen its traditional geo-political primacy by virtue of its growing economic and military superiority. As far as Nepal is concerned, it still remains the largest of the three vital Himalayan states that have presented Jawaharlal Nehru's generation such a challenge. Among the more skeptical observers in India, Washington's increased involvement in Nepal has been anathema. The drive to advance Indian autonomy is certain to be felt in Nepal, where New Delhi is jealously guarding its version of the Monroe Doctrine.

U.S. and China: joined at the hip

Despite their profound differences China and the United States recognize that they need each other more than ever before. Most of the challenges confronting the United States – be it combating terrorism, limiting the proliferation and spread of weapons of mass destruction, reining in North Korea's nuclear ambitions, ensuring energy security, or protecting the global environment – cannot be managed without China's active and constructive participation. The United States relies on Chinese surpluses and savings to finance its huge budget deficit, while cheap Chinese-made imports help keep down U.S. inflation. Further integrating China into the global community offers the best hope of shaping China's interests and conduct in accordance with international norms on security, trade, finance, and human rights, and encourages a collaborative approach in confronting the challenges both countries face.

The equation, however, could change swiftly. News that China has replaced Japan as the world's second largest economy has intensified debate on Chinese intentions. China's defense budget rose to be the second highest in the world in 2008, and its naval build-up has, in the opinion of a leading American analyst, caused "the loss of the Pacific Ocean as an American lake."[28] This ambivalence had already led to major shifts in American policy. In a major reappraisal in 2006, the Bush administration clubbed south and central Asia together as a single bureau within the State Department. The expanded department now deals with U.S. foreign policy and relations with eight of the 14 nations sharing a land border with China. By contrast, only four have land borders with India. Afghanistan has thus become a bridge between these two volatile regions.

Some Chinese experts dismiss the notion that India could be used to counterbalance their country. Their conclusions are based less on an appreciation of New Delhi's benign intentions vis-à-vis its northern neighbor than on Chinese perceptions of India's self-interest. India, like China, is an old civilization that has ambitions to become one of the main poles in a multipolar world.[29] Those who see India as a part of a strategy to contain China, too, warn that New Delhi would be the ultimate loser in such an alliance.[30] Beijing can be expected to play on New Delhi's nationalist instincts and its visceral aversion to foreign powers. Yet the Chinese recognize the benefits India would see in letting an informal alliance to take shape. In Beijing's view Washington might not be averse to allowing the informality to persist.[31] Perhaps out of these mixed feelings, Chinese commentators have warned Indians not to view New Delhi's unwillingness to align itself with the United States as a favor to Beijing.[32]

From the Chinese perspective the United States used the Maoist insurgency to build its presence in Nepal as part of the wider post 9/11 global military build-up. Washington's stress on the identity of views with New Delhi on Nepal, in the Chinese view, was more of a ploy to overcome Indian opposition.[33] Kathmandu saw one of the biggest American embassy build-ups in the post 9/11 era. The Obama administration's recent budget requests for the State Department included more funding for positions in the Kathmandu embassy. Yet by allowing the Americans some leeway in Nepal, Beijing may hope to dilute Indian influence and chip away at the containment alliance. The Obama administration, too, has played along. Its decision to confer on Beijing a stakeholder status in Nepal, equivalent to that which New Delhi has traditionally reserved for itself, underscores the scope for Sino-U.S. co-operation.

China and India: mutual interests

Skepticism about Washington has exacerbated Beijing and New Delhi's challenge of stabilizing their own bilateral relationship. At the same time there is a growing recognition of their mutual interests. Despite their dramatic rise, China and India, based on their per capita GDP, are likely to belong to the category of developing countries for many decades. This suggests that they will also have the motives and concerns that are faced by both developed *and* developing countries. They are likely to lean towards the developed world, or the developing world, depending on the issue involved.[34] The conflict in Iraq, Iran's nuclear weapons programme, global trade and the environment are just some of the issues that have positioned China and India together against U.S. policy.

Admittedly, the prospects on the Sino-Indian bilateral front are thus wide, entailing enough of a mixture of co-operation, competition and confrontation to engage optimists as well as pessimists. However, neither India nor China stands to benefit from an open rivalry, given their current strategies of accumulating power through economic growth and forging international links. Quiet competition – economic/political co-operation and muted strategic rivalry whenever possible – appears the likeliest outcome of bilateral relations over the next couple of decades.[35]

When Chinese leaders, officials and academics underscore how their country is some distance from becoming a global power, the emphasis is broadly aimed at countering the "China threat" school. But it also underscores the urgency with which Beijing desires to prevent India from joining any attempt at containing China. On the other hand, much as India has reason to suspect an expansion of Chinese influence in the region in the name of bolstering its periphery, it confronts another imperative. Despite its own improving ties with the U.S., Japan, Russia and the European Union, India cannot overlook the imperative of preventing the expansion of extra-regional influence in a way that could raise Chinese anxieties, thereby impinging on its own interests.

That imperative is in play in Nepal. Both countries played an important role in constructing a United Nations mission (UNMIN) with a limited mandate, despite their own unwillingness to set a precedent for their own countries. The strategic dialogue at foreign secretary level has allowed them to exchange views on stabilizing the situation. But the involvement of the European Union, Japan, Russia and Pakistan, among other nations, prevents broad-stroke interpretations and rationalizations.

China's motives and intentions in Nepal have long been open to diverse interpretations. Beijing, too, has often promoted ambiguity in order to calibrate its response to shifting dynamics. Still, some basic tenets of its policy are discernible. China does not see itself merely as a beneficiary of Nepal's desire to balance its relationship with India. Chinese academics and officials stress that the two countries have a 2,000-year history of traditional friendship and contact. Beijing notes that both countries, in their different ways, have been the victims of imperialism and colonialism. Such commonalities, in its view, provide the basis for an enduring relationship. Beijing is cognizant of the suspicions with which Nepalese view Chinese intentions.[36] It has been candid in asserting that, for a variety of reasons, it has not done enough to help Nepal in the past.[37]

Beijing's current assertiveness in Nepal is likely to grow because it represents the convergence of several Chinese policies. The maintenance of internal stability, the "Go West" development campaign, the reunification of the motherland, with its strong emphasis on Tibet and Taiwan, have become important Chinese concerns that are likely to become even more so. The People's Liberation Army has grown more assertive in these areas, amid growing calls to extend its role to safeguard China's "boundaries of national interests."[38]

After declining for much of the 1990s, the Sino-Nepalese economic partnership has grown. From a total of $140,000 in 2004–2005, China has raised its aid commitment to Nepal to $35.5 million in 2010–2011. While that amount is smaller than the $92.6 million India has pledged, Beijing's aid quantum represents a more than 250-fold increase compared to India's nearly 11-fold increase during the same period. (India is allowed to directly spend up to $700,000 in development/welfare activities without informing the Nepalese authorities.)[39] In recent years the structure of the Sino-Nepalese partnership has changed from one that comprised of grants focusing on light industries with pronounced political symbolism. Today Chinese companies are becoming increasingly involved in such diverse Nepalese sectors as mining and energy development, and the services sector. Tourism has become an essential component, with some 35,000 Chinese visiting Nepal annually, second only to the number of Indian visitors. Cultural diplomacy, traditionally promoted through exchange of dance and musical troupes, as well as academic and sports delegations, has been aggressively boosted through the Confucius Institute.[40] The announcement by a Beijing-backed foundation that it plans to spend $3 billion to transform Lumbini, Lord Buddha's birthplace, into a magnet for Buddhists around the world, marked a new high in China's quest to deploy soft power in Nepal, prompting fresh questions of its strategic and political motives as well.[41]

China's focus on deploying its soft power has not diminished the role of hard power. What is significant is that the military relationship, long stymied because of India's fierce opposition, has grown exponentially in recent years. Beijing continues to dispatch a bevy of military delegations to Nepal, seeking to build institutional partnerships. Beijing's military assertiveness must be viewed within five overall objectives behind the development of military power: regime security, territorial integrity, national unification, maritime security, and regional stability.[42] Four out of the five areas have links to Nepal. The March 2008 demonstrations and riots in Tibetan areas serves only to reinforce the view that threats to regime security such as ethnic unrest is a strategic issue that influences national unification, social stability and economic development.

The Tibet litmus test

Officially, every government in Kathmandu has adhered to the "One China" policy. But repeated reaffirmations by Nepal do not seem to have assuaged China. The frequency with which China expresses its concerns on this matter, and the fact that Nepal feels the need to continually reiterate its adherence, demonstrates the elusiveness of stability on this vital front. China has become candid in articulating how it sees Nepal's position on Tibet as a litmus test of its ties, and innovative in seeking to secure proper respect for its sensitivities. But Sino-Nepalese relations today cover an entire gamut of issues, with Beijing becoming an increasingly influential player in the China–Nepal–India regional dynamic. China's behavior is clearly reflective of a power that has used every opportunity to expand its influence and relative power over its smaller neighbor.[43] Securing a stable and friendly Nepal has always been one of the core elements of China's south Asia strategy.[44] That imperative has grown commensurately with south Asia's growing geo-political value to China.

India is apprehensive of the planned extension of the Qinghai–Lhasa railway to the Nepalese border. The main purpose of the railway is to integrate Tibet more closely to the Chinese economy. Critics insist it militarily strengthens China's hold over Tibet. India, for its part, sees the railway strengthening China's offensive military capability against India. A planned extension from Lhasa to Shigatse, in the words of a leading Indian strategic analyst, would boost China's military transport and reinforcement capabilities against India. At short notice the People's Liberation Army could intensify military pressure on Indian by rapidly mobilizing up to 12 divisions.

This enhanced capability comes amid a string of new Chinese military airfields along the frontier with India, and an increase in Chinese missile strength on the Tibetan plateau. Furthermore, the railroad helps augment China's missile-transport capability by facilitating the transport of intermediate-range missiles, but also by allowing China to rail-base and conceal the location of its intercontinental ballistic missiles.[45] Once expanded to the Nepalese border, many Indians fear, this in itself will have a major impact on China's influence in Nepal, Bhutan, and on the northeast Indian states.

China is about to complete an ultra-modern dry port in Gyirong (Chinese for Kerong), through which the lucrative trans-Himalayan trade once thrived. The local government of the Tibet Autonomous Region (TAR) has said that the Gyirong Port located in TAR's Xigaze (Shigatse) Prefecture will begin operations in 2011, although some portion of the construction work will continue even after it is opened to public. With road and rail access to the Nepalese border available, Chinese goods, investment, migration, and tourism in these Himalayan fringe-lands will increase.

Nepal's expectations of reclaiming part of its profitable legacy of a trans-Himalayan entrepot have faced tensions. The southern Nepalese plains bordering India were quiet for much of the Maoist insurgency. But the Chinese are now complaining of the growing lawlessness there.[46] Implicit in that concern is a fear that that the open border might turn into a no-go area akin to the Afghan–Pakistan border, which would undermine Beijing's broader objective of easier access to the south Asian heartland.[47] There have been reports of Chinese agents crossing the porous India–Nepal border for the purpose of infiltrating Tibetan exile groups in India and monitoring the activities of the Dalai Lama and his associates.

All the diverse elements of the Sino-Indian rivalry play into each other because Nepal offers the major place where India feels it can challenge China. For its part, China knows that Nepal is susceptible to punitive Indian pressures but understands the value of being assertive there, because, despite India's ability to intervene more substantially in Nepal's domestic politics, any overt Indian intervention would be a strategic mistake. Such a move would almost certainly bring China's opposition and involvement. Conversely, lack of Indian initiative and involvement in Nepal carries its own risks. Nepal's social and economic development could be undermined by continued political violence and instability, providing further fuel for insurgency. Indian strategists worry that a weak, unstable, and "failing" Nepal might provide China with opportunity to directly interfere in south Asia.[48]

Maoist leader Dahal sought to tap into this anxiety by calling for strategic co-operation between China and India on Nepal, to boost regional stability. It was immediately unclear whether Dahal, who made the proposal after a visit to China, reflected the views of his hosts. But subsequent comments in the Chinese and Indian press were sympathetic. China's decision to appoint as its new ambassador in Kathmandu someone with experience in multilateral diplomacy on the Korean Peninsula is also viewed as part of this objective.

Conclusion

Tibet will continue to play an important role in Nepal's evolution as the territory becomes an ever more key factor in India–China relations. Nepal sees the rapid transformations in China's western regions as opportunities to expand ties with China and beyond through the emerging physical connections.[49] Nepal sees this process as irreversible and seeks Indian participation for wider regional advantage. While expressing sympathy for Nepal's developmental aspirations, India is alarmed by China's military build-up and infrastructure development in the region, as well as reported plans to divert or dam rivers that rise in Tibet and flow into India. China's territorial claims on India, its deepening alliance with

Pakistan and a perceived shift in China's position on Kashmir has led to a hardening of India's position on Tibet. Chinese insecurity about Tibet, on the other hand, will remain an important determinant of its approach toward India. New Delhi, which has been unable to allay Beijing's fears resulting from the presence of the Dalai Lama and a large Tibetan refugee population in India, is even less likely to quell them now that more voices than ever are seeking to use the issue as a bargaining chip in the overall bilateral relationship.[50] Nepal, however, will also increasingly find itself caught in the other elements underpinning the India–China rivalry.

Complicating this equation is the mutual skepticism of China and India of the United States. In Nepal, Washington already completes – to paraphrase the words of a prominent American analyst used in a different context – a "romantic" triangular contest that is inherently unstable.[51] The post 9/11 years have seen the United States bolster military relations with the Nepalese army, build a new and modern embassy complex, ostracize and then engage with the Maoists. Kathmandu, under a government including the Maoists, in May 2011 announced it would send troops to Iraq while Washington has evinced interest in signing a permanent Status of Forces Agreement with Nepal, which would establish the rights and privileges of American personnel present in the host country in support of the larger security arrangement. Thus, growing U.S. involvement in Nepal could impel the regional giants to co-operate, to some degree, over Nepal. The nature and scope of this triangular contest will be influenced by the increasing prominence of the European Union, Japan, Pakistan and Russia, as well as non-government international advocacy groups, all of which have their independent interests in Nepal.[52]

As China's global power grows, its policy towards Nepal is likely to be increasingly characterized by two clear trends: the return of what Martin Jacques has called the Middle Kingdom mentality, and the assertiveness of the People's Liberation Army. As its power and influence grows, China is likely to maintain its traditionally strong hierarchical view of the world, based on a combination of racial and cultural attitudes, which will play a fundamental role in shaping how China views other nations and peoples and its own position at the top of the ladder. As a civilizational state possessing a past that casts a huge shadow over its present, China is unlikely to keep Nepal – the last tributary to the Celestial Empire – out of its sights. While it is unlikely that China would resurrect any of its irredentist claims, its attitudes and approaches to Nepal could draw heavily from the legacy of the tributary relationship.

The second fact is the growing role of the People's Liberation Army in the formulation of Chinese foreign policy. Nepal has become the focus of the convergence of several Chinese policies such as the maintenance of internal stability, its "Go West" development campaign and the re-unification of the motherland with its strong emphasis on Tibet and Taiwan. The fact that the People's Liberation Army has grown more assertive in these areas, amid growing calls to extend its role to safeguard China's "boundaries of national interests,"[53] has tremendous implications for Nepal. While the external focus has fallen on possible Chinese perceptions of the benefits arising from a friendly Maoist-led Nepal, Beijing's interest in the restoration of the monarchy as a force of stability should not be discounted.[54]

China enjoys its greatest asset in the form of the Nepalese people's fierce sense of independence from India. Even the Indians have become candid in acknowledging that China gives the impression of non-interference yet at the same time manages to get its way most of the time. Meanwhile India makes its interests in Nepal known and is increasingly viewed as a domineering neighbor meddling in Nepal's policies and politics.[55] Beijing can be expected to continue reminding the Nepalese of their proud legacy of independence and dangle the prospect of economic and social prosperity to win over public opinion. Chinese assertiveness, however, carries its risks. Of the two key characteristics of the tributary system, Nepal would have little problem in acknowledging the over-whelming size of China compared to her neighbors. But Nepal's willingness to accept Chinese benevolent superiority – in the traditional sense of the Chinese tributary system – will be based on the intensity of its desire to ward off Indian pressure. If the Chinese become as meddlesome as the Indians, then the Nepalese people could become less deferential to the Chinese.

Any Nepalese perception of Chinese imperial behavior – on military-security co-operation, on Nepal's treatment of Tibetan exiles' political rights, on overall attitudes towards the Nepalese – is something that India would certainly seek to benefit from. In the post-monarchy years, China's newfound activism has engendered the kind of media and public scrutiny of its motives that was traditionally reserved for India. If the Sino-Indian rivalry in the past focused on the rulers, the arena has clearly shifted to winning Nepalese hearts and minds.

Notes

1 Trails of truth and trade

1 N. Bhattarai, *Nepal and China: A Historical Perspective*, 2010, pp. 1–2.
2 J.K. Fairbank, *China: A Modern History*, 1992, p. 75; V.K. Manandhar, *Cultural and Political Aspects of Nepal–China Relations*, 1999, pp. 1–2.
3 L. Petech, *Northern India According to The Shui-Ching-Chu*, pp. 35–6; N.N. Pandey, *Nepal–China Relations*, 2005, pp. 53–4.
4 Contrary to some assertions that Buddhabhadra was born in central India or Kashmir, Nepalese scholars maintain he was born in Kapilvastu, before moving to Jalalabad and Kashmir. See M.B. Shakya, *The Life of Nepalese Buddhist Master Buddhabhadra (359–429 CE.): From Chinese Sources*, 2009.
5 V.K. Manandhar, *Cultural and Political Aspects*, 1999, pp. 8–9.
6 S.H. Wriggins, *The Silk Road Journey with Xuanzang*, 2004, pp. 101–4.
7 R. Shaha, "Ancient and Medieval Nepal," *Kailash*, 14:3–4, 1988, p. 159.
8 J. Keay, *China: A History*, 2009, pp. 240–2.
9 Some scholars, failing to obtain credible Nepalese sources, have long thought Bhrikuti was a mythological figure (G. Tucci, "The Wives of Srong-btsan-sgam-po," *Oriens Extremus*, Vol. 9, 1962, pp. 121–6). However, some Tibetan accounts make Bhrikuti the daughter of Amsuvarma, while others list her as Udaya Dev's daughter, thus making her Narendra Dev's sister.
10 T.W.D. Shakabpa, *Tibet: A Political History*, 1967, p. 26.
11 N. Bhattarai, *Nepal and China*, 2010, p. 22.
12 L.E. Rose, *Nepal: Strategy for Survival*, 1971, p. 11.
13 D.R. Regmi, *Ancient Nepal*, 1960, p. 214.
14 B.R. Acharya, *Nepalko Samkshipta Brittanta* [A Concise Account of Nepal], 1966, p. 8.
15 Tan Chung, "Ageless Neighbourliness Between India and China," *China Report* 15:2, 1979, p. 11; T.R. Manandhar and T.P. Mishra, *Nepal's Quinquennial Missions to China*, 1986, pp. 3–4.
16 V.K. Manandhar, *A Comprehensive History Of Nepal–China Relations Up To 1955 A.D.*, Vol. 1, 2004, p. 38.
17 Ibid., p. 51. The more enterprising Chinese travelers were not discouraged. Yijing, a monk who likely witnessed Xuanzang's death and grand funeral in Changan, used a circuitous land and sea route to India in AD 671 during a journey that took him to Lumbini. Yijing was the first Chinese source to record that Hindus believed Manjusri came from China. See I-Tsing, *A Record of the Buddhist Religion*, trans. J. Takukusu, 1896, p. 136.
18 A second Nepalese monk, Vimoksasena, had reached China in the sixth century. S. Thapa, "Buddhist Sanskrit Manuscripts of Nepal," Dec. 2009.
19 J. Whelpton, *A History of Nepal*, Cambridge, 2005, p. 29.

20 Wang Hongwei, "Some Thoughts On Sino-Nepal Relations," *Spotlight* magazine, Oct. 20–26, 2000, p. 24; V.K. Manandhar, *Comprehensive History*, Vol. 1, 2004, p. 52.
21 A. Paludan, *Chronicle of the Chinese Emperors*, 1998, p. 151.
22 J. Waley-Cohen, *The Culture of War in China*, 2006, pp. 51–2.
23 V.K. Manandhar, *Comprehensive History*, Vol. 1, 2004, p. 55.
24 T.L. Guta. "Aniko: Image Weaver," *Contributions to Nepalese Studies*, 24:1, January 1997, p. 72.
25 One of Arniko's assistants committed the iconographic precepts to paper. His "Canon of the measurements for making statues" has since remained the standard manual for casting Lamaist Buddhist images in China. See H.A. van Oort, *The Iconography of Chinese Buddhism in Traditional China, Part 1*, 1986, p. 6.
26 V.K. Manandhar, *Comprehensive History*, Vol. 1, 2004, pp. 64–5.
27 Manandhar and Mishra, *Quinquennial Missions*, 1986, p. 6; Rose, *Strategy for Survival*, 1971, p. 12.
28 E. Bretschneider, *Medieval Researches from Eastern Asiatic Sources*, Vol. 2, 1888, p. 222.
29 Ibid., pp. 222–3.
30 Shih-shan Henry Tsai, *The Eunuchs in the Ming Dynasty*, 1996, p. 121.
31 *Dictionary of Ming Biography 1368–1644*, 1976, pp. 552–3.
32 Shih-shan Henry Tsai, *The Eunuchs*, 1996, p. 127.
33 *Dictionary of Ming Biography*, 1976, pp. 552–3.
34 Manandhar and Mishra, *Quinquennial Missions*, 1986, pp. 6–7.
35 Fairbank, *China*, 1992, pp. 137–40.
36 T. Laird, *The Story of Tibet: Conversations with the Dalai Lama*, 2006, p. 145.
37 Shakabpa, *Tibet*, 1967, p. 111.
38 Ibid., pp. 112–13.
39 W.W. Smith, *Tibetan Nation*, 1996, p. 113.
40 Waley-Cohen, *Culture of War*, 2006, p. 52.
41 P.R. Shakya, *Nepal and China: International Relations and Trans-Himalayan Trade in the 18th Century*, 2002, p. 87.
42 C.R. Markham, G. Bogle and T. Manning, *Narratives of the Mission of George Bogle to Tibet and of the Journey of Thomas Manning to Lhasa*, 2nd ed., 1879, p.liv.
43 W. Digby, *1857. A Friend in Need. 1887. Friendship Forgotten*, 1890, p. 21.
44 For a discussion of this arrangement, see Rose, *Strategy for Survival*, 1971, pp. 13–14.
45 I. Joshi. "Nepal-Tibbat Sambandha: Aitihasik Simhabolokan" [Nepal-Tibet Relations: An Historical Review], *Ancient Nepal*, No. 147, June 2001.
46 M.C. Goldstein, *The Snow Lion and the Dragon*, 1997, p. 15.
47 L. Petech, *China and Tibet in the Early Eighteenth Century*, 1950, p. 70.
48 Goldstein, *Snow Lion*, 1997, p. 18.
49 Manandhar and Mishra, *Quinquennial Missions*, 1986, p. 7.
50 L.F. Stiller, *The Rise of the House of Gorkha*, 1973, pp. 117–18.
51 Ibid., pp. 101–2.

2 Bubbling between boulders

1 P. Landon, *Nepal*, Vol. 1, 1928, p. 67.
2 R. Shaha. *Nepali Politics: Retrospect and Prospect*, 1978, p. 104.
3 L.E. Rose, *Nepal: Strategy for Survival*, 1971, p. 25.
4 P.R. Shakya, *Nepal and China: International Relations and Trans-Himalayan Trade in the 18th Century*, 2002, pp. 129–32.
5 The condition was that the raja must pay for the operation, and the British would thereafter gain control of his state and receive over half its annual revenue. K. Teltscher, *The High Road to China*, 2006, p. 16.

6 P.R. Uprety, *Nepal–Tibet Relations 1850–1930*, 2nd ed., 1998, p. 30.

7 Teltscher, *High Road*, 2006, p. 18.

8 J. Rowland, *A History of Sino-Indian Relations*, 1967, p. 15.

9 C.R. Markham, G. Bogle and T. Manning, *Narratives of the Mission of George Bogle to Tibet*, 2nd ed, 1879, pp. 157–8.

10 Ibid., p. lxvii.

11 Ibid., pp. 150–1.

12 Ibid., p. 205.

13 B.R. Acharya. "The Reign Of King Pratap Simha," *Regmi Research Series*, Year 6, No. 2, 1974, pp. 34–5; Rose, *Strategy for Survival*, 1971, p. 32.

14 P.R. Shakya, *Nepal and China*, 2002, pp. 45–6.

15 L.F. Stiller, *The Rise of the House of Gorkha*, 1973, p. 148.

16 Teltscher, *High Road*, 2006, p. 154.

17 A. Lamb, *British India And Tibet, 1766–1910*, 1986, pp. 11–12.

18 Rose, *Strategy for Survival*, 1971, p. 38; P.R. Shakya, *Nepal and China*, 2002, p. 47.

19 Even after attaining majority, the Dalai Lama refused to assume direct control. T.W.D. Shakabpa, *Tibet: A Political History*, 1967, pp. 155–6.

20 W. Kirkpatrick, *An Account of the Kingdom of Nepal*, 1811, p. 340.

21 T.R. Manandhar and T.P. Mishra, *Nepal's Quinquennial Missions to China*, 1986, p. 11.

22 P.R. Shakya, *Nepal and China*, 2002, p. 111.

23 Rose, *Strategy for Survival*, 1971, pp. 40–1.

24 V.K. Manandhar, *A Comprehensive History Of Nepal–China Relations Up To 1955 A.D.*, Vol. 1, 2004, pp. 80–1.

25 Manandhar and Mishra, *Quinquennial Missions*, 1986, p. 12.

26 See V.K. Manandhar, *Comprehensive History*, Vol. 1, 2004, p. 83.

27 For details of this mission, see V.K. Manandhar, *Cultural and Political Aspects of Nepal–China Relations*, 1999, pp. 13–15.

28 P.R. Shakya, *Nepal and China*, 2002, p. 168.

29 V.K. Manandhar, *Comprehensive History*, Vol. 1, 2004, pp. 86–7; Shakabpa, *Tibet*, 1967, pp. 162–5.

30 P.R. Shakya, *Nepal and China*, 2002, p. 171.

31 C.D. Boulger and M.W. Hazeltine, *China*, 1901, p. 236.

32 E. H. Parker, "Nepaul And China," *The Imperial And Asiatic Quarterly Review And Oriental And Colonial Record*, 7:13–14, 1899, p. 70; D. Strand and M.K. Chan, "Militarism and Militarization in Modern Chinese History," 1982, p. 54.

33 V.K. Manandhar, *Comprehensive History*, Vol. 1, 2004, p. 95; Rose, *Strategy for Survival*, 1971, p. 58.

34 M.J. Kunwar, "China and War in the Himalayas, 1792–1793," *The English Historical Review*, 77:303, 1962, p. 290.

35 V.K. Manandhar, *Comprehensive History*, Vol. 1, 2004, pp. 95–6.

36 *Qinding Guoerkajilu* [Official Summary Account of the Pacification of Gorkha], 1992, original Chinese and English translation quoted in P.R. Shakya, *Nepal and China*, 2002, p. 129.

37 Damodar Pande was the son of a key commander of Prithvi Narayan Shah's army who perished during the first attack on Kirtipur. In recognition of his service, Prithvi Narayan granted the Pande family responsibility for Tibetan affairs in perpetuity. Stiller, *House of Gorkha*, 1973, p. 61.

38 In August 1792, Bahadur Shah sought ten guns and ten European artillery officers. The following month he requested two battalions each of Europeans and sepoys, complete with military stores and a suitable number of guns. L.F. Stiller, "The Role of Fear in the Unification of Nepal," *Contributions to Nepalese Studies*, 1:2, 1974, p. 72.

39 Kirkpatrick, *Nepal*, 1811, pp. 348–9.

40 Ibid., pp. 349–50.

41 T. Smith. *Narrative of a Five Years' Residence at Nepaul*, Vol. 1, 1852, pp. 160–1.
42 Kirkpatrick, *Nepal*, pp. 351–2.
43 Landon, *Nepal*, Vol. 1, 1928, p. 69.
44 Exactly when the Sino-Nepalese treaty was signed remains in dispute. Rose (*Strategy for Survival*, 1971, p. 64) suggests the end of September, while Nepalese military sources state that the final battle was fought on October 5, 1792.
45 P.J. Rana, in his *Life of Maharaja Sir Jang Bahadur* (1909) quotes the key provisions of the treaty. But no Nepalese record corresponds to them. A leading Nepalese historian suggests that no treaty was ever drawn up or signed at the cessation of the Sino-Nepalese war in 1792 (C.R. Nepali, "Nepal-Chin Yuddha," *Sharada*, 1956, pp. 202–16). There were only exchanges of letters between the Chinese commander and the Nepalese Durbar. On the Chinese side, the terms of the agreement are found scattered through Fukangan's reports to the emperor and letters to the Nepal Darbar. (Rose, *Strategy for Survival*, 1971, p. 65).
46 The Chinese had initially demanded that the king or regent lead the tribute mission, but Kathmandu cited the difficulties of distance and time. The court pledged to send someone with the rank of *kaji*, usually a leading noble ranking third or fourth in the administrative hierarchy. See V.K. Manandhar, *Comprehensive History*, Vol. 2, 2004, p. 66.
47 H.A. Oldfield, *Sketches From Nipal*, Vol. 1, 1880, pp. 283–4.
48 V.K. Manandhar, *Comprehensive History*, Vol. 1, 2004, p. 176.
49 Ibid., pp. 148–9.
50 L. Boulnois, "Chinese Maps and Prints on the Tibet Gorkha War of 1788–92," *Kailash*, 1989, p. 98.
51 Strand and Chan, "Militarism and Militarization," 1982, p. 54.
52 J.D. Spence, *The Search for Modern China*, 1991, p. 112. Yingcong Dai, "Military Finance of the High Qing Period: An Overview," in N.D. Cosmo (ed.), *Military Culture in Imperial China*, 2009, p. 312.
53 Quoted in P.R. Shakya, *Nepal and China*, 2002, p. 180.
54 H.E.M. James, *The Long White Mountain*, 1888, pp. 413–14.
55 Teltscher, *High Road*, 2006, p. 250.
56 Manandhar and Mishra, *Quinquennial Missions*, 1986, pp. 49–50.
57 The proscription would last until 1963 when, following a request from the 16th Karmapa, the Tibetan Government-in-Exile lifted the ban.
58 P.C. Perdue, *China Marches West: The Qing Conquest of Central Eurasia*, 2005, p. 440.
59 V.K. Manandhar, "The Nepalese Quinquennial Missions Of 1792 And 1795 To China," *Ancient Nepal*, No. 145, July 2000, p. 10.
60 Ibid., p. 11.
61 Parker, *Nepaul and China*, 1899, p. 77.
62 B.R. Acharya, *Aba Yasto Kahile Na Hos* [May This Never Happen Again], 2006, p. 16.
63 Ibid., pp. 17–18.
64 L.E. Rose and J.T. Scholz, *Nepal: Profile of a Himalayan Kingdom*, 1980, p. 16.
65 Stiller, *House of Gorkha*, 1973, pp. 173–4.

3 Containment and carnage

1 E.H. Parker, "Nepaul And China," *The Imperial And Asiatic Quarterly Review And Oriental And Colonial Record*, 7:13–14, 1899, p. 77.
2 "The Assassination of Rana Bahadur Shah," *Regmi, Research Series*, Year 3, No. 5, 1971, pp. 101–2.
3 T.R. Manandhar and T.P. Mishra, *Quinquennial Missions*, 1986, pp. 23–4.
4 L. James, *Raj: The Making and Unmaking of British India*, 1997, p. 69.

5 T.R. Manandhar, "British Residents at the Court of Nepal During the 19th Century," *Voice of History*, Vol. 17–20 (1), 2005, p. 6.

6 A. Lamb, *British India And Tibet, 1766–1910*. 1986, pp. 28–9.

7 L.F. Stiller, *The Rise of the House of Gorkha*, 1973, p. 307.

8 H.A. Oldfield, *Sketches From Nipal*, Vol 1, 1880, p. 292.

9 For instance, the ambans refused a leading member the Pande cabinet asylum in Tibet. V.K. Manandhar, *A Comprehensive History Of Nepal-China Relations Up To 1955 A.D.*, Vol. 1, 2004, p. 186.

10 Stiller, *House of Gorkha*, 1973, p. 321.

11 F. Hamilton, *An Account of the Kingdom of Nepal: And of the Territories Annexed to this Dominion by the House of Gorkha*, 1819, p. 176.

12 Yingcong Dai, "Military Finance of the High Qing Period: An Overview," in N.D. Cosmo (ed.), *Military Culture in Imperial China*, 2009, p. 309.

13 Manandhar and Mishra, *Quinquennial Missions*, pp. 24–5.

14 L.E. Rose and J.T. Scholz, *Nepal: Profile of a Himalayan Kingdom*, 1980, p. 36.

15 Manandhar and Mishra, *Quinquennial Missions*, 1986, p. 25.

16 R.S. Gundry, *China and Her Neighbours*, 1893, pp. 120–2.

17 V.K. Manandhar, *Comprehensive History*, Vol. 2, 2004, pp. 69–70.

18 Gundry, *China and Her Neighbours*, 1893, pp. 120–2.

19 V.K. Manandhar, *Comprehensive History*, Vol. 2, 2004, pp. 69–70 and 77.

20 E.M. Tappan (ed.), *China, Japan, and the Islands of the Pacific* [Vol. I of The World's Story: A History of the World in Story, Song, and Art], 1914, p. 189.

21 V.K. Manandhar, *Comprehensive History*, Vol. 1, 2004, pp. 188–9.

22 W.W. Hunter, *Life of Brian Houghton Hodgson*, p. 99.

23 Rose, *Strategy for Survival*, 1971, p. 85; D. Twitchett and J.K. Fairbank (eds), *The Cambridge History of China. Vol. 10, Late Ch'ing, 1800–1911, Part 1*, 1978, p. 105; T.W.D. Shakabpa, *Tibet: A Political History*, 1967, p. 174.

24 D. Wright, *History of Nepal*, 1877, p. 53.

25 V.K. Manandhar, *Comprehensive History*, Vol. 1, 2004, p. 195.

26 T. Gould, *Imperial Warriors: Britain and the Gurkhas*, 1999, p. 70.

27 L. James, *Raj*, 1997, p. 65.

28 V.K. Manandhar, *Comprehensive History*, Vol. 1, 2004, p. 191; Rose, *Strategy for Survival*, 1971, p. 86.

29 D.J. Waller, *The Pundits: British Exploration of Tibet and Central Asia*, 2004, p. 175.

30 Twitchett and Fairbank, *Cambridge History of China*, 1978, p. 396.

31 V.K. Manandhar, *Comprehensive History*, Vol. 1, 2004, pp. 193–4.

32 In the event, the issue of the Nepal war did not seem to have come up during the Amherst mission. Lamb, *British India and Tibet*, 1986, p. 36.

33 The emperor was reported to have been highly indignant at the tone and language of Hastings in his cautionary address, exclaiming: "These English seem to look upon themselves as kings, and upon me as merely one of their neighboring Rajahs." (See R.M. Martin, *China; political, commercial, and social; an official report. Vol II*. 1847, p. 25.)

34 P. Landon, *Nepal*, Vol. 1, London: Constable, 1928, p. 78.

35 Oldfield, *Sketches From Nipal*, Vol. 1, 1880, p. 300.

36 For detailed discussion of this episode, see Rose, *Strategy for Survival*, 1971, pp. 89–91.

37 V.K. Manandhar, *Comprehensive History*, Vol. 1, 2004, pp. 206–8.

38 H.E.M. James, *The Long White Mountain*, 1888, pp. 414–15.

39 T. Smith, *Narrative of a Five Years' Residence at Nepaul*, Vol. 2, 1852, p. 86.

40 Ibid., p. 88; H. James, *The Long White Mountain*, 1888, p. 415.

41 Qingying Chen, *Tibetan History*, 2003, pp. 82–3.

42 L. James, *The Rise and Fall of the British Empire*, 1994, p. 135.

43 Ramakant, *Indo-Nepalese Relations 1816–1877*, 1968, pp. 46–51; L.F. Stiller, *The Silent Cry*, 1976, p. 104.

44 One leading historian believes Bhimsen and Queen Regent Lalita Tripurasundari deliberately delayed the request of a doctor from the British residency. (B.R. Acharya, "General Bhimsen Thapa And The Samar Jung Company," *Regmi Research Series*, Year 4, No. 9, September 1972 p. 164.)
45 Rose, *Strategy for Survival*, 1971, p. 95.
46 J. Whelpton, *A History of Nepal*, 2005, p. 43.
47 Rose, *Strategy for Survival*, 1971, p. 95; V.K. Manandhar, *Comprehensive History*, Vol. 1, 2004, p. 223.
48 Manandhar and Mishra, *Quinquennial Missions*, 1986, p. 95.
49 V.K. Manandhar, *Comprehensive History*, Vol. 1, 2004, p. 186; R.K. Douglas, *China*, 1887, p. 244.
50 Manandhar and Mishra, *Quinquennial Missions*, 1986, p. 26.
51 For a detailed discussion, see Stiller, *Silent Cry*, 1976, pp. 88–94.
52 R. Rana, "B.H. Hodgson as a Factor for the Fall of Bhimsen Thapa," *Ancient Nepal*, No. 105, April-May 1988, p. 16.
53 Ibid., p. 19.
54 Rose, *Strategy for Survival*, 1971, p. 98.
55 Landon, *Nepal*, Vol. 1, 1993, p. 86.
56 Ibid., pp. 89–90.
57 Ibid., p. 99.
58 Ibid., p. 91.
59 Rose, *Strategy for Survival*, 1971, p. 99.
60 J. Keay, *China: A History*, 2009, p. 460.
61 J.Y. Wong, *Deadly Dreams: Opium, Imperialism, and the Arrow War (1856–1860) in China*, 1998, p. 39.
62 Rose, *Strategy for Survival*, 1971, p. 100.
63 Whelpton, *A History of Nepal*, 2005, p. 44.
64 B.R. Acharya, *Aba Yasto Kahile Na Hos* [May This Never Happen Again], 2006, pp. 67–8.
65 Rose, *Strategy for Survival*, 1971, p. 100.
66 Ibid., p. 101.
67 From Wei Yuan's 1842 treatise, "Plans for a Maritime Defense," quoted in H. Kissinger, *On China*, pp. 60–3.
68 Whelpton, *A History of Nepal*, 2005, p. 44.
69 Ibid.
70 Rose, *Strategy for Survival*, 1971, p. 102.

4 Crowns and empires

1 The early contention of some British historians that Jang Bahadur had called off that mission to please the British has been challenged by Nepalese historians, most notably by G.M. Nepal, "Jang Bahadur ko Bidesh Niti Ra 1904 ko Peking jane pratinidhi mandal," *Contributions to Nepalese Studies*, 8:2, June 1981, pp. 175–206.
2 Ibid., p. 181.
3 V.K. Manandhar, *Comprehensive History*, Vol. 2, 2004, p. 23.
4 T.R. Manandhar and T.P. Mishra, *Quinquennial Missions*, 1986, p. 27.
5 D. Wright, *History of Nepal*, 1877, p. 59.
6 For a discussion of the motives and experiences of Jang Bahadur see J. Whelpton, *Jang Bahadur in Europe: The First Nepalese Mission to the West*, 1983.
7 R. Shaha, *Essays in the Practice of Government in Nepal*, 1982, pp. 68–9.
8 G.M. Nepal, "Jang Bahadur ko bidesh niti," 1981, p. 181.
9 Manandhar and Mishra, *Quinquennial Missions*, 1986, p. 56.
10 Ibid., p. 58.
11 Shaha, *Essays*, 1982, pp. 72–3.

12 L.E. Rose, *Nepal: Strategy for Survival*, 1971, pp. 109–10.
13 Quoted in V.K. Manandhar, *Comprehensive History*, Vol. 1, 2004, pp. 264–5.
14 Ibid., p. 254.
15 Ibid., p. 252. The Chinese objected. How could a tributary of China also be a tributary to Nepal, itself a Qing tributary? Jang insisted that the Tibetans had agreed to the provision and that, moreover, he considered the treaty as a package. Rejection of a provision would mean the repudiation of the entire treaty. Registering their objection, the Chinese nevertheless went along.
16 W.W. Hunter, *The Imperial Gazetteer of India*, 1886, p. 104.
17 V.K. Manandhar, *Comprehensive History*, Vol. 1, 2004, pp. 269–70.
18 Manandhar and Mishra, *Quinquennial Missions*, 1986, p. 28.
19 V.K. Manandhar, *Comprehensive History*, Vol. 1, 2004, p. 268.
20 P. Landon. *Nepal*, Vol. 1, 1928, p. 153 and pp. 246–7.
21 Manandhar and Mishra, *Quinquennial Missions*, 1986, p. 29.
22 A. Lamb, *British India And Tibet, 1766–1910*, 1986, p. 108.
23 J.W.S. Wyllie and W.W. Hunter, *Essays on the External Policy of India*, 1875, pp. 197–8.
24 Manandhar and Mishra, *Quinquennial Missions*, 1986, p. 29 and p. 60.
25 Around this time, in a missive to Beijing, the governor of Sichuan wrote of the need to engage with Nepal to fortify Tibet and Sichuan. See Ch'ing-Chi-Ch'ou-Tsang-Tsou-Tu (Memorials and correspondence concerning the arrangement of affairs during the latter part of the Ch'ing dynasty), Peiping, National Academy, 1938, Vol. 1, p. 162: Memorial from Ting Pao-chen to Emperor, Nov. 15, 1877.
26 For details, see P.R. Uprety, *Nepal–Tibet Relations 1850–1930*, 2nd ed., 1998, pp. 90–2.
27 N. Bhattarai, *Nepal–Chin Sambhanda* [Nepal–China Relations], 2001, p. 193.
28 K. Mojumdar, *Political Relations Between India and Nepal, 1877–1923*, 1973, p. 51.
29 Landon, *Nepal*, Vol. 2, 1928, p. 64.
30 P.S. Rana, *Rana Intrigues*, 1995, pp. 89–91.
31 Rose, *Strategy for Survival*, 1971, p. 143.
32 Manandhar and Mishra, *Quinquennial Missions*, 1986, p. 30.
33 W. Digby, *1857. A Friend in Need. 1887. Friendship Forgotten*, pp. 100–1 and 144–6.
34 V.K. Manandhar, *Comprehensive History*, 2004, Vol. 2, p. 77.
35 Rose, *Strategy for Survival*, 1971, p. 145.
36 V.K. Manandhar, *Comprehensive History*, Vol. 1, 2004, pp. 286–7.
37 Ibid.
38 Ibid., p. 289.
39 A. Andreyev, *Soviet Russia & Tibet: The Debacle of Secret Diplomacy, 1918–30s*, 2003, pp. 25–6.
40 K.E. Meyer and S.B. Brysac, *Tournament of Shadows: The Great Game and the Race for Empire in Central Asia*, 2006, p. 279.
41 Lamb, *British India and Tibet*, 1986, p. 206; Rose, *Strategy for Survival*, 1971, p. 152. Earlier, Bir Shamsher had politely rebuffed Lord Curzon's request to visit Kathmandu, insisting he could not ensure the viceroy's safety.

5 Games great and small

1 T.P. Manandhar and T.R. Mishra, *Quinquennial Missions to China*, 1986, p. 30.
2 K.E. Meyer and S.B. Brysac, *Tournament of Shadows: The Great Game and the Race for Empire in Central Asia*, 2006, p. 278.
3 Ibid., p. 280. "The Buddhist faith of the Tibetan people is threatened by enemies and oppressors from abroad – the English," the Dalai Lama wrote. "Be so kind as to instruct my ambassadors how they may be reassured about their pernicious and foul activities."

4 D.S. Van Der Oye, "Tournament of Shadows: Russia's Great Game in Tibet," in A. McKay (ed.), *The History of Tibet: The Modern Period: 1895–1959*, 2003, p. 53.

5 P. Addy, *Tibet on the Imperial Chessboard*, 1984, p. 72.

6 D. Gilmour, *Curzon: Imperial Statesman*, 2006, p. 273.

7 L.E. Rose, *Strategy for Survival*, 1971, pp. 155–6.

8 Addy, *Tibet on the Imperial Chessboard*, 1984, p. 92.

9 T.P. Mishra, "Sri Teen Maharaj Chandra Shamsher ra Chiniya Samman" [Chandra Shamsher and Chinese Honor] *Ancient Nepal*, No. 98–99, 1987, p. 10.

10 P. Addy, "Imperial Prophet or Scaremonger?: Curzon's Tibetan Policy Reconsidered," *Asian Affairs*, Vol. 14, 1983, p. 59.

11 P. Landon, *Nepal*, Vol. 2, 1928, p. 110.

12 "Thibet To Be Invaded," *New York Times*, November 17, 1903.

13 E. Kawaguchi, *Three Years in Tibet*, 1909, pp. 522–3.

14 F.E. Younghusband, *India and Tibet*, 1910, pp. 133–7.

15 A.T. Grunfeld, *The Making of Modern Tibet* (Revised ed.), 1996, p. 59.

16 V.K. Manandhar, *Comprehensive History* Vol. 1, 2004, pp. 296–7.

17 M.C. Goldstein, *The Snow Lion*, 1997, p. 24.

18 J. Keay, *China: A History*, 2009, pp. 501–2.

19 In the words of Charles Bell, the British diplomat who would play a central role in subsequent developments, "Nepal helped the British toward a result which has worked to its own detriment." See Charles Bell, *The People of Tibet*, 1928, pp. 233–4.

20 Addy, "Imperial Prophet or Scaremonger?," 1983, p. 66.

21 V.K. Manandhar, *Comprehensive History*, Vol. 1, 2004, p. 304.

22 T.P. Mishra, "Chandra Shamsher," 1987, pp. 10–11; V.K. Manandhar, *Comprehensive History*, Vol. 1, 2004, pp. 314–15.

23 Manandhar and Mishra, *Quinquennial Missions*, 1986, p. 30; M.B. Yahuda, *China's Role in World Affairs*, 1978, p. 24.

24 The Nepalese mission members were reportedly lodged in the extreme north of the city under the surveillance of Chinese troops. The British minister at Beijing believed the Chinese did so to keep the Nepalese away from other foreigners. Manandhar and Mishra, *Quinquennial Missions*, 1986, p. 60.

25 Landon, *Nepal*, Vol. 2, 1993, p. 120.

26 P.S. Rana. *Rana Intrigues*, 1995, pp. 154–5.

27 Goldstein, *Snow Lion*, 1997, p. 27; M.C. Wright (ed.), *China in Revolution: The First Phase, 1900–1911*, 1968, p. 5; H.E. Richardson, *Tibet and Its History*, 2nd revised ed., 1984, pp. 95–8.

28 V.K. Manandhar, *Comprehensive History*, Vol. 1, 2004, pp. 308–9.

29 Younghusband, *India and Tibet*, 1910, p. 388; T.W.D. Shakabpa, *Tibet: A Political History*, 1967, p. 227; V.K. Manandhar, *Comprehensive History*, Vol. 1, 2004, pp. 308–9.

30 Once the Chinese consolidated their hold on Tibet, the Thirteenth Dalai Lama told the British, Beijing would assert claims over Nepal and Bhutan. See V.K. Manandhar, *Comprehensive History*, Vol. 1, 2004, p. 312; T. Laird, *The Story of Tibet. Conversations with the Dalai Lama*, 2006, p. 235.

31 Rose, *Strategy for Survival*, 1971, p. 165.

32 Ibid., p. 166. The British were prepared to confirm Lord Elgin's pledge, made in 1894, that they had "no intention or design of interfering with Nepal's autonomy," but they were not willing to surrender their right to exercise ultimate guidance over Nepal's foreign policy. The resident was instructed to inform Chandra Shamsher that Nepal's status lay somewhere between that of independent Afghanistan and the "feudatory States of India."

33 Ibid., pp. 165–7.

34 V.K. Manandhar, *Comprehensive History*, Vol. 1, 2004, pp. 315–16.

35 Goldstein, *Snow Lion*, 1997, p. 31.

36 Ibid., pp. 30–1.
37 C. Harris and T. Shakya, *Seeing Lhasa*, 2003, p. 95; H.L. Showers, "Eighteen Months In Nepal," *Blackwood's Edinburgh Magazine*, Vol. 199, May 1916, p. 606.
38 Rose, *Strategy for Survival*, 1971, p167.
39 A. Lamb, "The McMahon Line" in A. McKay (ed.), *The History of Tibet: The Modern Period: 1895–1959*, 2003, pp. 110–11.
40 Rose, *Strategy for Survival*, 1971, p. 171.
41 W.F. O'Connor, *On the Frontier and Beyond: A Record of Thirty Years' Service*, 1931, p. 309.
42 Rose, *Strategy for Survival*, 1971, pp. 171–2.
43 M. Yahuda, "The Changing Faces of Chinese Nationalism" in Michael Leifer (ed.) *Asian Nationalism*, 2000, p. 27.
44 Goldstein, *Snow Lion*, 1997, pp. 34–5.
45 C. Bell, *Tibet Past and Present*, 1992, p. 233.
46 The National Archives, U.K. Government, "The Nepal–Tibet Dispute," CAB 24/211, April 5, 1930.
47 D.J. Lee, "National China Re-Establishes Relations with the Kingdom of Nepal," *The China Weekly Review*, 55:27, 1930, p. 148.
48 M.C. Van Walt Van Praag. *The Status of Tibet*, 1987, pp. 77–8.
49 P.S. Rana, *Rana Intrigues*, 1995, pp. 166–8.
50 D.J. Lee, "The Prime Minister of Nepal Decorated By China," *The China Weekly Review*, Vol. 60, 9 April 1932, p. 188.
51 Laird, *The Story of Tibet*, 2006, pp. 282–3.
52 I. Prasad, *The Life and Times of Maharaja Juddha Shumsher Jung Bahadur Rana of Nepal*, 1996, pp. 104–5.
53 V.K. Manandhar, *Comprehensive History*, Vol. 2, 2004, pp. 161–2.
54 Prasad, *Juddha Shumsher*, 1996, pp. 109–10. There was little reason yet for Juddha Shamsher to squirm. Hitler had not revealed his war plans to the secret Hossbach Conference and the announcement of the Anschluss with Austria was months away. British Prime Minister Neville Chamberlain had yet to travel to Munich for talks with Hitler, much less bear the opprobrium of 'appeasement'.
55 Heinrich Himmler, the chief of the dreaded Waffen-SS force, among others, believed Tibet might harbor the last of the original Aryan tribes, the legendary forefathers of the German race, whose leaders possessed supernatural powers that the Nazis could use to conquer the world. See A. McKay, "Hitler and the Himalayas: the SS Mission to Tibet," *Tricycle*, 10:3, 2001, pp. 64–8 and 90–3.
56 Meyer and Brysac, *Tournament of Shadows*, 2006, pp. 519–20.
57 For details, see P. Hyer. "Japanese Expansion and Tibetan Independence" in L. Narangoa and R. Cribb (eds.), *Imperial Japan and National Identities in Asia, 1895–1945*, 2003, pp. 83–4.
58 T. Gould, *Imperial Warriors: Britain and the Gurkhas*, 1999, p. 110.
59 N. Bhattarai. *Chin Ra Tyasasita Nepal Ko Sambandha* [China and Its Relations with Nepal], 1961, p. 231; A. Husain, *British India's Relations with the Kingdom of Nepal*, 1970, p. 222.
60 Ilia Tolstoy, the OSS team leader, changed his mind on the grounds the "present Tibetan government is most unfavorably minded toward any opening of Tibet ... [and regards] ... motor vehicles as modern and anti-Tibetan." See J.K. Knaus, *Orphans of the Cold War*, 2000, p. 10.
61 M.C. Goldstein, *A History of Modern Tibet, 1913–1951*, 1989, pp. 385–90.
62 L. Hsiao-ting, "War or Stratagem? Reassessing China's Military Advance towards Tibet, 1942–1943," *The China Quarterly*, Vol. 186, June 2006, pp. 446–62.
63 Three Nepalese battalions fought as part of the Fourteenth Army in Burma, while another 200,000 Nepalese served with British Indian Gurkha units or in the Indian military police. Apart from Burma, Gurkha units fought primarily in the Middle

Eastern and North African theaters. Total Gurkha casualties in the two world wars exceeded 43,000 and 13 soldiers won Victoria Crosses. See J. Whelpton, *A History of Nepal*, 2005, p. 67.

64 T.R. Ghoble, *China–Nepal Relations and India*, 1986, p. 32, and K.B. KC, *Nepal After the Revolution of 1950*, Vol. 1, 1976, p. 54.

65 Knaus, *Orphans*, 2000, p. 5.

66 D.S. Rana, *Nepal: Rule and Misrule*, 1978, p. 201; "Chiangs Get Many Gifts," *New York Times*, May 14, 1947.

67 M.P. Koirala, *A Role In a Revolution*, 2008, pp. 187–93.

68 Several high-level Indian officials, including Deputy Prime Minister Sardar Vallabhai Patel, were reported to have urged at one time the accession of the border states to the Indian Union on the same basis as the Indian "native states." See Rose, *Strategy for Survival*, 1971, p. 195.

69 L.E. Rose, "India, China, the Himalayan Border States and Afghanistan: 1947–57," *South Asian Survey*, 4:1, 1997, p. 82.

70 G. Jain, *India Meets China in Nepal*, 1959, p. 17.

71 B.L. Joshi and L.E. Rose, *Democratic Innovations in Nepal*, 1966, p. 70.

72 Rose, *Strategy for Survival*, 1971, p. 186.

6 Cold War contortions

1 C. Jian, "The Tibetan Rebellion of 1959 and China's Changing Relations with India and the Soviet Union," *Journal of Cold War Studies*, 8:3, Summer 2006, pp. 58–60.

2 M.M. Sheng, "Mao, Tibet, and the Korean War," *Journal of Cold War Studies*, 8:3, Summer 2006, p. 16.

3 King Tribhuvan later told Prime Minister Matrika Prasad Koirala that he had deliberately left Prince Gyanendra behind to test whether the Ranas would have the "temerity to wipe out the entire dynasty or would they use the child as a last resort." M.P. Koirala, *A Role In a Revolution*, 2008, p. 128.

4 G. Jain, *India Meets China in Nepal*, 1959, p. 108.

5 L.E. Rose, *Strategy for Survival*, 1971, p. 192.

6 London had seemed prepared to recognize Gyanendra on the grounds that the Rana regime was "firmly established and was in effective control of the country." However, the cabinet was split between those unwilling to go against the Indians, who were better positioned to recognize the realities on the ground, and those who were against India treating Nepal as a satellite state. See Government of UK National Archives. Online. Available at: www.nationalarchives.gov.uk (accessed June 24, 2010).

7 B. Chatterji, *People, Palace And Politics*, 1980, pp. 85–6; and B. Chatterji, *A Study of Recent Nepali Politics*, 1967, p. 145.

8 M. Hoftun, W. Raeper and J. Whelpton, *People, Politics and Ideology: Democracy and Social Change in Nepal*, 1999, p. 35.

9 G.B. Devkota, *Nepal ko Rajnitik Darpan* [Political Mirror of Nepal], 1959, p.63.

10 M. Hoftun, W. Raeper and J.Whelpton, *People Politics and Ideology*, 1999, p. 38.

11 Central Intelligence Agency, *Consequences of Communist Control Over South Asia*, October 3, 1952.

12 Ramakant, *Nepal-China and India*, 1976, p. 79; V.K. Manandhar, *A Comprehensive History Of Nepal–China Relations Up To 1955 A.D.*, Vol. 2, 2004, p. 220.

13 One report suggested the Tibetans had agreed to send the rebels back but were overruled by the Chinese. See V.K. Manandhar, *Comprehensive History*, Vol. 2, 2004, p. 195.

14 "Nepali Rebel Said To Plan New Attack," *New York Times*, May 9, 1952.

15 "Robin Hood of the Himalayas," *Time*, August 5, 1957. There was an eerie parallel with another Asian monarchy. The Chinese had already granted refuge to Pridi Banomyong, a former prime minister of Thailand, who, like Singh, was not known for

communist sympathies when he fled into exile. See F. Low, *Struggle for Asia*, 1955, p. 225.

16 W. Levi, "Government and Politics in Nepal: II," *Far Eastern Survey*, 22:1, January 14, 1953, p. 7.

17 N. Goyal, *Political History of Himalayan States: India's Relations with Himalayan States Since 1947*, 2nd ed., 1964, p. 29.

18 In letters to Prime Minister Koirala, Nehru praised Chinese Premier Zhou Enlai for his "high intelligence" and "receptiveness to new ideas ... by no means the narrow-minded person communists often are." See M.P. Koirala, *A Role in a Revolution*, 2008, p. 309.

19 Ibid., p. 295.

20 F. Moraes, *The Revolt in Tibet*, 1960, p. 127.

21 R. Shaha, *Modern Nepal: A Political History 1769–1955*, Vol.2, 1990, p. 307.

22 W. Levi, "Nepal in World Politics," *Pacific Affairs*, 30:3, September 1957, pp. 243–4.

23 G.P. Bhattachacharjee, *India and the Politics of Modern Nepal*, 1970, p. 89.

24 Zhou reportedly agreed to continue respecting Indian paramountcy in Nepal but asserted China's intention to establish diplomatic relations with Nepal. See V.K. Manandhar, *Comprehensive History*, Vol. 2, 2004, pp. 238–9.

25 Ramakant, *Nepal-China and India*, 1976, p. 89.

26 G. Jain, *India Meets China in Nepal*, 1959, p. 112.

27 M.P. Koirala, *A Role in a Revolution*, 2008, pp. 233–4 and 287.

28 Tribhuvan's plan to visit the United States initially posed a dilemma to Washington, considering that American immigration law allowed visas to one wife at a time. See "2 Wives Pose U.S. Problem If King Visits" (*Washington Post*, November 5, 1954). The State Department subsequently ruled Tribhuvan admissible ("King Ruled Admissable," *New York Times*, December 2, 1954).

29 Based on my conversations with several palace officials who served under King Mahendra in the 1950s and 1960s.

30 Mahendra had written a personal letter to Mao affirming his readiness to relinquish the throne and even become a communist if that would help Nepal preserve its independence. Distrustful of palace aides, he chose an obscure communist leader who delivered the letter to Mao. The Chinese leader pledged full support for Nepal's aspirations to neutrality. See K.J. Gurung, "Mahendra ko sandesh Mao lai" [Mahendra's Message To Mao], *Nepal Weekly* (Kathmandu), June 27, 2010, p. 11.

31 V.K. Manandhar, *Comprehensive History*, Vol. 2, 2004, pp. 246–7.

32 King Mahendra had played the most important role in the negotiations and was anxious to keep India out of the process. The king involved only a handful of very close associates in the negotiations. For details, see V.K. Manandhar, *Comprehensive History*, Vol. 2, 2004, pp. 249–56.

33 The Chinese government announced it could keep him no longer because he had threatened hunger strike and suicide if he could not return home. W. Levi, "Politics in Nepal," *Far Eastern Survey*, 25:3, March 1956, p. 41.

34 Interesting details of K.I. Singh's life in China emerged. He said he had led a secluded life there, had no chance to study Chinese administration, and therefore could not describe conditions in that country. One of his followers added that Singh never met Mao or Zhou. See B.L. Joshi and L.E. Rose, *Democratic Innovations in Nepal: A Case Study of Political Acculturation*, 1966, pp. 258–9; Levi, "Politics in Nepal," 1956, p. 41. Dr. Singh later repeated some of those observations in conversations with me.

35 B.L. Joshi and L.E. Rose, *Democratic Innovations in Nepal*, 1966, p. 240.

36 Some reports suggested that the decision came after some communist leaders secretly met Mahendra and gave assurances that they would not oppose the monarchy. See Hoftun *et al.*, *People, Politics and Ideology*, 1999, p. 49. Two palace advisers serving at the time suggested to me that King Mahendra had spent several sessions with these leaders, essentially claiming that he was a "communist with a crown."

37 A.M. Rosenthal, "Grim Shadows Over The Cobra Throne," *New York Times*, May 27, 1956.
38 The choice was significant. An ethnic Mongolian rising in national politics after the promulgation of the People's Republic of China's constitution two years earlier, Ulanfu was also the chairman of the State Council Nationalities Affairs Commission and a member of the National Defense Council.
39 "The Taste of Northern Spy," *Time*, October 8, 1956.
40 Rose, *Strategy for Survival*, 1971, p. 212. In more private conversations with Chinese leaders, however, Prime Minister Acharya expressed concern about Nepal being squeezed to death by the two giants. Zhou tried to allay his fears by assuring him that China as well as India had their hands full for the next 25 years and that Nepal had nothing to worry about. See W. Levi. "Nepal in World Politics," *Pacific Affairs*, 30:3, September 1957, p. 237; Ramakant, *Nepal–China and India*, 1976, p. 102.
41 G. Jain, *India Meets China in Nepal*, 1959, p. 112.
42 J.B. Roberts and E.A. Roberts, *Freeing Tibet*, 2009 pp. 11–12.
43 Ibid., p. 126.
44 Ibid., p. 10.
45 C. Willis (ed.), *A Lifetime of Wisdom: Essential Writings By and About the Dalai Lama*, 2002, p. 252.
46 T. Shakya, *The Dragon in the Land of Snows*, 1999, p. 213.
47 H.F. Armstrong, "Where India Faces China," *Foreign Affairs*, Vol. 37, July 1959, p. 619.
48 A. Gupta, *Politics in Nepal: A Study of Post-Rana Political Developments and Party Politics*, 1964, pp. 148–9. The palace initially received the support of India, which even advised Koirala not to seek the job. But Koirala eventually got Nehru on his side. See M.D. Dharamdasani, "A Study of New Delhi's Role and Attitude Towards the Democratic Forces in Nepal" in *Looking to the Future: Indo-Nepal Relations in Perspective* in Lok Raj Baral (ed.), 1996, p. 94.
49 D.R. Clarridge and D. Diehl, *A Spy for All Seasons: My Life in the CIA*, 1997, p. 69.
50 *Kalpana* Weekly (Kathmandu) April 3, 1959. Surya Prasad Upadhyaya and Ganesh Man Singh, the two general secretaries, criticized China for violating the 1951 Sino-Tibetan treaty as well as other treaties signed by China with other nations. They equated the Tibetan uprising with the Hungarian revolt of 1956. The events in Tibet, the duo declared, provided a warning to all the nations of Asia.
51 Rose, *Strategy for Survival*, 1971, p. 220.
52 Ramakant, *Nepal-China and India*, 1976, p. 117.
53 Rose, *Strategy for Survival*, 1971, p. 220.
54 Ibid., p. 220.
55 Ramakant, *Nepal-China and India*, 1976, p. 116.
56 Rose, *Strategy for Survival*, 1971, p. 221.
57 G.P. Bhattachacharjee, *India and the Politics of Modern Nepal*, 1970, p. 107.
58 S.K. Jha, *Uneasy Partners: India and Nepal in the Post Colonial Era*, 1975, pp. 37–9.
59 "Red Chinese Troops Rumored Inside Nepal," *Christian Science Monitor*, December 1, 1959.
60 "Chinese Said To Infiltrate Nepal," *Washington Post*, December 11, 1959.
61 J.W. Garver, *Protracted Contest: Sino-Indian Rivalry in the Twentieth Century*, 2001, p. 148.
62 "The Value of Nepal," *Christian Science Monitor*, December 19, 1959.
63 Ramakant, *Nepal–China and India*, 1976, p. 132.
64 Rose, *Strategy for Survival*, 1971, p. 225.
65 B.P. Koirala, *Bisweshwar Prasad Koiralako Atmabritanta*, 1998, pp. 251–2.
66 Ibid., pp. 252–53.
67 Ibid.

68 "Nepal Bars Red Claim to Everest," *Washington Post.* April 5, 1960.
69 Joshi and Rose, *Democratic Innovations*, 1966, pp. 370–1.
70 Ramakant, *Nepal–China and India,* 1976, p. 145.
71 "Peking Apology Satisfies Nepal," *Washington Post*, July 5, 1960.
72 J.K. Knaus, "Official Policies and Covert Programs," *Journal of Cold War Studies*, 5:3, 2003, p. 71.
73 U.S. Department of State, *Foreign Relations of the United States, 1969–1976.*
74 A.T. Grunfeld, *The Making of Modern Tibet*, (Revised ed.), 1996, p. 160.
75 D.D. Eisenhower, *Waging Peace: The White House Years: A Personal Account 1956–1961*, 1965, p. 582.
76 B.P. Koirala, *Atmabritanta*, 1998, pp. 260–1.
77 Ibid., pp. 277–8. Documents seized from the principal organizer appeared to implicate the palace. While King Mahendra was away on an extended foreign trip, Koirala made that information public. After returning to Kathmandu. Mahendra privately reprimanded Koirala.
78 Joshi and Rose, *Democratic Innovations*, 1966, pp. 384–5.

7 Perilous pragmatism

1 B.P. Koirala, *Atmabritanta*, 1998, p. 230.
2 M.P. Koirala, *A Role In a Revolution*, 2008, pp. xi–xii.
3 Quoted in L.E. Rose, *Strategy for Survival*, 1971, pp. 233–4.
4 Ibid., p. 236.
5 P.K.Padmanabhan, "Nepal Has Importance Far Beyond Its Size," *Los Angeles Times*, March 1, 1961.
6 J.K. Knaus, *Orphans*, 2000, p. 246.
7 J.B. Roberts and E.A. Roberts, *Freeing Tibet*, 2009, p. 96.
8 For a discussion of the psychological dimensions of Nepal's relations with China, see L.E. Rose, "King Mahendra's China Policy" in S.D. Muni (ed.), *Nepal: An Assertive Monarchy*, 1977, pp. 219–39.
9 J.F. Copper, *China's Foreign Aid*, 1976, p. 9.
10 G.P. Deshpande, "China and the Himalayan States," *China Report*, 3:2, 1967, pp. 19–20.
11 Rose, *Strategy for Survival*, 1971, p. 239.
12 W. Wilcox, "China's Strategic Alternatives in South Asia," in Tang Tsou, (ed.), *China in Crisis, Volume 2*, 1968, p. 404.
13 Both accounts are drawn from my separate conversations with some leading members of the delegation.
14 Rose, *Strategy for Survival*, 1971, p. 240.
15 Acharya subsequently denied making the road proposal. Ramakant, *Nepal–China and India*, 1976, p. 105.
16 Rose, *Strategy for Survival*, 1971, p. 241.
17 Ramakant, *Nepal-China and India*, 1976, p. 190.
18 J.W. Garver, *Protracted Contest*, 2001, pp. 147–8.
19 How much of this softening was influenced by Nehru's threat to use military force to incorporate the Portuguese territory of Goa into the union was unclear. But when the Indian military moved in on December 18 and annexed the territory in a 36-hour operation, the development shook the royal regime.
20 Central Intelligence Agency, National Intelligence Estimate Number 100–2–60, *Sino-Indian Relations*, May 17, 1960, p. 5.
21 U.S. Department of State, *Foreign Relations of the United States, 1961–1963*, Volume XIX, South Asia, Document 88, undated.
22 Rose, *Strategy for Survival*, 1971, pp. 244–5.
23 Ibid., p. 245

24 S.K. Jha, *Uneasy Partners*, 1975, p. 171

25 J. Sharma, *Nepal: Struggle for Existence*, 1986, p. 185.

26 R.J. McMahon, *The Cold War on the Periphery*, 1994, p. 288.

27 U.S. Department of State, *Foreign Relations of the United States, 1961–1963*, Volume XIX, South Asia, Document 190. November 3, 1962.

28 "Rebels Suspend Nepal Movement," *New York Times*, November 9, 1962.

29 For a detailed discussion on this subject, see D.B. Bista, "Nepalis in Tibet," *Contributions to Nepalese Studies*, 8:1, 1980, pp. 1–19.

30 M. Moynihan, "Tibetan Refugees in Nepal," in D. Bernstorff and H. Welck (eds.), *Exile As A Challenge: The Tibetan Diaspora*, 2003, pp. 313–14; T. Shakya, *The Dragon in the Land of Snows*, 1999, p. 284.

31 Roberts and Roberts, *Freeing Tibet*, 2009, p. 95.

32 C. McGranahan, "Tibet's Cold War," *Journal of Cold War Studies* 8:3, Summer 2006, pp. 120–1.

33 M. Liu, T. Clifton, P. Roberts and T. Laird, "A Secret War on the Roof of the World," *Newsweek*, 134:7, August 16, 1999.

34 Copper, *China's Foreign Aid*, 1976, p. 5.

35 E.B. Mihaly, *Foreign Aid and Politics in Nepal*, 1965, p. 152; Wilcox, *China's Strategic Alternatives in South Asia*, p. 404.

36 L.E. Rose, "Nepal: The Quiet Monarchy," *Asian Survey*, 4:2, 1964, p. 728.

37 L.E. Rose, "Nepal: Under Same Management, Business as Usual," *Asian Survey*, 5:2, 1965, pp. 74–8.

38 Rose, *Strategy for Survival*, 1971, p. 262.

39 Quoted in S.C. Bhatt. *The Triangle India–Nepa–China: A Study of Treaty Relations*, 1996, p. 134.

40 McGranahan, "Tibet's Cold War," 2006, p. 122.

41 A.T. Grunfeld, *The Making of Modern Tibet*, (Revised ed.), 1996, pp. 160–1.

42 L.E. Rose, "Nepal in 1965: Focus on Land Reform," *Asian Survey*, 6:2, 1966, p. 89.

43 For details, see Rose, *Strategy for Survival*, 1971, p. 264; and Garver, *Protracted Contest*, 2001, p. 149.

44 G. Jain, "China's Dual Approach," *China Report*, 6:4, 1970, p. 14.

45 Rahul, "India's Changing China Policy," *China Report*, 6:4, 1970, p. 19.

46 P. Van Ness. *Revolution and Chinese Foreign Policy*, 1970, pp. 223–4.

47 Ramakant, *Nepal–China and India*, 1976, p. 192.

48 "China-Nepal Friendship Highway Completed," *Beijing Review*, June 2, 1967.

49 Rose, *Strategy for Survival*, 1971, p. 264.

50 Rose, *Strategy for Survival*, 1971, pp. 264–5.

51 R. Shaha, *Nepali Politics: Retrospect and Prospect*, 1978, p. 127

52 Rose, *Strategy for Survival*, 1971, p. 265.

53 Based on my conversations with a leading Nepalese Foreign Ministry official at the time.

54 *Translations On People's Republic of China*, Washington: Joint Publications Research Service, Sep 5–7, 1967, p. 58.

55 Based on my conversations with a senior Nepalese bureaucrat serving then.

56 K.J. Conboy and J. Morrison, *The CIA's Secret War in Tibet*, 2002, p. 147.

57 Several palace officials, including some who served under both Kings Mahendra and Birendra, related this view to me in separate conversations.

58 Based on my conversations with Nepalese and American diplomatic sources who were directly involved at the time.

59 Quoted in D. Norbu, "Strategic Development in Tibet: Implications for Its Neighbors," *Asian Survey*, 19:3, March 1979, pp. 245–9.

60 F. Gaige, Nepal: The Search for National Concensus, *Asia Survey*, 10:2, February 1970, p. 105.

61 *The Rising Nepal* (Kathmandu), June 24, 1969.

62 Ibid.
63 "Nepal's Public Opinion Supports Bista in Condemning Indian Government's Expansionist Policy," *Beijing Review*, July 11, 1969, p. 29.
64 "Nepalese Ambassador to China Gives Reception," *People's Daily*, June 12, 1969, and *Beijing Review*, June 20, 1969.
65 Zhou did attend a dinner at the Nepalese embassy in Beijing where he praised Nepal for its "glorious tradition of resisting foreign aggression" and "foreign policy of independence." *The China Quarterly*, No. 42, April–June 1970, pp. 182–3.
66 U.S. Department of State, *Foreign Relations of the United States, 1969–1976, Volume XVII*, China, 1969–1972.
67 N. Khadka, "Chinese Foreign Policy toward Nepal in the Cold War Period: An Assessment," *China Report*, 35:1, 1999, p. 65.
68 Indira Gandhi was reported to have held a series of meetings with former Gurkha soldiers in the Indian Army who had become prominent community leaders, some closely allied to the palace. K.J. Gurung, *Indira Gandhi lai bhetda* [Meeting Indira Gandhi], *Nepal Weekly* (Kathmandu), July 11, 2010, p. 11.
69 S.P. Gyawali, *Byakti ra Bicchar: Ek Vakil ko Samsmaran ra Chintan* [Person and Thoughts: The Remembrance and Contemplation of a Lawyer], 1998, pp. 169–70.
70 Y.N. Khanal. "Nepal in 1972: A Search for a New Base-Camp?" *Asian Survey*, 13:2, February 1973, p. 211.

8 Reforms and recriminations

1 M.R. Josse, "Sino-US Relationship and its Global Implications with Special Reference to Nepal," December 18, 2003.
2 Quoted in S.C. Bhatt, *The Triangle India–Nepa–China: A Study of Treaty Relations*, New Delhi: Gyan Publishing House, 1996, p. 84.
3 Based on my conversations with palace officials.
4 A. Lustgarten, *China's Great Train*, 2008, p. 57.
5 A.T. Grunfeld, *The Making of Modern Tibet*, (Revised ed.), 1996, p. 163.
6 Earlier in the year, the U.S. ambassador in New Delhi, Daniel Patrick Moynihan, had written to the State Department in Washington on how the Soviets had been in touch with Tibetan refugees in Nepal and in India. But Moscow apparently wanted to act independently of New Delhi, and was not willing to provide any open support to the Tibetan cause at international forums. All this would work against the putative alliance. For details on this period of Soviet–Tibetan interaction, see C. Arpi, "Dalai Lama & the Russian Card," *The Statesman*, May 29, 2010; J.K. Knaus, *Orphans of the Cold War*, 2000, pp. 297–8; and C.M. Andrew and V. Mitrokhin, *The World Was Going Our Way*, 2005, p. 278.
7 J. Chang and J. Halliday, *Mao: The Untold Story*, 2005, p. 584. The picture appears in the book.
8 Grunfeld, *The Making of Modern Tibet*, 1996, p. 163.
9 At the time Beijing Radio's Nepali-language shortwave radio broadcasts regularly made these warnings in its own commentaries and those it carried from other official Chinese publications.
10 M. Dunham, *Buddha's Warriors*, 2004, p. 389.
11 J.B. Roberts and E.A. Roberts, *Freeing Tibet*, 2009, p. 154; Dunham, *Buddha's Warriors*, p. 384.
12 In the past, Wangdu had decided against joining the Special Frontiers Troops, sensing that it was established as a tool further Indian, not Tibetan, interests. See Dunham, *Buddha's Warriors*, 2004, p. 387.
13 For details on the Nepalese military's Mustang operation and aftermath, see J.F. Avedon, *In Exile from the Land of Snows*, 1984, pp. 126–9.
14 L.E. Rose and J.T. Scholz, *Nepal: Profile of a Himalayan Kingdom*, 1980, p. 132.

15 The long gap between Birendra's enthronement and formal coronation is explained by the extensive search for an astrologically propitious moment.
16 S.D. Muni. *India and Nepal: A Changing Relationship*, 1992, p. 69.
17 These are my personal impressions gathered from conversations with American diplomats and academics in Kathmandu.
18 One particularly scathing commentary held that internationally New Delhi had "thrown itself into the lap of Soviet revisionist social-imperialism, which has brought about increasing colonialization of India's economy." See "Indira Gandhi Government's Ferocious Features Fully Exposed," *People's Daily*, June 29, 1975.
19 This reversal was attributed by some Nepalese to growing influence of a group of palace administrators and technocrats sharing a Marxist background, who effectively vetoed the more liberal recommendations put forward by a king-appointed commission.
20 U.S. Department of State, Foreign Relations of the United States, 1969–1976, Volume XVIII, China, 1973–1976.
21 J.T. Scholz, "Nepal in 1976," *Asian Survey*, 17:2, 1977, p. 203.
22 R. Shaha, *Nepali Politics: Retrospect and Prospect*, 1978, p. 177.
23 N. Sen, "Setting of the Red Sun," *China Report*, 29:2, 1993, p. 209.
24 J.T. Scholz, "Nepal in 1977," *Asian Survey*, 18:2, February 1978, p. 203.
25 J. Sharma, *Nepal: Struggle for Existence*, 1986, p. 242.
26 J.P. Anand, "Nepal's Zone of Peace Concept and China," China Report, 13:6, 1977, p. 9.
27 "Indian General Election and Soviet Setback in South Asia," *Beijing Review*, April 8, 1977, pp. 23–4.
28 Quoted in D.V. Praagh, *The Greater Game: India's Race with Destiny and China*, 2003, p. 362.
29 Prime Minister Kirti Nidhi Bista broke with protocol and went to the airport to receive Deng. King Birendra not only cut short his visit to western Nepal but also attended a banquet given by Bista in honor of the vice-premier. *The Statesman* (Calcutta), February 4, 1978.
30 *People's Daily*, February 5, 1978.
31 J.W. Garver, *Protracted Contest*, 2001, p. 151.
32 M. Regmi, "Chiniya ruchie ko artha" [The Realities Behind China's New Interest], *Nepal Weekly*, December 21, 2008.
33 L.R. Baral, "Nepal in 1978," *Asian Survey*, 19:2, 1979, pp. 202–3.
34 L.R.Baral, *Nepal: Problems of Governance*, 1993, p. 167.
35 Parmanand, "China's Nepal Policy," *IDSA Journal*, 17:1, 1984, p. 83
36 L.R. Baral, "Nepal in 1979," *Asian Survey*, 20:2, 1980, pp. 203–4.
37 Garver, *Protracted Contest*, 2001, pp. 65–6.
38 T. Shakya, *The Dragon in the Land of Snows*, 1999, pp. 43 and 264.
39 Ibid., p. 46.
40 Ibid., p. 376.
41 M.C. Goldstein, *The Snow Lion*, 1997, p. 67.
42 T. Shakya, *The Dragon in the Land of Snows*, 1999, p. 384.
43 As chairman of the Sichuan Revolutionary Committee, Zhao had escorted the king to various projects in the province in 1976. See M.R. Josse, *Nepal and the World: An Editor's Notebook, Vol. 1*, 1984, p. 73.
44 "Premier Zhao on Current International Issues," *Beijing Review*, June 15, 1981, p. 9.
45 Garver, *Protracted Contest*, 2001, pp. 150–1.
46 T.P. Uprety, "Nepal in 1982," *Asian Survey*, 23:2, 1983, pp. 147–8.
47 K.S. Sharma, "Nepal in 1983," *Asian Survey*, 24:2, 1984, p. 262.
48 J.G. Roberts, *Aid Programmes by the Governments of India and China to Nepal*, Master's dissertation, University of Hong Kong, 1997, p. 51.
49 J. Mann, "China Moves to Limit Foreign Access to Tibet," *Los Angeles Times*, July 25, 1985.

50 Garver, *Protracted Contest*, 2001, p. 151.
51 Y.N. Khanal, "Nepal in 1985," *Asian Survey*, 26:2, 1986, p. 252.
52 Tibet Justice Centre, *Tibet's Stateless Nationals: Tibetan Refugees in Nepal*, 2002, p. 38.
53 For a detailed account of the Dalai Lama's 1981 visit to Lumbini and how Nepal and China managed to work that out, see Avedon, *In Exile*, 1984, pp. 183–8.
54 L.R. Baral, "Nepal in 1986," *Asian Survey*, 27:2, 1987, p. 178.
55 L.R. Baral, "Nepal in 1987," *Asian Survey*, 28:2, 1988, p. 176.
56 A senior official in the royal entourage gave me this information.
57 A.J. Singh, "How the Tibetan Problem Influenced China's Foreign Relations," *China Report*, 28:3, 1992, pp. 285–6.
58 L.E. Rose, "Nepal as a Link Country," in P. Gaeffke and D.A. Utz (eds), *The Countries of South Asia*, 1988, p. 162.
59 Garver, *Protracted Contest*, 2001, p. 151.
60 When Nepal requested the purchase of anti-aircraft guns in 1972 and 1976, New Delhi refused, saying that the kingdom had no need for them. Another request in the early 1980s went unanswered for years. Garver, *Protracted Contest*, 2001, pp. 152–3.
61 Ibid.
62 Ibid.
63 Ibid.
64 A.J. Singh, "How the Tibetan Problem Influenced," 1992, p. 286.
65 T. Shakya, *The Dragon in the Land of Snows*, 1999, pp. 428–9.
66 United States Committee for Refugees and Immigrants, 2001.
67 Garver, *Protracted Contest*, 2001, p. 157.
68 Ren Yujun, "Will Nepal–India Relations Improve?" *Beijing Review*, 24–30 July 1989, pp. 15–16.
69 Garver, *Protracted Contest*, 2001, p. 153. How little headway the meeting made became apparent days later. During a meeting with President Mitterrand in Paris on his way back home, the monarch was quoted as describing Gandhi's "soothing" words in the Yugoslav capital as "double talk." See J. Sharma, *Democracy Without Roots*, 1998, p. 26.
70 Roberts and Roberts, *Freeing Tibet*, 2009, p. 189.
71 Garver, *Protracted Contest*, 2001, p. 159.
72 N. Koirala, "Nepal in 1989," *Asian Survey*, 30:2, 1990, p. 140.
73 "Dalai Lama, Accepting Prize, Urges Peaceful Tibet Solution," *New York Times*, December 11, 1989.
74 T. Frängsmyr and I. Abrams (eds.), *Nobel Lectures: Peace: 1981–1990*, 1997, p. 261.
75 *Zheng ming*, No. 151, May 1990, p. 18, quoted in Garver, *Protracted Contest*, 2001, p. 162. Under the constitutional provisions of the time, the president's role was largely symbolic, with formal executive power wielded by the premier and the general secretary of the Chinese Communist Party. Although initially supportive of Zhao Ziyang's efforts to deal with the Tiananmen protests, Yang had subsequently joined the hardliners who believed it was a foreign-inspired effort to spread instability. Yang, as noted earlier, had been closely associated with China's Tibet policy after the communist takeover. Vice-chair of the Central Military Affairs Commission, he had deeper ties with the People's Liberation Army and was reported to be closely associated with China's arms sales policy.
76 Ibid., p. 165.

9 Realpolitik to regicide

1 J.W. Garver, *Protracted Contest*, 2001, p. 157.
2 N. Koirala, "Nepal in 1990: End of an Era," *Asian Survey*, 31:2, February 1991, p. 138.

3 Ibid., p. 163.
4 The Nepalese government insisted it knew nothing about the visit. The organizers challenged that contention, claiming they had requested security arrangements well in advance.
5 J. Sharma, *Democracy Without Roots*, 1998, p. 199.
6 N. Khadka, "Geopolitics and Development," *Asian Affairs*, Fall 1992, 19:3, p. 155.
7 *The Times of India* (New Delhi), October 20, 1992.
8 *The Statesman* (Calcutta), October 18, 1992.
9 P. Mehra, "China and South Asia," *China Report*, 1994, p. 305.
10 J. Sharma, *Democracy Without Roots*, 1998, p. 204.
11 Ibid., p. 202.
12 For a perceptive discussion on this phase, see J.W. Garver, "China and South Asia," *The ANNALS of the American Academy of Political and Social Science*, Vol. 519, 1992, pp. 72–3.
13 K. Hachhethu, "Nepal's India Policy Under Communist Government," *Contributions to Nepalese Studies*, 25:2, July 1999, p. 230.
14 J. Sharma, *Democracy Without Roots*, 1998, pp. 268–9.
15 Ibid., pp. 264–5.
16 Ibid., p. 269.
17 R. Lostumbo, "Tibetan Refugees in Nepal," *Georgetown Immigration Law Journal*, 9:4, 1995, p. 916.
18 Tibetans with Nepalese refugee cards did not enjoy the civil and legal rights of Nepalese citizens and had no defined legal status. Tibetan women who married Nepalese automatically became citizens, although the converse was not the case. Children born to Tibetan refugees generally did not have a right to acquire Nepalese citizenship. Most Tibetans, however, never attempted to become citizens because of the hurdles in the process. But, more importantly, many felt that to do so would be to compromise the Tibetan national identity. For details on the so-called "Gentleman's Agreement," see *Tibet's Stateless Nationals: Tibetan Refugees in Nepal*, 2002, pp. 90–2.
19 P. Adhikari, *Ties That Bind: An Account of Nepal–China Relations*, 2010, pp. 93–6.
20 L.E. Rose, "Nepal and Bhutan in 1998," *Asian Survey*, 39: 1, 1999, p. 157.
21 K.V. Rajan, "Nepal–India Relations," *South Asian Journal*, No. 7, 2005.
22 Many Nepalese who had seen Bhutan's king accorded that honor twice over the decades pressed the point that it was so only because India was anxious to project Bhutan as an independent country despite its being a virtual Indian protectorate.
23 *Spotlight Weekly* (Kathmandu), September 17, 1999.
24 J. Pomfret, "Go West, Young Han," *Washington Post*, September 15, 2000.
25 Zhang Li, *To Manage Conflict in South Asia*, October 2009, pp. 78–9.
26 "Karmapa's travel through Nepal confirmed," *People's Review*, January 20, 2000.
27 Ibid.
28 M.Fathers, "Thunder Out of China," *Time*, 17 January, 2000.
29 S.S. Rana, "Nepal's Strategic Importance Underscored," *People's Review*, January 18, 2001, p. 1.
30 A. Roy, *Prachanda: The Unknown Revolutionary*. 2008, pp. 68–9.
31 "A Significant Milestone!" *People's Review*, February 8, 2001.
32 "President Jiang Meets Nepali and Cuban Guests," *Beijing Review*, March 15, 2001.
33 *China Report*, 37:3, 2001, p. 424.
34 S.S. Rana, "Nepal's Strategic Importance Underscored," 2001, p. 1.
35 M.R. Josse. "Business as usual: China gives, Nepal takes," *People's Review*. May 17, 2001.
36 "We May See the Recurrence of a New Cold War in our Region," *Nepali Times*, May 11, 2001.
37 Based on my conversations with Chinese diplomats and journalists.

38 "Chinese Premier Zhu Rongji's South Asia Tour, 11–22 May 2001," *China Report*, 37:4, 2001, p. 543.
39 General Vivek Shah, King Birendra's military secretary, wrote in his memoirs a decade later that the monarch was in the process of garnering western, Chinese and Indian support for his intervention that was aimed at ending the Maoist insurgency. V. Shah, Maile dekhe ko darbar: Sainik sachib ko samsmaran [The Palace I Saw: Memoirs of a Military Secretary], 2010, pp. 56–8.
40 "Nepal's King Birendra's murder and the Chinese revelation," *The Telegraph Online*, November 13, 2008.

10 Mao versus monarchy

1 "India's Nepal Worries." *Business Week*, June 18, 2001.
2 B.R. Bhattarai "Naya kot parba lai manyata dina hudaina" [Do Not Legitimize the New Kot Parba], *Kantipur*, June 6, 2001.
3 "China's new friend in Nepal," *Stratfor Global Intelligence Update*, June 7, 2001; A. Ghosh, "Subcontinental Drift: The China Card," Time.com, June 5, 2001, 2009); "Nepal: Challenge for India and China," *Asia Times*, June 8, 2001. Some people who knew King Gyanendra sought to refute those suggestions. See "King Gyanendra Is Not Anti-Indian," www.rediff.com, June 11, 2001.
4 "Nepali Army Head Reaffirms Support for One-China Policy," *People's Daily Online*, September 2, 2001.
5 "Nepal Committed to Enhancing Friendship with China," *Xinhua*, September 4, 2001.
6 L.R. Baral, "Nepal in 2001," *Asian Survey*, 42:1, 2002, p. 201.
7 For perspectives on the origins and growth of the insurgency, see M. Lawoti and A. K. Pahari (eds.), *The Maoist Insurgency in Nepal*, 2010; M. Hutt (ed.), *The Himalayan People's War*, 2004; and Deepak Thapa (ed.), *Understanding the Maoist Movement of Nepal*, 2003. For the ethnic dimension of the insurgency and Nepalese politics in general, an excellent single-author volume is S.I. Hangen, *The Rise of Ethnic Politics in Nepal*, 2010.
8 D.V. Praagh, *The Greater Game: India's Race with Destiny and China*, 2003, p. 342.
9 R. Manchanda. "Emergency and a Crisis," *Frontline*. March 2–15, 2002.
10 "China to discuss US military presence with Nepal," *Press Trust of India*, April 28, 2002.
11 K.P. Nayar, "Delhi Leaves Nepal Gate Ajar," *The Telegraph* (Calcutta), June 23, 2002.
12 P. Pan, "China Backs Nepal Over Maoist Rebels," *Washington Post*, July 14, 2002.
13 Ibid.
14 DebkaFile, a Jerusalem-based English language open source military intelligence website, reported that the Maoist insurgency in Nepal may be one of the last surviving operations of a little known Chinese intelligence organ known as the Ministry of Foreign Liaison, a body the Chinese Communist Party set up in Mao Zedong's day for the export of revolution through covert operations and the political indoctrination of indigenous cadres. "Beijing's Finger in Nepal's Maoist Revolt," May 28, 2002. A leading Indian expert on China subsequently pointed to ultra-leftist elements in the People's Republic of China (PRC), claiming absolute loyalty to the late leader Mao Zedong, for supporting Maoist movements in Nepal and India. See D.S. Rajan, "China: Signs of Ultra-Leftist Support To Maoists Of India And Nepal," *South Asia Analysis Group*, Paper No. 1565 May 10, 2005.
15 "Nepal Committed to Enhancing Friendship with China," *Xinhua*, September 4, 2001.
16 "Nepal to Fully Support One China Policy:FM," *People's Daily Online*, December 9, 2002.
17 A. Baruah, "Nepal Needs To Be Transparent for Better Ties," *The Hindu* (Madras), February 14, 2003.

18 The move was in response to the Maoists' involvement in the murder of two Nepalese security officers working for the American Embassy. S. Sharma, "Nepal Rebels Slam US Terror Label," BBC News Online, May 2, 2003.
19 U.S. Embassy statement, November 1, 2003.
20 R. Maitra, "Nepal Bows to China's Demands," *Asia Times Online*, June 17, 2003.
21 D. Lai. "Great Power Peace and Stability in Asia: China's Emerging Role," in A. Gupta (ed.), *Strategic Stability in Asia*, 2008, pp. 34–5.
22 *Indo-Asian News Service*, August 8, 2003.
23 *Patterns of Global Terrorism*, US Department of State. April 2004, p. 14.
24 P. Soren, "US Interest in Nepal: Politics of Military Aid," *ORF Strategic Trends*, 2:16, April 26, 2004.
25 "Nepal Itself Can Resolve Current Crisis: Chinese envoy," *Kantipur Online*, May 14, 2004.
26 "New Delhi Must Play a More Assertive Role," *The Times of India*, May 28, 2004.
27 S. Chandrasekharan, "Deuba's Visit and Thereafter," *South Asia Analysis Group*, September 29, 2004.
28 S. Ramachandran, "India Moves With the King," *Asia Times Online*, January 22, 2005.
29 "China Hopes Nepal to Realize Social Security: FM Spokesman," *Xinhua*, February 1, 2005.
30 There were reports that the Chinese had pressed Crown Prince Paras on the matter during his visit to Beijing the previous year. "Nepal's Royal Coup: Making a Bad Situation Worse," International Crisis Group, February 9, 2005, p. 14.
31 A. Wolfe, "International Spotlight on Nepal," *Power and Interest News Report*, March 11, 2005.
32 F. Stakelbeck Jr., "Is China grooming 'another Tibet?'" *Washington Times*, December 29, 2005.
33 D. Dillon, "China's Zombie Countries," *National Review Online*, May 10, 2005.
34 S. Ramachandran, "Nepal's Maoists Air Their Dirty Laundry," *Asia Times Online*, May 17, 2005.
35 A. Acharya, "Wen Jiabao's South Asian Sojourn," *China Report*, 41:3, 2005, p. 317.
36 "China Rolls Out Red Carpet for King," *The Telegraph* (Calcutta), April 25, 2005.
37 J. Hemanth, "Koirala Freed to Calm India," *The Telegraph* (Calcutta), April 2, 2005.
38 J.S Pocha, "China Rolls Out Red Carpet For King," *The Telegraph* (Calcutta), April 25, 2005.
39 R. Devraj, "Emergency Lifted as Nepal King's China Card Fails," *Inter-Press Service*, May 1, 2005.
40 "Maoists Say Prachanda Tape is 'Propaganda'," *Indo-Asian News Service*. May 22, 2005.
41 S. Sarkar, "India Takes Up Tape Issue With Nepal Army," *The Statesman* (Calcutta), May 25, 2005.
42 A. Mukul. "Indian Spooks Host Nepal Rebel," The *Times of India Online*, May 24, 2005. Online.
43 S.Sarkar, "China Pledges £12.3 mn Aid to Nepal," *Indo-Asian News Service*, August 16, 2005.
44 S. Shukla, "The Gulf Widens, *India Today*, September 19, 2005, p. 30.
45 Ibid.
46 One Indian newspaper, perceived as sympathetic to the Nepalese monarchy, suggested that New Delhi had encouraged the ceasefire to prevent Gyanendra from internationalizing his roadmap, K. Gupta, "Maoist Ceasefire in Nepal After Talks in India," *The Pioneer Online*, September 4, 2005.
47 "Parliamentary Polls Talk Another Ploy: Leaders," *The Kathmandu Post*, October 15, 2005.

48 "China, Nepal Pledge Further Military Exchanges," *People's Daily Online*, October 21, 2005.
49 "China Offers India Help on Maoist Rebels," *United Press International*, October 27, 2005.
50 P.B. Samanta, "China is Nepal's Spanner to Kabul's Entry," *Indian Express Online*. November 13, 2005.
51 "The King and We," *Indian Express Online*, November 28, 2005.
52 For details of these developments and the dimensions of India's ambivalence, see Muni, S.D., *India's Foreign Policy: The Democracy Dimension*, 2009. pp. 90–3.
53 Based on my conversations with Indian politicians and bureaucrats.
54 "Prevent Chinese, Pakistani Arms Supplies To Nepal," *Indo-Asian News Service*. December 20, 2005.
55 For example, "Himalayan Tyranny," *Indian Express*. January 21, 2006.
56 D. Adhikary, "Nepal Still In A State of Flux," *Asia Times Online*, October 24, 2006. Online.
57 "India Growing Concerned by Growing China–Nepal Links," *United Press International*, December 20, 2005.
58 "India Expresses Concern to China over Political Turmoil in Nepal," *Press Trust of India*, January 10, 2006.
59 S.Sarkar, "Is China Changing its Stance Towards Nepal?" *Indo-Asian News Service*, February 12, 2006.
60 "Party-Maoists partnership wrongheaded: Moriarty," *The Kathmandu Post*, February 17, 2006.
61 Zhang Song and Zhang Jiye, "US forces Nepal to accept the National Endowment for Democracy to offset China's Influence," *Global Times* (Chinese), January 16, 2006; Zhang Li, *To Manage Conflict in South Asia*, October 2009, p. 87.
62 Based on my interviews with Chinese and Nepalese officials.
63 Zhang Li, *To Manage Conflict*, 2009, p. 78.
64 R. Deshpande, "Save Monarchy, But Restore Democracy," *The Times of India*, April 19, 2006.
65 "Karan's Feedback: King Not Averse To Interim Govt," *Indian Express*. April 21, 2006.
66 J.W. Garver and Fei-Ling Wang, "China's Anti-encirclement Struggle," *Asian Security*, 6:3, 2010, p. 241.
67 Based on my conversations with two Chinese academics.

11 Scramble for new allies

1 S.Sarkar, "China Irked As Nepal Trumps King Card," *The Statesman* (Calcutta), April 28, 2006.
2 "Nepal To Construct Highway To Link With China," *Xinhua*, May 28, 2006.
3 "China Unhappy Over Tibet Refugees," *The Kathmandu Post*, July 4, 2006.
4 C. McGranahan, *Arrested Histories*, 2010, p. 264.
5 S.Sarkar, "Nepal's King Traded Tibetan Refugees for US support: WikiLeaks," *Indo-Asian News Service*, January 15, 2011.
6 The story is detailed in J. Green, *Murder in the High Himalaya*, 2010.
7 T. Pokharel, "China for 6-month U.N. mission," *The Kathmandu Post*, January 13, 2007.
8 UN Department of Public Information Press Release, February 26, 2007.
9 "MPRF Expresses Sorrow over Gaur Incident," *The Kathmandu Post*, March 23, 2007.
10 "Maoists Not to Join Koirala-led Govt: Gurung," *The Himalayan Times*, March 25, 2007.
11 "Nepal Favors Inclusion of China," *The Hindu* (Madras), April 4, 2007.

12 Liang Yan, "The Guerrilla Leaders Going Out of the Jungle," *Global Times*, July 15, 2006. China's pre-eminent academic expert on Nepal was seen seated among Nepalese People's Liberation Army commanders wearing one of their combat jackets. (See B. Bhat, "Chiyars! Naya Nata" [Cheers! New Relations], *Nepal Weekly*, June 17, 2007.)

13 Wang Hongwei, "Chin Chup Lagera Basdaina" [China Won't Sit Silently By], *Nepal Weekly*, November 5, 2007. This was a sentiment I heard repeated in separate conversations with two Chinese officials before Professor Wang made it publicly in the Nepalese media.

14 "Koirala Appeals for Railway Link with China," *The Telegraph Weekly*, December 25, 2007, p. 3.

15 "Arms from US and China, What For?" *The Telegraph Weekly*, February 8, 2008, p. 1.

16 P.D. Samanta, "Pro-China Centres, Calling for Reduced Ties with Delhi, Sprout Along Nepal Border With India," *Indian Express*, February 10, 2008.

17 "Prachanda Defends Chinese Crackdown on Tibetans," *Press Trust of India*, March 23, 2008.

18 "Appeasing China: Restricting the Rights of Tibetans in Nepal," *Human Rights Watch*, July 23, 2008.

19 "China Begins Building Tibet–Nepal Rail Link: Official," *Agence France Presse*, April 26, 2008.

20 Ren Yan Song, "US–India Eye Nepal Changes," *Global Times*, April 28, 2008.

21 "China Unhappy Over Nepal's Response To Anti-China Demonstrations," *Deutsche Presse Agentur*, May 13, 2008.

22 Nepalese authorities reportedly made an estimated 8,350 arrests of Tibetans, out of an estimated total population of some 20,000 Tibetan refugees, exiles, and asylum seekers, during the period between March 10 and July 18, 2008. See B. Vaughn, *Nepal: Political Developments and Bilateral Relations with the United States*, 2011, p. 10.

23 "Equidistance with India, China will be maintained," Prachanda interview with Karan Thapar, CNN-IBN, May 18, 2008.

24 S. Sarkar, "Prachanda's China Trip Will Send Negative Message to India: Yadav," *Indo Asian News Service*, August 20 2008. Sharad Yadav, leader of the Janata Dal-United party, who headed a delegation of the Indo-Nepal Friendship Forum to attend the oath-taking ceremony of the new Nepalese premier, said that in Kathmandu.

25 In 2002, China wanted King Gyanendra to visit Beijing before New Delhi ostensibly as a gesture of reassurance that he would maintain the friendly policies of his father and brother. The monarch, however, visited India first. V. Shah, *Maile dekhe ko darbar: Sainik sachib ko samsmaran* [The Palace I Saw: Memoirs of a Military Secretary], 2010, p. 85.

26 S. Sarkar, "China's Cold War On Tibet," *ISN Security Watch*, December 4, 2008. Online.

27 S. Sarkar, "Gyanendra Says China Card Brought His Downfall: Report," *Indo-Asian News Service*, December 3, 2008.

28 "China Trying to Influence Nepal's Army?" *Press Trust of India*, January 11, 2009.

29 D. Adhikary, "A Middle Path Opens Up To Nepal," *Asia Times Online*, March 20, 2009.

30 A.K. Mehta, a retired general in the Indian Army, and K.V. Rajan, a former Indian ambassador to Nepal, made such comments during interviews with the BBC Nepali Service. Ashok K. Mehta, BBC Nepali Service interview, March 11, 2009 (my transcription). "Rajanspeak," *Nepali Times*, Issue 450, May 8, 2009. Moreover, the man the Maoists had appointed as the new army chief, General Kul Bahadur Khadka, was reported to have pro-Chinese leanings. See "Nepal: A Political Crisis and Indo-Chinese Tensions," *Stratfor*, May 4, 2009.

31 S. Varadarajan, "Delhi Missed Chance to Resolve Nepal Crisis," *The Hindu* (Madras), May 11, 2009.

32 "Dalai Lama Invited To Visit Nepal," *The Telegraph*, July 2, 2009.

33 P. Kafle, "Chin le kasdai cha" [Chinese Noose Tightening], *Naya Patrika*, August 15, 2009.

34 M.R. Josse, "Zhang Gaoli's Banquet Speech," *People's Review*, September 24, 2009.

35 N.P. Upadhyaya, "Beijing To Meet Delhi in Kathmandu," *The Telegraph Weekly*, September 9, 2009.

36 "Nepal To Deploy Police On Tibet Border: Minister," *Agence France-Presse*, October 4, 2009.

37 *China's National Defense in 2008*, Beijing: Information Office of the State Council of the People's Republic of China, January 2009, p. 6.

38 "India dismisses Prachanda report on anti-China activities," *Indo-Asian News Service*, October 6, 2009.

39 Wang Hongwei, interview with BBC Nepali Service, October 21, 2009, (my transcription).

40 Hu Shisheng, a researcher of Southern Asian studies at the China Institutes of Contemporary International Relations, quoted in Zuo Xuan, "India Covets Dalai Lama's Visit," *Global Times*, November 9, 2009.

41 In subsequent months, Chakra Prasad Bastola, foreign minister at the time of the 2001 palace killings, and General Bibek Shah, military secretary to King Birendra, would claim that the massacre was part of an international conspiracy.

42 Zhang Li, *To Manage Conflict in South Asia*, October 2009, p. 80.

43 Dai Bing. "India Building a Security Barrier Against China," *China.org.cn*, February 8, 2010.

44 The fact that the departing Indian Ambassador, Rakesh Sood, and his presumptive successor, Jayanta Prasad, both served as their government's envoy in Kabul was considered more than coincidental. For informed Nepalese perspectives on Yang Houlan's appointment, see M.R. Josse, "Sino-Nepal Ties Upgraded to New Strategic High," *People's Review* (Kathmandu), June 2, 2011; and A. Upadhyay, "China's New Ambassador," *The Kathmandu Post*, June 6, 2011.

45 Wang Hongwei, interview with BBC Nepali Service, October 21, 2009.

46 Based on my conversations and email communication with Chinese sources.

47 T.R. Aryal. "Nepali Maoists In China's Eyes," *Republica*, August 9, 2010.

12 Beyond Tibet

1 Zhao Gancheng, "South Asia's Position in the International Order and Choice Before China," *South Asian Studies* (Chinese), No. 1, 2010.

2 One prominent Indian analyst believes China is in the third phase of the security and foreign policy objectives in Nepal set forth by Mao Zedong. In this phase, he writes, Beijing has adopted an aggressive posture to weaken New Delhi's hold on Nepal with a wider focus on encircling India. Kumar, S. "China's Expanding Footprint in Nepal: Threats to India," *Journal of Defence Studies*, 5:2, pp. 77–89.

3 I have treated the perceptual and contextual factors hindering Nepal–India relations in an earlier book. S. Upadhya, *The Raj Lives: India in Nepal*, 2008.

4 J. Lamont and K. Hille, "Chinese Essay Sparks Outcry in India," *Financial Times*, August 12, 2009.

5 Zhu Shansan, "90% in Online Poll Believe India Threatens China's Security," *Global Times*, June 12, 2009.

6 B. Verma, "Unmasking China," *Indian Defence Review*, 24:3, 2009.

7 Since these territories were never part of India for the British to have granted independence, supporters of the Greater Nepal movement maintain that the British should have returned them to Nepal. While Indians dismiss such claims, in private

conversations with me, a few academics and officials have conceded that the Chinese could try to take advantage, especially amid a general deterioriation of Sino-Indian relations.

8 A. Scobell, "'Cult Of Defense' And 'Great Power Dreams': The Influence Of Strategic Culture On China's Relationship With India" in Michael R. Chambers (ed.), *South Asia In 2020: Future Strategic Balances And Alliances*, November 2002, p. 346.

9 B. Emmott, *Rivals: How the Power Struggle Between China, India and Japan Will Shape Our Next Decade*. 2008, p. 257.

10 W. Lam, "Hu's 'New Deal' with Tibet: Chinese Characteristics and Tibetan Traits?" *China Brief*, 10:2, January 21, 2010.

11 R. Sikri, *Challenge and Strategy: Rethinking India's Foreign Policy*, 2009, p. 104; S. Ganguly, "Assessing India's Response To The Rise of China: Fears and Misgivings" in C.W. Pumphrey (ed.) *The Rise of China in Asia*, 2002, pp. 101–2.

12 For an excellent overview of the Karmapa Lama's exile and its implications see T. Johnson, *Tragedy in Crimson*, 2011, pp. 137–58.

13 Lan Jianxue, "21st Century China–Nepal Relations," *South Asian Studies* (Chinese), 2009.

14 D.N. Dhungel and S.B. Pun (eds.), *The Nepal–India Water Relationship: Challenges*, 2009, pp. 8–9.

15 P.K. Gautam, "Sino-Indian Water Issues," *Strategic Analysis*, 32:6, 2008, pp. 969–74.

16 K. Sibal, "India–China Relations, Some Reflections," *Indian Defence Review*, 23:1, January–March 2008, pp. 200–4.

17 Lei Guang, "From National Identity to National security," *The Pacific Review*, 17:3, 2004, pp. 399–422.

18 M.W. Frazier, "Quiet Competition and the Future of Sino-Indian Relations," in F.R. Frankel and H. Harding (eds.), *The India–China Relationship: What the United States Needs to Know*, 2004, p. 310.

19 Addressing a closed-door security conference in December 2009, Indian army chief General Deepak Kapoor was quoted as saying that India's new war doctrine planned for fighting China and Pakistan simultaneously, prompting a particularly strong reaction from Islamabad. Beijing, by contrast, was relatively quiet.

20 Frazier, *Quiet Competition*, 2004, p. 310.

21 Emmott, *Rivals*, 2008, p. 2.

22 B. Chellaney, *Asian Juggernaut*, 2010, p. 239.

23 Ibid., pp. 238–9.

24 J. Hoagland, "As Obama Bets on Asia, Regional Players Hedge," *Washington Post*, February 14, 2010.

25 Chellaney, *Asian Juggernaut*, 2010, p. 249.

26 C.R. Mohan, "India and the Balance of Power," *Foreign Affairs*, 85:4, 2006.

27 M. Malik, "Eyeing the Dragon," in S.P. Limaye (ed.), *Asia's China Debate*, December 2003, pp. 6–8.

28 R.D. Kaplan, "The Geography of Chinese Power," *Foreign Affairs*, 3:89, May–June, 2010.

29 S. Randol, "How to Approach the Elephant," *Asian Affairs*, 34:4, 2008, pp. 211–26.

30 "India's Unwise Military Moves," *People's Daily Online*, June 11, 2009.

31 Based on my conversations and email communication with Chinese officials.

32 Li Hongmei, "Veiled Threat or Good Neighbor?" *People's Daily Online*. June 19, 2009.

33 Based on my conversations with Chinese analysts.

34 M. Jacques, *When China Rules the World*, 2009, pp. 229–32.

35 For a full discussion of the various scenarios, see Frazier, "Quiet Competition," 2004, pp. 294–318.

36 Wang Hongwei, "Sino-Nepal Relations in the 1980s," *Asian Survey*, 25:5, May 1985, p. 513.

37 Wang Hongwei, in an email interview with me.
38 See, for example, commentary by Huang Kunlun, "Safeguarding National Security Needs to Transcend the Territorial Space," *PLA Daily*, January 4, 2009.
39 My calculations based on open source material. I owe particular debt to Chandan Ghimire, joint secretary of Nepal's Ministry of Industry and Commerce.
40 P.S. Palit, "China's Soft Power in South Asia," *RSIS Working Paper No. 200*, June 8, 2010.
41 The Asia Pacific Exchange and Co-operation Foundation said it planned to raise $3 billion at home and abroad to build temples, an airport, a highway, hotels, convention centres and a Buddhist university in Lumbini and transform it into an attraction for Buddhists around the world in the same way as Mecca is to Muslims and the Vatican for Catholics.
42 M.T. Fravel, "China's Search for Military Power," *The Washington Quarterly*, 31:3, 2008, p. 127.
43 M. Dabhade and H.V. Pant, "Coping With Challenges to Sovereignty," *Contemporary South Asia*, 13:2, 2004, p. 162.
44 Zhang Li, *To Manage Conflict in South Asia*, October 2009, p. 90.
45 Chellaney, *Asian Juggernaut*, 2010, pp. 192–3.
46 S. Acharya, 'Chin ko Nepal Najar' [China's View of Nepal], *Nepal Weekly* (Kathmandu), May 17, 2009.
47 Based on my conversations with two Chinese experts.
48 K.C. Dash, *Regionalism in South Asia*, 2008, p. 73.
49 For an incisive discussion on this subject, see B. Koirala, "Sino-Nepalese Relations: Factoring In India," *China Report*, 46:3, 2010, pp. 231–42.
50 For a recent Indian perspective, see R. Sikri, "The Tibet Factor in China–India Relations," *Journal of International Affairs*, 64:2, 2011, pp. 55–72.
51 H. Harding, "The Evolution of the Strategic Triangle," in F.R. Frankel and H. Harding (eds.) *The India–China Relationship*, 2004, p. 322.
52 For an informed Indian perspective on the diverse interests and influences of foreign powers and their impact on New Delhi, see N. Nayak, "Involvement of Major Powers in Nepal Since the 1990s," *Strategic Analysis*, 33:1, 2009, pp. 41–53.
53 See, for example, Huang Kunlun, "Safeguarding National Security," *PLA Daily*, January 4, 2009.
54 Several Nepalese academics and journalists visiting China over the past three years have spoken to me of the great interest their semi-official hosts have shown in the possibility of the restoration of the monarchy and its impact on building stability in Nepal and the region.
55 U. Parashar, "India Losing Little Great Game," *Hindustan Times*, September 5, 2010.

Bibliography

"2 Wives Pose U.S. Problem If King Visits," *Washington Post*, November 5, 1954.

Acharya, A., "Wen Jiabao's South Asian Sojourn," *China Report*, Vol. 41, Issue 3, 2005, pp. 315–26.

Acharya, B.R., *Nepalko Samkshipta Brittanta* [A Concise Account of Nepal], Kathmandu: Pramod Shamsher and Nir Bikram 'Pyasi', 1966.

Acharya, B.R., "General Bhimsen Thapa And The Samar Jung Company," *Regmi Research Series*, Year 4, No. 9, Kathmandu, September 1972.

Acharya, B.R., "The Reign Of King Pratap Simha," *Regmi Research Series*. Year 6, No. 2, Kathmandu: February 1, 1974.

Acharya, B.R., *Aba Yasto Kahile Na Hos* [May This Never Happen Again], Kathmandu: Sri Krishna Acharya, 2006.

Acharya, S., 'Chin ko Nepal Najar' [China's View of Nepal], *Nepal Weekly* (Kathmandu), May 17, 2009.

Addy, P., "Imperial Prophet or Scaremonger?: Curzon's Tibetan Policy Reconsidered," *Asian Affairs*, Vol. 14, 1983, pp. 54–67.

Addy, P., *Tibet on the Imperial Chessboard: The Making of British Policy Towards Lhasa, 1899–1925*, Calcutta: Academic Publishers, 1984.

Adhikari, P., *Ties That Bind: An Account of Nepal-China Relations*, Kathmandu: Sangam Institute, 2010.

Adhikary, D., "Nepal Still In A State of Flux," *Asia Times*, October 24, 2006. Online. Available www.atimes.com/atimes/South_Asia/HJ24Df01.html (accessed December 23, 2009).

Adhikary, D., "A Middle Path Opens Up To Nepal," *Asia Times*, March 20, 2009. Online. Available www.atimes.com/atimes/South_Asia/KC20Df02.html (accessed April 1, 2009).

Anand, J.P., "Nepal's Zone of Peace Concept and China," China Report, 13:6, 1977, pp. 6–10.

Andrew, C.M. and V. Mitrokhin, *The World Was Going Our Way: The KGB and the Battle for the Third World*, New York: Basic Books, 2005.

Andreyev, A., *Soviet Russia & Tibet: The Debacle of Secret Diplomacy, 1918–30s*, Leiden: Brill, 2003.

"Appeasing China: Restricting the Rights of Tibetans in Nepal," *Human Rights Watch*, July 23, 2008.

"Arms from US and China, What For?" *The Telegraph Weekly*, February 8, 2008, p. 1.

Armstrong, H.F., "Where India Faces China," *Foreign Affairs*, Vol. 37, July 1959, pp. 617–25.

Arpi, C., "Dalai Lama & the Russian Card," *The Statesman* (Calcutta), May 29, 2010.

Aryal, T.R., "Nepali Maoists In China's Eyes," *Republica*, August 9, 2010.

Avedon, J.F., *In Exile from the Land of Snows*, New York: Alfred A Knopf, 1984.

Bajracharya, B.R., *Bahadur Shah, the Regent of Nepal, 1785–1794*, New Delhi: Anmol Publications, 1992.

Baral, L.R., *Nepal: Problems of Governance*, New Delhi: Konark, 1993, p. 167.

Baral, L.R., "Nepal in 1978: Year of Hopes and Confusions," *Asian Survey*, Vol. 19, No. 2, February 1979, pp. 198–204.

Baral, L.R., "Nepal in 1979: Political System in Crisis," *Asian Survey*, Vol. 20, No. 2, February 1980, pp. 197–205.

Baral, L.R., "Nepal in 1986: Problem of Political Management," *Asian Survey*, Vol. 27, No. 2, February 1987, pp. 173–80.

Baral, L.R., "Nepal in 1987: Politics without Power," *Asian Survey*, Vol. 28, No. 2, February 1988, pp. 172–79.

Baral, L.R., "Nepal in 2001: The Strained Monarchy," *Asian Survey*, Vol. 42 No. 1, January–February 2002, pp. 198–203.

Baruah, A., "Nepal Needs To Be Transparent for Better Ties," *The Hindu* (Madras), February 14, 2003.

BBC Nepali Service, interview with A.K.Mehta and K.V. Rajan, March 11, 2009.

BBC Nepali Service, interview with Wang Hongwei, October 21, 2009, (my transcription).

"Beijing's Finger in Nepal's Maoist Revolt," DEBKA, May 28, 2002. Online. Available www.debka.com/article.php?aid=83 (accessed April 4, 2006).

Bell, C., *The People of Tibet*, Oxford: Clarendon, 1928.

Bell, C., *Tibet Past and Present*, New Delhi: Motilal Banarasidas, 1992.

Bhat, B., "Chiyars! Naya Nata," [Cheers, New Relations] *Nepal Weekly* (Kathmandu), June 17, 2007.

Bhatt, S.C., *The Triangle India–Nepa–China: A Study of Treaty Relations*, New Delhi: Gyan Publishing House, 1996, p. 84.

Bhattachacharjee, G.P., *India and the Politics of Modern Nepal*, Calcutta: Minerva, 1970.

Bhattarai, B.R., 'Naya kot parba lai manyata dina hudaina' [Do Not Legitimize the New Kot Parba], *Kantipur*, June 6, 2001.

Bhattarai, N., *Chin Ra Tyasasita Nepal Ko Sambandha* [China and Its Relations with Nepal], Kathmandu: Nepal Academy, 2018 B.S [1961].

Bhattarai, N., *Nepal and China: A Historical Perspective*, New Delhi: Adroit Publishers, 2010.

Bhattarai, N., *Nepal–Chin Sambhanda* [Nepal–China Relations], Kathmandu, Sajha Prakashan, 2058 [2001].

Bista, D.B., "Nepalis in Tibet," *Contributions to Nepalese Studies*, Vol. 8 No. 1, 1980, pp. 1–19.

Boulger, C.D. and M.W. Hazeltine, *China*, New York, Peter Fenelon Collier, 1901.

Boulnois, L., "Chinese Maps and Prints on the Tibet Gorkha War of 1788–92," *Kailash*, Vol. 15, Nos. 1–2, 1989, pp. 83–112.

Bretschneider, E., *Medieval Researches from Eastern Asiatic Sources*. Vol. 2, London: Trubner, 1888.

Central Intelligence Agency, National Intelligence Estimate Number 100–2–60, *Sino-Indian Relations*, May 17, 1960, p. 5. Online. Available www.foia.cia.gov/docs/DOC_0001098216/DOC_0001098216.pdf (accessed December 23, 2009).

Central Intelligence Agency, Special Estimate SE-32, *Consequences of Communist Control Over South Asia*, October 3, 1952. Online. Available www.foia.cia.gov/docs/DOC_0000010597/DOC_0000010597.pdf (accessed December 23, 2009).

Ch'ing-Chi-Ch'ou-Tsang-Tsou-Tu (Memorials and correspondence concerning the arrangement of affairs during the latter part of the Ch'ing dynasty), Vol. I, Peiping, National Academy, 1938.

Chandrasekharan, S., "Deuba's Visit and Thereafter." Nepal Update No. 55. *South Asia Analysis Group*, September 29, 2004. Online. Available www.saag.org/common/uploaded_files/note240.html (accessed July 2, 2011).

Chang, J. and J. Halliday. *Mao: The Untold Story*, New York: Alfred Knopf, 2005.

Chatterji, B., *A Study of Recent Nepali Politics*, Calcutta: World Press, 1967.

Chatterji, B., *People, Palace And Politics*, New Delhi: Ankur, 1980.

Chellaney, B., *Asian Juggernaut: The Rise of China, India and Japan*, New York: HarperCollins, 2010.

Chen Jian, "The Tibetan Rebellion of 1959 and China's Changing Relations with India and the Soviet Union," *Journal of Cold War Studies*, Vol. 8, No. 3, Summer 2006, pp. 54–101.

"Chiangs Get Many Gifts," *New York Times*, May 14, 1947.

"China Begins Building Tibet–Nepal Rail Link: Official," *Agence France Presse*, April 26, 2008.

"China Hopes Nepal to Realize Social Security: FM Spokesman," *Xinhua*, February 1, 2005.

"China Offers India Help on Maoist Rebels," *United Press International*, October 27, 2005.

"China to discuss US military presence with Nepal," *Press Trust of India*, April 28, 2002.

"China Trying to Influence Nepal's Army?" *Press Trust of India*, January 11, 2009.

"China Unhappy Over Nepal's Response To Anti-China Demonstrations," *Deutsche Presse Agentur*, May 13, 2008.

"China Unhappy Over Tibet Refugees," *The Kathmandu Post*, July 4, 2006.

"China-Nepal Friendship Highway Completed," *Beijing Review*, June 2, 1967.

"China, Nepal Pledge Further Military Exchanges," *People's Daily Online*, October 21, 2005.

China's National Defense in 2008, Beijing: Information Office of the State Council of the People's Republic of China, January 2009.

"Chinese Said To Infiltrate Nepal," *Washington Post*, December 11, 1959.

Clarridge, D.R. and D. Diehl, *A Spy for All Seasons: My Life in the CIA*, New York: Scribner, 1997.

Conboy, K.J. and J. Morrison, *The CIA's Secret War in Tibet*, Lawrence: University Press of Kansas, 2002.

Copper, J.F., *China's Foreign Aid*, Lexington, Mass.: Lexington Books, 1976.

Dabhade, M. and H.V. Pant, "Coping With Challenges to Sovereignty: Sino-Indian Rivalry and Nepal's Foreign Policy," *Contemporary South Asia*, Vol. 13, No. 2, 2004, pp. 157–69.

Dai Bing, "India Building a Security Barrier Against China," *China.org.cn*, February 8, 2010. Online. Available www.china.org.cn/opinion/2010–02/08/content_19387164.htm (accessed March 1, 2010).

"Dalai Lama Invited To Visit Nepal," *The Telegraph*, July 2, 2009. Online. Available www.telegraphnepal.com/headline/2009–07–01/dalai-lama-invited-to-visit-nepal (accessed August 10, 2011).

"Dalai Lama, Accepting Prize, Urges Peaceful Tibet Solution," *New York Times*, December 11, 1989.

Dash, K.C., *Regionalism in South Asia: Negotiating Cooperation, Institutional Structures*, London and New York: Routledge, 2008.

Deshpande, G.P., "China and the Himalayan States," *China Report*; Vol. 3, No. 2, 1967, pp. 18–20.

Deshpande, R., "Save Monarchy, But Restore Democracy," *The Times of India*, April 19, 2006.

Devkota, G.B., *Nepal ko Rajnitik Darpan* [Political Mirror of Nepal], Kathmandu, 1959.

Devraj, R., "Emergency Lifted as Nepal King's China Card Fails," *Inter-Press Service*, May 1, 2005.

Dharamdasani, M.D., "A Study of New Delhi's Role and Attitude Towards the Democratic Forces in Nepal" in *Looking to the Future: Indo-Nepal Relations in Perspective.* Baral, L.R. (ed.). New Delhi: Anmol Publications, 1996.

Dhungel, D.N. and S.B. Pun (eds), *The Nepal-India Water Relationship: Challenges*, Berlin: Springer, 2009.

Dictionary of Ming Biography 1368–1644, Ann Arbor: Association of Asian Studies, 1976.

Digby, W., *1857. A Friend in Need. 1887. Friendship Forgotten.* London: Indian Political Agency, 1890.

Dillon, D., "China's Zombie Countries," *National Review Online*, May 10, 2005. Online Available www.nationalreview.com/comment/dillon200505100804.asp (accessed January 5, 2006).

Douglas, R.K., *China*, London: Society for Promoting Christian Knowledge, 1887.

Dunham, M., *Buddha's Warriors, The Story of the CIA-Backed Tibetan Freedom Fighters, the Chinese Invasion, and the Ultimate Fall of Tibet*, New York: Jeremy P. Tarcher/Penguin, 2004.

Eisenhower, D.D., *Waging Peace: The White House Years: A Personal Account 1956–1961*, New York: Doubleday, 1965.

Emmott, B., *Rivals: How the Power Struggle Between China, India and Japan Will Shape Our Next Decade*. New York: Harcourt Inc, 2008.

"Equidistance with India, China will be maintained," Prachanda interview with Karan Thapar, *CNN-IBN*, May 18, 2008. Online. Available www.in.com/videos/watchvideo-equidistance-with-india-china-will-be-maintained-695541.html (accessed August 10, 2011).

Fairbank, J.K., *China: A New History*, Cambridge Mass.: Harvard University Press, 1992.

Fathers, M., "Thunder Out of China," *Time*, 17 January, 2000.

Frängsmyr, T. and I. Abrams (eds), *Nobel Lectures: Peace: 1981–1990*, Singapore: World Scientific Publishing Co., 1997.

Frankel, F.R., and H. Harding (eds), *The India-China Relationship: What the United States Needs to Know*, New York: Columbia University Press, 2004.

Fravel, M.T., "China's Search for Military Power," *The Washington Quarterly*, Vol. 31 No. 3, 2008, pp. 125–41.

Frazier, M.W., "Quiet Competition and the Future of Sino-Indian Relations," in Frankel, F.R. and H. Harding (eds), *The India–China Relationship: What the United States Needs to Know*, New York: Columbia University Press, 2004.

Gaige, F., Nepal: The Search for National Concensus, *Asia Survey*, 10:2, February 1970, pp. 100–6.

Ganguly, S., "Assessing India's Response To The Rise of China: Fears and Misgivings." In C.W. Pumphrey (ed.), *The Rise of China in Asia: Security Implications*, Carlisle, PA: Strategic Studies Institute, 2002, pp. 95–104.

Garver, J.W., "China and South Asia," *The ANNALS of the American Academy of Political and Social Science*, Vol. 519, 1992.

Garver, J.W., *Protracted Contest: Sino-Indian Rivalry in the Twentieth Century*, Seattle and London: University of Washington Press, 2001.

Garver, J.W. and Fei-Ling Wang, 'China's Anti-encirclement Struggle', *Asian Security*, 1555–2764, Vol. 6, Issue 3, 2010, pp. 238–61.

Gautam, P.K., "Sino-Indian Water Issues," *Strategic Analysis*, Vol. 32, No. 6, 2008, pp. 969–74.

Ghoble, T.R., *China-Nepal Relations and India*, New Delhi: Deep and Deep Publications, 1986.

Ghosh, A., "Subcontinental Drift: The China Card," *Time.com*, June 5, 2001. Online. Available www.time.com/time/world/article/0,8599,129176,00.html (accessed July 10, 2009).

Gilmour, D., *Curzon: Imperial Statesman*, New York: Farrar, Straus and Giroux Paperbacks, 2006.

Goldstein, M.C., *A History of Modern Tibet, 1913¬1951: The Demise of the Lamaist State*, Berkeley: University of California Press, 1989.

Goldstein, M.C., *The Snow Lion and the Dragon: China, Tibet and the Dalai Lama*, University of California Press, Berkeley, 1997.

Gould, T., *Imperial Warriors: Britain and the Gurkhas*, London, Granta Books, 1999.

Goyal, N., *Political History of Himalayan States: India's Relations with Himalayan States Since 1947*, 2nd ed., New Delhi: Cambridge Book and Stationery Stores, 1964.

Green, J., *Murder in the High Himalaya: Loyalty, Tragedy, and Escape from Tibet*, New York: Public Affairs, 2010.

Grunfeld, A.T., *The Making of Modern Tibet*, (Revised edition) Armonk, NY: M.E. Sharp 1996.

Gundry, R.S., *China And Her Neighbours*, London: Chapman And Hall, 1893.

Gupta, A., *Politics in Nepal: A Study of Post-Rana Political Developments and Party Politics*, New Delhi: Allied Publishers Pvt. Ltd., 1964.

Gupta, K., "Maoist Ceasefire in Nepal After Talks in India," *The Pioneer Online*, September 4, 2005.

Gurung, K.J., "Mahendra ko sandesh Mao lai" [Mahendra's Message To Mao], *Nepal Weekly* (Kathmandu), June 27, 2010, p. 11.

Gurung, K.J., *Indira Gandhi lai bhetda* [Meeting Indira Gandhi], *Nepal Weekly* (Kathmandu), July 11, 2010, p. 11.

Guta, T.L., "Aniko: Image Weaver," *Contributions to Nepalese Studies*. Vol. 24 No. 1, January 1997, pp. 71–78.

Gyawali, S.P., *Byakti ra Bicchar: Ek Vakil ko Samsmaran ra Chintan* [Person and Thoughts: The Remembrance and Contemplation of a Lawyer], Kathmandu: Jagadamba Publications, 1998.

Hachhethu, K., "Nepal's India Policy Under Communist Government," *Contributions to Nepalese Studies*, Vol. 25 No. 2, July 1999, pp. 227–38.

Hamilton, F., *An Account of the Kingdom of Nepal: And of the Territories Annexed to this Dominion by the House of Gorkha*. London: A. Constable, 1819.

Hangen, S.I., *The Rise of Ethnic Politics in Nepal: Democracy in the Margins*, New York: Routledge, 2010.

Harris, C. and T. Shakya, *Seeing Lhasa: British Depictions of the Tibetan Capital 1936–1947*, Chicago: Serindia Publications, 2003.

Hemanth, J., "Koirala Freed to Calm India," *The Telegraph* (Calcutta), April 2, 2005.

"Himalayan Tyranny," *Indian Express.* January 21, 2006. Online. Available www.indian-express.com/oldStory/86307/ (accesssed August 10, 2011).

Hoagland, J., "As Obama Bets on Asia, Regional Players Hedge, *Washington Post,* February 14, 2010.

Hoftun, M., W. Raeper and J. Whelpton, *People, Politics and Ideology: Democracy and Social Change in Nepal,* Kathmandu: Mandala Book Point, 1999.

Holslag, J., *China and India: Prospects for Peace,* New York: Columbia University Press, 2010.

Hsiao-ting, L., "War or Stratagem? Reassessing China's Military Advance towards Tibet, 1942–1943," *The China Quarterly,* Vol. 186, June 2006.

Huang Kunlun, "Safeguarding National Security Needs to Transcend the Territorial Space," *PLA Daily,* January 4, 2009.

Human Rights Watch, "Appeasing China: Restricting the Rights of Tibetans in Nepal," New York, July 23, 2008.

Hunter, W.W., *The Imperial Gazetteer of India,* London: Trübner & Co., 1886.

Hunter, W.W., *Life of Brian Houghton Hodgson,* London: John Murray, 1896.

Husain, A., *British India's Relations with the Kingdom of Nepal,* London: George Allen and Unwin Ltd., 1970.

Hutt, M. (ed.), *The Himalayan People's War: Nepal's Maoist Rebellion,* Bloomington and Indianapolis: Indiana University Press, 2004.

Hyer, P., "Japanese Expansion and Tibetan Independence" in Li Narangoa and Robert Cribb (eds), *Imperial Japan and National Identities in Asia, 1895–1945,* New York: RoutledgeCurzon, 2003.

I-Tsing, *A Record of the Buddhist Religion,* translated by J. Takakusu, Oxford: Clarendon Press, 1896.

Imperial Gazetteer of India: Provincial Series, Volume 1. Afghanistan and Nepal. Calcutta: Superintendent of Government Printing, 1908.

"India dismisses Prachanda report on anti-China activities," *Indo-Asian News Service,* October 6, 2009.

"India Expresses Concern to China over Political Turmoil in Nepal," *Press Trust of India,* January 10, 2006.

"India Growing Concerned by Growing China-Nepal Links," *United Press International,* December 20, 2005.

"India's Unwise Military Moves," *People's Daily Online,* June 11, 2009.

"Indian General Election and Soviet Setback in South Asia," *Beijing Review,* April 8, 1977, pp. 23–4.

"Indira Gandhi Government's Ferocious Features Fully Exposed," *People's Daily,* June 29, 1975.

International Crisis Group, "Nepal's Royal Coup: Making a Bad Situation Worse," *Crisis Group Asia Report No, 91,* Brussels/Kathmandu, February 9, 2005.

Jacques, M., *When China Rules the World: The End of the Western World and the Birth of a New Global Order,* New York: The Penguin Press, 2009.

Jain, G., *India Meets China in Nepal,* New York: Asia Publishing House, 1959.

Jain, G., "China's Dual Approach," *China Report,* Vol. 6, Issue 4, 1970, pp. 12–15.

James, H.E.M., *The Long White Mountain.* London: Longmans, Green & Co., 1888.

James, L., *The Rise and Fall of the British Empire,* New York: St. Martin's Press, 1994.

James, L., *Raj: The Making and Unmaking of British India,* New York: St. Martin's Press, 1997.

Jha, S.K., *Uneasy Partners: India and Nepal in the Post Colonial Era*. New Delhi: Manas, 1975.

Jian, C., "The Tibetan Rebellion of 1959 and China's Changing Relations with India and the Soviet Union," *Journal of Cold War Studies*, 8:3, Summer 2006.

Johnson, T., *Tragedy in Crimson: How the Dalai Lama Conquered the World But Lost the Battle with China*, New York: Nation Books, 2011.

Joshi, B.L. and L.E. Rose, *Democratic Innovations in Nepal: A Case Study of Political Acculturation*, Berkeley and Los Angeles: University of California Press, 1966.

Joshi, I., "Nepal–Tibbat Sambandha: Aitihasik Simhabolokan" [Nepal–Tibet Relations: An Historical Review], *Ancient Nepal*, No. 147, June 2001.

Josse, M.R., *Nepal and the World: An Editor's Notebook, Vols. 1&2*, Kathmandu: Author, 1984.

Josse, M.R., "Business As Usual: China Gives, Nepal Takes." *People's Review Weekly* (Kathmandu). May 17, 2001.

Josse, M.R., *Sino-US Relationship and its Global Implications with Special Reference to Nepal*, paper presented at a conference organized by China Study Center, Kathmandu December 18, 2003.

Josse, M.R., "Zhang Gaoli's Banquet Speech: Crammed With Important Messages," *People's Review Weekly*, September 24, 2009.

Josse, M.R., "Sino-Nepal Ties Upgraded to New Strategic High," *People's Review Weekly*, June 2, 2011.

Kafle, P., "Chin le kasdai cha" [Chinese Noose Tightening], *Naya Patrika*, August 15, 2009.

Kaplan, R.D., "The Geography of Chinese Power," *Foreign Affairs*, Vol. 3 No. 89, May/June 2010, pp. 22–41.

"Karan's Feedback: King Not Averse To Interim Govt," *Indian Express*. April 21, 2006.

Kawaguchi, E., *Three Years in Tibet*, London: Theosophical Publishing Society, 1909.

KC, K.B., *Nepal After the Revolution of 1950*, 2 Vols., Kathmandu: Sharada Prakashan Griha, 1976.

Keay, J., *China: A History*, New York: Basic Books, 2009.

Khadka, N., "Chinese Foreign Policy toward Nepal in the Cold War Period: An Assessment," *China Report*, Vol. 35, Issue 1, 1999, pp. 61–81.

Khadka, N., "Geopolitics and Development: A Nepalese Perspective," *Asian Affairs*, Vol. 19, No. 3, 1992, pp. 134–67.

Khanal, Y.N., "Nepal in 1985: An Uneasy Year," *Asian Survey*, Vol. 26, No. 2, February, 1986, pp. 246–52.

"King Gyanendra Is Not Anti-Indian," The Rediff Interview/Former foreign secretary Romesh Bhandari, June 11, 2001, Online. Available www.rediff.com/news/2001/jun/11inter.htm (accessed July 10, 2009).

"King Ruled Admissable: U.S. Consul Supports Entry of Tribhubana of Nepal," *New York Times*, December 2, 1954.

Kirkpatrick, W., *An Account of the Kingdom of Nepal*. London: W. Bulmer & Co. for William Miller, 1811.

Kissinger, H.A., *On China*, New York: The Penguin Press, 2011.

Knaus, J.K., *Orphans of the Cold War: America and the Tibetan Struggle for Survival*, New York: PublicAffairs, 2000.

Knaus, J.K., "Official Policies and Covert Programs: The U.S. State Department, the CIA, and the Tibetan Resistance," *Journal of Cold War Studies*, Vol. 5, No. 3, 2003, pp. 54–79.

"Koirala Appeals for Railway Link with China," *The Telegraph Weekly*, December 25, 2007, p. 3.

Koirala, B., "Sino-Nepalese Relations: Factoring In India," *China Report*, Vol. 46, Issue 3, 2010, pp. 231–42.

Koirala, B.P., *Bisweshwar Prasad Koiralako Atmabritanta*, Sharma, Ganesh Raj (collector). Jagadamba Prakashan, Kathmandu 2055 B.S.[1998].

Koirala, M.P., *A Role In a Revolution*. Kathmandu: Jagadamba, 2008.

Koirala, N., "Nepal in 1989: A Very Difficult Year," *Asian Survey*, Vol. 30, No. 2, February 1990, pp. 136–43.

Koirala, N., "Nepal in 1990: End of an Era," *Asian Survey*, Vol. 31, No. 2, February 1991, pp. 134–39.

Kumar, S. "China's Expanding Footprint in Nepal: Threats to India," *Journal of Defence Studies*, Vol 5. No 2. April 2011, pp. 77–89. Online. Available http://idsa.in/system/files/jds_5_2_skumar.pdf (accessed August 10, 2011).

Kunwar, M.J., "China and War in the Himalayas, 1792–1793," *The English Historical Review*, Vol. 77, No. 303, 1962, pp. 283–97.

Lai, D., "Great Power Peace and Stability in Asia: China's Emerging Role," in A. Gupta (ed.) *Strategic Stability in Asia*, Aldershot, UK: Ashgate Publishing, 2008.

Laird, T., *The Story of Tibet. Conversations with the Dalai Lama*. Grove Press, New York, 2006.

Lam, W., "Hu's 'New Deal' with Tibet: Chinese Characteristics and Tibetan Traits?" *China Brief*, Vol. 10 Issue 2, Washington DC: The Jamestown Foundation, January 21, 2010. Online. Available www.jamestown.org/programs/chinabrief/single/?tx_ttnews%5Btt_news%5D=35930&tx_ttnews%5BbackPid%5D=25&cHash=32e2b6280c (Accessed August 10, 2011).

Lamb, A., *British India And Tibet, 1766–1910*. London and New York: Routledge dy Kegan Paul. 1986.

Lamb, A., "The McMahon Line" in A. McKay (ed.), *The History of Tibet: The Modern Period: 1895–1959*, London: RoutledgeCurzon, 2003, pp. 101–26.

Lamont J., and K. Hille, "Chinese Essay Sparks Outcry in India," *Financial Times*, August 12, 2009.

Lan Jianxue, "21st Century China–Nepal Relations: The Perspective of National Interests," *South Asian Studies* (Chinese), No. 4, 2009.

Landon, P., *Nepal 2 Vols*, London: Constable. 1928. Reprint. New Delhi: Asian Educational Services, 1993.

Lawoti, M. and A.K. Pahari (eds), *The Maoist Insurgency in Nepal: Revolution in the Twenty First Century*, New York: Routledge, 2010.

Lee, D.J., "National China Re-Establishes Relations with the Kingdom of Nepal," *The China Weekly Review*, 55:27, 1930.

Lee, D.J., "The Prime Minister of Nepal Decorated By China," *The China Weekly Review*, Vol. 60, 9 April 1932.

Lei Guang, "From National Identity to National security: China's Changing Responses Toward India in 1962 and 1998, *The Pacific Review*, Vol. 17 No. 3, 2004, pp. 399–422.

Levi, W., "Government and Politics in Nepal: II," *Far Eastern Survey*, Vol. 22, No. 1, January 14, 1953, pp. 5–10.

Levi, W., "Politics in Nepal," *Far Eastern Survey*, Vol. 25, No. 3, March 1956, pp. 39–46.

Levi, W., "Nepal in World Politics," *Pacific Affairs*, Vol. 30, No. September 3, 1957, pp. 236–48.

Li Hongmei, "Veiled Threat or Good Neighbor?" *People's Daily Online.* June 19, 2009. Online. Available http://english.peopledaily.com.cn/90002/96417/6682302.html (accessed July 15, 2009).

Liang Yan, "The Guerrilla Leaders Going Out of the Jungle," *Global Times*, July 15, 2006.

Lin Hsiao-ting, "War or Stratagem? Reassessing China's Military Advance towards Tibet, 1942–1943," *The China Quarterly*, Vol. 186, June 2006, pp. 446–62.

Liu, M., T. Clifton, P. Roberts and T. Laird, "A Secret War on the Roof of the World," *Newsweek*, Volume 134, Issue 7, August 16, 1999.

Lostumbo, R., "Tibetan Refugees in Nepal: From Established Settlements to Forcible Repatriation," *Georgetown Immigration Law Journal.* Vol. 9, No. 4. 1995, pp. 911–17.

Low, F., *Struggle for Asia*, London: Frederick Muller, 1955.

Lustgarten, A., *China's Great Train*, New York: Times Books, 2008.

Maitra, R., "Nepal Bows to China's Demands," *Asia Times Online*, June 17, 2003. Online. Available www.atimes.com/atimes/South_Asia/EF17Df04.html (accessed February 1, 2009).

Malik, M., "Eyeing the Dragon: India's China Debate," in S.P. Limaye (ed.), *Asia's China Debate*, Honolulu: Asia-Pacific Center for Security Studies, December 2003.

Manandhar, T.R., "British Residents at the Court of Nepal During the 19th Century," *Voice of History*, Vol. 17–20 No. 1, 2005, pp. 5–22.

Manandhar, T.R. and T.P. Mishra, *Nepal's Quinquennial Missions to China.* Kathmandu: Purna Devi Manandhar and Pushpa Mishra, 1986.

Manandhar, V.K., *Cultural and Political Aspects of Nepal-China Relations.* New Delhi: Adroit Publishers, 1999.

Manandhar, V.K., "The Nepalese Quinquennial Missions Of 1792 And 1795 To China," *Ancient Nepal*, No. 145, July 2000, pp. 7–18.

Manandhar, V.K., *A Comprehensive History Of Nepal–China Relations Up To 1955 A.D.*, 2 *Vols.*, New Delhi: Adroit Publishers, 2004.

Manchanda, R., "Emergency and a Crisis," *Frontline.* March 2–15, 2002. Online. Available www.frontlineonnet.com/fl1905/19050500.htm (accessed January 13, 2009).

Mann, J., "China Moves to Limit Foreign Access to Tibet," *Los Angeles Times*, July 25, 1985.

"Maoists Not to Join Koirala-led Govt: Gurung," *The Himalayan Times*, March 25, 2007.

"Maoists Say Prachanda Tape is 'Propaganda'," *Indo-Asian News Service.* May 22, 2005.

Markham, C.R., G.Bogle and T.Manning, *Narratives of the Mission of George Bogle to Tibet and of the Journey of Thomas Manning to Lhasa*, 2d ed. London: Trübner and Co., 1879.

Martin, R.M., *China: Political, Commercial, and Social; An Official Report. Vol II.* London: James Madden, 1847.

McCarthy, R.E., *Tears of the Lotus.* Jefferson, NC: McFarland & Company, Inc., 1997.

McGranahan, C., "Tibet's Cold War: The CIA and the Chushi Gangdrug Resistance, 1956–1974," *Journal of Cold War Studies* Vol. 8, No. 3, Summer 2006, pp. 102–30.

McGranahan, C., *Arrested Histories: Tibet, the CIA and Memories of a Forgotten War*, Durham, N.C.: Duke University Press, 2010.

McKay, A., "Hitler and the Himalayas: the SS Mission to Tibet," *Tricycle*, Vol. 10 No. 3, 2001, pp. 64–8, 90–3.

McMahon, R.J., *The Cold War on the Periphery: The United States, India, and Pakistan*, New York: Columbia University Press, 1994.

Mehra, P., "China and South Asia: Some Reflections on the Past and the Future," *China Report*, Vol. 30, Issue 3, 1994, pp. 295–307.

Meyer, K.E. and S.B. Brysac, *Tournament of Shadows: The Great Game and the Race for Empire in Central Asia*, New York: Basic Books, 2006.

Mihaly, E.B., *Foreign Aid and Politics in Nepal*. London: Oxford University Press, 1965.

Mishra, T.P., "Sri Teen Maharaj Chandra Shamsher ra Chiniya Samman." [Chandra Shamsher and Chinese Honor] *Ancient Nepal*, Number 98–99, February–May 1987, pp. 4–13.

Mohan, C. R., "India and the Balance of Power," *Foreign Affairs*, Vol. 85, No. 4, 2006, pp. 17–32.

Mojumdar, K., *Political Relations Between India and Nepal, 1877–1923*, New Delhi: Munshiram Manoharlal, 1973.

Moraes, F., *The Revolt in Tibet*, New York: Macmillan, 1960.

Moynihan, M., "Tibetan Refugees in Nepal, in Bernstorff, Dagmar and Hubertus von Welck (eds.), *Exile As A Challenge: The Tibetan Diaspora*, Hyderabad, India: Orient Longman, 2003.

"MPRF Expresses Sorrow over Gaur Incident," *The Kathmandu Post*, March 23, 2007.

Mukul, A., "Indian Spooks Host Nepal Rebel," *The Times of India*, May 24, 2005. Online. Available http://timesofindia.indiatimes.com//india/Indian-spooks-host-Nepal-rebel/articleshow/1120698.cms (accessed August 10, 2011).

Muni, S.D., *India's Foreign Policy: The Democracy Dimension*, New Delhi: Foundation Books, 2009.

Nayak, N., "Involvement of Major Powers in Nepal Since the 1990s: Implications for India," *Strategic Analysis*, Vol. 33, Issue 1, 2009, pp. 41–53.

Nayar, K.P., "Delhi Leaves Nepal Gate Ajar," *The Telegraph* (Calcutta), June 23, 2002.

"Nepal Bars Red Claim to Everest," *Washington Post*, July 5, 1960.

"Nepal Committed to Enhancing Friendship with China," *Xinhua*, September 4, 2001.

"Nepal Favors Inclusion of China," *The Hindu* (Madras), April 4, 2007.

"Nepal Itself Can Resolve Current Crisis: Chinese envoy," *Kantipur Online*, May 14, 2004.

"Nepal To Construct Highway To Link With China," *Xinhua*, May 28, 2006.

"Nepal To Deploy Police On Tibet Border: Minister," *Agence France-Presse*, October 4, 2009.

"Nepal to Fully Support One China Policy:FM," *People's Daily Online*, December 9, 2002. Online. Available http://english.peopledaily.com.cn (accessed February 1, 2009).

Nepal, G.M., "Jang Bahadur ko bidesh niti ra 1904 ko Peking jane pratinidhi mandal" [Jang Bahadur's Foreign Policy and the 1847 Mission to China] *Contributions to Nepalese Studies*, Vol. 8, No. 2, June 1981, pp. 175–206.

"Nepal: A Political Crisis and Indo-Chinese Tensions," *Stratfor*, May 4, 2009.

"Nepal: Challenge for India and China," *Asia Times*, June 8, 2001. Online. Available http://atimes.com/editor/CF08Ba01.html (accessed July 10, 2009).

"Nepal's King Birendra's Murder and the Chinese Revelation," *The Telegraph Online*, November 13, 2008. Online. Available www.telegraphnepal.com/news_det.php?news_id=4353 (accessed November 15, 2008).

"Nepal's Public Opinion Supports Bista in Condemning Indian Government's Expansionist Policy," *Beijing Review*, July 11, 1969, p. 29.

"Nepalese Ambassador to China Gives Reception," *People's Daily*, June 12, 1969, and *Beijing Review*, June 20, 1969.

"Nepali Army Head Reaffirms Support for One-China Policy," *People's Daily Online*, September 2, 2001.

"Nepali Rebel Said To Plan New Attack," *New York Times*, May 9, 1952.

Nepali, C.R., *Shri Panch Rana Bahadur Shah*, Kathmandu: Mary Rajbhandari, 1964.

"New Delhi Must Play a More Assertive Role," *The Times of India*, May 28, 2004.

Norbu, D., "Strategic Development in Tibet: Implications for Its Neighbors." *Asian Survey*, Vol. 19, No. 3, Mar. 1979, pp. 245–59.

O'Connor, W.F., *On the Frontier and Beyond: A Record of Thirty Years' Service*, London, 1931.

Oldfield, H.A., *Sketches From Nipal. 2 Vols.* London: W.H. Allen and Co., 1880.

Padmanabhan, P.K., "Nepal Has Importance Far Beyond Its Size," *Los Angeles Times*, March 1, 1961.

Palit, P.S., "China's Soft Power in South Asia," RSIS Working Paper No. 200, Singapore: S. Rajaratnam School of International Studies, June 8, 2010.

Paludan, A., *Chronicle of the Chinese Emperors*, London: Thames and Hudson, 1998.

Pan, P., "China Backs Nepal Over Maoist Rebels," *Washington Post*, July 14, 2002.

Pandey, N.N., *Nepal–China Relations*. Kathmandu: Institute of Foreign Affairs, 2005.

Parashar, U., "India Losing Little Great Game." *Hindustan Times*, September 5, 2010.

Parker, E.H., "Nepaul And China," *The Imperial And Asiatic Quarterly Review And Oriental And Colonial Record*, Third Series-Volume VII No 13 & 14, January–April, Woking, England: The Oriental University Institute, 1899, pp. 64–82.

"Parliamentary Polls Talk Another Ploy: Leaders," *The Kathmandu Post*, October 15, 2005.

Parmanand, "China's Nepal Policy," *IDSA Journal*, 17:1, 1984, p.83.

"Party-Maoists partnership wrongheaded: Moriaty," *The Kathmandu Post*, February 17, 2006.

Patterns of Global Terrorism. Washington DC: US Department of State. April 2004, p. 14 Available at www.state.gov/s/ct/rls/crt/2003/.

"Peking Apology Satisfies Nepal," *Washington Post*, July 5, 1960.

Perdue, P.C., *China Marches West: The Qing Conquest of Central Eurasia*, Cambridge, Mass.: Harvard University Press, 2005.

Petech, L., *China and Tibet in the Early Eighteenth Century*, Leiden: E.J. Brill, 1950.

Petech, L., *Northern India According to The Shui-Ching-Chu*, ISMEO, Roma, 1950.

Pocha, J.S., "China Rolls Out Red Carpet For King," *The Telegraph* (Calcutta), April 25, 2005.

Pokharel, T., "China for 6-month U.N. mission," *The Kathmandu Post*, January 13, 2007.

Praagh, D.V., *The Greater Game: India's Race with Destiny and China*, Montreal: McGill-Queen's University Press, 2003.

"Prachanda Defends Chinese Crackdown on Tibetans," *Press Trust of India*, March 23, 2008.

Prasad, I., *The Life and Times of Maharaja Juddha Shumsher Jung Bahadur Rana of Nepal*, New Delhi: Ashish Publishing House, 1996.

"Premier Zhou on Current International Issues," *Beijing Review*, June 15, 1981, p. 9.

"President Jiang Meets Nepali and Cuban Guests," *Beijing Review*, March 15, 2001.

"Prevent Chinese, Pakistani Arms Supplies To Nepal," *Indo-Asian News Service*. December 20, 2005.

Pumphrey, C.W. (ed.), *The Rise of China in Asia: Security Implications*, Carlisle, Penn.: U.S. Army War College, Strategic Studies Institute, 2002.

Qingying Chen, *Tibetan History*, Beijing: China Intercontinental Press, 2003.

Rahul, "India's Changing China Policy," *China Report*, Vol. 6. Issue 4, 1970, pp. 16–20.

Rajan, D.S., "China: Signs of Ultra-Leftist Support To Maoists Of India And Nepal," *South Asia Analysis Group*, Paper No. 1565, May 10, 2005. Online. Available www. saag.org/common/uploaded_files/paper1565.html (accessed December 23, 2009).

Rajan, K.V., "Nepal–India Relations," *South Asian Journal*, No. 7, January–March 2005. Online. Available www.southasianmedia.net/Magazine/Journal/7_nepal-india_relations.htm (accessed 16 October 2009).

"Rajanspeak," *Nepali Times*, Issue 450, May 8, 2009.

Ramachandran, S., "India Moves With the King," *Asia Times Online*, January 22, 2005. Online. Available www.atimes.com/atimes/South_Asia/GA22Df06.html (accessed February 3, 2009).

Ramachandran, S., "Nepal's Maoists Air Their Dirty Laundry," *Asia Times Online.* May 17, 2005. Online. Available www.atimes.com/atimes/South_Asia/GE17Df01.html (accessed September 10, 2009).

Ramakant, *Indo-Nepalese Relations 1816–1877*, New Delhi: S. Chand and Co., 1968.

Ramakant, *Nepa–China and India*, New Delhi: Abhinav Publications, 1976.

Rana, D.S., *Nepal: Rule and Misrule*, New Delhi: Rajesh Publications, 1978.

Rana, P.J.B., *Life of Maharaja Sir Jung Bahadur*, Allahabad: Pioneer Press, 1909.

Rana, P.S., *Rana Intrigues*, Kathmandu: R. Rana, 1995.

Rana, R., "B.H. Hodgson as a Factor for the Fall of Bhimsen Thapa," *Ancient Nepal*, No. 105, April–May 1988, pp. 13–20.

Rana, S.S., "Nepal's Strategic Importance Underscored," *People's Review*, January 18, 2001, p. 1.

Randol, S., "How to Approach the Elephant: Chinese Perceptions of India in the Twenty-first Century," *Asian Affairs*, Vol. 34 No. 4, 2008, pp. 211–26.

"Rebels Suspend Nepal Movement," *New York Times*, November 9, 1962.

"Red Chinese Troops Rumored Inside Nepal," *Christian Science Monitor*, December 1, 1959.

Regmi, D.R., *Ancient Nepal*, Calcutta: Firma K.L. Mukhopadhyay, 1960.

Regmi, M., "Chiniya ruche ko artha" [The Realities Behind China's New Interest], *Nepal Weekly*, December 21, 2008.

Ren Yan Song, "US–India Eye Nepal Changes," *Global Times*, April 28, 2008.

Ren Yujun, "Will Nepal–India Relations Improve?" *Beijing Review*, July 24–30 1989, pp. 15–16.

Richardson, H.E., *Tibet and Its History*, 2nd revised ed., Boulder: Shambhala, 1984.

Roberts, J.B. and E.A. Roberts, *Freeing Tibet: 50 Years of Struggle, Resilience and Hope*, New York: Amacom Books, 2009.

Roberts, J.G., *Aid Programmes by the Governments of India and China to Nepal*, Master's dissertation, University of Hong Kong, 1997, p. 51. Online. Available at: http://hub.hku.hk/bitstream/10722/40436/1/FullText.pdf (accessed December 22, 2009).

"Robin Hood of the Himalayas," *Time*, August 5, 1957.

Rose, L.E., "Nepal: The Quiet Monarchy," *Asian Survey*, Vol. 4, No. 2, February, 1964, pp. 723–8.

Rose, L.E., "Nepal: Under Same Management, Business as Usual." *Asian Survey*, Vol. 5, No. 2, February, 1965, pp. 74–8.

Rose, L.E., "Nepal in 1965: Focus on Land Reform," *Asian Survey*, Vol. 6, No. 2, February 1966, pp. 86–89.

Rose, L.E., *Nepal: Strategy for Survival*. Berkeley: University of California Press, 1971.

Rose, L.E., "King Mahendra's China Policy" in S.D. Muni (ed.), *Nepal: An Assertive Monarchy*, New Delhi: Chetana Publications, 1977, pp. 219–39.

Rose, L.E., "Nepal as a Link Country," in Peter Gaeffke and David A. Utz, (eds), *The Countries of South Asia: Boundaries, Extensions, and Interactions*, Proceedings of the South Asia Seminar, Department of South Asia Regional Studies, University of Pennsylvania, 1988.

Rose, L.E., "India, China, the Himalayan Border States and Afghanistan: 1947–57," *South Asian Survey*, Vol. 4, Issue 1, 1997, pp. 81–94.

Rose, L.E., "Nepal and Bhutan in 1998: Two Himalayan Kingdoms," *Asian Survey*, Vol. 39, No. 1, Jan-Feb 1999, pp. 155–62.

Rose, L.E. and J.T. Scholz, *Nepal: Profile of a Himalayan Kingdom*. Boulder, Colo.: Westview Press, 1980.

Rosenthal, A.M. "Grim Shadows Over The Cobra Throne," *The New York Times*, May 27, 1956.

Rowland, J., *A History of Sino-Indian Relations: Hostile Co-existence*. Princeton, NJ: D. Van Nostrand, 1967.

Roy, A., *Prachanda: The Unknown Revolutionary*. Kathmandu: Mandala Book Point, 2008.

Samanta, P.B., "China is Nepal's Spanner to Kabul's Entry," *Indian Express*, November 13, 2005. Online. Available www.indianexpress.com/oldStory/81898/ (Accessed August 10, 2011).

Samanta, P.B., "Pro-China Centres, Calling for Reduced Ties with Delhi, Sprout Along Nepal Border With India," *Indian Express*, February 10, 2008. Online. Available www.indianexpress.com/news/prochina-centres-calling-for-reduced-ties/271636/ (accessed August 10, 2011).

Sarkar, S., "India Takes Up Tape Issue With Nepal Army," *The Statesman* (Calcutta), May 25, 2005.

Sarkar, S., "China Pledges £12.3 mn Aid to Nepal," *Indo-Asian News Service*, August 16, 2005.

Sarkar, S., "Is China Changing its Stance Towards Nepal?" *Indo-Asian News Service*, February 12, 2006.

Sarkar, S., "China Irked As Nepal Trumps King Card," *The Statesman* (Calcutta), April 28, 2006.

Sarkar, S., "Prachanda's China Trip Will Send Negative Message to India: Yadav," *Indo Asian News Service*, August 20, 2008.

Sarkar, S., "Gyanendra Says China Card Brought His Downfall: Report," *Indo-Asian News Service*, December 3, 2008.

Sarkar, S., "China's Cold War On Tibet," *ISN Security Watch*, December 4, 2008.

Sarkar, S., "Nepal's King Traded Tibetan Refugees for US support: WikiLeaks," *Indo-Asian News Service*, January 15, 2011.

Scholz, J.T., "Nepal in 1976: Problems with India Threaten Birendra's New Order," *Asian Survey*, Vol. 17, No. 2, February, 1977, pp. 201–7.

Scholz, J.T., "Nepal in 1977: Political Discipline or Human Rights," *Asian Survey*, Vol. 18, No. 2, February 1978, pp. 135–41.

Scobell, A., "'Cult Of Defense' And 'Great Power Dreams': The Influence Of Strategic Culture On China's Relationship With India" in M.R. Chambers (ed.), *South Asia In 2020: Future Strategic Balances And Alliances*, Carlisle, Penn.: U.S. Army War College Strategic Studies Institute, November 2002, pp. 329–59.

Sen, N., "Setting of the Red Sun," *China Report*, Vol. 29, Issue 2, 1993, pp. 197–211.

Shah, V., *Maile dekhe ko darbar: Sainik sachib ko samsmaran* [The Palace I Saw: Memoirs of a Military Secretary], Kathmandu: Yeti Publications, 2010.

Shaha, R., *Nepali Politics: Retrospect and Prospect*, New Delhi: Oxford University Press, 1978.

Shaha, R., *Essays in the Practice of Government in Nepal*, New Delhi: Manohar, 1982.

Shaha, R., "Ancient and Medieval Nepal," *Kailash*, Vol. 14, Nos. 3 and 4, 1988.

Shaha, R., *Modern Nepal: A Political History 1769–1955*, 2 Vols. Maryland, USA: Riverdale, 1990, p. 307.

Shakabpa, T.W.D., *Tibet: A Political History*, New Haven and London: Yale University Press, 1967.

Shakya, M.B., *The Life of Nepalese Buddhist Master Buddhabhadra (359–429 CE.): From Chinese Sources*, Kathmandu: China Study Center, 2009.

Shakya, P.R., *Nepal and China: International Relations and Trans-Himalayan Trade in the 18th Century*, Ph.D. dissertation, Tokyo University of Foreign Studies, 2002. Online. Available http://repository.tufs.ac.jp/handle/10108/35598?mode=full&metadis pmode=lang (accessed December 22, 2009).

Shakya, T., *The Dragon in the Land of Snows: A History of Modern Tibet Since 1947*, New York: Columbia University Press, 1999.

Sharma, J., *Nepal: Struggle for Existence*, Kathmandu: Communication Inc., 1986, p. 185.

Sharma, J., *Democracy Without Roots*, New Delhi: Book Faith India, 1998.

Sharma, S., "Nepal Rebels Slam US Terror Label," BBC News Online, May 2, 2003.

Sheng, M.M., "Mao, Tibet, and the Korean War," *Journal of Cold War Studies*, Vol. 8, No. 3, Summer 2006, pp. 15–33.

Shih-shan Henry Tsai, *The Eunuchs in the Ming Dynasty*, Albany, N.Y.: SUNY Press, 1996.

Showers, H.L, "Eighteen Months In Nepal," *Blackwood's Edinburgh Magazine*, Edinburgh, Vol. 199, May 1916, pp. 595–613.

Shukla, S., "The Gulf Widens, *India Today*, September 19, 2005, p. 30.

Sibal, K., "India–China Relations, Some Reflections," *Indian Defence Review*, Vol. 23, No. 1, January-March 2008, pp. 200–204. Online. Available www.indiandefencere-view.com/geopolitics/India-China-Relations-Some-Reflections.html (accessed August 10, 2011).

Sikri, R., *Challenge and Strategy: Rethinking India's Foreign Policy*, New Delhi: Sage Publications, 2009.

Sikri, R., "The Tibet Factor in China–India Relations," *Journal of International Affairs*, Vol. 64, No. 2, Spring/Summer 2011, pp. 55–72.

Singh, A.J., "How the Tibetan Problem Influenced China's Foreign Relations," *China Report*, Vol. 28, Issue 3, 1992, pp. 261–89.

Smith, T., *Narrative of a Five Years' Residence at Nepaul. 2 Vols*, London: Colburn and Co., 1852.

Smith, W.W., *Tibetan Nation.* Boulder, CO: Westview Press, Inc. 1996.

Soren, P., "US Interest in Nepal: Politics of Military Aid," *ORF Strategic Trends*, Vol. 2 Issue. 16, April 26, 2004.

Spence, J.D., *The Search for Modern China*, New York: W.W. Norton, 1991.

Stakelbeck, F., "Is China grooming 'another Tibet?" *Washington Times*, December 29, 2005. Online. Available www.washingtontimes.com/news/2005/dec/28/20051228–095200–7650r/ (accessed January 5, 2006).

Stiller, L.F., *Prithwinarayan Shah in the Light of Dibya Upadesh*, Kathmandu: 1968.

Stiller, L.F., *The Rise of the House of Gorkha*, New Delhi: Manjusri, 1973.

Stiller, L.F., "The Role of Fear in the Unification of Nepal," *Contributions to Nepalese Studies*, Vol. 1, No. 2, 1974, pp. 42–89.

Stiller, L.F., *The Silent Cry: The People of Nepal – 1816–1839*, Sahayogi Prakashan, Kathmandu, 1976.

Stiller, L.F., *Letters from Kathmandu: The Kot Massacre*, Kathmandu, Center for Nepal and Asian Studies, 1981.

Strand, D. and M.K. Chan, "Militarism and Militarization in Modern Chinese History." In *The Military and Society: Reviews of Recent Research*, New York: Haworth Press, 1982.

Tan Chung, "Ageless Neighbourliness Between India and China: Historical Perspective and Future Prospects," *China Report*, Vol. 15, No. 2, 1979, pp. 3–37.

Tappan, E.M. (ed.), *China, Japan, and the Islands of the Pacific* [Vol. I of The World's Story: A History of the World in Story, Song, and Art] Boston: Houghton Mifflin, 1914.

Teltscher, K., *The High Road to China: George Bogle, the Panchen Lama, and the First British Expedition to Tibet*, New York: Farrar, Straus and Giroux, 2006.

Thapa, D. (ed.), *Understanding the Maoist Movement of Nepal*. Kathmandu: Martin Chautari, 2003.

Thapa, S., "Buddhist Sanskrit Manuscripts of Nepal and Expansion of Mahāyāna Buddhism in the North with Special Reference to China," Paper presented at the International symposium on "Buddhist Light: Buddhism and Sino-Nepal Cultural Linkage, Jinan University, Guangzhou, China," December 2009. Online. Available www.scribd. com/doc/24973491/Thapa-s-Bud-Skt-Lit-of-Nepal-and-Expansion-Mahayana-Buddhism-in-the-North-With-Reference-to-China (accessed March 14, 2010).

"The King and We," *Indian Express Online*, November 28, 2005. Online. Available www.indianexpress.com/oldStory/82813/ (Accessed August 10, 2011).

The National Archives, U.K. Government, "The Nepal-Tibet Dispute," CAB 24/211, April 5, 1930. Online. Available www.nationalarchives.gov.uk/documentsonline/ details-result.asp?queryType=1&resultcount=1&Edoc_Id=8044820 (accessed December 23, 2009).

The National Archives, U.K. Government, Cabinet 77 (50), CONCLUSIONS of a Meeting of the Cabinet, November 23, 1950, The National Archives: CAB/128/18. Online. Available www.nationalarchives.gov.uk (accessed June 24, 2010).

"The Taste of Northern Spy," *Time*, October 8, 1956.

"The Value of Nepal," *Christian Science Monitor*, December 19, 1959.

"Thibet To Be Invaded," *New York Times*, November 17, 1903.

Tibet's Stateless Nationals: Tibetan Refugees in Nepal, Berkeley: Tibet Justice Center, 2002.

Translations On People's Republic of China. Washington: Joint Publications Research Service, September 5–7, 1967.

Tucci, G., "The Wives of Srong-btsan-sgam-po," *Oriens Extremus*, Vol. 9, 1962, pp. 121–26.

Twitchett, D. and J.K. Fairbank (eds), *The Cambridge History of China. Vol. 10, Late Ch'ing, 1800–1911, Part 1*, Cambridge: Cambridge University Press, 1978.

U.N. Department of Public Information Press Release, "US Envoy to Nepal Calls into Question June Polls Unless Political Concensus Reached Soon," February 26, 2007.

U.S. Department of State, *Foreign Relations of the United States, 1961–1963*, Volume XIX, South Asia, Document 88, "United States Relations With South Asia: Major Issues And Recommended Courses Of Action," undated. Online. Available http:// history.state.gov/historicaldocuments/frus1961–63v19/d88 (accessed December 23, 2009).

U.S. Department of State, *Foreign Relations of the United States, 1961–1963*, Volume XIX, South Asia, Document 190, "Memorandum From the President's Deputy Special Assistant for National Security Affairs (Kaysen) to President Kennedy," November 3, 1962. Online. Available http://history.state.gov/historicaldocuments/frus1961–63v19/d190 (accessed December 23, 2009).

U.S. Department of State, *Foreign Relations of the United States, 1969–1976, Volume XVII*, China, 1969–1972, Document 176, Memorandum of Conversation. Online. Available http://history.state.gov/historicaldocuments/frus1969–76v17/d176 (accessed December 23, 2009).

U.S. Department of State, *Foreign Relations of the United States, 1969–1976, Volume XVII*, China, 1969–1972, Document 278, Memorandum Prepared for the 40 Committee. Online. Available http://history.state.gov/historicaldocuments/frus1969–76v17/d278 (accessed December 23, 2009).

U.S. Department of State, *Foreign Relations of the United States, 1969–1976, Volume XVIII*, China, 1973–1976, Document No. 136. Memorandum of Conversation. Online. Available http://history.state.gov/historicaldocuments/frus1969–76v18/d136 (accessed December 23, 2009).

United States Committee for Refugees and Immigrants, *U.S. Committee for Refugees World Refugee Survey 2001*: Nepal, 20 June 2001. Online. Available www.unhcr.org/refworld/docid/3b31e1670.html (accessed January 20, 2011).

Upadhya, S., *The Raj Lives: India in Nepal*, New Delhi: Vitasta Pub., 2008.

Upadhyay, A., "China's New Ambassador," *The Kathmandu Post*, June 6, 2011.

Upadhyaya, N.P., "Beijing To Meet Delhi in Kathmandu," *The Telegraph Weekly* (Kathmandu), September 9, 2009.

Uprety, P.R., *Nepal-Tibet Relations 1850–1930*. 2d Ed. Kathmandu: Ratna Pustak Bhandar, 1998.

Uprety, T.P., "Nepal in 1982: Panchayat Leadership in Crisis," *Asian Survey*, Vol. 23, No. 2, February, 1983, pp. 143–48.

Van Der Oye, D.S., "Tournament of Shadows: Russia's Great Game in Tibet. in A. McKay (ed.), *The History of Tibet: The Modern Period: 1895–1959*, London: RoutledgeCurzon, 2003, pp. 43–56.

Van Ness, P., *Revolution and Chinese Foreign Policy*, Berkeley: University of California Press, 1970.

Van Oort, H.A., *The Iconography of Chinese Buddhism in Traditional China, Part 1*, Leiden: Brill, 1986.

Van Walt Van Praag, M.C. *The Status of Tibet*, Colorado: Westview Press, 1987.

Varadarajan, S., "Delhi Missed Chance to Resolve Nepal Crisis," *The Hindu* (Madras), May 11, 2009.

Vaughn, B., *Nepal: Political Developments and Bilateral Relations with the United States*, Washington DC: Congressional Research Service, April 7, 2011.

Verma, B., "Unmasking China." *Indian Defence Review*, Vol 24:3, July-September 2009. Online. Available www.indiandefencereview.com/2009/08/unmasking-china.html (accessed November 15, 2009).

Waley-Cohen, J., *The Culture of War in China: Empire and the Military under the Qing Dynasty*, New York: I.B. Tauris, 2006.

Waller, D.J., *The Pundits: British Exploration of Tibet and Central Asia*, Lexington: University Press of Kentucky, 2004.

Wang Hongwei, "Sino-Nepal Relations in the 1980s," *Asian Survey*, Vol. 25, No. 5, May 1985, pp. 512–20.

Wang Hongwei, "Chin Chup Lagera Basdaina" [China Won't Sit By Silently], *Nepal Weekly*, November 5, 2007.

Wang Hongwei, "Some Thoughts On Sino-Nepal Relations," *Spotlight* magazine, Oct. 20–26, 2000, p. 24.

"We May See the Recurrence of a New Cold War in our Region," *Nepali Times*, May 11, 2001.

Whelpton, J., *Jang Bahadur in Europe: The First Nepalese Mission to the West*. Kathmandu: Sahayogi Press, 1983.

Whelpton, J., *A History of Nepal*. Cambridge: Cambridge University Press, 2005.

Wilcox, W., "China's Strategic Alternatives in South Asia," in T. Tsou, (ed.) *China in Crisis, Volume 2: China's Policies in Asia and America's Alternatives*, Chicago: The University of Chicago Press, 1968.

Willis, C. (ed.)., *A Lifetime of Wisdom: Essential Writings By and About the Dalai Lama*, New York: Marlowe & Company, 2002.

Wolfe, A., "International Spotlight on Nepal," *Power and Interest News Report*, March 11, 2005. Online. Available www.pinr.com (accessed December 12, 2008).

Wong, J.Y. *Deadly Dreams: Opium, Imperialism, and the Arrow War (1856–1860) in China*. Cambridge Studies in Chinese History, Literature, and Institutions. Cambridge (England) and New York: Cambridge University Press, 1998.

Wriggins, S.H., *The Silk Road Journey with Xuanzang*, Colorado: Westview Press, 2004.

Wright, D., *History of Nepal*. London: Cambridge University Press, 1877.

Wright, M.C. (ed.), *China in Revolution: The First Phase, 1900–1911*, New Haven, Conn.: Yale University Press, 1968.

Wyllie, J.W.S. and W.W. Hunter, *Essays on the External Policy of India*. London: Smith, Elder, & Co., 1875.

Yahuda, M., "The Changing Faces of Chinese Nationalism" in M. Leifer (ed.) *Asian Nationalism*, London: Routledge, 2000.

Yahuda, M., *China's Role in World Affairs*, London: Croom Helm, 1978.

Yingcong Dai, "Military Finance of the High Qing Period: An Overview." In N.D. Cosmo (ed.), *Military Culture in Imperial China*, Cambridge, Mass.: Harvard University Press, 2009.

Younghusband, F.E., *India and Tibet*, London: John Murray, 1910.

Zhang Li, *To Manage Conflict in South Asia: China's Stakes, Perceptions and Inputs*, Stockholm, Sweden: Institute for Security and Development Policy, October 2009. Online. Available www.isdp.eu/images/stories/isdp-main-pdf/2009_li_to-manage-conflict-in-south-asia.pdf (accessed December 23, 2009).

Zhang Song and Zhang Jiye, "US forces Nepal to accept the National Endowment for Democracy to offset China's Influence," *Global Times* (Chinese), January 16, 2006.

Zhao Gancheng, "South Asia's Position in the International Order and Choice Before China," *South Asian Studies* (Chinese), No. 1, 2010.

Zhu Shansan, "90% in Online Poll Believe India Threatens China's Security," *Global Times*, June 12, 2009.

Zuo Xuan, "India Covets Dalai Lama's Visit," *Global Times*, November 9, 2009. Online. Available www.globaltimes.cn/world/asia-pacific/2009–11/483521.html (accessed December 10, 2009).

Index